Arthur Innes

Britain and her rivals in the eighteenth century

1713-1789

Arthur Innes

Britain and her rivals in the eighteenth century
1713-1789

ISBN/EAN: 9783337282615

Printed in Europe, USA, Canada, Australia, Japan

Cover: Foto ©ninafisch / pixelio.de

More available books at **www.hansebooks.com**

BRITAIN
AND HER RIVALS
IN THE EIGHTEENTH CENTURY.
1713–1789.

BY

ARTHUR D. INNES, M.A.,
SOMETIME SCHOLAR OF ORIEL COLLEGE, OXFORD.

LONDON:
A. D. INNES & CO.,
BEDFORD STREET.
1895.

PREFACE.

The eighteenth century is probably the period of English History with which Englishmen are least familiar. It lacks the pageantry and picturesqueness of earlier times, while the problem of the British Constitution was practically settled with the expulsion of the Stuarts. Consequently the years between the wars of Marlborough and the wars of Bonaparte are commonly regarded as uninteresting ; in spite of the fact that during those years was fought out the great struggle which in the end rent the British race in two, but not till it had secured to the English-speaking peoples the empire over North America and India ; an empire which resisted the mighty onslaught of Napoleon, has since expanded over Australasia, and bids fair to absorb no small part of Africa.

If the history of this period is supposed to be uninteresting, it ought not to be so ; for though it has unattractive features, dreary phases, and some sordid details, it nevertheless abounds in stirring episodes, and is perhaps richer than any other in political lessons of the highest import to-day. Not the least striking of these lessons has recently been brought, none too soon, into special prominence by the invaluable volumes of Captain Mahan.

It can hardly be said that historians have neglected the eighteenth century : the great work of Mr. W. H. Lecky is a standing proof to the contrary. But the curiously small space, relatively, allotted to it in popular or school histories is evidence of the extent to which it is commonly overlooked ; or was at any rate overlooked before Professor Seeley, some twelve years ago, aroused a new interest in the story of the Expansion of England, by the book which bears that title.

My object in writing this volume has been to present such an outline of this period as may serve to ordinary people, not historical specialists, as a groundwork for, and possibly an incentive to, further study. It was Sir John Seeley's work which suggested to me the need of such a volume; and if I have succeeded in my aim, I should myself choose to regard this book as a tribute to his memory, though I never had the honour of his acquaintance. But if I have not succeeded, I sincerely trust that some more able writer will renew the attempt with better results: since I am persuaded that, however interesting the wars of early monarchs may have been, however valuable a knowledge of the growth of the British Constitution may prove, both the interest and the value of the history of the growth of the British Empire should be at least as great to any man who is proud to call himself a citizen of that Empire.

In the preparation of this work, it would be impossible for me to say how much I owe to the various writers whose books I have consulted. But besides the more obvious volumes, such as those already referred to, I should like to direct the particular attention of students to Sir Alfred Lyall's admirable works dealing with the advance of the British in India.

I have further to thank Messrs. Longmans for their courtesy in permitting me to make special use of their maps for the Seven Years' War and the campaigns of Washington: and, finally, to acknowledge my great personal obligation to Mr. A. H. Johnson, of Merton College, Oxford, who very kindly read nearly the whole of my manuscript, and to whom I am indebted for many valuable suggestions and corrections.

A. D. I.

January, 1895.

CONTENTS.

PROLOGUE.

THE SITUATION AFTER UTRECHT.

Results of the war—Relative position of the five oceanic Powers; in America, in India, in the South Seas—Possible combinations—Nature of the coming contest; its conditions—Maritime strength; of England, France, Spain—The German states—The French succession—The Italian duchies—English power of inaction 1

BOOK I.

THE HOUSE OF HANOVER.

CHAPTER I.

THE HANOVERIAN SUCCESSION.

1713–1716.

Parties in 1713—The Whigs—The Tories—Jacobitism—Party effects of Utrecht—The Commercial Treaty—1714: Bolingbroke's difficulties—Uncertainty of the party—The Schism Act—Fall of Oxford—The queen's death—Triumph of the Whigs—The new king; instability of his position—1715: Jacobite intrigues—Death of Louis XIV.—Mar raises the clans—The rising in England—The collapse of Preston—Sheriffmuir—1716: Break-up of Mar's army—After the 'Fifteen—Characteristics of the rebellion . . . .

CONTENTS.

CHAPTER II.
THE FRENCH ALLIANCE.
1716-1726.

Establishment of the new dynasty—Drawbacks of the Hanoverian connection--1716: The Whig disruption—Hanover and the Northern Powers—The French succession—The Triple Alliance—Alberoni and Elizabeth Farnese—Charles XII. —1717: Spain attacks Sardinia—Temporary compromise—Alberoni's intrigues—The Quadruple Alliance—1718: Spain attacks Sicily—Battle of Cape Passaro; its effects—1719: Failure of Alberoni's schemes; his fall—1723: The Duke of Bourbon regent in France—1725: Austro-Spanish Alliance —The Treaty of Hanover 23

CHAPTER III.
FLEURY AND WALPOLE.
1726-1739.

Fleury—1727: Accession of George II.—1731: Treaty of Vienna —Fleury's Bourbon policy—Walpole's objects—War of the Polish succession—British non-intervention—Results of the war—Spain and Portugal—The First Family Compact, 1733; its deficiencies as a plan; Fleury's real purpose; Walpole's place in it—Walpole's peace policy; the alternative; its weak point—Why the peace-policy broke down— The quarrel with Spain—Jenkins's ears—Preparations for war—Feeling in England—Declaration of war 40

CHAPTER IV.
THE PREMONITORY WAR, AND THE END OF JACOBITISM.
1739-1748.

Inefficient measures—Anson—Vernon—The German states— 1740: Death of the Emperor—1741: Frederick of Prussia and Maria Theresa—War of the Austrian succession—1742: Peace of Breslau—The British navy—Its effects—Fall of Walpole—1743: Battle of Dettingen—1745: Battle of Fontenoy—Jacobite schemes—James—Charles Edward— The conditions of the '15 and the '45 compared—Importance attached to the dynastic question—Danger of its remaining unsettled—Its intrinsic consequence—Attitude of

English Jacobites—Landing of Charles—Capture of Edinburgh—Preston Pans—The march to Derby—Position of Charles—The retreat—1746: Falkirk—Culloden—The end of Jacobitism—The war in Europe, and at sea—1748: Treaty of Aix-la Chapelle 54

BOOK II.

THE STRUGGLE FOR EMPIRE.

CHAPTER I.

THE COMING STORM.

1748-1756.

Meaning of the last war: state of Europe after it—Importance of individuals — Pelham — Newcastle — Pitt — Affairs in America; in India—Maria Theresa and Frederick—The new grouping of allies—Confusion in England—Frederick takes the initiative. 71

CHAPTER II.

THE WAR IN EUROPE.

1756-1761.

Interesting features of the war—Frederick attacks Saxony—Capture of Dresden—1757: The Austrian alliances—Position of Hanover—Battle of Prague—Battle of Kolin—Convention of Kloster Seven—Frederick's danger—Battle of Rossbach—Battle of Leuthen—Russians and Swedes—Pitt comes into power—1758: Military position of Frederick—Battle of Zorndorf—Battle of Hochkirchen—Prince Ferdinand—1759: Minden—Frederick's exhaustion—Battle of Kunersdorf—Capture of Dresden—1760: Battles of Liegnitz and Torgau—Campaign of 1761 82

CHAPTER III.

BRITAIN AND FRANCE.

1754-1761.

British and French in America—Opening hostilities—Panic in England—1756: Byng at Minorca—Pitt in office—1757:

Coalition of Pitt and Newcastle—Pitt's naval policy—Effects of sea-power—Gibraltar—1758: The new maritime policy—Canada—Montcalm—Choiseul in France—1759; Boscawen and De la Clue—The Brest fleet—Battle of Quiberon, Nov. 28th—The French navy crushed—Wolfe in Canada—Effect of naval control—Wolfe takes Quebec, Sept. 18th—1760: Completion of conquest of Canada—Accession of George III.—Prospect of Spanish intervention—1761: Pitt resigns ... 96

CHAPTER IV.

INDIA BEFORE THE STRUGGLE.

1707-1740.

Popular misconception of Indian history—India not a nation—The Mogul empire—Principal Indian states—Four main divisions—Conditions of a European conquest—Sea-power the controlling factor—The rival European powers—Chartered companies: the Dutch; the French; the English—Comparison of the French and English companies—French governors—La Bourdonnais—Ultimate certainty of English success 111

CHAPTER V.

INDIA: DUPLEIX.

1741-1754.

Dupleix's scheme—Position of the rival companies—1743: Effect of the declaration of war between France and England—1746: Dupleix and La Bourdonnais—Capture of Madras—1747: Rupture between Dupleix and the Nawab—French military successes—1748: Pondicherry threatened by Boscawen—Effects of the peace of Aix-la-Chapelle—Influence of sea-power—New phase of the contest—1749: Rival claimants to native thrones—Plan of Dupleix—The English join in—Success of Dupleix—1751: Robert Clive—1752: Successes of Clive and Lawrence—Dupleix at bay—1754: His recall—The situation in 1754 122

CHAPTER VI.

INDIA: ESTABLISHMENT OF THE BRITISH.

1754-1761.

Renewal of hostilities—1758: Lally—1759: Siege of Madras—Colonel Ford—Isolation of Lally—1760: Battle of Wandewash—The French power crushed—*Bengal*—1756: The Black Hole—1757: Clive and Watson at Calcutta—Intrigues against Suraj-ud-Daulah—Omichund—Battle of Plassey—1759: Capture of Masulipatam—Clive's position—Shah Alum—The Dutch interposition—1760: Clive's application of Dupleix's policy—The new conditions 135

CHAPTER VII.

THE WINDING UP OF THE WAR.

1761-1763.

Position of the combatants—1762: Withdrawal of Russia—Catharine of Russia—Recovery of Silesia—1761: Second Family Compact—1762: The West Indies—Portugal—Bute's desire for peace—He alienates Prussia—1763: Peace of Paris—Triumphant position of Britain—William Pitt—Features of the war—British naval policy—Its effect—England's debt to Pitt 148

BOOK III.

SURVEY OF THE WHIG SUPREMACY.

CHAPTER I.

THE CONSTITUTION.

1714-1760.

George I.—1716: The Septennial Act—1719: The Peerage Bill—Walpole—*George II.* and Queen Caroline—From Walpole to the coalition—Ministerial responsibility—*George III.*—Attack on the Whig oligarchy; by Pitt; by George III.; by the democrats 159

CHAPTER II.

ENGLAND.

1714-1760.

Whigs and Tories—1720: The South Sea Bubble—Towshend and Walpole—Walpole's finance—1733: His excise scheme—His opportunism—His attitude to the Nonconformists—Causes of his power—His opponents—System of corruption—Results of his rule—1743: The Pelhams—Influence of Pitt 170

CHAPTER III.

SCOTLAND.

1707-1760.

Scotland at the Union—The clans—The Lowlands—Scots and English—Religious and educational legislation—The Union—Effects of the 'Fifteen—Discontent with the Union—Effects of the 'Forty-five—Heritable jurisdictions: in the Lowlands; in the Highlands—Break-up of the clan system; result—Progress made possible—Scots in England . . . 181

CHAPTER IV.

IRELAND.

1714-1760.

Scotland and Ireland compared—The Catholic population—Commercial repression—Landlords and tenants—Representation—Education—Catholic inaction—English control—1724: Wood's half-pence—Signs of revival 193

CHAPTER V.

GREATER BRITAIN.

1714-1763.

The American colonies—Colonial constitutions—The colonial theory—Dangers from the French—Results of the great war—Restrictions on trade—Attitude of Walpole—Change in the situation—*India*—Break-up of the Mogul Empire—

Disorganisation of native powers—Rivalry between French and English—Three stages of the contest—The British advance inevitable—The new order 202

CHAPTER VI.

EUROPE.

1714-1775.

The Anglo-French alliance—The Bourbon union—Fleury and Walpole—The French error—Walpole's error—Tangles of French policy—From Walpole to Pitt—Fleury's successors—Pitt and Choiseul—Subsequent isolation of England—Development of French naval policy—Difficulties and opportunities of France 212

BOOK IV.

GEORGE THE THIRD.

CHAPTER I.

BUTE TO NORTH.

1760-1770.

Bute—His antagonism to Pitt—1761: Fall of Pitt—1762: Fall of Newcastle—Bute's triumph—1763: Its fall—The Triumvirate—The Bedford ministry—Wilkes—1765: The Stamp Act—The Regency Bill—The King and the Bedfords—The Rockingham ministry—1766: Pitt takes office—Pitt becomes Earl of Chatham—His plans—His illness—1767: Charles Townshend—1768: Chatham's resignation—Anti-colonial ministry—1769: Re-appearance of Chatham—1770: North's ministry 221

CHAPTER II.

KING, PARLIAMENT, AND PEOPLE.

1760-1774.

Ministerial fluctuations—Break-up of the Whigs—Corruption—The king and his ministers—Parliamentary representation—Wilkes and liberty—1763: *The North Briton*—Number

—Clinton's embarrassments—Cornwallis in the south— 1778-9: D'Estaing at Savannah—Position of the British in 1780—*The War in the West Indies*—1778: Santa Lucia captured—1779: D'Estaing and Byron—1780: Arrival of De Guichen and Rodney 295

CHAPTER III.

THE STRUGGLE FOR LIFE.

1779-1783.

Spain joins the allies—Naval superiority of the allies—1780: Rodney and the Spanish Fleet—Rodney and De Guichen in the West Indies—July, 1780: The situation—The Northern Army—1780-1: Cornwallis in the south—1781: Cornwallis retreats to Yorktown—1780: The armed neutrality—War with Holland—1781: Arrival of De Grasse in the West Indies—His failure to crush the British fleet—July: position of the British in America—The opposing fleets at the Chesapeake—Surrender of Yorktown—Change in British sentiment—Strength of the rival navies—1782: Siege of Gibraltar—The relief by Lord Howe—1781: Suffren sails for India—1782-3: Suffren and Hughes—1782: De Grasse and Hood at St. Kitt's—Arrival of Rodney—Battle of The Saints—Results of the struggle—Desire for peace—Preliminaries signed—1783: Final treaties 310

CHAPTER IV.

THE RETENTION OF INDIA BY WARREN HASTINGS.

1772-1785.

The northern provinces—The Mahrattas—The Nizam—Hyder Ali—The sea—Bengal—Hastings and Oudh—1773: The Rohillas—1774: Aspects of the Rohilla war—Policy of Hastings—1774: Bombay and the Mahrattas—Action of Hastings—1777: French overtures—Bombay blunders—Goddard and Popham—French declaration of war, 1778—Hyder Ali; his annoyance—1780: He falls on the Carnatic—1781: Eyre Coote—Critical position of the British—1782:

Arrival of Suffren—The Mahratta pacification—Death of Hyder Ali—1783: Peace with France, and end of the crisis —Summary 327

CHAPTER V.
INDIAN ADMINISTRATION UNDER WARREN HASTINGS.
1772-1785.

Objects of North's Regulating Act; its provisions—The Supreme Court—Confusion of authority—1774: The new members of council—1775: The council and Oudh—Nuncomar—1777: Hastings becomes predominant—1780: Duel of Hastings and Francis—1778: The Madras council—Financial difficulties of Hastings—The council and the judges—The Rajah of Benares—1783: The Oudh begums—1784—The work of Hastings; his retirement. 310

CHAPTER VI.
IRELAND: THE VOLUNTEERS.
1776-1784.

1778: Relaxation of the penal code—Demand for free trade—Rise of the volunteers—Effect of the movement—1779: Demand for redress of grievances—Free trade granted—1780: Demand for legislative independence—Grattan—The Mutiny Bill—The Mutiny Act made perpetual—1781: Lord Carlisle viceroy—Reception of the news of Yorktown—The volunteers at Dungannon—1782: The Constitution of 1782—"Simple Repeal"—1783: the Renunciatory Act—Grattan and Flood—The Bishop of Derry—The volunteer convocation in Dublin—Demand for parliamentary reform—Rejection of the Reform Bill 352

CHAPTER VII.
THE CONFLICT OF PARTIES.
1772-1784.

King George's rule, through North—Catholic emancipation—1780: The Gordon riots—Strength of the ministry—Parliamentary corruption—Economic reform—1782: North resigns

—Second Rockingham administration—Fox and Shelburne—Measures of reform—The Shelburne ministry—1783: Coalition of Fox and North—The ministry of Portland—Fox's India Bill; it arouses violent opposition—Intervention of the King—The Younger Pitt Prime Minister—1784: Government in a minority—Pitt's increasing popularity—Dissolution—Pitt's triumph. 364

EPILOGUE.

BEFORE THE FRENCH REVOLUTION.

1784-1789.

William Pitt—Foreign affairs—The Commercial Treaty with France, 1786—Pitt's finance; taxation; loans; sinking fund—End of Parliamentary reform, 1785—The Regency Bill, 1788—*Ireland:* reform—Progress—Commercial restrictions—Pitt's proposals; their failure, 1785—*India*—Pitt's India Bill, 1784—Concluding remarks 376

LIST OF MAPS

At the End of the Volume.

THE WORLD, SHOWING DISTRIBUTION OF COLONIAL POSSESSIONS IN 1714 AND 1785.
EUROPE [WESTERN], 1714.
EUROPE [NORTH CENTRAL]; FOR THE WARS OF FREDERICK THE GREAT.
{ INDIA: SHOWING THE MOGUL EMPIRE.
{ INDIA [SOUTHERN].
INDIA: BENGAL, THE UPPER PROVINCES, AND MAHRATTA DOMINION.
{ AMERICA [NORTH AND CENTRAL].
{ AMERICA: UNITED STATES AND CANADA.
{ AMERICA: NEW YORK AND PHILADELPHIA.
{ THE WEST INDIES, 1778.

PLAN FOR SIEGE OF QUEBEC 107

CHRONOLOGICAL CHART OF ALLIANCES AND WARS, 1716-1749.

	17 16	17	18	19	20	1	2	3	4	5	6	7	8	9	30	1	2	3	4	5	6	7	8	9	40	1	2	3	4	5	6	7	8
General.		England and France in Alliance.													First Family Compact.											Premonitory Wars.							
England.	Stanhope Whigs.												Walpole.													Pelham.							
France.			Orleans Regency.					Bourbon.							Fleury.													Poupadour.					
Spain.	Alberoni.								Spain turns to Austria.									Spain draws to France.								Bourbon Alliance.						
Wars.		Spanish Wars.																			War of Polish Succession.						Anglo - Spanish War.					
																										Austrian Succession War.				France v. England.	The "Forty Five."	
India.																																Duplex: 1st. Period.

CHRONOLOGICAL TABLE FOR THE GREAT WAR, 1756–1763.

Year.	Belligerents.	Ministers.	The War— in Europe.	Sea and Canada.	in India.
1756.		Newcastle.	Saxony taken.	*Byng at Port Mahon.*	*Black Hole.*
1757.	Austria with Russia and Sweden and England against Prussia and France and		Prague. *Kolin. Hastenbeck.* Rossbach. Leuthen.	BLOCKADE OF	CLIVE IN BENGAL. Plassey.
1758.			Zorndorf. *Hochkirchen.*	FRENCH PORTS.	*Fort St. David lost.*
1759.		William Pitt.	Minden. *Kunersdorf. Dresden lost. Maxen.*	Lagos. Quebec. Quiberon.	Madras relieved. Masulipatam. Patna relieved. Dutch expelled.
1760.			Liegnitz. Torgau.	BRITAIN MISTRESS	Wandewash.
1761.			*Silesia lost.* Kirchdenkern.	OF THE SEAS. West	Pondicherry taken.
1762.	Spain joins Russia withdraws.	Bute.	Burkersdorf. Silesia recovered.	Indian Conquests.	
1763.			Peace of Paris.		

Italics denote British or Prussian reverses.

BRITAIN AND HER RIVALS.

CORRIGENDA.

Page 9, eight lines from bottom, *for* "grandfather" *read* "great-grandfather."
  ,, 295, heading, *for* "1789" *read* "1780."

BRITAIN AND HER RIVALS

IN THE

EIGHTEENTH CENTURY.

PROLOGUE.

THE SITUATION AFTER UTRECHT.

Results of the war—Relative position of the five oceanic Powers; in America, in India, in the South Seas—Possible combinations—Nature of the coming contest; its conditions—Maritime strength; of England, France, Spain—The German states—The French succession—The Italian duchies—English power of inaction.

THE war of the Spanish succession, which was terminated by the Treaty of Utrecht in 1713, was, on the face of it, concerned with the balance of power in Europe: and, being essentially European, England's share in it has an appearance of wantonness; and her withdrawal from it, of rational prudence. But, in fact, the interests ultimately at stake, as concerned England, were not European. It did not matter very greatly which of the countries of Europe was strongest; but it did matter very much whether France and Spain should act independently or in concert as the rivals of England beyond seas. The war gave us a great deal. It gave us Newfoundland and Nova Scotia, and the invaluable naval stations of Gibraltar and Minorca in the Mediterranean. But the peace which established a Bourbon on the throne of Spain prepared the way for that union of those two powers which it had been

The conclusion of the war.

the precise purpose of Whig statesmen to prevent. For France and Spain were now the two rivals of Great Britain in colonial enterprise; they stood second to her as naval powers: in combination they might endanger her naval supremacy, and, with it, her colonial expansion.

The rivalry in oceanic commerce and colonial expansion is the true key to the political history of the century. It is often obscured, because the ostensible motives of statesmen frequently have very little to do with the ultimate interests at stake.

Probably there was no one of the Powers which had definitely grasped the fact that a struggle for transmarine empire was approaching. Till Pitt came into power, no single statesman appears to have fully realised it. In England men's minds were fixed on the question whether the Stuarts were coming back again. The ambition alike of France and of Spain was for continental aggrandisement in the first place. Nevertheless, nothing was more certain than that sooner or later commercial rivalry would lead to a desperate struggle for transmarine, and therefore for naval, supremacy.

Five Powers, in effect, shared the oceanic commerce at this time. But of these five, Portugal had already fallen out of all chance of competition, and Holland had reached the limits of her capacity for expansion. Spain had already secured for herself territories so vast and so rich that she had no need to go farther afield; but, as a great monopolist, she was in constant danger of having her monopolies interfered with, and any attempt at such interference would tend to produce a serious collision. In the relations of Spain, France, and England lay the causes which were certain to lead to a great struggle.

The rival oceanic Powers;

For wherever the English flag had been planted, the French flag was floating not very far off. In North America the greater part of the continent was disputed territory. Modern statesmen are attempting

in America;

to solve in Africa a problem of a somewhat similar character by the system of definitely limited spheres of influence. It is conceivable that a precise and complete treaty of partition might have made it possible to avoid the great collision. But, at that day, statesmen at home paid so little attention to colonial matters that such a method of averting hostilities never came within the range of practical politics. Moreover, modern methods of arbitration had not been established; while the difficulty of rapid communication with the mother country must in any case have seriously interfered with the prospect of composing incidental quarrels between rival colonists: nor is it at all probable that any scheme of partition could have been proposed to which both sides would have agreed.

The American seaboard from the St. Lawrence to Florida was inhabited by highly organised British colonies. But on the north in Canada, on the south in Louisiana, the country was French. Inland lay a vast unconquered territory, which English and French both coveted. Both desired to expand, but neither could do so unless at the cost of the other. Even the limits of what each might already claim for her own were unsettled in Nova Scotia and in Georgia. The rights of the rival nations in regard to fishing and to various privileges were subjects of constant dispute. So that between French and British colonists there existed an abundance of those minor sources of friction which are so often the occasion of conflicts in which far larger issues are at stake. It is difficult for a rivalry on so large a scale to be conducted without an appeal to force. When constant quarrels on minor points stir up continual animosities, the prospect of continuous peace vanishes.

That the continent of North America was sure, in no very long time, to become the object of fierce contention might have been recognized even at this time. But it was not so obvious that in the East also there was in India; to be a duel for empire, with results not less startling nor less important than in the West. For in India as yet there was no antagonism of organised British and French states. There, practically, the whole peninsula owned the suzerainty of the Moguls: the Europeans merely occupied trading stations here and there on the coast; they had hardly dreamed as yet of political influence, much less of territorial expansion. Yet there were those who had seen visions. And here, also, it might safely have been prophesied by one who perceived the disintegration which was creeping over the Mogul empire, and the paralysis which had already set in at head-quarters, that some day a Frenchman or an Englishman would be at the head of affairs in Pondicherry or in Madras, who would see that those visions were possible to realise, and would attempt to realise them. Nor would it have required much foresight to prophesy that, when once the attempt was made, whether by English or French, the others would promptly set about counteracting the attempt in their own interests. The mere trade rivalry of companies seeking to obtain this or that concession, would give place to a struggle in which each would seek to annihilate the other.

It was inevitable, therefore, that both in North America and in India, either England or France would have to withdraw and leave the field clear for the other; and it was most improbable that either would withdraw, except after a life-and-death struggle.

Now the colonial and commercial rivalry of France was with England only. The field in which England was her competitor was sufficiently large to occupy all her energies, and even then the competition was a greater strain upon her resources than on those of England. But with England it was otherwise. Her enterprise carried her still farther afield, and she challenged the monopoly of Spanish trade in the southern seas. She did not seek territorial expansion at the expense of Spain, but she did seek a share in Spanish commerce, which Spain was not willing to resign to her. Already, to her shame, she

in the South Seas.

had wrung from Spain the monopoly of the slave-trade, and had secured certain other concessions : but she was not content with these ; and, since she could obtain no more by legal means, she sought it by illicit traffic. Hence Spain, as well as France, viewed her commercial aggrandisement with intense jealousy ; and England had two rivals, who, having no mutual colonial jealousies, might easily act in concert against her whenever their European differences did not stand in the way.

Thus the prize for which the great war was to be fought was the greatest for which rival powers had ever contested since the days of Hannibal. There have been, of course, wars of equal importance—wars in which the hordes of barbaric invaders were held at bay or proved triumphant ; struggles for life between rival races and rival religions ; wars of conquest or annihilation. But the contest of the eighteenth century was one between civilised Powers of equal rank ; not for the destruction of one, or the dominion of one over the other, but for a prize which each desired to win from the other—the empire of East and West.

Britain, then, stood alone as against France and Spain in the colonial rivalry. Her interests and those of France were in such direct opposition that, in the long run, the alternatives could only be, either a duel, or the withdrawal of one party from the field. No adjustment was practicable. As concerned Spain, England wished for concessions which Spain could only grant at the expense of her monopolies, and the granting of which would have rankled as a continual grievance. It is difficult to see how an alliance on such terms could have been firm or lasting. Practically, therefore, there was no prospect of the rivalry being settled by a strong alliance between England and either one of the other two powers. On the other hand, her naval superiority made it sure that, in war carried on by sea, or over seas, Britain would get the better of either France or Spain single-handed, unless civil discord

Possibilities of alliance.

prevented her activity abroad. The great danger to her lay in the risk of a close combination of France and Spain; and her salvation in the fact that no such close combination was actually formed till the battle was already decided, though it was constantly on the verge of formation, and, apart from continental politics, would have been entirely advantageous both to Spain and to France.

The contest, then, was inevitable; but the fact was not as yet altogether patent, nor had the rivals realised the conditions under which it would have to be fought. Yet those conditions are clear enough. First, so far as the contest would be fought out in America or in India, the advantage was certain to lie with the competitor who could keep up communications with the base: and that power depended on control of the seas. Secondly, it was from transmarine commerce that the rivals mainly obtained the sinews of war; the one which controlled the seas could cut off the supplies of the other, while securing her own. Thirdly, so far as the war should be waged at home, a direct attack could only be made by invasion; and here again, England being an island, the possibility of invasion depended on control of the seas. Therefore it was only by one side or the other developing complete naval supremacy, though only for a time, that the battle could be fought out to a decisive conclusion.

Conditions of the contest.

Now, at the peace of Utrecht, England's fleet was far stronger than that of any other Power. But in the colonial struggle she required to be able to cope with France and Spain in combination. On the other hand, the prospects of France and Spain depended on their acting together, and developing an adequate joint fleet, or else each individually bringing her fleet up to the English standard. It was singularly fortunate for England that France and Spain were in opposition to each other for fourteen years; that when they were on the friendliest terms they still never succeeded in

Relative strength of the Powers.

acting harmoniously; that France never realised, until it was too late, the importance of naval efficiency; that Spain's attempts at recuperation of her fleet were time after time made abortive by a series of disasters; and that the English navy never had to deal with the combined strength of France and Spain until the maritime forces of the former had been all but annihilated. Thus the British fleet never at any time had to cope with a fleet of equal force; and so, even under incompetent war ministers, she was able to hold her own; while, so soon as a competent war minister was at the helm, she could exert and profit by a quite overwhelming supremacy of the seas. The final struggle did not begin till 1756, forty-three years after the Treaty of Utrecht, but we shall presently observe in detail, not merely the paramount effects of British naval supremacy after that date, but its important influence in the premonitory conflicts.

When we turn to the political conditions within Europe, and the domestic problems before English statesmen, we shall find that they combine rather curiously to foster precisely that naval supremacy on which Britain's success in the hardly foreseen colonial contest was to depend.

To Englishmen at home, the one pressing question to which everything else was subordinate was that of the succession to the throne. Till that question was finally settled there was a perpetual risk of civil war. The wealthiest and most powerful sections of the community were all in favour of the Hanoverian succession; and the Stuarts, if restored, would have to lean on foreign support. As a matter of fact, the Stuarts were not restored; but the House of Hanover lived in perpetual fear that a restoration, by means of foreign support, would be attempted. Consequently, it was at all times necessary to be fully prepared for the danger of a foreign invasion, to which end the maintenance of an adequate defensive fleet was again a necessity.

But for at least five and twenty years France never felt the pressing necessity of keeping up her fleet. She left the colonial contest out of her calculations; for nearly thirty years after the death of Louis XIV., in 1715, she never proposed to invade England; and during the greater part of that time she was in sufficiently close alliance with England to leave in the hands of that Power the conduct of any naval operations which their joint continental policy demanded. Spain, on the other hand, deteriorated instead of advancing. Thoroughly exhausted, her whole system thrown completely out of gear by the war just ended, it was only possible for her to recover by the exercise of rigid economy, coupled with thorough administrative reorganisation. But these were conditions which her rulers refused to recognize, with the exception of Alberoni, whose plans were frustrated. So Spain plunged into wars prematurely, exhausting herself afresh when she should have been husbanding her strength. Isolated as she was, each war brought disaster, and lost her all the ground she might have previously gained, leaving her at the same time less capable of efforts at reconstruction.

<small>France and Spain.</small>

Thus circumstances which were quite unconnected with colonial relations combined to make England comparatively careful of her navy, and France careless of hers; while they completely frustrated any attempts on the part of Spain to correct the balance of naval power. But while they also led England, apart from her fleet, to concentrate her energies on the accumulation of a great reserve of wealth, they led both France and Spain to expend their energies and their reserves on the prosecution of European quarrels, and on schemes of continental aggrandisement.

Until 1746 the leading incentive of Great Britain's attitude to the European powers was her desire to avoid such a rupture with any of them, but especially with France, as would secure to the Jacobites active foreign support. At the same time, her previous relations to

<small>The German States.</small>

Austria, coupled with the Austrian sympathies of the House of Hanover, made her discountenance aggression aimed against that power, and so, entirely apart from colonial questions, led her to view with disfavour as threatening to the Empire any marked *rapprochement* between France and Spain.

Of the German principalities, none was as yet of first-class importance; but one, Prussia, was being so organised that, in thirty years' time, she suddenly stepped to the front and assumed the position of a leading state. When she did so come forward, the previous theory of the balance of powers was upset, and the political calculations of European statesmen were completely distorted. The establishment of Prussia on the European continent in the middle of the century was a fact second only in importance to the establishment of the British race in America and India at the same time.

The complications of European politics will be found to turn mainly, for twenty years or more, on the questions of the succession to the throne of France, and the inheritance of sundry Italian dukedoms and kingdoms; and, later, on the succession of Maria Theresa to the Hapsburg possessions.

<small>Sources of friction.</small>

On examination it will appear that, in most cases, the disturbing influence, in one way or another, was the court of Spain.

The Treaty of Utrecht secured on the Spanish throne Philip, grandson of Louis XIV. of France; and uncle of the heir apparent, at that time a child. When Louis XV. succeeded his grandfather in 1715, Philip became heir presumptive as far as kinship was concerned. He had formally renounced his right of succession, as condition of receiving the Spanish crown; but he himself was never satisfied in conscience that his renunciation was valid or justifiable. Hence, until the boy king was grown up, married, and had a son, it was never certain that the Spanish king might not claim the throne

<small>The French succession.</small>

when it became vacant. Such a course would probably have plunged France into civil war, as the House of Orleans would have challenged his title; and further, Europe would have been in arms to prevent the junction of the Spanish and French crowns. It followed, therefore, that Philip could never feel friendly to French ministers who were opposed to his succession; while none who favoured his claim could obtain power in France. Thus, until the young king had a son, no close alliance between France and Spain was possible.

Further, in 1714, Philip married, as his second wife, Elizabeth Farnese, daughter of the late, and niece of the reigning (but childless) Duke of Parma and Piacenza; and her will dominated Spanish policy. Elizabeth claimed the succession, not only to Parma and Piacenza, but also to Tuscany: the reversions of which were claimed, on the other hand, by Austria. Moreover, as an Italian, Elizabeth was intensely desirous of the expulsion of Austria from Italy altogether, and especially from the two Sicilies. At this time, Sicily itself belonged to the Duke of Savoy; Naples and Sardinia were both in the hands of Austria. The Italian idea was that the Duke should exchange Sicily for Sardinia; so that the above-named Italian dukedoms and the kingdoms of Naples and Sicily would become the bones of contention between Austria on one side, and, on the other side, Spain and her queen as heir of the Farnesi.

The Italian duchies.

Thus, so long as Philip and his consort were both living, there was constant hostility between Spain and Austria, varied by intervals when the Spanish queen had expectations of gaining her ends in Italy by means of an Austrian alliance. There was constant friction between Spain and England, varied by intervals when the Spanish court had hopes of obtaining English assistance against Austria, by means of commercial concessions. Nor was there ever any cordiality between the French and Spanish courts, although the theory of a Bourbon combination as a thing to be aimed at was very much present in the background of French policy after Fleury came into power.

These considerations show that to the Spanish court Austria, not England, was the most obvious enemy. Elizabeth was more concerned with Italy than with American commerce. Similarly, for a long time the French court was more concerned with securing reciprocal support from the English government in the matter of the succession than in looking forward to future subjects of rivalry. And when the question of succession ceased to be pressing, she was still more occupied with anti-Austrian schemes on the continent than with anti-English schemes in the colonies. The division of their interests, the strain of continental wars, and continual naval decay, placed both France and Spain at a disadvantage with England when the collision arrived—a disadvantage which would have been less, but for their incapacity for joint action. On the other hand, England for five and twenty years wasted her resources comparatively little on superfluous wars, and accumulated great wealth; while she was compelled to maintain her navy tolerably, though by no means in that state of thorough efficiency which was possible, and would have ultimately rendered her decisive triumph much more rapid and less expensive than it actually was.

England's power of inaction.

BOOK I.
THE HOUSE OF HANOVER.

CHAPTER I.

THE HANOVERIAN SUCCESSION.

1713–1716.

Parties in 1713—The Whigs—The Tories—Jacobitism—Party effects of Utrecht—The Commercial Treaty—1714: Bolingbroke's difficulties—Uncertainty of the party—The Schism Act—Fall of Oxford—The queen's death—Triumph of the Whigs—The new king; instability of his position—1715: Jacobite intrigues—Death of Louis XIV.—Mar raises the clans—The rising in England—The collapse of Preston—Sheriffmuir—1716: Break up of Mar's army—After the 'Fifteen—Characteristics of the rebellion.

THE position of parties in England at the close of Queen Anne's reign was peculiarly complex; because, of the two great divisions, one, the party actually in power, had not made up its mind on the most pressing of all public questions, that of the succession to the throne.

The parties and the succession.

The Whigs were perfectly clear on the matter. They had ejected James II., and had effected the "glorious Revolution." For them a Stuart restoration could mean nothing but political annihilation, unless perhaps for a few who might be adroit enough to secure themselves by private preliminary intriguing. The great body of the party was thoroughly bent on securing the Protestant succession.

The Whigs.

But among the Tories opinion was divided. There was a small section of genuine Jacobites who held the high legitimist doctrine. There were some who foresaw that, if the Elector of Hanover succeeded to the throne, he must rest on the Whigs, and that consequently their own political prospects rested on the chance of a Stuart restoration. These were, for the most part, privately committed to the Jacobite policy, though to a large section of the party, that policy was honestly repugnant, except on terms of James embracing the Protestantism.

The Tories.

The position of this last body was particularly difficult, because, in fact, if their heads were on one side, their hearts were on the other. They were Churchmen, and the voice of the clergy was almost unanimously given in support of the doctrine of passive obedience, in defiance of which the Revolution had been effected. They could not free themselves from that sentiment of loyalty, and that secret belief in divine right for which their fathers had fallen in the Great Rebellion. The idea of allegiance to a German prince who could, at best, only be regarded as an expedient institution, and to whom could attach none of the glamour of hereditary royalty, none of the divinity that doth hedge a king, was abhorrent. And yet it was impossible to be blind to the danger of re-establishing a Roman Catholic upon the throne. The experience of what that might mean was only some five and twenty years past. The risk of being obliged to repeat the work of 1688, and of perhaps failing to repeat it, was too much to face. Therefore they halted between two opinions; in their secret hearts leaning to one, in their public avowals to the other. And thus, while it is undoubtedly true that the judgment of the nation at large was altogether in favour of the House of Hanover, it is also true that the sentiment of the nation at large was in favour of the House of Stuart. If anything should occur, either to rouse sentiment so that it should outweigh judgment, or to produce a revised judgment which could be reconciled with sentiment, it was quite possible that the policy of restoration might carry the day.

The Tories being divided in mind on this question, it was of primary importance that they should keep the final decision of it in their own hands; and the immediate results of the Treaty of Utrecht were all in their favour. If France had, in fact, obtained practically what she had fought for in securing the Bourbon succession in Spain, the objection to her doing so had become much less palpable than it would have been at an earlier stage of the war; for the rival claimant had himself succeeded to the Hapsburg dominions, and had been elected Emperor in the interval. On the other hand, England actually profited more than any other of the belligerents. The cost in honour counted for little in the existing degraded state of public feeling. And so, while what England gained had been due to the Whigs who conducted the war, the credit for it went to the Tories, who negotiated the peace. At the same time, the dangerous power of the Duke of Marlborough—for the time identified with the Whig party—was greatly curtailed, while his opportunities for acquiring fresh prestige were removed.

The Tory peace.

Although the chiefs of the Tory party, Oxford and Bolingbroke, had reason to congratulate themselves on the result, there was one part of their policy which very seriously endangered their popularity, and that was the proposed Commercial Treaty with France. England and France were to admit each other's goods on the same terms as the "most favoured nation;" that is, goods of the same class were not to be admitted from other countries with a lower duty upon them: so that, for instance, French and Portuguese wines would compete in the market on even terms. At the present day, few economists would question the soundness of the principle; but a different theory dominated the public mind at this time. According to the "mercantile theory," the object

The Commercial Treaty.

of foreign commerce was to bring as much bullion into the country as possible. Now, if English imports from France exceeded in value the goods she exported to France, it is clear that the balance would have to be made up in the precious metals. It followed, according to the mercantile theory, that commercial arrangements between France and England resulting in an excess of imports over exports would be destructive to English wealth, because they would drain away the precious metals from England to France. It was certain that, under the treaty, there would be an enormous increase of French imports; and it was supposed that there would be no corresponding increase of exports. Thus, not only would England suffer by her increased commerce with France, and suffer more and more as her commerce went on increasing; but she would lose her lucrative trade with Portugal. For since the Portuguese wines would now have to compete on even terms with French wines, England would import less from Portugal, and, by way of retaliation, Portugal would raise the duties on English wool, and there would be a serious diminution in English exports to Portugal. But in the Portuguese trade our exports had hitherto considerably exceeded our imports; the balance had been made up in bullion. So we were about to exchange a commerce which had brought bullion into the country, for a commerce which would take bullion out of it. The commercial classes were furious; the Whigs, who especially leaned on the commercial classes, were not slow to make political capital out of a measure to whose inherent advantages Walpole, at least, must have been sufficiently alive. The commercial treaty was thrown out; but the Tory position was seriously weakened.

Still the representation of parties in Parliament was not materially affected at the general election which ensued. Oxford and Bolingbroke retained their majority, but the task before them was one of extraordinary difficulty.

As the time drew nearer when the final decision between

James and George must be made, the situation was growing extremely critical.

Bolingbroke had made up his own mind. For him the restoration was a necessity. The Whig chiefs had the ear of George, and whoever else might obtain the confidence of the Elector, it was quite certain that Bolingbroke would not. But, as yet, an avowal of the Stuart cause would be fatal. James steadily refused to change his religious faith; his supporters had no choice but to profess unswerving adherence to the Act of Settlement. What might have occurred if they had dared to unite and openly throw off the mask, it is hard to say; but the risk was too great, and they did not dare. Moreover, Bolingbroke was himself desperately hampered by the attitude of Oxford, who delayed, and temporised, and would not definitely commit himself. And with him at the head of the Tory ministry, it followed that the party could not be decisively manipulated so as to be brought into line. Meantime, the Whigs were making the most of the position, forcing their opponents to repeated declarations of loyalty to the Hanoverian succession, and challenging every act which could be construed into a sign of the opposite intention.

<small>Bolingbroke.</small>

The problem for Bolingbroke, therefore, was to organise the Tories into a Jacobite party, to popularise the Jacobite theory, and to gag the Hanoverians; and all the time to proclaim himself a Hanoverian, until his organisation should be complete enough to enable him to throw off the mask and effect a *coup d'état* which might be carried through by an outburst of popular sentiment on one side in the face of the apathy of the other side, whose cause was at least unlikely to arouse popular enthusiasm.

Accordingly, the first step of the ministry, when the new parliament met in January, 1714, was to attack Steele for a pamphlet in which it was affirmed that he had charged the queen with the intention of upsetting the Act of Settlement—an accusation which he had, in fact, brought against ministers. As a counter to this, the Lords—in which House the majority was decisively anti-Jacobite—attacked a Tory pamphlet (written by Swift, though the authorship was concealed) which had caused violent offence to the Scots. This they followed up by an address to the crown in favour of the Catalans, amounting to a vote of censure on ministers for their disgraceful desertion of their allies in the Treaty of Utrecht.

Ministers further weakened their own position by the next move—a proposal to make it high treason to bring foreign troops into the country. The avowed intention was to prevent invasion by the Chevalier; but the measure was so obviously aimed in reality at the Elector that it had to be stopped, and, in fact, gave the more colour to the charge, openly brought forward in a resolution of both Houses in April, that, under the existing government, the Hanoverian succession was in danger. The resolution was defeated, but a large number of Tories voted against the government.

Feeling that the popularity of the ministry was in jeopardy, Oxford and Bolingbroke made a bid for the support of that section of the Church party from whom most could be hoped in the way of inflammatory proceedings, by the Schism Act, which forbade any Dissenters to teach, under severe penalties. That such a measure would be widely unpopular was clear enough; but the prospects of a *coup d'état* turned on the possibility of a sudden outburst of feeling, and the Sacheverell riots had already shown in what quarters and by what means such an outburst would have the best chance of being aroused. {The Schism Act.}

On the other hand, apart from this chance, the measure was injurious to the government; and, at the same time, Bolingbroke was no nearer to getting the control of his principal colleague than he had been. Nothing would induce Oxford to make up his mind. His influence, indeed,

C

was fast failing: with the queen he was out of favour; the queen's favourite, Mrs. Masham, was violently hostile to him; and it was evident that he would have to go ere long: but the state of Anne's health was so bad that Bolingbroke's chief danger lay in the difficulty of removing him soon enough. The opportunity did not come till after the close of the session. On July 27th there was a meeting of the council; the queen was present; the meeting was stormy. When it broke up, at two o'clock in the morning, Oxford had been dismissed, and the task of forming a new administration was assigned to his rival.

Dismissal of Oxford.

Bolingbroke's chance had come. Even now he made a vain show of conciliating the Whig leaders; but the scheme of his new administration was too palpably Jacobite to allow any real doubt as to its meaning. He was himself to be Secretary of State; Wyndham, whose Jacobitism was never very doubtful, was at the head of the Treasury; Bishop Atterbury was to be Privy Seal; Ormond was to control the army, and Mar Scotland. Every post of consequence was in Jacobite hands.

Formation of Jacobite ministry;

But at the very moment when the cup was raised to his lips it was dashed from his grasp. At two o'clock in the morning of July 28th, Oxford had fallen; on the morning of the 30th the queen was seized with an apoplectic fit, probably a consequence of the extremely agitating events of the night of the 27th. It was the moment for which Bolingbroke should have been ready, but he had had only two days to prepare for it. The shock of the emergency was paralysing. On the same morning, the 30th, while the council, consisting, according to practice, only of the high officers specially summoned, was sitting to consider what was to be done, the doors were suddenly thrown open, and two great Whig peers, Argyll and Somerset, entered. They had come, they said, to offer their assistance—which they seem to have been entitled to do as members of the Privy Council. The Duke of Shrewsbury,

its collapse.

a peer whose attitude on the question of the succession had been open to doubt, one of the most astute and incalculable of intriguers, promptly rose to thank them. On the physicians' report of the state of the queen's health being brought, it was forthwith proposed that Shrewsbury should be made Lord Treasurer. Bolingbroke could only assent. It is, indeed, uncertain whether he did not himself make the proposal.

A deputation at once proceeded to the presence of the queen, who had recovered consciousness. She acquiesced, handing the white staff to the new Treasurer with the words, "Use it for the good of my people." A special summons was immediately sent to all members of the Privy Council within reach, many of them Whigs. Instant measures were taken to prevent any possibility of a rising or an invasion. On the 31st the queen had relapsed into a state of lethargy, and all was in readiness to proclaim her successor. The next morning, within five days of Oxford's fall, she was dead. Atterbury still believed that the position might be retrieved by a bold stroke, and urged that King James should be proclaimed, offering himself to head the procession in his lawn sleeves. But the rest were more prudent, or more pusillanimous, and King George was proclaimed without disturbance. *The Queen's death.*

The Whigs had, in fact, managed the situation with entire success. They had practically convicted the heads of the other party of desiring the Stuart restoration, if not of actually conspiring to that end; and with the chiefs, the whole body of Tories were generally included in the suspicion of Jacobitism. It was certain that none but Whigs could have the confidence of the new dynasty, so that they were assured of a complete triumph if the new dynasty succeeded. And when the crisis arrived, they were enabled to turn the tables on Bolingbroke and effect a *coup de main* themselves, instead of allowing him to do so. The fallen statesman summed *The Whigs triumphant.*

up the position accurately in the words: "The grief of my soul is this: I see plainly that the Tory party is gone."

The new king had drawn up his list of the "Lords Justices" who were to conduct the government until his arrival. Practically all were Whigs, and all the Whigs of prominence were there except three—Somers, who was too infirm; Marlborough, whose double-dealing was too notorious; and his son-in-law, Sunderland. It only remained for the Tories to do what they might to retrieve their position, by vying with their successful opponents in expressions of loyalty to the new régime; and in the face of this unexpected turn of affairs, the continental courts, one after the other, acknowledged the Hanoverian succession.

It was not till the middle of September that the king himself arrived in his new dominions; and he promptly confirmed the expectation that the Tories would be entirely excluded from power. Townshend and Stanhope were made Secretaries of State, and the other principal offices were all bestowed on leading Whig peers. The position at first occupied by Walpole was subordinate, but he rapidly rose in importance as the most powerful of all the Whig speakers in the House of Commons, and a year later became First Lord of the Treasury.

The Whigs, however, were not content with having thoroughly carried out the doctrine of "Spoils to the victors;" they resolved to go further, and crush the vanquished. Parliament was dissolved; the proclamation calling a new one was a presage of the course they intended to take; and the country endorsed their policy by returning an overwhelming Whig majority. From the debate on the address, it became evident that vigorous proceedings would be taken, certainly against Bolingbroke and Oxford, probably against Ormond and others. The first promptly and secretly fled from the country, and took service with James.

In April a committee was appointed to examine the conduct of the late ministry in regard to the negotiations for the Utrecht Treaty, and the resulting report was a tremendous indictment of broken pledges and scandalous bad faith. On the strength of it, the three Tory chiefs already named were impeached. Ormond was not prepared to risk the consequences, and followed Bolingbroke; Oxford chose to abide the storm. The two fugitives were attainted, but the impeachment was never carried through, since it appeared too dangerous a precedent to base charges of high treason on the conduct of negotiations which had already received the sanction of two parliaments.

But although the Whigs had secured the complete control of parliament and the public offices, King George's throne was not as yet by any means secure. The leaders of the Jacobite intrigue were crushed, but there was considerable Jacobite feeling in the country. The personality of the new monarch was not calculated to counteract the sentimental loyalty to the Stuarts. He was a German of the Germans. The average Englishman finds it hard to feel real respect for a foreigner, and George could not even speak English. Moreover, he brought a train of foreign favourites, and foreign favourites are always unpopular—and of foreign mistresses, which did not, indeed, shock public morality, but did shock public taste. The Stuarts had always an extraordinary power of winning personal popularity, but it was quite impossible for George to be personally popular. It still appeared that with skilful organisation a Jacobite rising might overthrow the new dynasty.

Instability of the new dynasty.

On the other hand, it was felt that if an effective blow was to be struck, it must be struck at once. Help from France was one condition of a successful rising, and French help could hardly be hoped for when once Louis XIV. should be dead; for the good will of Orleans, who would become regent on his death, could not be counted upon. Louis, however, whose good will, at any rate, was certain, might be inveigled into committing himself more deeply than he was disposed to do; and Bolingbroke conducted a very active intrigue with a view to drawing the king into a new English war. But again he was disappointed by the death of the French king before his plans were matured. The last effort of Jacobitism for the time collapsed in the abortive rising known as "the 'Fifteen."

Although it was tolerably certain before the actual demise of Louis, in September, 1715, that French assistance could not be counted on, Mar, the leading Scottish Tory noble, received instructions to raise Scotland. What precise share James had in pushing matters on—how far he hoodwinked Bolingbroke in doing so—is uncertain. But Mar, apparently, without arousing suspicion, travelled north, collected the leading Jacobite chiefs of the clans, and persuaded them to proclaim King James. Many of them were fully aware of the hopelessness of the effort; but sheer loyalty to an idea, and jealousy of the ascendancy of the Whig Duke of Argyll—the intensity of clan hostilities is not easy for an Englishman to realise—enabled Mar to muster a considerable army, with which he made haste to do nothing. Argyll was sent north with all speed; but a little promptitude and energy on Mar's part would have made him powerless, and the whole country north of the Cheviots would have been in the hands of the Jacobites.

The 'Fifteen.

The Scotch rising should have been attended by risings in England; but here it was comparatively easy for the government to strike. The fleet was ready for action; in the south, Wyndham and six other members were seized on suspicion; while the other leading Jacobites were allowed to feel that any movement on their part could be crushed before it had time to gather strength.

In the north of England Lord Derwentwater, Thomas Forster, and a few other gentlemen raised the standard of King James, chiefly moved thereto by the intelligence that warrants were out against them. In the south of Scotland, Lord Kenmure, who was joined by the Earls of Nithisdale,

Winton, and Carnwath, proclaimed James; and these two handfuls of men, together amounting only to a few hundreds, joined forces. At Kelso the numbers and intelligence of the insurgents were increased by the arrival of Brigadier M'Intosh with a detachment from Mar's army. M'Intosh, the solitary officer possessed of any military knowledge or skill, had crossed the Forth by a clever manœuvre, and had nearly succeeded in capturing Edinburgh Castle on the way.

The army at Kelso now numbered altogether some two thousand men. They might have marched south, and engaged General Carpenter, the government commander, who had only some nine hundred raw troops; but the Highlanders objected. They might have marched north, co-operating with Mar, and have crushed Argyll; but the English objected. So they marched along the border, doing nothing, till they could make up their minds.

In the course of time they did make up their minds, and decided to invade Lancashire. Five hundred of the Highlanders refused to accompany them. The main body, however, marched south, meeting with no resistance; the Posse Comitatus of Cumberland ran away, having conceived an alarming idea of the ferocity of the Highlanders. The numbers of the insurgents had been considerably increased by miscellaneous, half-armed, and wholly untrained recruits, before they reached Preston.

Meantime, Carpenter had been following them. General Wills, who had also been sent north by the government, was at Wigan, and resolved to march on Preston, while Carpenter was to make a flank attack. When the news was brought to Forster, who held the commission to command the Jacobite army in England, that incompetent officer had retired to bed, and was with difficulty roused, and stirred into making some preparations for defence. Even then he confined himself to barricading the streets; but his men successfully repulsed the attack of General Wills

Preston.

(on the 12th of November). Carpenter arrived the next day, bringing the number of the government troops up to about a thousand. Forster then offered to treat: Wills would only promise that the rebels should not be cut to pieces if they surrendered at discretion; which they did.

On the same day, November 13th, a battle was fought in Scotland, at Sheriffmuir, between Argyll and Mar, who had at last been stirred up to move. The battle was summed up in the popular rhyme:—

Sheriff-muir.

> "There's some say that we wan
> And some say that they wan,
> And some say that none wan at a', man!
> But ae thing I'm sure,
> That at Sheriffmuir
> A battle there was that I saw, man;
> And we ran and they ran,
> And they ran and we ran,
> And we ran and they ran awa', man."

There was some hard fighting on Mar's left wing, where Argyll won, and dispersed the insurgents. On the other hand, Argyll's left wing was scattered by the rush of the Highlanders. Mutual jealousies, and irritation at Mar's want of energy, had so disheartened and demoralised the Jacobites, that the Seaforth Mackenzies simply ran away, and the Camerons and Appin Stuarts retired without striking a blow. Both sides claimed the victory; but, as Mar withdrew from the field, Argyll had on the whole the better title to such credit as there was.

Mar went back to Perth. The clansmen began to go home. The insurrection in England was ended. No rising had been attempted in Ireland. Some of Mar's supporters were inclined to try making terms privately. Six thousand Dutch troops had been sent over in the mean time, according to compact, to assist the government. At this juncture, James himself arrived in Scotland, and joined the army at Perth, whereby the drooping spirits of the insurgents were slightly raised. But they were in no condition to take the offensive. When, in January, it became evident that, despite the rigour of the season, the enemy had resolved to take active measures, and were marching on Perth, the Jacobite army was obliged to retreat to Dundee, and thence to Montrose. James, reluctantly giving way to the urgent persuasions of his advisers, embarked secretly for France; and the army continued to retreat and dwindle, till finally it broke up altogether.

Thus this most abortive of rebellions, stupid in its inception, and desultory in its execution, terminated in a collapse worthy of the complete disorganisation and absence of management which characterised it from one end to the other. Mar, and the gentlemen who had been with him, escaped to France. Many of those who so escaped, were attainted. Of those who had been taken at Preston, the peers were impeached and condemned to death. Lord Nithisdale, however, escaped, by the courageous stratagem of his wife; and although ministers were convinced of the necessity for dealing vigorously with the rebels, the opposition was so strong, especially in the Upper House, that they found it advisable to recommend the respite of Lords Nairn, Carnwath, and Widdrington. As Lord Wintoun also succeeded in breaking prison, Kenmure and Derwentwater were the only peers who were beheaded. Of the commoners, some escaped from prison; only twenty-six were hanged, though several of those taken at Preston, being half-pay officers, had been summarily shot as deserters. James seized the opportunity to put the finishing stroke to his own fortunes, by dismissing the one man of real ability on his side—Bolingbroke; who, if he had been untrustworthy before, was driven by this step to separate himself finally and defiantly from the Jacobite party.

End of the rising.

The whole story of the 'Fifteen—the whole picture it presents—is pitiful and ignominious from every point of view. There is a glow of romance about those Highland chiefs who embraced the lost cause in the face of their conviction that it

Considerations on the rebellion.

was lost; there is a touch of pathos about the heir of the
Stuarts arriving in the gloom of a bitter winter in the camp
of his supporters, merely to find them already all but
desperate, and divided only between counsels of making
a last rally and dying in the field, or throwing up the
struggle and fleeing into exile: yet these cast but a
transient flash of light upon a story of recklessness, vacillation, bickering, half-heartedness, and sheer folly, which it
would be difficult to parallel. Nothing is more striking
than the blank apathy, the utter absence of any sort of
enthusiasm with which the country looked on, while armies
of a few hundred men were allowed to decide a question on
which hung the destiny of a nation. The government,
indeed, took their measures with some wisdom, and, by
concentrating their energies in the south, prevented any
attempt at a rising there, and successfully checked any
danger of French invasion; but if either Mar or Forster
had been endowed with a fragment of military capacity, the
slackness of the measures taken in the north might easily
have led to disaster. And in the moment of triumph
generosity was the last thing the victors thought of. The
captives from Preston marched through London with their
arms bound, and a band playing a triumphal march. The
victorious party refused to allow Lord Wintoun, who was
"of feeble intellect," to be heard by Counsel. The judges
scolded juries for acquitting prisoners of high treason: they
scolded the prisoners themselves for being Roman Catholics.
If mercy were shown to some of the peers, it was because
those peers had influential connections. King George
distinguished himself by the boorishness of his treatment
of two countesses, who, when their husbands were in prison,
awaiting the doom of high treason, entrapped him into a
private audience to plead for pardon. Throughout there is
an undercurrent of consciousness that, until the rebellion
was finally crushed, and all chance of a French invasion
thoroughly at an end, half the men of position in the

country were chiefly anxious to avoid committing themselves too far, in case by any chance the other side should get the best of it. Marlborough is known to have actually supplied money to aid the insurrection. Even so trusted a Whig as Argyll did not escape suspicion. But the rising was suppressed ; and with its suppression, following on the death of Louis XIV., and accompanied by the dismissal of Bolingbroke, all immediate danger of a fresh rebellion disappeared.

CHAPTER II.

THE FRENCH ALLIANCE.

1716-1726.

Establishment of the new dynasty—Drawbacks of the Hanoverian connection—1716: The Whig disruption—Hanover and the Northern Powers—The French succession—The Triple Alliance—Alberoni and Elizabeth Farnese—Charles XII.—1717: Spain attacks Sardinia—Temporary compromise—Alberoni's intrigues—The Quadruple Alliance—1718: Spain attacks Sicily—Battle of Cape Passaro; its effects—1719: Failure of Alberoni's schemes; his fall—1723: The Duke of Bourbon regent in France—1725: Austro-Spanish Alliance—The Treaty of Hanover.

Establishment of the House of Hanover.
THE failure of the insurrection of 1715 saved Great Britain from a restoration which would in all probability have resulted in continuous civil strife. Fortunately it came at a moment when France was unusually well disposed towards England, and disinclined to support the claims of the Stuarts. Hence it was long before the Hanoverian succession could again be seriously threatened, and the new dynasty was firmly established during a quarter of a century of alliance with France, of freedom from prolonged wars, and of rapidly increasing commercial prosperity.

Disadvantages of the Hanoverian connection.
Still the accession of a foreign prince to the English throne was not without drawbacks. George was a Hanoverian, and all his personal interests were Hanoverian, not English. So far as this led to an almost entire withdrawal of royal interference in domestic politics, this was gain. But whenever the interests of Hanover on the continent clashed with the interests of

England, the king's inclination was to favour the electorate. He was ready to press the power of England into the service of Hanover; and his strong feelings as a prince of the Empire led him, as it led his son, into a partisan support of Austria, which it required all the strength of Walpole to restrain. Consequently there was no cry more easily raised, and more popular when raised, by English malcontents than that ministers were pursuing a Hanoverian policy, whether the cry happened to be raised with reason or without. As a rule, the policy which best suited England was best for Hanover also; but even so it was obviously easy for the Opposition to prove to their own satisfaction that the motive of the measures taken was not British but Hanoverian.

One result of the king's preference for Hanover is important primarily because it led to a split in the Whig party. To that split was due the somewhat fortunate removal of Walpole from office, at a period when an active foreign policy was desirable, and his still more fortunate return to power precisely at the time when a great peace minister was required. And the source of this division was the withdrawal of the king himself to Hanover, whither he took Stanhope, leaving his son in England with Townshend and Walpole. Every king of the Hanoverian House has been to a considerable extent at feud with his eldest son. King George at a distance was ready to believe that the ministers he left behind him were forming a party with Prince George at home. Stanhope, separated from his colleagues and influenced strongly by personal contact with the king, did not support Townshend as he ought to have done. Sunderland, joining the king, and taking his view of the political situation, widened the rift while increasing his own influence. Therefore, from 1716 to 1720, Stanhope and Sunderland directed affairs, and Townshend and Walpole were practically in Opposition. In 1720 the South Sea Bubble burst, and the ministry

The Whig disruption.

collapsed ; but Townshend and Walpole, who would have
been in the ministry and have fallen with it but for the
rift, were enabled to resume power.

On the other hand, in these early years there were two
specific occasions on which George's Hanoverian predilections
produced strained relations with foreign powers without
adequate reason from a British point of view. The first
of these was in 1715, when George acquired Bremen and
Verden for the electorate, from Denmark. The acquisition
was in some respects useful to England, and was extremely
useful to Hanover, but it involved entering a coalition
against Charles XII. of Sweden, and thereby making a bitter
foe of the Northern monarch.

A year later George aroused the hostility of Russia.
The Czar, seeking aggrandisement, threatened Mecklenburg ; and, by so doing, in George's view, threatened
Hanover. The king wished to draw England into the
quarrel, and threatened to send a British fleet to the Baltic.
The opposition of ministers at home prevented extreme
measures being actually taken, and the mere threat proved
in fact sufficient to check the Czar—a somewhat striking
testimony to the advantage of unqualified naval predominance,—but the result was that, purely in the interests of
Hanover, George had united Charles and Russia in enmity
to England, and especially to the Hanoverian succession.

But the great feature in foreign politics between 1715 and
1739 was the steady alliance between England and France.

When Louis XIV. died, in 1716, he left as his successor
on the French throne his great-grandson, a sickly child,
whose life was extremely uncertain. The next in
blood was Philip of Spain, who was barred from
the succession by the formal renunciation of his
claim, which had been the condition of his receiving the
Spanish crown, so that the heir presumptive was the Duke
of Orleans, who was regent. But the legal validity of
Philip's renunciation was denied by French lawyers, on the

The French succession.

ground that the title was indefeasible; and Philip himself was inclined to believe, as a point of conscience, that he was bound to assert his claim in spite of the renunciation. The regent therefore felt that his succession was extremely likely to be disputed, and was by no means sure of the support of the nation. It was evidently of great importance that the new dynasty in England should be able to rely on the French government for support as against the Stuarts. It was quite worth while for the regent to promise that support in exchange for British support of his own claim to the succession in France. The alliance therefore rested, in the first instance, on a dynastic bargain. By the diplomacy of Stanhope and Dubois, the Triple Alliance was effected between England, France, and the Netherlands, whereby each of the two leading powers guaranteed the succession for the other. The great advantages, however, rested with England, to whom France transferred certain trading rights with Spanish America, at the same time agreeing to demolish the fortifications at Mardyke, which were intended to serve instead of those at Dunkirk. The result of these provisions was to effectually check any tendency towards increased naval activity on the part of France, and thus to accentuate and develop England's naval supremacy.

Anglo-French alliance.

At this time Spain was recovering rapidly from her exhaustion, under the able administration of Alberoni. But, powerful as he was, he was obliged to submit his own policy to the domination of the queen. The queen's hostility was directed in the first place against the emperor, whom she wished to displace in Italy; and, in the second place, against the French regent, whom she wished to displace from the succession. Alberoni, with a far truer perception of the Spanish national interests, would have preferred to secure a free hand in Italy by buying England with trading concessions, and, at the same time, to develop a systematic Spanish commerce, to which latter

Alberoni.

purpose he would probably have preferred devoting the main energies of the country. But the attitude of the Spanish court towards the French government made it necessary for England to choose between two alliances. To have joined Spain would have forced France to a close coalition with Austria and an energetic support of the Stuarts. The danger was too great. England held by the French alliance, preferring safety from the Stuarts to commercial privileges. Alberoni therefore felt that, if the queen's Italian schemes were to have effect, England must be prevented from interfering, and Spain must be able, if necessary, to fight her.

The Spanish minister was therefore very well pleased to find George exciting the animosity of both Russia and Sweden. Görtz, the minister of Charles XII., conceived the idea of an attack on England in the interest of the Stuarts, and the idea found much favour in English Jacobite circles—partly because the reliance of the exiled family on France had always been something of a stumblingblock, partly because, under the peculiar circumstances, the support of a Protestant power was particularly likely to be popular. But early in 1717 this conspiracy was detected by the interception of correspondence, and both Görtz and the Swedish ambassador, Gyllenborg, were arrested.

<small>Charles XII.</small>

Alberoni wanted time to complete the reorganisation of the Spanish navy, and the construction of a northern alliance against England; but time was not allowed him. Austria was engaged in a war with the Turks, which forced her to withdraw troops from Italy, and the chance for an attack seemed to Elizabeth too good to lose.

So in 1717 Spain made a sudden swoop on Sardinia, with a view to exchanging that island for Sicily. But the failure of Görtz's plot left England free to act, and neither England nor France was disposed to have the European peace broken. England and France, accordingly, interposed jointly to press terms on Austria

<small>Spanish attack on Sardinia.</small>

and Spain. They proposed that Elizabeth's son, Don Carlos, should be recognized as heir to the disputed duchies of Tuscany, Parma, and Piacenza, but that these should be definitely separated from the Spanish crown; and Austria was further to resign her claim to the Spanish crown. On the other hand, Spain was to resign her claims on the Sicilies, the Milanese, and the Netherlands, and was to restore Sardinia to Austria; which, again, was to be allowed to exchange it for Sicily with the Duke of Savoy, who was to be compensated by having his own succession to the Spanish crown (in case of the failure of Philip's issue) guaranteed. *A compromise effected.*

The compromise was open to one objection—that all the parties to it thought they were entitled to what they received, and to a good deal which they gave up as well. Therefore, though they acquiesced sullenly, having indeed very little choice, neither of the principal parties were by any means satisfied. Austria was too much occupied with the Turkish war to be very restive; but Alberoni only intended to use the temporary check to complete his organisation. He accordingly proceeded with the preparation of his navy and of armaments for transport, and at the same time renewed his intrigues with the Northern powers, and set on foot an active conspiracy in France. According to his plans, Sweden and Russia were brought into agreement. As soon as Charles had completed the conquest of Norway, and recovered Bremen and Verden, Russia and Sweden were to combine in an attack on Britain for the purpose of restoring the Stuarts, relying on the assistance of the Jacobites in Scotland and England. The activity of the anti-Orleanist faction in France was to keep that nation thoroughly occupied; while Austria, with a Turkish war on her hands, would be unable to check the progress of the Spanish arms in Italy, supported as these would be by the good will of the native population. *Alberoni's intrigues.*

England, however, was not idle. Alberoni could not

prepare great armaments secretly, and it was quite evident that active measures of some sort were intended. Before any overt steps were taken, England succeeded in mediating between Austria and the Turks, and sent a fleet of twenty sail of the line under Byng to the Mediterranean. Moreover, she induced Austria to accept definitely the terms she had proposed, and the Triple Alliance became a Quadruple Alliance by a treaty signed on August 18 (1718). At the same time, in the hope of securing a peaceful issue, she even made overtures to Spain for the restoration of Gibraltar, though it is not clear how far the proposal was made conditional on compensatory concessions.

But Spain was not in a mood for compromise. If her schemes went well in France and in conjunction with Sweden and Russia, she need give up nothing of her claims. About the middle of 1718, Alberoni's armament sailed under sealed orders, and suddenly descended upon Sicily. The Spanish troops swept the island. Messina was the only place where serious resistance was to be looked for, and on July 31st the siege commenced.

Spanish attack on Sicily.

The Austrians in Naples, well aware that they would be the next object of attack, were thoroughly alarmed; when Byng with his twenty vessels appeared. He took 2000 Austrian troops to Reggio, with a view to the relief of Messina, and invited the Spanish commander to suspend hostilities. That officer declined. Whereupon Byng went in search of the Spanish ships.

He found them off Cape Passaro, and bore down on them. The English fleet, though numerically somewhat inferior, was considerably superior in weight of metal and in seamanship, the Spanish sailors being as yet insufficiently trained. Although war had not been declared, it was quite evident that a battle was intended, and it is a poor defence, if defence of Byng's action is needed, to urge that the Spaniards fired the first shot. As for the engagement itself, the English fleet sailed in upon

Battle of Cape Passaro;

the Spanish fleet, and annihilated it. Only one English
vessel was seriously damaged; only ten Spanish ships
escaped. The rest were all sunk or captured. Captain
Walton, who had been sent after some which attempted
to escape, gave an account of what occurred in a historic
despatch. "Sir," he wrote, "we have taken and destroyed
all the Spanish ships which were upon the coast; the
number as per margin."

This victory did not effect the immediate object in view
—the relief of Messina, which surrendered at the end of
September. But, as compared with the collapse of
the Spanish fleet, the fall of Messina was of no *its effect.*
importance. To carry on a war for any length of time,
communication must be kept up with the source of supplies.
But, unless she had command of the Mediterranean, it was
impossible for Spain to keep up communications properly
with Italy; and Passaro left her completely cut off. Much
had been done to restore the Spanish fleet. With some
more training, it might very well have become extremely
formidable, as it had been in the past. But a single blow
had shattered the prospect. And, although Alberoni was
only roused to fresh efforts, the battle of Cape Passaro was
in effect the death-blow to his policy. It is curious that
neither the battle itself nor Alberoni's measures of reprisal,
in seizing British goods and vessels in Spanish ports, were
regarded as a declaration of war.

No less complete was the failure of Alberoni's companion
schemes. The attack on England by Sweden and Russia
was not to be made till Charles had conquered
Norway; and, instead of conquering it, he was *Failure of Alberoni's*
killed by a stray bullet before Friedrichshalle. *other*
His death was promptly followed by a revolution, *schemes.*
in which the party opposed to Görtz was successful, and
that minister was executed, and his policy reversed; while
the arrival of an English fleet in the Baltic effectually prevented any activity on the part of Russia.

A similar collapse attended the projects of the anti-Orleanist party in France. Dubois discovered the chief agents in the conspiracy, bided his time, and seized them and their papers (though the most compromising had probably been destroyed), when the hour was ripe. The complicity of the Spanish court in the plot was sufficiently established, and war was formally declared against Spain by England on December 17th (old style), and by France on January 9, 1719 (new style).

Thus Alberoni's schemes had been foiled in every quarter. He had thought to raise a fleet which should dispute the supremacy of the seas with England: his plan had collapsed at Cape Passaro. He had thought to combine the Northern powers and the Jacobites: his plan had collapsed at Friedrichshalle. He had attacked Austria when she was crippled by the Turkish war: that war had come to an end. He had stirred up a conspiracy in France: the conspiracy had been defeated and brought to nothing. Yet he was not disposed to own himself beaten. He prepared a new expedition, destined this time to invade England, and to act in concert with the Jacobites.

England made ready for the invasion. Austrian and Dutch troops were brought over; the soldiers were disposed in the north and west with a view to checking any rising at the very beginning; Admiral Norris was ready with a squadron in the Channel. But the preparations were superfluous. Alberoni might have declared that the stars in their courses fought against him. His fleet set sail, and was ruined by a storm in the Bay of Biscay before coming in sight of an enemy. Two of the ships reached Scotland, but there was no rising, though a few clansmen joined the invaders. They were left alone for some while, but were presently dispersed by a few troops under General Wightman.

Alberoni at bay.

On the other hand, France prepared to take the offensive. A campaign was planned on the Pyrennean frontier. Marshal Villars, who hated the English alliance, refused to lead the

French troops; Berwick, a natural son of James II., and an excellent officer, was placed in command. Though acting obviously against his political views, he placed his duty as a marshal of the French army above all other considerations. The French arms were completely successful. In the course of the campaign, nine large ships of war, which were nearly completed, and the materials for seven more, were burnt The work of Byng at Cape Passaro and of the storm in the Bay of Biscay was completed. A Spanish fleet was no longer a possibility.

To add to the sum of disasters, an English expedition attacked Vigo, and destroyed there a quantity of the stores which had been intended for the invasion. Nor did affairs in Sicily offer much prospect of consolation to the Spanish minister. Cut off from supplies and reinforcements by the destruction of the fleet, the army there held its own in spite of the arrival of Austrian troops; but it could do no more. Alberoni began to make overtures for peace, yet even now he was so little willing to recognize his position as hopeless that he demanded the cession by England of Minorca and Gibraltar. But the allies were not likely to make concessions. They insisted on the acceptance of the terms of the Quadruple Alliance, and on the dismissal of Alberoni himself as a necessary condition. Crushed by the series of overwhelming reverses, Philip consented, feeling that resistance was no longer possible. He promised —and kept the promise—to withdraw from Sicily and Sardinia; he accepted the territorial divisions which the allies had laid down, though still refusing to recognize their justice; and the career of the great minister, whose schemes, if it had been possible to carry them out, would have restored the former power of Spain, was closed for ever, so far as concerns the larger political interests. Europe was once more at peace, and, though the peace was uneasy, it remained almost unbroken for the next twelve years, while nearly twenty years passed before England was again

Fall of Alberoni.

involved in a real war. Philip's decree, announcing his
accession to the Quadruple Alliance, was issued on January
26, 1720.

This position of affairs, however, was not satisfactory
either to Spain or to Austria. Charles was jealous of the
power of Hanover, which was becoming too independent
through the English connection. Moreover, he was anxious
about the succession to his own principalities, as the title of
the daughter who was his heir was certain to be disputed
unless guaranteed by the Powers. Spain, on the other hand,
was greatly aggrieved by the recent action both of France
and England. A personal insult, as often happens, brought
affairs to a head. In 1723 Orleans died, and the Duke of
Bourbon came to the head of affairs. The duke was no
friend to the young Duke of Orleans, who was now heir
presumptive to the French throne. Louis, the young king,
was betrothed to the Spanish infanta, who was a child of
six; and his health was poor. Consequently the prospect
of another heir appearing was extremely uncertain. Determined to secure an immediate marriage, and so to exclude
Orleans from the succession, the duke broke off the Spanish
match, and married the young king to Mary, the

Austro-Spanish alliance. daughter of Stanislaus, ex-king of Poland. The
Spanish court was furious, and, when it found that
England would not drop the French alliance, proceeded to
make overtures to Austria, which resulted in the Treaty of
Vienna. Avowedly, the terms of the alliance were a series
of concessions by Spain to Austria, including the guarantee
of the Pragmatic Sanction, *i.e.* the right of succession of
Maria Theresa, the emperor's daughter, and the recognition
of the Ostend Company—a trading association established
by Austria, and calculated to interfere with the commercial
advantages secured to England and Holland by the Treaty of
Westphalia. This was a serious matter for England; but
more serious still were the secret articles which came to the
cognizance of George and his ministers (though they could

not be made generally known) whereby Austria was pledged to support Spain in a peremptory demand for the restoration of Gibraltar and Minorca, and both Powers, in the event of refusal, were to aim at a Stuart restoration ; while a union was contemplated between Maria Theresa and Don Carlos, extremely disturbing to the balance of power.

The answer of England was an alliance with France and with Prussia, known as the Treaty of Hanover—the work chiefly of Townshend, who, with Walpole, had returned to power in 1720. This was denounced as a "Hanoverian" measure ; the explanation, however, is that ministers knew, and the Opposition did not know, of the secret articles in the Treaty of Vienna, and its essentially anti-British character. But the inclination of Russia to join the allies of Vienna lent an additional plausibility to the attacks of the Opposition, because the enmity of Russia was directed far more against Hanover than England. *The Treaty of Hanover.*

Thus, in 1726, matters were exceedingly threatening, and the outbreak of a new war seemed imminent—a war in which the two monarchs whose rival claims to the throne of Spain had deluged Europe with blood, were to be combined against France and England.

CHAPTER III.

FLEURY AND WALPOLE.

1726–1739.

Fleury—1727: Accession of George II.—1731: Treaty of Vienna—Fleury's Bourbon policy—Walpole's objects—War of the Polish succession—British non-intervention—Results of the war—Spain and Portugal—The First Family Compact, 1733; its deficiencies as a plan; Fleury's real purpose; Walpole's place in it—Walpole's peace policy; the alternative; its weak point—Why the peace-policy broke down—The quarrel with Spain—Jenkins's ears—Preparations for war—Feeling in England—Declaration of war.

ALREADY, in 1720, the return to power of Townshend and Walpole had imported a strong pacific influence into the councils of Great Britain. In 1726 there was a ministerial crisis in France; the young king declared himself of age, dismissed the Duke of Bourbon, and called Cardinal Fleury, who was already seventy-two years of age, to the post of first minister. The cardinal's aims, the motives of his policy, were different from those which had actuated the regent; but there was as yet no outward change in the path pursued.

Fleury.

The schemes of the Austro-Spanish alliance were directed more against England than against France, though indignation with the latter country had been the main cause of their inception. Little activity, however, was displayed in carrying them out. Austria was lukewarm at the best: and once again England's naval supremacy placed her practically out of reach of serious attack. She was able to send one fleet to the Baltic, which, as usual, sufficed to keep Russia quiet; and another to blockade Cartagena, thus intercepting the treasure-ships on which Spain depended for her supplies. With all this, she retained so complete a command of the Mediterranean that Spain could do no more than attempt to besiege Gibraltar from the land side, an operation which could not but prove entirely futile.

Under these circumstances, the emperor was somewhat helpless; and in February, 1727, he signed preliminaries of peace. The hopes of Spain were rekindled by the news of the death of George I., which, it was thought, would result in the fall of the Whig ministry, and perhaps in a Jacobite rising. But nothing of the kind occurred. George II. succeeded George I. without disturbance, and within a week Walpole, who had secured the unswerving support of Queen Caroline, was established in power more firmly than ever. But, in spite of the aimless character of the war, it was not till November, 1729, that it was definitely terminated by the treaty of Seville. The claim to Gibraltar was simply ignored, some disputed trade questions were settled, and Spain was allowed to garrison with her own troops certain towns in the duchies already allotted to Don Carlos. The business was completed at the Treaty of Vienna in March, 1731, when Austria acceded to the proposals, and agreed to abolish the Ostend Company. In return, Walpole guaranteed the Pragmatic Sanction, on condition that Maria Theresa should not be married to a Bourbon, or to any other prince of sufficient weight to disturb the balance of power. *Succession of George II.* *Treaty of Vienna.*

In fact, these treaties were the firstfruits of what was in truth a new policy on the part of France. Fleury, like Walpole, was pre-eminently a peace minister; but his schemes were aggressive, though he sought to carry them out by diplomacy instead of war. Primarily, indeed, he was well aware that the first necessity for France *Policy of Fleury.*

was to recover from the strain of the great war, and organise her resources. For these ends peace was essential. It was, therefore, supremely desirable to recover the friendship of Spain, without losing that of England. But beyond the policy of domestic prosperity was that of continental aggression, the basis of which must be an alliance between the two Bourbon dynasties of France and Spain. This the marriage of Louis XV. had now made practicable, by removing the presumption that Philip might find himself actually nearest heir by blood to the French throne when it should fall vacant. That such an alliance might be effected, it was necessary most carefully to avoid any sort of rupture with England, lest that power should be driven to a league with Austria. Fleury, in fact, felt that the larger interests of France and Spain were identical, but that they could be attained only by means of a persistently peaceful policy; so that delay in an understanding with Spain was preferable to a premature rupture with England. His policy, therefore, fell in thoroughly with that of the English minister. **Policy of Walpole.** Walpole, like Fleury, was bent on preserving European peace as far as possible, but, at any rate, on keeping England out of any embroilments. The security of the Hanoverian dynasty was in his eyes of the first importance; and foreign war was the opportunity of Jacobitism. On all accounts, the accumulation of wealth was to be desired; and war at once drains the national coffers and cuts off the sources of replenishment by checking commerce. Again, the accumulation of wealth not only means the accumulation of strength, but also the general spread of contentment with things as they are, which makes the task of government comparatively easy. The Stanhope Whigs had pursued a "spirited" foreign policy, by which they had succeeded in destroying the prospect of Spain taking the seas against England on anything like equal terms. Walpole followed up the advantage by pursuing a peace policy, which gave England an enormously greater reserve of wealth to draw upon when the great collision took place than she could have had otherwise.

For the time, therefore, both Fleury and Walpole had succeeded in their objects, and Fleury had effected the reconciliation, which was the first step towards an alliance with Spain.

European affairs were thus settling down into a condition which, if uneasy, still showed no immediate threatening of a disturbance, when a fresh conflagration was suddenly kindled. The King of Poland died. Stanislaus, his predecessor on the throne, and father of the young Queen of France, was elected by half the country; the other half proclaimed Augustus of Saxony, son of the late king. Russia was bent on supporting the latter candidate; Austria took the same side; France, as a matter of course, favoured Stanislaus. The question was no possible concern either of England or of Spain; but whereas the former country was bent on peace, the latter saw an opportunity for turning a war to account in Italy. Fleury—perhaps with some reluctance—was drawn into the struggle. Thus Austria and Russia were ranged on the side of Augustus, France and Spain on that of Stanislaus. On the Rhine and in Italy the emperor met with a series of reverses. In Poland, on the other hand, Augustus, with the assistance of a Russian army, met with complete success; but no sooner was it obtained than Russia, having secured her own objects, withdrew; Austria was again isolated. *War of the Polish succession.*

In England, George was longing to plunge into the war in support of the emperor; the queen's judgment was equally strong on the same side, and the queen ruled the king: but Walpole ruled the queen, and nothing would induce him to countenance such a policy. England absolutely refused to fight. Austria had no choice but to give in, if she could do so with a fair show of honour. Walpole brought to bear on both sides all the pressure he could to put an end to the conflict. Fleury, at least, had no desire to fight when he could see his way to a diplomatic success.

The Queen of Spain, the prime instigator of the war, was anxious chiefly to secure the kingdom of Naples for her son, Don Carlos. There was no reason for protracting hostilities. Negotiations, however, lasted a long time. When they were **Conclusion** concluded, it was Fleury again who had achieved **of the war.** the most important success. Spain was satisfied by the retention of Naples and Sicily for Don Carlos. Austria, besides carrying her candidate for Poland, was soothed by the restitution of Parma, and the resignation of the claims of Don Carlos as heir presumptive to the Grand Duchy of Tuscany. The master-stroke of Fleury was in inducing the Duke of Lorraine, who was about to marry Maria Theresa, to take the reversion of Tuscany, and give up Lorraine itself, as compensation for the recognition of Augustus as King of Poland, to Stanislaus; on whose death it would devolve to the crown of France. Every one appeared to have got an equivalent for anything given up, while France got Lorraine without giving up anything at all. Finally, in case it should appear to the emperor that his equivalents were not adequate, France guaranteed the Pragmatic Sanction. The treaty was finally signed in 1737.

A separate complication, which went near to involving England in spite of Walpole, arose out of a quarrel between **Spain and** Spain and Portugal in 1735. On this occasion, **Portugal.** Sir John Norris was sent with twenty-five ships of the line to the Tagus, in the hope that so imposing a demonstration would be sufficient to check extreme measures on the part of Spain. By the help of energetic mediation on the part of France, matters were patched up for the time; but the circumstances were a significant indication of troubles to come.

The war of the Polish succession is an interesting example of the value to England of her extra-continental position. In spite of the eagerness of King George to join in it, it remained possible for England to continue as an onlooker, increasing her commerce and gathering wealth; while

France, in spite of the naturally pacific inclinations of Fleury, was unable to resist the impulse to plunge into the quarrel. The conclusion of the war is a tribute to the diplomatic skill of the French minister, who managed to appropriate all the gains to France or Spain. The advancement of the Bourbons being the general object, the peace secured it so far as continental affairs were concerned. But it was done at the expense of a strain on both French and Spanish exchequers, while England was storing up wealth; France and Spain were less than ever able to devote any considerable expenditure to their navies; and they were, in fact, less prepared for a struggle with England after the war than before it.

It is perfectly clear that at this period the great problem of the future was the mastery of the New World. It is no less clear that the true policy for France and Spain was, combination with a view to the complete suppression of English rivalry. And it is certain that a league, having precisely this as its ostensible object, was formed between France and Spain in the secret treaty of 1733, known as the First Family Compact. This was an agreement that the Bourbon Powers should further each other's interests in every possible way, as against the German Powers on the one hand, and England on the other, and that they should unite in recovering for Spain the English naval stations in the Mediterranean, and in destroying the English oceanic commerce. Under the circumstances it would be natural to see in this Family Compact a Bourbon conspiracy, having as its object the suppression of England, the one serious colonial rival of the Bourbon powers. *The First Family compact.*

But in spite of the prominence of the anti-British features in the compact, the evidence seems to show that neither the French nor the Spanish government gave it the first place in their calculations. Elizabeth, at any rate, however angry she might be periodically at the retention by England of Gibraltar and *Its deficiencies as a political scheme.*

Minorca, and at the British illicit traffic with Spanish America, was in the first place Italian, and cared more to turn Italy into an appanage of her own family, and to drive Austria out of it, than to wreak vengeance on England. Fleury was no exception to the general rule, in accordance with which French statesmen have almost always allowed the colonial aspirations of a part of the nation to be overweighted by continental rivalries. And the *prima facie* proof that this was the case is to be found in the systematic neglect of the French navy. Nothing could be more certain than that in a war *à outrance* between France or France and Spain, on one side, and England on the other for colonial possessions, the relative strength of the two navies must decide the victory. But France made no kind of attempt, either to reconstruct her own fleet, or to encourage Spain in that course. On the contrary, France and Spain exhausted their resources on a purely continental war which did nothing to weaken England. Whatever the ultimate intention may have been, it is quite clear that this course was about the worst that could have been followed with a view to carrying out the avowed intention of the Secret Treaty of 1733.

Hence, apart from the terms of that treaty, the action of both France and Spain points to the continent, rather than the colonies, as the field of aggression. Fleury wished to avoid war, to develop France at home, to spend as little as possible. If he had an attack on England in view, it was not an immediate attack. There was much animosity towards England at the Spanish court, but while there was a chance of pushing forward in Italy the Spanish rulers were content to leave England alone. For both the Bourbon Powers Austria was the rival from whom most might be extracted at the least cost. Practically it was Austria that lost what the Western kingdoms gained by the war of the Polish succession; and while that war was going on, neither France nor Spain was making ready for a prospective war with the great naval power.

The explanation, then of the Family Compact would be as follows : Fleury, on general grounds, wished for an alliance of the Bourbon dynasties ; but one which should *Fleury's* not drive the other powers into an anti-Bourbon *real aims.* league. The primary purpose of that alliance would be to weaken the Empire. When this object was satisfactorily accomplished, England might be taken in hand, and the Bourbons be made supreme beyond sea as well as in Europe. Spain also desired first to bring pressure to bear on the Empire ; but she was quite ready to set aside her chief purpose under the influence of temporary excitement. Now, at the time when the secret treaty was signed, the Spanish court had been violently irritated by the reports of the frequent collisions and quarrels between Spanish coast-guards and British trading vessels in the South American seas. Therefore she forced the anti-British purposes of the league to the front, in framing the compact. Fleury trusted to circumstances, and to his own diplomatic skill, to keep those purposes actually in the background ; as being ultimately desirable, but immediately impracticable. It appears, indeed, very probable that, according to Fleury's own scheme of operations, the success of the Franco-Spanish programme on the continent, accompanied and followed by judicious domestic administration, would immensely strengthen the combined Bourbons ; Britain, meantime, by standing neutral, would have forfeited Austrian sympathy, and, when the Bourbons turned upon her, she would be isolated. Walpole's intense aversion to war was known ; his present belief that England would be worsted in a contest with France and Spain together was known. The inference was that, before very long, he would be so much afraid of risking such a war that diplomatic pressure would secure to the Bourbons by degrees all that they chose to demand. The expenditure involved in strengthening the French fleet with a view to the contingency of a war under such circumstances, might thus be very well deferred, and could very likely be dispensed with altogether. In the mean time, England was to be kept neutral, while Austria was being sufficiently disabled.

If this be the correct view of the plan of the Family Compact, the prominence of its anti-British position is somewhat deceptive. It was due to the immediate irritation of one party to the compact; and the intentions expressed in it were really secondary, and were not based on an adequate idea of the vital importance of its policy: as is proved by the complete neglect of the steps necessary to carrying that policy out except on the hypothesis that Britain had no power of resistance.

Walpole's policy then, up to the time when his hand was forced by popular clamour, will appear to be justified in all but one particular.

First, the immense advantages of a consistent peace-policy throughout these years is very apparent. A peace-policy was the one security against violent domestic dissensions, and active foreign support of the Stuarts. It was the one means of gathering a store of wealth which should enable the country to bear the strain of a great war if one should be forced upon her. It is quite true that it was to Walpole's personal interest to maintain the policy, because as a finance minister he was unrivalled, while as a war minister he was incompetent. On the other hand, by refusing to give way to the more warlike councils of the king, he risked losing the royal favour. If Walpole's policy was sound, the fact that it was on the whole in his personal interest to maintain it cannot reasonably be made a ground of reproach.

Walpole's peace-policy.

The question is whether the advantages of a warlike policy might not have been greater. Walpole had the secret treaty before him, in spite of all the precautions of the Bourbons. In view of the fact that what may fairly be called a Bourbon conspiracy was on foot, it has been held that true statesmanship demanded

The alternative.

that it should be directly counteracted. But the evidence
of the conspiracy was not sufficient to justify a league which
should attempt to crush the Bourbons. The effect of any
attempt in that direction would have been merely to check
the continental aggrandisement of these powers, to make
England and the Hanoverian dynasty the first object of
their animosity instead of the second, and to drive them
into closer agreement with each other. By letting things
alone, they were allowed to expend their energies on objects
not directly injurious to England, while she was steadily
gathering strength, and arriving at a condition in which she
would, comparatively speaking, be well able to support the
strain of war. The serious mistake in Walpole's management was that he made no actual preparations for the war when it should come. It was certain that, sooner or later, the combined Bourbons would turn on England. It was needful that, when the time came, she should at once be able to make adequate resistance. And a statesman with larger ideas might have foreseen, that not merely adequate resistance would be needed, but positive mastery. The English navy only required to be kept in a state of thorough efficiency to secure complete predominance over the decaying maritime forces of France and Spain. A policy of parsimony could not make it inferior to its rivals, but did make its superiority needlessly ineffective. *Its weak point.*

Thus from Fleury's point of view, which underrated the struggle of the future and calculated on England showing no resistance, the neutrality of England on the continent seemed all gain. Walpole, however, perceived that this neutrality, by giving the power of resistance, would in the long run upset Fleury's policy. But while with admirable skill he maintained the neutrality, he failed to make of it all that he might have made. Both the English and the French statesmen were playing a waiting game, each counting on being ready before the actual collision should occur, each *Breakdown of Walpole's and Fleury's policy.*

reckoning on the other's aversion to war when it should occur, each trusting to diplomacy backed by the threat of war as the means by which he would ultimately triumph, each believing that he would in the end get the better of the other without actual recourse to arms. And the schemes of both were frustrated, because at the critical moment each lost control. Spain broke away from Fleury, and England broke away from Walpole, when neither was in the least prepared for a mortal combat. The theory that the national instinct discovered that it was time to incapacitate Spain before France could support her seems to want an adequate basis. What actually happened was that both Spain and England arrived at a stage of mutual irritation, which made each uncontrollably eager to fly at the other with very little regard to the consequences. There is no sign that either England, Spain, or France perceived how much might depend on the issue of the quarrel, or weighed her own fitness for entering on it.

The origin of the outbreak lay in the collisions extending over a series of years between the English traders—occasionally legitimate, but more often illicit—and the Spanish coastguard ships. Under the earlier commercial treaties, Spain preserved a complete monopoly of the Spanish-American trade. English ships might not touch the coast unless driven by stress of weather. But by the Assiento, conferring the monopoly of the slave trade on the English South Sea Company, the facilities for illicit traffic had been greatly increased ; and the additional right, transferred to England at the time of the French alliance in 1716, of sending one regular trading vessel to the Spanish colonies had soon become liable to similar abuse. It is said that the English ship used to lie at anchor, and to be constantly relieved of her cargoes and supplied with fresh goods by other vessels. This contraband traffic was the handle now used by Spain. Frequent complaints had been made, and, on the other side, English captains complained

The Anglo-Spanish quarrel.

that the Spaniards had exceeded their proper powers, and exercised their right of search on the high seas. There could be no doubt whatever that Spain was technically justified in exercising the right of search to the full in the Spanish seas. There is no legitimate excuse for the contraband traffic which was consistently winked at, if not encouraged, at home. But Spain now chose to exercise her rights with rigour and arrogance, and, it can hardly be doubted, with the deliberate intention of causing as much irritation and offence as she could. All manner of stories were told of the ill-treatment to which English sailors were subjected, and of the insolence of Spanish officials. As time went on, the stories grew and multiplied. The English, who were undoubtedly, in point of law, the original offenders, easily convinced themselves that they were the aggrieved party. The Spanish method of correcting and applying rights was calculated to cause the very existence of those rights to be felt as an insult. As the immediate interest of the war of the Polish succession grew less, the Spanish court turned its attention more and more to the complaints of the American Spaniards. Spain protested, and made demands for restitution. Meantime the tales of Spanish insolence and violence were passing from mouth to mouth in England, and the populace was in a ferment of indignation, not the less dangerous because partly unreasoning. Walpole was set against war, but the country began to clamour for it. The queen died, and the minister, bereft of his great ally, was terribly weakened. The climax came when the war party produced a captain named Jenkins, with a grim story of outrage. Six years Jenkins's ears. before, the Spanish coastguard had boarded his vessel, charged him with smuggling, and, failing to find evidence, had torn off one of his ears, bidding him send it to the king. The ear was produced. He was asked what his feelings had been; and, with excellent dramatic effect, replied: "I commended my soul to God, and my cause to my country."

Naturally, the Opposition lost no opportunity of utilising popular feeling to the utmost, for party purposes. Their position was strengthened by the hostile attitude assumed by Spain towards the new colony of Georgia—a premonition of the coming struggle for supremacy in North America. Nevertheless, Walpole strove his hardest. Though he sent a fleet to the Mediterranean, and otherwise made preparations for war, it was evident that he would not fight if he could possibly help it. A commission inquired into the claims and counter-claims for compensation between Spain and England; and the balance was found to be heavily in favour of England. Thereupon Spain put in a claim on the English government for sums due from the South Sea Company in respect of the Assiento, a claim denied by the company. Still, a convention was signed in which even this was half conceded. But the questions of the right of search, and of the delimitation of Georgia were not settled by it; and, to the intense wrath of the "patriots" in parliament, the aggressive commanders of the Spanish coastguard were allowed to go unpunished.

<small>Preparations for war.</small>

Walpole succeeded in carrying the address in favour of the convention, in both houses. But, even in parliament, he only just held his own. His difficulties were increased, and the Opposition were supplied with fresh matter for patriotic clamour, by the fact that at this time England granted a subsidy to Denmark, on terms of that country holding six thousand troops ready for English service if required. Avowedly this was a counter-move to an alleged attempt on the part of France to draw Denmark into an anti-English alliance. But Spain, not France, was the object of popular suspicion and indignation. The allegation was generally disbelieved; the Opposition cried out that this was merely another "Hanoverian" measure, to induce Denmark to acquiesce in the acquisition from Holstein by Hanover of the fortress of Steinhorst. Walpole knew, and the Opposition did not know, of the Family

Compact of 1733; there may have been more truth in the charge against France than is generally supposed, and a real justification for Walpole's measure; still the effect was to give his parliamentary opponents a fresh cry against him. It became clear that the alternatives before him were war or resignation, and he chose war. *[Declaration of war.]*

The country was wild with joy. When the declaration of war was published in October, 1739, the bells were set ringing in every steeple. "They are ringing the bells now," said Walpole; "they will be wringing their hands soon."

CHAPTER IV.

THE PREMONITORY WAR, AND THE END OF JACOBITISM.

1739-1748.

Inefficient measures—Anson—Vernon—The German states—1740: Death of the Emperor—1741: Frederick of Prussia and Maria Theresa—War of the Austrian succession—1742: Peace of Breslau—The British navy—Its effects—Fall of Walpole—1743: Battle of Dettingen—1745: Battle of Fontenoy—Jacobite schemes—James—Charles Edward—The conditions of the '15 and the '45 compared—Importance attached to the dynastic question—Danger of its remaining unsettled—Its intrinsic consequence—Attitude of English Jacobites—Landing of Charles—Capture of Edinburgh—Preston Pans—The march to Derby—Position of Charles—The retreat—1746: Falkirk—Culloden—The end of Jacobitism—The war in Europe, and at sea—1748: Treaty of Aix-la-Chapelle.

Inefficient war-measures. THE war which broke out in 1739 was entered upon by Walpole with extreme reluctance. He had only Spain to fight against, but he knew that the participation of France was merely a question of time. Yet nothing like adequate vigour was applied to the conduct of affairs. No clear plan of naval strategy was adopted. Two expeditions were fitted out, one commanded by Anson, the other by Vernon. The equipment of the two squadrons was far from creditable. Anson, however, has at least the credit of having done his work with a skill, courage, and dogged perseverance which have won well-deserved fame for his voyage round the world; although, beyond bringing home a certain amount of treasure, and doing considerable damage here and there on the Spanish American coasts, the expedition had small practical result.

Vernon's six ships began operations by capturing Porto Bello, destroying the fortifications, and withdrawing to Jamaica. A large additional fleet was then sent out to join him, with a body of soldiers under command of General Wentworth. It was resolved to capture Cartagena; but the attempt failed, admiral and general each laying the blame on the other. The same thing happened at Sant Iago. The presence of English fleets in Spanish waters interfered with Spanish commerce, but no blow was struck, and the whole of the operations are a melancholy record of futility. The object of a fleet may be considered as being either the control of the sea or the protection and possession of points on land. On the former theory, on which every great English admiral has acted, it is broadly speaking the first business of the fleet to find and demolish the enemy's ships. On the latter theory, generally held in favour by French commanders, it is the business of the fleet to avoid naval engagements, and devote itself to covering or attacking strong places. There are conditions under which the latter policy may be the right one; in this case it certainly was not. But it does not seem to have occurred to Vernon, that, as an object of destruction or capture, hostile ships were of much more importance than the fortifications of Porto Bello or Cartagena.

<small>The naval war.</small>

This desultory war, however, was soon merged in a European conflagration.

If Walpole had been inclined to inaugurate a vigorous anti-Bourbon policy while he was still master of England, he would have had two leading difficulties: the half-heartedness of Austria, which was beguiled by France into a belief in her friendliness; and the uncertain attitude of the German states. For the German princes were more anxious each to advance his

<small>Attitude of German States.</small>

private interests than to form a solid combination against a Bourbon alliance which was hardly suspected of existing. On the death of the Emperor Charles and the accession to the Austrian inheritance of Maria Theresa, his daughter, the complicated character of the position revealed itself.

Every one of the great Powers had guaranteed the Pragmatic Sanction, whereby Maria Theresa was to succeed to her father's dominions. But the Elector of Bavaria, besides aspiring to the imperial crown, was the rival claimant to the Hapsburg succession; and had never given the guarantee. He was therefore prepared to resist. Frederick of Prussia, who had recently come to his throne, and found himself at the head of a state which had in effect been organised into a first-class military power by his father, wanted the Austrian province of Silesia. Spain, of course, wanted to absorb some more of Italy. France recognized her opportunity in the weakness of her great rival on the continent. On the other hand, to Hanover, it was important to support Austria: to England it had become important to break the Bourbon combination.

Charles died in October, 1740. It was Frederick of Prussia who fired the conflagration. In December, he marched into Silesia, and invited Maria Theresa to cede the province to him, offering in return to support her against all other claimants. The queen refused to treat with him; he proceeded to reduce the province. In April of the following year the Prussian and Austrian armies met at Mollwitz, and Frederick was completely victorious. He again offered Maria Theresa his alliance if she would give up Lower Silesia and Breslau; again she refused, though pressed by England (to which she was already indebted for subsidies) to accede. On the failure of negotiations, Frederick entered on an alliance with France. France was to assist the Elector of Bavaria in his claim, and Sweden was to be embroiled with Russia to keep them out of the complications in Central Europe.

War of the Austrian succession.

England had entered on a war with Spain; but with Walpole still in the cabinet, she was in no hurry to plunge into the European war. France sent an army to threaten Hanover which frightened George into a treaty of neutrality for a year; and another to invade Austria as an auxiliary of Bavaria. By the end of September, Saxony had joined against Austria, and Spain was attacking the Austrian dominions in Italy. Thus isolated, the queen threw herself on the protection of her Hungarian subjects; who responded to the appeal, though only at the price of important concessions. At the same time, France did not hasten to crush her, being afraid of making Bavaria too strong. The Austrian General Niepperg made a secret compact with Frederick, whereby the former was enabled to withdraw from Silesia and advance against the opposing allies who were most inefficiently commanded; while the conquests they had made in Upper Austria were threatened by a second army, under Khevenhüller.

Thus, since both France and Prussia held their hands, by the end of February the Elector of Bavaria, who had just succeeded in obtaining the chief goal of his ambition, the imperial crown, found that his future prospects depended on Frederick's support.

Frederick, in turn, saw that Austria showed no intention of carrying out Niepperg's compact, so held himself free to renew his attack. The battle of Czeslau, in May, **Peace of** was decisive. It was followed by the Peace of **Breslau.** Breslau, by which Maria Theresa surrendered nearly all Silesia with Glatz (June, 1742).

It is to be noted that all this time the only country with which England had declared war was Spain, and that France was not formally at war with Austria, but only **The** sent her troops as "auxiliaries" of Bavaria. The **British** naval proceedings of the time are instructive. **Navy.** While Vernon had a great fleet frittering away its energies on the Spanish main, Admiral Haddock was in command of a fleet in the Mediterranean, which was occupied in blockading a Spanish flotilla at Cadiz. But when Spain sent a squadron, joined by a French one, for the furtherance of her designs in Italy, the English admiral was not strong enough to attack the combined forces. However, a little later, when Matthews took the command in the Mediterranean, one of his captains pursued a Spanish flotilla into a French harbour, and, despite the "neutrality" of France, burnt it there; and another, Captain Martin, suddenly appeared at Naples with five ships, and required the king (Don Carlos) to withdraw his troops from the Spanish armies, and to enter into an engagement to take no part in the war in Italy. Moreover, he announced that, if the engagement were not signed in an hour, he would bombard Naples; and the engagement was signed. It was clear, in fact, that, the moment vigour was shown, England's control of the Mediterranean was complete; France and Spain were powerless. And Fleury realised that, even for the purposes of his purely continental policy, he had made a serious blunder in allowing the French navy to sink so low. For the Mediterranean is the true military highway between Spain and Italy; and just as Spain had before lost all chance of successful operations in Sicily and Italy when her fleet was destroyed at Passaro, so now she was rendered hopelessly ineffective in Italy by a tolerably managed squadron of English ships in the Mediterranean.

The circumstances of the case throughout this time necessarily made England a keen partisan of Austria; **Fall of Walpole.** equally, of course, the parliamentary Opposition were on the lookout for "Hanoverian" actions on the part of ministers. The Hanoverian treaty of neutrality, made at a time when England was subsidising the Austrian armies, gave rise to angry comment. Walpole's unpopularity grew rapidly, and at last, in February, 1742, he resigned. The administration of foreign affairs passed into the hands of Carteret.

The result appeared in the greatly increased activity of England in the war. English troops joined in it; Hanoverian troops were subsidised by England. Of course the Hanoverian outcry broke out again, to be made fiercer as time went on by the jealousies of English and Hanoverian soldiers. The death of Fleury in January, 1743, at the age of ninety, followed two months later by that of Walpole, removed a factor which made for peace. The cardinal had followed an aggressive policy, but the methods he always preferred were those of diplomacy. Meantime, since the peace of Breslau, the Austrian arms had been generally successful. By May (1743) the English and Hanoverian troops were joined by an Austrian force, and in June they won the battle of Dettingen, famous for the tactical blunders of the commanders and the courageous conduct of the troops on both sides, but best remembered on account of the personal valour shown by George II., and the fact that it was the last battle in which an English king fought in person. By the end of the summer the arms of the Austrians and their allies were everywhere triumphant. *England joins in the Continental war.* *Dettingen.*

But success did not dispose Maria Theresa to peace; and, on the other hand, Frederick of Prussia felt that it was time for him to be on guard again. France attempted to negotiate with Austria, but was met with an arrogance which made it practically impossible to treat. In the spring of 1744 France and Prussia came to terms, and the former power dropped the curious fiction hitherto maintained, that she was merely an "auxiliary," and declared war against England. Again, however, the year's campaigns were all in favour of Austria, whose troops were ably commanded by Traun in fact, and by Prince Charles of Lorraine in name. *Frederick rejoins the war.*

The death of the emperor in January, 1745, followed by a compact between his son and Maria Theresa, demolished the fiction of "loyalty to the emperor" as a motive for

Prussian hostility to Austria; for this was the formal plea on which Frederick, as a prince of the Empire, had justified his action. Nevertheless, the war continued to be carried on in three different quarters. The Austrian troops were chiefly occupied in fighting Frederick of Prussia, and in Italy, and no longer prospered. France carried her arms into the Netherlands, where she was met by English, Hanoverian, and Dutch troops. But though the Duke of Cumberland was a brave soldier he was no match for Saxe in the field. At Fontenoy the unflinching courage of the British troops was scarcely more remarkable than the futility of the operations in which it was displayed. Later in the year, when the success of Frederick's campaign forced Austria to come to terms with him, and he withdrew from the contest, the gain to the allies of having the Austrian army thus set free was practically neutralised by the withdrawal of English troops, owing to the Jacobite rising under Charles Edward.

Fontenoy.

Frederick withdraws.

It had always been recognized by Walpole and the peace party that our embroilment in a European war would be the opportunity of the Jacobites; and, in particular, that war with France would insure French support of the Stuarts. So long as England and France were nominally at peace, the French court was bound to recognize its treaty obligations to the reigning house. But the declaration of war was the signal for renewed and active intriguing. The exiled house, as well as their British supporters, had not considered a rising practicable without French assistance; but in 1744 active assistance was promised. Charles Edward was to invade England with a French army under the command of Saxe. The fleet even put to sea; but when Sir John Norris with the Channel squadron appeared, so that the invaders found that a sea-fight with a strong opponent would have to be risked— and when, further, a storm arose which scattered and seriously damaged the expeditionary fleet—the enterprise was

Jacobite schemes.

abandoned ; and it soon became evident that such energies as Louis was disposed to spare for the war would be devoted to the campaign in the Netherlands, and that no further assistance would be given to the Stuarts. This change of front was in fact due, probably, to the natural incapacity of a despotic government to understand the meaning of English party politics. The party outcry against Hanover and "Hanoverian" measures had been taken as a sign of violent discontent with the Hanoverian dynasty ; whereas by this time the immense mass of the country had quite learned, after an apathetic fashion, to identify the national interests with the Hanoverian succession. The threat of invasion for the moment put an end to the clamours of the parliamentary Opposition, which consisted mainly, not of Jacobites, but of Whigs who wanted office. When Louis discovered that invaders would not, as he had expected, be welcomed with open arms, the official project of invasion was dropped.

The natural despondency of James was at all times a check on the enthusiasm of the advocates of his cause. But Prince Charles Edward was a man of different mettle. Young and enthusiastic, he possessed to the full that power of inspiring personal devotion so strangely characteristic of the Stuarts. To his deliberate resolve to cast policy to the winds and trust everything to enthusiasm we owe one of the most romantic episodes in history. {Charles Edward.}

At the time of his rising, its termination must have appeared to every sober spectator a foregone conclusion. The rising of 1715 had been planned under circumstances which gave some promise of success. It followed hard on the accession of a monarch for whom there was no sort of personal loyalty ; when the High Church party, with their doctrine of non-resistance were extremely powerful. Numbers were ready to join if affairs opened well. It was abortive because it was the most stupidly conducted rebellion on record. But the {Conditions of the 'Fifteen and the 'Forty-five.}

'Forty-five at the outset seemed utterly hopeless. The cause could inspire no general enthusiasm. The House of Hanover had been reigning for thirty years, and the country had enjoyed unexampled material prosperity under it. There was no kind of adequate Jacobite organisation. There was now no chance of help from France. There was no reasonable ground to expect a rising in England. There was no commander of experience to help the insurgents. But there was one element present in the 'Forty-five which was entirely absent from the 'Fifteen—the element of personal devotion, the wild and enthusiastic loyalty which breathes in the Jacobite songs of Scotland. And this was due to the somewhat enigmatical personality of Charles Edward Stuart. To this must be attributed the fact that, though he failed, he came dangerously near to success. For, unaided though he was, it has been held by shrewd judges that, if Charles had been allowed his own way, and the insurgents had not turned back at Derby, the House of Hanover might have been overthrown.

Some historians have been in the habit of writing as if a Stuart restoration at this time would have meant a fierce renewal of the old constitutional struggles; as if the hard-won liberties of the nation were at stake. To others it has appeared that the whole question was mainly personal to the great Whig houses who had been primarily responsible for turning the Stuarts out and keeping the Hanoverians in, and it has been argued that the importance of the success or failure of Prince Charles's rising has been altogether over-estimated. Neither view appears to be altogether sound.

The Stuarts were a singularly obstinate and impracticable race, with an unusual capacity for following the worst advice
Political importance of a restoration; given to them. But they had received a series of very practical lessons in the danger of goading the people too much, of going too far in defiance of popular sentiment. It was not a hundred years since one of them had lost his head; not sixty since another

had found it advisable to fly the country. It is not likely that they would have been prepared to face a repetition of either experience ; and had they been restored, and attempted to repeat experiments in absolutism, the results would hardly have been more disastrous than those of George III.'s efforts in the same direction. By this time, the constitutional theory was too firmly established to have been very seriously endangered. The vital matter was not so much whether we were to have a Stuart or a Hanoverian on the throne, as to have the question settled for good and all, so that the perpetual threat of a civil war might be finally got rid of. The apathy with which the country at large viewed the rising was largely attributable to the consciousness that this was the case.

But, while the victory of the government did settle the question, it is very doubtful whether the victory of the Stuarts would have done so ; not because the constitution would have been in danger, but because far the larger part of the powerful families would have been brought into permanent opposition to the crown. The Tories would have expected the spoils, and the Whigs would have been constantly on the lookout for an opportunity of reinstating themselves, which could only have been brought about by a fresh revolution. In the interest of domestic peace therefore, the practical destruction of Jacobitism was exceedingly fortunate. Moreover, foreign relations were assuming a very complicated aspect. We were on the eve of a war the importance of which can hardly be overrated, and it is extremely doubtful whether any man but William Pitt could have saved it from a termination at least comparatively disastrous. It is possible that he would have controlled the helm if the Stuarts had won, but it is exceedingly improbable. Moreover, it is all but certain that a restoration by French aid would have so altered our relations to France that the whole results of the Seven Years' War would have been completely changed, and the situation in

North America and India entirely reversed. And even if Charles had effected the restoration without French assistance, the Stuarts would have been compelled to rely on French support for the security of the dynasty, to an extent which must have changed the whole character of any struggle between the two countries.

There are, therefore, these three main grounds on which it may be argued that a Stuart restoration would have been dangerous: it would have threatened the constitution; it would have produced perpetual unrest by driving the most important sections of the country into opposition; it would have changed our foreign relations at a great international crisis, with disastrous consequences to us. The first of these three arguments, at the time and generally since, has been allowed far more weight than it is entitled to. The second weighed more than anything else with the politicians of the day, because to them it was a matter of personal interests, though to us it is of consequence mainly as affecting the third argument, which by contemporaries was left almost out of sight, but in spite of its comparatively speculative nature is far the most important. How speculative it is we shall see at once by recognizing that it turns to an immense extent on the personality of Charles Edward, whose complete collapse after the failure of his enterprise affords no reasonable criterion of what he might have become had that great crisis in his life had a different termination.

<small>its real and imaginary dangers.</small>

The English Jacobites did not favour the idea of a rising unless solid assistance from France was guaranteed. France was not prepared to assist a rising unless the Jacobites could show that they were strong enough to make failure a practical impossibility. Therefore neither English Jacobites nor France were inclined to make the first move. Nevertheless, Prince Charles Edward was resolved to wait no longer. He sent notice to certain friends, who replied by urging him to remain quiet. He disregarded their advice, and sailed, almost unattended, for Scotland. In July, 1745, he reached the coast. Macdonald of the Isles and Macleod declined to assist him or to meet him. Macdonald of Clanranald and Macdonald of Kinloch Moidart met him. They began by telling him that his enterprise was mere madness, they ended by vowing themselves to his service. Cameron of Lochiel came to urge his immediate withdrawal, and left to collect his clansmen. Lochiel's adherence turned the scale. No single chief had been prepared to support the prince; now chief after chief came in; those who hesitated paused no longer when once they had come into the presence of Charles. He had been three weeks in Moidart already before the Edinburgh authorities knew that anything was going on. On August 19th he raised the standard. Sir John Cope, the commander-in-chief, was sent against him, but mistook his intentions and marched past him to Inverness. Charles marched on Edinburgh; the town was seized with a panic. Gardiner's dragoons ran away at Coltbrigg without striking a blow. Envoys were sent from the city; the carriage which had conveyed them to and fro passed out of the gates again at five o'clock in the morning, and a party of Highlanders seized the opportunity to walk in, overpower the guard, and quietly take possession of the other gates. When the citizens rose in the morning, they found the insurgents in command of the town, though the castle remained impregnable. A few days later, Sir John Cope reappeared on the scene. Charles took his little army out to meet him at Preston Pans. On September 20th they faced each other. Early on the next morning, while the mist was lying, the Highlanders were guided across the marshes which separated the armies, formed up, and made the attack. The battle was decided in ten minutes, and, for the time, Scotland was in effect once more in the hands of the Stuarts.

 Charles spent the next five weeks in Edinburgh, collecting

[sidenotes: Landing of Charles Edward. Capture of Edinburgh. Preston Pans.]

F

money and forces, waiting for a Jacobite rising and the landing of French troops in England. But no Jacobites rose, and no troops landed. On the other hand, the government were completing their organisation in England. General Wade was at Newcastle, and the Duke of Cumber-
The march to Derby. land was collecting troops in the south. With some reluctance the Highland chiefs agreed to march on England without further delay. The little army of six thousand men started. Making a feint of marching on Newcastle to fight Wade, they turned aside, and entered the country by way of Carlisle, which promptly surrendered. They marched on, unopposed by Wade, through Lancashire, which received them with nothing more substantial than good wishes. Cumberland was tricked as Wade had been, and they reached Derby. London was before them, guarded, as was supposed, by an army at Finchley. Cumberland and Wade were behind them. Charles believed, not without reason, that if he pursued the dictates of sheer audacity, the Jacobites in the south would still rise, French troops would land, and the restoration would be effected. No single officer favoured his view. After angry debate he submitted, and the army turned to march north again.

All this time there had been absolutely no spontaneous movement on either side in England. The country simply
Position of Charles. sat at home, looked on, and wondered whether the Highlanders were really cannibals. Here and there only an enthusiast had joined the insurgents. In Scotland, on the other hand, Lord President Forbes, the shrewdest as well as the kindliest of Scottish statesmen, had persuaded three or four important chiefs, notably Lord Lovat, Macdonald of the Isles, and Macleod of Macleod, to hold aloof, and was now setting the Sutherlands and other northern Whigs in motion.

Scotland was no longer secure. In England the question was whether the victory could be won by sheer audacity.

So far, it was sheer audacity which had carried the day. To drop that policy might be necessary, but it meant in effect giving up the effort. Whether Charles would have won if he had advanced, no one can tell: there were plenty of acute onlookers who believed that he would; there were plenty who believed there was no hope in any case. But, when once he turned his back upon Derby, he never had any chance left at all.

The army had left Edinburgh on October 31st; on December 26th it was back at Glasgow. Only once on the way had Cumberland attempted to molest its movements, and that one attempt had been a signal failure. *The retreat.* A week later Charles marched to besiege Stirling, where his forces were raised to about nine thousand in number. Meantime General Wade had been superseded by Hawley, the duke having been recalled from fear of an army being landed in the south. Charles resolved to give battle; Hawley fancied he could make short work of Highlanders, but discovered at Falkirk that he was in error. *Falkirk.* Still, complete as the rout was, it did Charles more harm than good, for it brought Cumberland north to replace Hawley, and brought the dissensions among the insurgent officers to a head—with the practical effect that, on February 1st, the prince was compelled to relinquish the siege of Stirling, and marched towards Inverness. The operations during the next two months were desultory; but early in April Cumberland was in motion, the Lowlands being sufficiently garrisoned with foreign soldiers. The government troops had ample supplies from the sea; the insurgents were by no means equally well off.

On the night of April 15th Charles was with his army on Culloden Moor. Cumberland was at hand. It was bitter weather; the Highlanders had had only one biscuit served out to them that day. Still, a *Culloden.* night attack was resolved upon. But delays occurred. It became evident by two o'clock in the morning that a surprise would be impossible. The Highlanders, who had been marching all night, were obliged to march back again to Culloden.

Nevertheless, hungry and weary as they were, the memory of past victories, and a certain wild but splendid chivalry, determined the prince and his followers to give battle. But Cumberland had found a way to meet them. Time after time the Highlanders had won battles by the fury of their onset, breaking the enemy's line and flinging them into confusion. Cumberland drew up his army—their superior numbers made it possible—in three lines. The clansmen's charge broke the first line, but the second was waiting for them, and received them with a deadly volley which threw them into utter confusion. No amount of desperate valour, and there was plenty of it, could save the day; the last hopes of the Stuart dynasty were finally quenched on Culloden Moor.

There is no need to dilate on the cruelties in which the victors indulged, whereby the Duke of Cumberland earned **After Culloden.** for himself the title of the "Butcher," and brought indelible infamy on a name which otherwise deserved to be held in respect at least, if not in honour. It would be a pleasanter task to trace the wanderings of the fugitive prince, to dwell on the many deeds of single-hearted loyalty, of pure devotion, of dauntless courage and endurance, whereby he and many of his followers were enabled to escape. The months that followed Culloden are full of incidents such as the most thrilling writers of romance could hardly match, of acts of heroism not to be surpassed. In spite of immense rewards offered, of tremendous temptations to a population so poor and so primitive as that of the Highlands, there are no records of betrayal or attempted betrayal, countless records of men and women who faced death or ruin in aiding and concealing fugitives from the triumphant arm of the government. In that period when, in public and private life alike, individual selfishness and self-seeking seem to have dominated morality so that any gleam of something higher comes as a welcome relief from the general sordidness and materialism, the annals of the White Cockade are a positive delight ; and although they have no political significance, it is with reluctance that one turns from them to the close of the European war.

At the outbreak of the insurrection, Frederick of Prussia had already retired from his alliance with France and Spain. The withdrawal of Cumberland, however, made it comparatively easy for the French troops to overrun the Netherlands. Otherwise, the campaigns on the continent were barren of result, partly because Philip of Spain died and was succeeded by Ferdinand, a son of his first wife, who cared but little for the advancement of the Bourbons in Italy. In America and in India, British and French were fighting ; the active contest for empire which was to be fought out during the next fifteen years had already begun. In America the advantage lay with the British, in India with the French. By sea, the superiority of England was emphasised in 1747 by a couple of naval victories, under Anson and Hawke ; and an attempt made by France to frighten the Dutch government was foiled in the same year, because it roused the people to overthrow the government, appoint William of Orange Stadtholder, and send him to join Cumberland, now returned, in the field. The combination, however, led to no very active results, as Marshal Saxe was more than a match for his opponents, who quarrelled. The war had become very desultory and very aimless. Louis commenced negotiations with Cumberland and the Dutch : but Maria Theresa, as usual, refused to hear of peace, and George, Cumberland, and a considerable English party were inclined to carry on the war. The result was that Marshal Saxe again proved his superior strategy, and it became more evident than ever that there was nothing to be gained by continuing. The peace party gained the day ; and though

The war on the continent ;

and at sea.

Maria Theresa continued her opposition, France, England, and Holland came into practical agreement, and she was forced to give in. In October, 1748, the Treaty of Aix-la-Chapelle was signed. Practically, the nett result of the whole period of the war was that Frederick got Silesia, and won for Prussia the position of a first-class power. Don Philip, brother of the kings of Spain and Naples, got Parma and Piacenza, which were to revert to Austria if he died without issue or succeeded to the Sicilies; and, for England, the Stuart bug-bear was practically disposed of, while nothing whatever was said about the original cause of quarrel with Spain. In India and America the position of the French and English remained practically unchanged; since Madras, which had been captured by the French, was restored in exchange for Louisberg, which had been taken by the English.

Treaty of Aix-la-Chapelle.

The finishing stroke to the cause of the Stuarts was given by Pelham's act abolishing hereditary jurisdictions in Scotland—a measure which destroyed the Clan system whereby alone the 'Forty-five had developed into a formidable rebellion.

BOOK II.
THE STRUGGLE FOR EMPIRE.

CHAPTER I.
THE COMING STORM.
1748-1756.

Meaning of the last war: state of Europe after it—Importance of individuals—Pelham—Newcastle—Pitt—Affairs in America; in India—Maria Theresa and Frederick—The new grouping of allies—Confusion in England—Frederick takes the initiative.

THE war which was concluded by the peace of Aix-la-Chapelle left the relative positions of England and France without material alteration, while it finally disposed of the Stuarts. It was, in fact, the commencement of the great duel for empire which ended in the expulsion of France from America and India; and, on the continent, of Prussia's bid for rank as a first-class power, which ended in her complete success. The immediate issues actually at stake in this premonitory war were, perhaps, never very great; for none of the belligerents was it a life-and-death struggle. But it was the warning of a life-and-death struggle about to be waged in every quarter of the globe.

Meaning of the war.

At the time of the Peace of Utrecht, France, Austria, Spain, and England were first-class powers, with Holland not quite relegated to a humbler position. The exceptional conditions following on the death of Louis XIV. had led to a strong Anglo-French alliance, which continued in appearance long after it had been in reality replaced by an alliance between France and Spain, directed almost equally against Austria and England. The unknown factor in the position had been Prussia, who utilised the contests of her neighbours to establish herself. So that the Peace of Aix-la-Chapelle left Europe under new conditions. Holland had fallen out of count; Spain, now scarcely in the front rank, under a new king who was less bellicose than his predecessor, was disinclined to war; and a new military state of the first class had been suddenly established in the middle of Europe, completely upsetting preconceived theories of the balance of power. At the same time, the colonial rivalries of England and France were rapidly coming to a head. England, however, had now a freer hand than in the earlier years, because she no longer had to fear that a foreign war would be accompanied by civil embroilments at home.

State of Europe.

It is interesting to observe the effect of individual personalities when political conditions become complicated. But for the brilliant abilities of one man, Frederick the Great, Prussia would hardly have been organised into a really first-class power. But for the same man's extraordinary activity and desperate resolution, she must have been crushed in the Seven Years' War; though, but for his unusual capacity for arousing the bitterest personal animosity, it may be doubted whether he would ever have been so fiercely attacked.

Importance of persons.

So it was the presence of a William Pitt in England, and the lack of one in France, which won the Empire. Pitt's four years of power raised England from a state of demoralisation, which seemed hopeless, to the highest pinnacle of glory. But if France had been controlled by any one who had realised in time that England must be beaten in America, in India, and above all on the sea, if any permanent advantage was to come of it, things might have gone very differently.

Again, once at least, Prussia was saved by the sudden withdrawal of Russia at a critical moment—due entirely to the different personal sentiments of the Czarina Elizabeth and her successor. Speaking roughly, the lesson of the period seems to be that the causes which make great struggles inevitable are not controlled by individuals, but it is mainly on individuals that the issue of these struggles depends. It is no more possible to extract an adequate view of history out of the personal ambitions and enthusiasms of a few great men, than to obtain it by treating the great men merely as necessary products of the existing political and social conditions.

In England, for a brief period following on the fall of Walpole, Carteret and Pulteney had been in the ascendant; the former being perhaps the minister whom King George preferred to any other. But Carteret's policy was too much that of a European statesman, too much coloured with Hanoverian conceptions, to be acceptable in England, and he had soon given place to Pelham and his brother Newcastle.

Pelham was no great statesman : he inherited Walpole's timidity in regard to foreign wars, and his fear of innovations at home; he was scarcely capable of initiating a policy, or of carrying one out with any great vigour : but he had immense tact and personal skill in reconciling discordant elements among ministers, and he had ready to hand, for all the dirty work of corruption, his brother Newcastle, who revelled in an occupation which, without requiring any excessive intelligence, made him feel himself to be wholly indispensable.

The Pelhams.

Pelham, as a general rule, managed to find some sort of office for any one whom it was dangerous to keep out. While he remained at the head of affairs, it was inevitable that there should be plenty of grumbling—for the young men who cared for politics, as apart from wirepulling, were necessarily jealous of the old men who were required for the sake of party organisation; but there was no danger of open sedition in the parliamentary ranks. The Pelhams could even utilise the 'Forty-five to force Pitt into office against the will of the king. It cannot be said that Pelham's administration was brilliant; but it was respectable and not discordant. It was timid, but not enough so to drive bolder politicians into open opposition; nor was it—as timid administrations often are—varied by occasional plunges into extreme rashness. And by his conciliatory system he was always able to secure the support or the silence of those whose opposition to Walpole had been vigorous enough to hamper him seriously, and had thus been enabled to carry out the policy of subsidising continental troops, which was necessary, but most unpopular.

Hence the years which immediately followed the peace of Aix-la-Chapelle were quiet though uneasy. It was not till Pelham's death, in 1754, that matters assumed a somewhat alarming appearance. Government till then had been a make-shift sort of affair, but it had served its turn without disaster.

The death of Pelham, however, left Newcastle at the head of the government, and a period of something like parliamentary anarchy ensued. Newcastle himself was grossly ignorant of politics, devoid of administrative capacity, and totally incapable of framing a definite policy, while he loved the sensation of power, and craved for a perfectly free hand in the bestowal of his favours.

Parliamentary chiefs; Newcastle,

In the Lower House, there were three men who were capable of taking the leadership; but of these, Murray, the Attorney-General, afterwards Lord Mansfield, had no intention of letting politics interfere with his professional ambitions. Henry Fox and William Pitt were the serious rivals.

Fox was a man of great ability, a master of debate, but emphatically an adventurer—a man who cared little for political principle, but a good deal for office, and more still for the stipends of office. William Pitt had long been distinguished for the vehemence and splendour of his oratory, for immense self-confidence and lofty ambition, and it was known that he cared extremely for power and very little for its emoluments. In the subordinate office of Paymaster he had won great popularity by refusing to follow the unvarying precedent of accepting those large percentages and perquisites which had made the post a peculiarly lucrative one. In the case of a rich man, this might have been regarded merely as a happy bid for popular favour; but Pitt was not a rich man, and his action then is in perfect accord with his habitual conduct. His scorn of pecuniary gains may have been ostentatious, and his methods were often theatrical; he very frequently did what is commonly described as "playing to the gallery;" but the sentiment was genuine for all that. And it was to this disinterestedness that Pitt owed very much of his subsequent success, in an age when very few politicians were disinterested. It inspired confidence even where he was disliked; whereas even where Fox was popular he was not trusted.

But neither Pitt nor Fox was popular in Parliament. If Fox was distrusted, Pitt was feared. And Newcastle probably felt that he could keep Fox faithful, but could never denominate his rival. Hence it was to Fox that he turned. There was the farther consideration that the king might be persuaded to tolerate Fox; but could not endure Pitt. At first the Prime Minister did not bid high enough, and Fox rejected his offer: so he had recourse to Sir Thomas Robinson, a hopelessly incompetent person; but when this produced the coalition of Pitt and Fox in an opposition conducted from the government benches, the conjunction was too formidable, and Fox was won over by renewed offers which appealed to his impecuniosity. A ministry was formed which was entirely incapable of dealing with anything like a crisis, but which could at least wear the appearance of carrying on the affairs of the country. But as the clouds thickened it became more and more evident: first, that ministers had no policy, and no mutual reliance; secondly, that no ministry could be a strong one from which Pitt was excluded; thirdly, that the country regarded him as the one competent man. The war had already commenced before Newcastle resigned, and a Pitt administration was formed—merely to prove that there was one way, and only one way, to form a government which should at once be strong in parliament and command the confidence of the country. Pitt and Newcastle were obliged to swallow their animosity and form a coalition, after Fox and Granville had made an abortive attempt; the king was obliged to accept a situation which was abhorrent to him, and, having accepted it, acted, as he did throughout his reign, with the utmost loyalty. But this was not till 1757, by which time England was giving signs of what can only be called imminent collapse. The history of the amazing reaction which followed will be traced in subsequent chapters.

While England was the scene of parliamentary intrigues and personal rivalries, the storm was gathering on the continent, in America, and in India.

In North America there was a large group of English colonies along the Eastern seaboard of what is now the United States, extending inland as far as the Alleghanies. Canada, on the north, was French; Louisiana, on the south, was French; Hudson Bay, Newfoundland, Nova Scotia or Acadia, were English, having been ceded at the Treaty of Utrecht: but the limits of Acadia had never been defined, and, of course, French and English took diametrically opposite views as to what was included under that name.

America.

To the west, the English claimed what we have learnt,

from the recent partition of Africa, to call the "Hinterland," *i.e.* the whole of the inland between the parallels of latitude at the northern and southern extremities of the seaboard of the original English colonies. But the French claimed all that lay west of what was actually held by English colonists, so joining Canada on the north to Louisiana on the south, and completely cutting off any possibility of expansion for their rivals. The English colonists altogether outnumbered the French, but the latter were better organised for military purposes; and both parties were in alliance with numerous Indian tribes, with whom the French seem to have been considerably more popular. Left entirely to themselves, the probabilities in a prolonged contest would, no doubt, have been in favour of the English, but the results would have been far from certain.

It has been held that the importance of the expulsion of France from America at this time is overrated, as the comparative strength of the rival populations made a prolonged competition impossible. That may be true of the colonies if they had been left to themselves. But, had the French home government adopted an active colonial policy, while the English home government continued indifferent for a little while longer, the whole of the conditions would have been changed.

As matters stood there was constant friction between the two parties, aggravated by the fact that neither of them kept in check their Indian allies, whose methods of warfare were unspeakably cruel.

Of affairs in India it will be better to treat consecutively later on; remarking here that there was a bitter rivalry between the English and French commercial companies, whose representatives were hardly waiting for an open declaration of hostilities to attack each other, while each was intriguing extensively with native rulers who were intended to be used as cat's-paws in the coming struggle.

<small>India.</small>

Under these conditions it was evident that, whatever else might happen, war between England and France at no distant date was inevitable.

Nor was a war between Austria and Prussia less certain.

Austria and Prussia. Traditionally, Austria was the great continental rival of France, and the not very cordial ally of England. But tradition had been completely overbalanced by the growth of Prussia. Those Italian provinces which had formed a bone of such fierce contention between Austria and Spain were no longer a subject of animosity, but Maria Theresa had set her heart on the recovery of Silesia and Glatz from Frederick. Moreover, being a person of exceedingly strong feelings, she was bent on annihilating Frederick, not merely as a question of policy, but out of personal rancour. If allied with Prussia and England, the one thing she longed for with her whole soul was the one thing she could not get. Moreover, with Prussia on her borders as an equal, Austria could no longer dominate the Empire. On the other hand, if Prussia and France should enter on a strong continental alliance, the chances of crushing the former would be very small. For it was, at any rate, certain that England would be intensely averse to any alliance of which the primary object was the destruction of Prussia.

To gain her ends, therefore, Austria required to initiate a new policy of a French alliance against Prussia; to be secure at least that there should not be a Franco-Prussian combination. Moreover, the Russian Czarina, Elizabeth, hated Frederick personally with a deadly hatred. With her active co-operation, and that of one or two minor German states, it seemed that Prussia, once isolated, must be completely crushed.

For a long time, however, France viewed the Austrian plan with disfavour. It would involve a complete breach of her traditional policy; it would result in the re-establishment of Austrian supremacy: besides which, France desired to

strike at England ; to do so on the continent meant
striking at Hanover ; and Prussia, if only she could be relied
upon, would be a much more efficient help than Austria in
attacking the Electorate.

Thus, as the collision between England and France
approached, great uncertainty prevailed as to the combination of the continental powers. George's first desire
was to renew the Hapsburg alliance ; but Kaunitz, the
Austrian minister, would not commit himself to the defence
of Hanover while there was still a chance of securing France.
England, therefore, in the interests of Hanover, was forced
to make overtures to Frederick ; and so it came about that
when France, still shy of Kaunitz, tried to open negotiations
at Berlin, she found herself too late. Frederick would not
trust her to carry on the war for his advantage after she
had secured her own ends ; while, on the other hand, English
subsidies would help him, or his enemies, more effectively
than French armies. He accepted the English alliance, the
more readily because he knew that otherwise a recently
concluded treaty between Russia and England would be
turned to his detriment ; and in January, 1756, the Treaty
of Westminster was signed.

France knew that she could not look for Spanish support
under the present King of Spain. She was not prepared for a
simple naval duel with England. The only alternative now
left her was to combine with Austria. Moreover, there were
considerations other than those of statesmanship which
weighed with Louis. His mistress, Madame de Pompadour,
had great influence with him ; and she was one of the many
people whose personal animosity Frederick had secured.
And, curious as it sounds, Louis had also an idea that, by
combining with Catholic against Protestant powers, he would
benefit the prospects of his own soul, and square the account
with Heaven for his private immoralities. In fine, it
appeared that if France acceded to the Austrian scheme,
Frederick would be so fully occupied in self-preservation,

that he could not possibly interfere in the English war, while England would lose her traditional ally. So Louis gave his adhesion. Austria was to have a free hand against Prussia; France was to have a free hand against England. The Treaty of Versailles, of which this was the practical sense, was signed on May 1, 1756; and Russia and Austria proceeded to negotiate for the partition of Prussia.

When these complicated conditions are summarised, we arrive at the following statement of the new European combination.

How were the two pairs of belligerents to be combined? Austria preferred the French alliance, because an Anglo-Prussian combination against her seemed less formidable than a Franco-Prussian one. Prussia preferred the English alliance, because France could not be relied on, while England would fight on the continent by means of subsidies. Austria's aloofness forced England into the arms of Frederick; the Anglo-Prussian alliance forced France into the arms of Austria. And so the camps were ranged, with England and Prussia on one side, and France and Austria on the other; with Russia prepared to act as energetically as her finances permitted, so far as attacking Frederick was concerned. Among the minor German states, Saxony was certain to support Austria, and Hanover to support Prussia.

Combination of the powers.

In the mean time, however, ministers in England had entirely failed to grasp the situation. The alliance with Austria was at an end, but the idea of the Austrian and French substitute for it seems to have been overlooked. A war with France was expected, and a subsidising treaty was made with Russia—as if Russia had any intention of allowing her troops to be used against any one but Frederick. At the very same time (January 16, 1756), a convention of neutrality was signed with Frederick at Westminster. The confusion of mind which allowed these hopelessly contradictory negotiations to go on simul-

Confusion in England.

taneously, without discovering that they were contradictory, is sufficient proof of the utter incompetence of the government.

But Frederick was thoroughly alive to all that was going on. He knew well enough that the time would come when Maria Theresa would endeavour to crush him, and he had spent his years of peace chiefly in making ready for war, training troops, and collecting treasure. He was aware now of the negotiations that were going on. He saw that his enemy was only waiting to make her arrangements irresistibly complete before declaring war. He was the last man in Europe to sit still and allow these arrangements to be completed. He decided not to wait, but to begin before Austria was ready—to act on the offensive before defence should become impossible.

Frederick.

CHAPTER II.

THE WAR IN EUROPE.

1756–1761.

Interesting features of the war—Frederick attacks Saxony—Capture of Dresden—1757 : The Austrian alliances—Position of Hanover—Battle of Prague—Battle of Kolin—Convention of Kloster Seven—Frederick's danger—Battle of Rossbach—Battle of Leuthen—Russians and Swedes—Pitt comes into power—1758 : Military position of Frederick—Battle of Zorndorf—Battle of Hochkirchen—Prince Ferdinand—1759 : Minden—Frederick's exhaustion—Battle of Kunersdorf—Capture of Dresden—1760 : Battles of Liegnitz and Torgau—Campaign of 1761.

Interest of the war in Europe.
THE Seven Years' War is the history of a nation at bay. It is politically important because it established the European Powers on the new basis. It is of importance from the military point of view, on account both of brilliant developments and tremendous blunders. As concerns administration, it illustrates over and over again the enormous advantage, at a crisis, of concentration. It is interesting, partly because a desperate resistance against seemingly overwhelming odds is always interesting, partly because of the extraordinary vicissitudes of fortune during its course. And to the political student it presents one more example of the danger to England of too intimate a connection with a continental state—seeing that, for practical purposes, we were as much hampered by the Hanoverian connection as if the electorate had been a British province ; and one more example, also, of the disastrous consequences to France of her usual blunder—the attempt to fight England on the continent.

The Prussian king had discovered the toils that were being laid for him. He had every reason to suppose that within twelve months he would find Russia, Austria, Saxony, and France making a combined attack and crushing attack upon him. If he broke the peace himself, no doubt he would be apparently putting himself in the wrong—but only until he could publish the documents, of the existence of which he knew, which in his expectation would prove the existence of the European conspiracy. Even had it not been so, when life is at stake nations are not in the habit of observing formalities. By striking at once, Saxony at any rate might be disabled, and, if all went well, it might even be possible to deal a blow at Austria which would seriously cripple her before the winter. Schwerin, his best officer, would co-operate from Glatz, and Prague might be captured.

Frederick attacks Saxony.

The plan could only be completely successful if Saxony collapsed at once. On August 29, 1756, Frederick entered Saxony. But the Electoral troops withdrew to a position at Pirna, where they were too strong to be attacked. A blockade became necessary, for Frederick could not afford to pass on at once to Bohemia and leave hostile Saxony to rise on his rear; and the Austrian army under Marshal Browne was soon ready to act.

The defence of Saxony thus effectually prevented the plan of surprise which had been contemplated. Still her own interests suffered. An attempt was made by Marshal Browne to relieve the blockade, his design being to fall on the rear of the Prussians, and so enable the Saxons to cut their way through. On October 1st a battle was fought at Lobositz between Browne and Frederick, who had left half his army behind to keep up the blockade; but the battle was indecisive, and Browne was able to continue his march. The ground, however, was too difficult, and the Prussian position too strong, to make the relief practicable; Browne had to retreat, and the Saxons to surrender

Capture of Saxony.

at discretion. So concluded the campaign for the year. The nett results were : the Dresden archives fell into the king's hands, and the public justification of his action followed ; Saxony no longer stood in the way of military operations, but, instead, materially helped to fill the Prussian treasury : and the troops which were to have been employed against Frederick were compelled to enter his service instead.

Kaunitz, the Austrian minister, employed the winter in pushing forward his alliances with great success. A fresh **Austrian alliances.** treaty was concluded with Russia (which had broken with England), involving the payment of a large subsidy to the Czarina, and, on May 1st, a treaty with France was signed at Versailles, in terms extraordinarily favourable to Austria. Prussia was to be partitioned for the benefit of Russia, Poland, Saxony, the Palatinate, and Austria ; all that France was to have was a portion of the Austrian Netherlands, including Ostend and Nieuport,—even that was to be contingent on the recovery of Silesia ; and, finally, Austria was to exchange with Don Philip, the younger brother of the Spanish king, the rest of the Netherlands—about which she cared little— for the Italian duchies of Parma, Piacenza, and Guastella— for which she cared a good deal. Perhaps the bargain was not quite so bad, from a wide Bourbon view, as it seems from a merely French one : for the Italian duchies were a constant source of irritation, and very little use ; while the Netherlands might prove of great advantage—of course on the assumption that, for military purposes, they would be practically at the service of France. But the alliance was to procure for Austria everything she could possibly want, including the destruction of Prussia ; while only in the event of complete success France was to have the Netherlands, her own part as a reward, and Don Philip's in exchange.

At the same time, George's ministers in Hanover very nearly wrecked everything, from a delusive hope that the electorate might come off scot-free by declaring itself neutral. Finally, however, an army of some fifty thousand men, drawn from various petty states, and paid for by Hanover, was drawn up behind the Weser under command of the Duke of Cumberland, to meet the approaching invasion of a large French army. To complete the circle of enemies, Sweden joined the allies with a view to securing Pomerania as her share of the spoils. <small>Hanover.</small>

It seems to have been expected that, against the enormous odds, Frederick's tactics would be purely defensive. He knew, however, that the only possible way of dealing effectually with his enemies, was to fall on them piece-meal with his whole force. Therefore, he beguiled the Austrians into a belief that he intended to devote himself to securing the position in Saxony; and they were utterly astonished by suddenly discovering that his whole army was converging for a dash upon Prague. He succeeded in forcing a battle (May 6, 1757) with the main army under Prince Charles—who, fortunately enough for Frederick, had superseded Browne,—before Daun with a second army could effect a junction; and, after a furious contest, in which both Browne and Schwerin were killed, the Imperial troops were completely defeated, and driven within the walls of Prague. <small>Battle of Prague.</small>

The king intended Prague to fall at once, but Prague held out. Daun was collecting reinforcements. Leaving just sufficient troops to maintain the blockade, Frederick marched against Daun. The opposing armies met at Kolin. The Prussian plan of attack was upset, because Prince Maurice of Dessau mistook his instructions, and General Mannstein exceeded his. On the other side were three Saxon cavalry regiments which had escaped the capitulation of Pirna, having been in Poland at the time. The commander of one of them saw his opportunity, and, without waiting for orders, charged at a critical moment. The battle was irretrievably lost, but the Austrians <small>Battle of Kolin.</small>

had been severely handled, and did not follow up the retreat. To remain in Bohemia, however, was hopeless ; the blockade of Prague was raised, and Frederick retired to Saxony. The Austrians followed as far as Zittau, just over the frontier. Frederick, however, could not entice them into a battle, and so was obliged to detach a portion of his army under Bevern, to watch them, while he proceeded to retrieve the situation on the western frontier ; a step made necessary by the disaster which had overtaken the Duke of Cumberland.

While Frederick had been winning the battle of Prague, and losing that of Kolin, Cumberland had been thoroughly mismanaging his task. Having taken up his position behind the Weser, he allowed the quite incompetent French general, D'Estrées, with a greatly superior army, to cross the river, without disputing the passage. A battle was fought at Hastenbeck, which could hardly be claimed as a victory by either party ; however, Cumberland thought it useless, apparently, to attempt opposition to the larger army of the French, and retired north with some precipitation, to Stade. Thus Hanover and Brunswick and the direct route to Berlin were left entirely unguarded.

Cumberland on the Weser.

D'Estrées was superseded by Richelieu, who was an equally incompetent commander, and allowed his troops to pillage very much as they liked. A good deal of time was wasted in plundering, before he set out in pursuit of Cumberland. The duke was in a *cul-de-sac*; he was in serious danger of being so shut in that he must surrender at discretion. A rescue from Frederick, after Kolin, could hardly be hoped for. On the other hand, Richelieu was not anxious to make terms which would drive his opponent to desperation, and winter was coming on. A convention was therefore concluded,—the King of Denmark acting as intermediary. The fact that Richelieu allowed it to be called a convention, instead of a capitulation, materially affected subsequent events, because a capitulation is a military act within the general's powers, but a convention is a diplomatic act, which, to become binding, requires the ratification of the home government. By this "Convention" of Kloster Seven (September 10th) the auxiliaries were dismissed, and the Hanoverians were to be allowed to go into winter quarters near Stade. Richelieu was left perfectly free to do as he liked: with two effective alternatives,—to proceed against the nearest Prussian territory, or to co-operate with Soubise, who was about to march on Saxony with a second French army, in conjunction with Imperial troops. He tried to do both, and did both badly.

<small>Convention of Kloster Seven.</small>

Frederick's position was now very alarming. He had been foiled in his attack on Prague, and had got back to Saxony with an Austrian contingent hanging on his rear, to find the army of defence neutralised at Stade, and the great allied force on its way into Saxony. As has already been related, he detached Bevern to keep the Austrians in play, and proceeded to see what could be done with the attack of Soubise from the west; while Richelieu's army, away further north, had to be left to the incompetence of its commander. Almost the only consolation left the king was in the knowledge that, whatever princes might wish to do, the feeling of the entire German population was on his side, and that there was no comparison between his own generalship and that of the allied commanders, or between the fighting capacity of their troops, enormously outnumbered though he was.

<small>Position of Frederick.</small>

But he could not sit still and wait for Soubise while Bevern waited for the Austrians. Bevern was not strong enough for that; he must get a battle out of the allies, and win a decisive victory: and Soubise was too much afraid of him to be at all inclined to give him an opportunity. Luckily a raid on Berlin by an Austrian contingent forced him to leave Soubise, and brought Soubise out of the hills to which he had withdrawn. The Austrians, however, **Battle of Rossbach.** did not wait for Frederick, who was thus enabled to return before the allied troops could withdraw again : and he caught them at Rossbach (Nov. 5th).

They had double his numbers, and thought they could outflank him. In making the attempt they exposed their own flank. The Prussian force seized its opportunity, fell on them while they were on the march, and shattered them to pieces, beyond all hope of present recovery.

For the immediate purpose, Cumberland's blunder had been retrieved, and the army of invasion broken up; but at the cost of leaving the Austrians in the south held in check only by Bevern. Owing to disputes between Prince Charles and Daun, comparatively little had been effected, but quite enough to make the situation in Silesia exceedingly grave. They captured Schweidnitz, defeated Bevern, and secured Breslau, and then Liegnitz ; unless Frederick could win another great battle against them, they would have most of Silesia before the winter set in, and the rest of it in early spring. Frederick had to march in all haste to join Bevern ; and by the time he reached the spot, the troops were demoralised, and Bevern was a prisoner himself. But Frederick and the men who had won Rossbach were prepared for anything. The odds were considerably more than two to one against them, but they must fight a battle and win it, or throw up the struggle. They were not going to throw up the **Silesia saved at Leuthen.** struggle. On December 3rd, Frederick found that Charles was preparing to give him battle. Next day he made the attack. The Austrians imagined that he meant to assault their right wing : he had fallen on their left and driven it back upon Leuthen before they found out their blunder. Then they supposed the Prussian flank to be unguarded, and attempted to fall upon it. But the Prussian cavalry were there ready, and fell upon them instead. The Austrians were beaten as thoroughly as their allies had been at Rossbach, without hope of recovery ; the battle of Leuthen broke up the allies in the south as completely as Rossbach had done in the west. Before the year was out, all Silesia except Schweidnitz—which, however, fell in the following spring—was in Prussian hands again.

Meantime, in the east, the Russians had defeated the army which had been sent to hold them in check ; but their general had withdrawn instead of making use of his victory, in the expectation that the Czarina was dying, and that her successor would support Prussia with an enthusiasm quite as great as her animosity had been. The Czarina did not die, but the Russian attack was completely wasted, and the opportunity given for driving back a Swedish attack on Pomerania. <small>Russians and Swedes.</small>

So far, then, Frederick had made an attack on his enemies, and been foiled at Kolin ; they had attacked him in the west and in Silesia, and been foiled at Rossbach and Leuthen. It was well for him that by this time Pitt had come into office with a free hand, owing to Newcastle's support ; for now there was to be no more vacillation. The British government recalled Cumberland, declined to ratify the Convention of Kloster Seven, subsidised Hanover, and entrusted the command of the Electoral troops to Ferdinand of Brunswick, a thoroughly competent general. With this army to hold invasion back on the west, and his treasury replenished by an English subsidy, Frederick's task of fighting off his enemies—and he could look for little more than that at the best—was rendered comparatively hopeful. Ferdinand had taken command of the Hanoverian troops immediately after Rossbach, and had already driven Richelieu behind the Aller before the campaign closed for the winter. <small>Pitt in power.</small>

Now, to follow the nature of the task before Frederick, it is necessary to have the points of attack clear. On the north-west, towards Hanover and Brunswick, was the French line of attack, held in check for the rest of the war by Ferdinand. Moving south and east, the <small>The points of attack.</small>

Imperial troops—those, that is, of the states of the Empire which supported Austria—were mainly occupied with Saxony; where, as a rule, they were kept in play by Prince Henry, Frederick's brother. Along the south, if Austria attacked Saxony, the king must meet her there; if she attacked Silesia, he must go and meet her there. On the east, north of Silesia, were the Russians; and in Pomerania, the comparatively unimportant Swedes.

Frederick commenced the campaign of 1758 by entering Austrian territory and besieging Olmütz in Moravia. The siege was a failure, partly because sieges never were Frederick's strong point, partly because a new Austrian commander was coming to the fore, in the person of Laudon. Daun, as usual, had a large army, but was more anxious to preserve it from disaster than to use it aggressively. Frederick, however, was obliged to raise the siege of Olmütz, and, although he advanced into Bohemia instead of retreating upon Silesia, the intelligence that the Russians under Count Fermor were threatening Brandenburg left him no choice but to hurry at top speed to join the contingent on the Oder to meet them. The **Battle of Zorndorf.** battle took place at Zorndorf (August 25th). The cruelties practised by the Cossacks had made the Prussians furious, and the fight was a singularly savage and bloody one. The Russian troops showed a stubborn courage which was quite unexpected, and they nearly saved the day by it in spite of bad handling: but they could not hold the field, and were forced to retreat into Poland; while Frederick hastened off to relieve Prince Henry.

For, meantime, Daun had turned his attention to Saxony when he was left free by Frederick's withdrawal to meet the Russians. He ought to have seized the opportunity to crush Prince Henry before the king could reappear; but he was, as usual, too slow. After a good deal of manœuvring, Frederick allowed his army temporarily to occupy a scarcely defensible position, counting on Daun's timidity; but for once the Austrian commander used his opportunity, and inflicted a defeat on him (at Hochkirchen, October 14th). This, however, seemed enough to Daun, who merely re-entrenched himself between the Prussians and Silesia, where a second Austrian army was having matters apparently all its own way. The king reorganised his troops, which had been defeated but not broken up; escaped past Daun, dashed into Silesia, relieved Neisse (which was being besieged), and was back again in Saxony before Daun had made any use of his temporary absence. {Battle of Hochkirchen.}

During the year, Ferdinand in the west had also done what was required of him. Already, before the winter, he had forced Richelieu behind the Aller; early in spring he drove the French back across the Rhine; and, in June, defeated Clermont, who had superseded Richelieu, at Crefeld. Soubise, however, had by this time recovered himself, and, with a second French army, made a diversion on Hesse, which made it necessary for Ferdinand to come back to Westphalia. Here he was joined by an English contingent of 8500 men: but the prospect was made less encouraging by the accession to power in France of an energetic minister, the Duc de Choiseul; whereby the era of court-favourite-commanders was closed, and the best French officers, Contades and the Duc de Broglie, were sent to the Rhine. {Prince Ferdinand.}

The year 1759 was one of triumph for the British arms in every quarter of the globe, and, owing in great part to the British contingent, for Ferdinand in Germany; while the French met with nothing but disaster. On the other hand, in this same year, Frederick himself suffered the most crushing reverse in his career.

The French, however, began successfully enough. Soubise captured Frankfurt, and Broglie foiled Ferdinand's attempt to recover it at Bergen (April 13th). Ferdinand had to fall back, the French captured Minden (July 9th), and Hanover was seriously threatened. To fight {Battle of Minden.}

and win a decisive battle was a necessity. Contades' position was a strong one, and he must be drawn out of it. The circumstances demanded audacity. In spite of his inferior numbers, Ferdinand detached ten thousand troops, and sent them round to the French rear, while he exposed his own left wing in a manner which invited attack; calculating that he would be able to bring up his supports before the attack was delivered. Contades came out of his position, made his arrangements under the impression that Ferdinand's plan had been a blunder instead of a trap, and delivered battle. A blunder was in fact made, because instructions were misunderstood and the English regiments were ordered to advance too soon; but the splendid discipline and courage which they displayed resulted in the rout of the French troops instead of the annihilation of the English. If Lord George Sackville, in command of the English and Hanoverian cavalry, had not positively refused to obey repeated orders to charge, the French would have been cut to pieces. As it was, they managed to withdraw to Minden, being cut off from their former strong position by the troops sent round beforehand; that night they had to evacuate Minden and cross the Weser, and the next day began to retreat as best they could upon Hesse Cassel. Hanover was saved by the battle of Minden (August 1st).

The close of 1758 had left Frederick in an unsatisfactory position. He had succeeded so far in preventing any of his enemies from getting a firm footing on his territories, but that was all. And he had done so only at the expense of a series of battles which had more than decimated his best troops, and these he could only replace by a system of forced recruiting that provided a very inferior type of soldier; whereas the Austrians had a very much larger stock of men to draw upon, and the quality of their troops was steadily improving. Moreover, by this time, Frederick's savings were exhausted, and

Weakness of Frederick.

he had to rely on the English subsidies to keep his treasury in a tolerable state of replenishment. In short, the strain of the war was telling more severely on Prussia than on the allies, and it was no longer possible for her to take the offensive. The only possible course was to watch whence the next attack was to be expected, and to meet it as promptly as possible when it came.

In 1759 the attack came from the Russian side. Soltikoff, who was now in command, advanced on the Oder. Laudon, with a contingent of eighteen thousand men, was on the way to join him. Frederick marched to Frankfurt (on the Oder), but Laudon effected the junction. Soltikoff was waiting for Frederick at Kunersdorf, with the Austrians ready to support him; Daun, with another Austrian force, was lingering a few marches away. **Battle of Kunersdorf.**

The odds were nearly two to one, as usual. However, on August 12th (a few days after Minden), Frederick attacked. He was successful at first, but unfortunately was determined to demolish his opponents at once. He continued to press the attack though his troops were thoroughly worn out; the superior numbers of his obstinate opponents began to tell; the advantage gained was turned into a defeat; fresh troops came to the succour of the Russians; the defeat became a rout, and the rout a flight. The Prussian army was completely and, to all appearance, hopelessly demolished. It had required courage enough to hold out after Kolin, to struggle through one campaign after another with a growing consciousness that every victory was but the staving off of final disaster. But Kunersdorf, for the first time, reduced the stubborn spirit of the great Frederick to despair. He resigned his command to Finck, appointed his brother Henry generalissimo, and evidently contemplated suicide.

Complete success was within the enemy's grasp, yet they failed to seize it. Soltikoff remained inactive; in part, probably, from the expectation that the Czarina was dying and Russian policy would veer round; in part, certainly, from disgust at the stolidity of Daun, who displayed his constitutional incapacity for acting ; while Laudon, being under his orders, was obliged to remain still. The result was that Frederick, finding that no one was going to interfere, took heart, resumed his command, and set about reorganising his army unmolested.

Recovery of Frederick.

Meantime, however, an Imperialist army had been besieging Dresden, which surrendered on the news of Kunersdorf. Daun, too, after an ineffectual pretence of co-operating with Soltikoff, moved off into Saxony, and the Russians withdrew into Poland. So far the allies had inflicted a tremendous defeat on their enemy at Kunersdorf, but had failed entirely to make use of it. They had captured Dresden, as an accidental result, but had made no more progress in Saxony. It even seems probable that they would have evacuated Dresden, and retired into winter quarters without having gained any ground in spite of their great victory, but for the fact that once more Frederick calculated too much on Daun's timidity. He sent Finck to Maxen to bar the way of the Austrians as they retired to Bohemia ; and Finck, instead of barring the way, was surrounded by overwhelming numbers and compelled to capitulate. The year ended in a futile attempt to recover Dresden by a winter campaign.

Thus, for the first time in the war, the allies, in 1760, commenced the year with a firm footing in Saxony. Ferdinand, in spite of his successes, had been unable to give Frederick any assistance beyond providing him with twelve thousand men for the winter campaign. His army was not large enough to do more than act as an efficient defence on the northwest. Frederick was becoming thoroughly exhausted. However, the strain was telling on the other side as well, and they continued to be thoroughly afraid of joining battle with their stubborn opponent. Hence they did not show such activity as might have been expected. Still, by the end of July (1760), they were making progress in Silesia ;

Frederick's exhaustion.

Glatz had fallen, Laudon was threatening Breslau, and the Russians came down to the Oder.

Frederick marched from Saxony, with Daun and a second Austrian army under Lacy following him, to attack the third Austrian division under Laudon, while the Russians looked on. He caught Laudon alone, defeated him at Liegnitz, August 15th, and then got rid of the Russians by allowing fraudulent despatches to fall into their hands, which caused them to retreat across the Oder again. Daun got back to Saxony before him; most of the electorate was in the hands of the allies; and Daun, with his main army, was strongly entrenched at Torgau. Here, on November 3rd, another battle was fought, and the Austrians were beaten and driven in upon Dresden. *Battles of Liegnitz and Torgau.*

The advantage gained by the allies in 1759 was retained; Frederick's two victories had only prevented their continued advance; but the process of exhaustion had gone further with both parties. In 1761 the Austrians again improved their position in Silesia by capturing Schweidnitz, but otherwise there were no military events of note, both sides being engaged in manœuvres which led to no results, except that the Russians had secured a footing in Pomerania. The operations of the French army on the west at one time proved threatening, but were successfully checked by Prince Ferdinand, who defeated Soubise and Broglie at Kirch Denkern. *Campaign of 1761.*

Up till 1759 the allies had failed to establish themselves in Prussian territory; then they had secured foothold in Saxony. At the end of 1761 they had it also in Silesia and Pomerania. To add to Frederick's difficulties, there was a new king in England with a new minister and a new policy and the end of the Prussian kingdom seemed at hand.

CHAPTER III

BRITAIN AND FRANCE.

1754–1761.

British and French in America—Opening hostilities—Panic in England—1756: Byng at Minorca—Pitt in office—1757: Coalition of Pitt and Newcastle—Pitt's naval policy—Effects of sea-power—Gibraltar—1758: The new maritime policy—Canada—Montcalm—Choiseul in France—1759: Boscawen and De la Clue—The Brest fleet—Battle of Quiberon, Nov. 28th—The French navy crushed—Wolfe in Canada—Effect of naval control—Wolfe takes Quebec, Sept. 18th—1760: Completion of conquest of Canada—Accession of George III.—Prospect of Spanish intervention—1761: Pitt resigns.

IN America the contest between England and France had commenced long before the two countries had formally declared war on each other. The French claim to the basin of the Ohio had led to the formation of an Ohio Company by the English colonists, in order to push their own counter-claim. The French sent out expeditions to set up forts, the English sent another to establish a fort where the Ohio River is formed; the French sent a larger party, who drove them back, established the fort themselves, calling it Fort Duquesne, and defeated, at Great Meadows, a second expedition sent out, under the command of George Washington, to support the first.

British and French in America.

This was in 1754. The home government began to realise that some importance attached to these proceedings, and sent out two regiments of the line, under General

Braddock, to help the colonists early in the following year. Braddock entirely over-estimated the superiority of his regulars, took for granted that he was going to carry matters as he liked, alienated the Indians, quarrelled with the colonial militia, and finally fell into an ambuscade and was annihilated, losing his own life in the fight. The disaster was by no means compensated by one or two minor successes a little later. Moreover, reinforcements came to the French in Canada. The fleet which carried them was followed up by an English squadron under Boscawen. Off Newfoundland the two fleets were separated by a fog, but two of the English had a fight with two of the French, which resulted in the capture of the latter. Still, the main purpose of the French expedition had been successfully carried out. The instructions to the English admiral had been that the French were to be attacked if it was found that the Bay of St. Lawrence was their goal. But even this engagement was not followed by an immediate declaration of war.

Commencement of hostilities.

In point of fact, the long period of political lethargy, jobbery, and administrative incapacity had by this time reduced the *morale* of the country to an extraordinarily low ebb. Ministers were desperately afraid of doing anything at all, and England was on the verge of hopeless panic—a state of affairs rarely, if ever, paralleled. A declaration of war was almost daily expected. A fleet was fitted out under Hawke, but ministers could not make up their minds what to do with it; and finally, still without a declaration of war, the admiral was instructed generally to capture French men-of-war and merchantmen wherever he might find them between Ushant and Cape Finisterre.

Panic in England.

At this time Fox was in office under Newcastle, while Pitt, who was directing the thunders of his invective against them, was growing in popularity. But it was not till the war had actually been declared that ministers would

H

resign, the opening event having evoked a storm of indignation which made their retention of office impossible.

The close of 1755 was full of rumours of an invasion, which produced unbounded alarm, but no attempt at arming. Instead, some Hanoverian troops were brought to England. It was known that French armaments were being fitted out: it was known also, early in the following year, that they were not destined for America, from the character of the supplies that were being collected. Warning of their true destination—Minorca—came from consuls abroad; but government turned a deaf ear to these, and would make no preparations. At last it became impossible to disbelieve, and a fleet of ten sail was precipitately equipped and sent out in April, 1756, under Admiral Byng, son of the Lord Torrington who had demolished Alberoni's fleet at Passaro. The French fleet from Toulon had started, however, and commenced operations against the island, which was insuffi-

Byng at Minorca. ciently garrisoned, before Byng appeared on the scene. The English fleet was a little inferior in weight of metal, and the English admiral, though personally brave enough, was so far possessed by the general demoralisation that he considered the chances of a victory too small, and its advantages too inadequate, to make it worth risking a defeat which might endanger Gibraltar as well. Therefore he left Minorca, one of the most valuable stations on the Mediterranean, to inevitable capture. About the same time war was openly declared.

When the news reached England, the public indignation knew no bounds. The government hoped to save itself by making a scapegoat of Byng, and concentrating the popular fury on him as the sole person responsible. But this contemptible course did not save them. Fox was the first to resign, and, before the close of the year, Newcastle was driven out of office, and the king compelled to accept Pitt.

Yet Pitt's favour in the country did not make him strong

in parliament; besides, he was disabled by gout. Still, the new ministry was animated by a very different spirit from the old one, and set about raising new regiments, remodelling the militia, and generally preparing to act with energy. Then Pitt's popularity was for a moment weakened by his magnanimous defence of Byng in defiance of the general clamour; he had no steady support, and was detested by the king and the Duke of Cumberland. In April he was dismissed, and once more disorganisation was supreme. The dismissal, however, only raised the national enthusiasm for him to double pitch. Yet it was not till three months had passed that the absolute necessity for a compromise which should combine Pitt and Newcastle was admitted, and one of the strongest and most successful administrations on record formed; in which "Pitt did what he liked, and Newcastle gave what he liked," Fox was made Paymaster and so was satisfied, and opposition fell to the ground. *Pitt takes office. The coalition.*

It was now July (1757), too late for the new government to make its policy actively felt in the war until Cumberland had already done what he could to cap the melancholy records of the time by the Convention of Kloster Seven; and some further failures have yet to be recorded before the turn of the tide. In America the French, under Montcalm, were making progress—without interference from Loudoun, the English commander, who could not make up his mind to attack Louisburg, the fortress on Cape Breton which commands the St. Lawrence; while the British admiral, Holbourne, refused to fight the relieving French fleet because they had eighteen ships to his seventeen. One more piece of mismanagement must be related to complete the tale, before Pitt had got his own policy thoroughly in hand, and found the men who were to carry it out. An expedition was planned against Rochefort in the Bay of of Biscay, one of the principal French arsenals. But the admiral, Hawke, and the general, Mordaunt, could not agree—the latter being beyond question to blame ; time was frittered away, the defences of the place were got into reasonable order, and, as success no longer seemed secure, the expedition returned home.

But with the last months of 1757 closes the first epoch of the war—the epoch of hesitating councils, of timid or incompetent commanders, of administrative in-capacity and desultory policy, of alternations between blind fury and blind alarm. From this time forward we find a definite policy carried out, with vigour in every detail—capable and brilliant officers in the important commands, activity in every department ; above all, the army, the navy, the whole nation infused with a new spirit of daring, of enterprise, of self-reliance. In 1758, the first year of the new order, the tide of failure is checked and turned ; the mastery is passing into the hands of England ; and the following years, to the close of of the war, are a record of unvarying triumph.

He initiates a definite policy.

"I am certain," Pitt had said to the Duke of Devonshire, the nominal head of his first brief administration, "that I can save the country, and that nobody else can." George had been bitterly opposed to the formation of the coalition ; but, when it was formed, Pitt said to him, "Sir, give me your confidence, and I will deserve it." "Deserve my confidence," answered the king, "and you shall have it." Pitt was the one man who could save the country, and, with the loyal and unanimous support of his colleagues and the king, he did it.

In brief, Pitt's policy was to support Frederick with money, but otherwise to make England herself play a wholly secondary part on the continent, while he concentrated his attention on developing an overwhelming mastery of the seas, and on the expulsion of the French from America. And it was by the mastery of the seas that we conquered both America and India, and turned the Kingdom of Great Britain and Ireland into the British Empire.

In the previous war our sea-power had been a controlling factor, as it had practically incapacitated Spain, neutralised Naples, and prevented a French invasion. But it had not been systematically developed. It was now to be so utilised that France was practically blockaded, her commerce cut off, her communications with India and America and her power of sending help thither destroyed; whereas English ships multiplied, commerce increased instead of diminishing, supplies were poured in wherever they were required, and our ally on the continent was furnished with those subsidies without which his desperate struggle against enormous odds must have collapsed. Incidentally, too, the unceasing danger of attacks on French ports all round the coast made it absolutely necessary for France to keep those ports in a state of defence, which crippled the powers of her army on the Rhine. Moreover, it was by the enormous naval superiority which we established at this time that the schemes of Napoleon were frustrated, and England saved, in the great wars to come. How immensely this same sea-power, even before its full development, had already influenced the course of events in India will be shown in the chapters treating of Indian affairs.

<small>Sea-power.</small>

In this connection, one strange blunder made by Pitt early in 1757 may be noted, though it led to no actually disastrous consequences. He proposed to give up Gibraltar to Spain as the price of her alliance and help in the recovery of Minorca. Minorca was valuable, but not so valuable as Gibraltar. Probably the object of this offer was to prevent Spain from joining France, and so weakening our naval preponderance; while it was thought worth while to give up Gibraltar to a naval ally who would thereby be secured to us, if Minorca was also recovered from the enemy. Fortunately, Pitt's overtures were rejected, while France was still too much engrossed with the continental war to realise the importance of at once pushing forward a policy of naval rivalry.

<small>Pitt and Gibraltar.</small>

The features, then, of Pitt's naval policy were these: first, the blockade of the French Channel and Atlantic ports, so that no fleets could get out either for the invasion of England or for the St. Lawrence; the protection of the Straits of Gibraltar, to prevent the French Mediterranean fleet from getting out; and flying attacks on various ports, to keep up a constant alarm and prevent progress of armament: secondly, as a result of the security thus obtained against the presence on the high seas of any strong naval force, the despatch of expeditionary fleets to assist in America and India, and to attack French colonies in the West Indies. The attendant results were an enormous growth of English shipping, and a diminution of French shipping; steady improvement in English seamanship, and deterioration in that of the French, owing to the latter being perpetually cooped up in port.

The new naval policy.

The unsuccessful expedition against Rochefort in 1757 was a somewhat discouraging commencement; but it was followed by a comparatively damaging attack on St. Malo; and throughout 1758 the policy of blockade was effectively carried out, though no engagements of importance took place.

In Canada, however, the changed conditions soon showed themselves. Loudoun was recalled, and replaced by Amherst, with Wolfe as second in command; the fleet was under Boscawen. The French squadron on the St. Lawrence was now reduced to five sail of the line. Thus unsupported, Louisburg, in spite of a stubborn resistance, was forced to capitulate before the close of July. Cape Breton and the Isle of St. John, rechristened Prince Edward's Island, fell into the hands of the English. The attempt, however, to make an inland entry into Canada failed.

Canada; Montcalm.

There were two possible routes into Canada: one by way of the sea, and the mouth of the St. Lawrence; the other inland, at the eastern end of the Great Lakes and by Lake

Champlain. But here the entry could not be made until the French forts which guarded the route were captured. Abercrombie, the principal officer left in charge when Loudoun was recalled, was entrusted with the task of attempting to reduce Ticonderoga. Though his forces were considerably superior to the enemy in numbers, the latter were commanded by Montcalm; the attack was very badly managed, and failed completely.

The effects, however, were fairly counterbalanced, not from the strictly military point of view, but as far as the public *morale* and feeling were concerned, by the capture of Fort Duquesne—hitherto connected only with disaster to the British arms—by another small expedition. The contest between the colonists of the two countries was chiefly caused by the dispute as to the ownership of the basin of the Ohio: the establishment of Fort Duquesne had been the practical method of asserting the French claim; and its capture and renaming as Pittsburg were a very practical reversal of the position.

British expeditions against Senegal and Goree, in Africa, resulted in the capture of both.

In 1759 the French army was shattered at Minden, as already narrated; the French navy was shattered at Quiberon; and the French power in Canada broken at Quebec. The conduct of our troops at Minden would have put heart into the English people if heart had been needed; but fine as that was, the triumphs of Quiberon and Quebec were even greater. _{1759.}

By the end of 1758, Choiseul had been summoned to power in France, and a very much more active policy was pursued in consequence. The energy of the continental army was revived, the necessity for a vigorous stroke of some kind was perceived, and steps were taken for the preparation of a powerful armament to invade England. Transports were prepared in the Channel and Atlantic harbours. A squadron was fitted out at Brest, _{Choiseul's policy.}

and another in the Mediterranean at Toulon, which were intended to combine. The result showed that France had allowed England by this time to attain a superiority, which ended in the annihilation of the French fleet instead of the invasion of England.

The attempt was made in the summer of 1759. Admiral Boscawen, in command of the Mediterranean squadron, had made an attack on some French frigates in Toulon, in consequence of which some of his vessels stood in need of repair, and he had to withdraw his fleet to Gibraltar, leaving look-out vessels on the way. The Toulon fleet seized the opportunity; hoping to evade him, pass the straits, and get away to Brest unmolested. In spite of a thick haze which favoured their movements, they were sighted near the straits by a lookout. The French Admiral, De la Clue, resolved to run for it; but his fleet became separated, five of the twelve ships making for Cadiz. In the morning, Boscawen's fleet of fourteen sail was in full pursuit of the other seven. They overtook the rear vessel, which delayed them considerably by making a desperate resistance; but the hope of escape was small. Of the remaining six ships, four were run ashore at Lagos, near Cape St. Vincent; and of these, Boscawen captured two, and burnt the others. The other two escaped. But the prospect of a junction between the Toulon fleet and that at Brest was at an end.

Destruction of the Toulon fleet.

The largest fleet still remained at Brest, where there were twenty-three ships of the line, besides frigates; blockaded, however, by Admiral Hawke. Now, a fleet at Brest suffered from the disadvantage that it could not come out of harbour while a heavy west wind was blowing, and it was needless for the English, under those conditions, to risk the damage of keeping at sea. When a westerly gale blew, they ran to Torbay; when the gale dropped, they came out and blockaded. It was therefore possible for other ships to get into Brest when a westerly

The Brest fleet;

wind was blowing, but not to come out. The transports which were to convey the invading army were harboured in the ports to the southward. The scheme of the French appears to have been, that the Brest fleet was to come out, beat the English, and so be free to convoy the transports without risking their loss. But their plan of action is somewhat obscure; for, when they did succeed in getting out on November 14th—Hawke, who came out of Torbay on the twelfth, having been beaten back by the wind,—they stood to the south instead of going in search of the English—perhaps with a view to dispersing Duff's smaller fleet, which was blockading Quiberon.

Hawke, however, had sailed again at the first available moment; and Conflans, the French commander, had hardly sighted Duff's squadron, when the leading vessels of Hawke's pursuing fleet were also sighted. A north-westerly gale was rising. Conflans, slightly out-numbered in ships, decided to make for Quiberon Bay, where the navigation was always difficult; believing that Hawke would not attempt to follow him, and, if he did, would only run his ships on the shoals and reefs. Hawke, however, was bent on demolishing the French fleet; and, to some extent, the course taken by them served as a guide for him. The English van overtook the French rear as they were getting in. On November 20th, in a heavy sea, with a gale blowing, where the navigation was exceptionally dangerous, was fought the battle which settled the fate of the French navy. Seven of the ships escaped into the mouth of the Vilaine—a feat which could only be performed at high tide, and was dangerous even then,—from which they did not get out again for more than a year; seven escaped to Rochefort; the rest were taken or destroyed. Two English ships were wrecked. The dispersed remnants of the French fleet were entirely powerless to act: instead of twenty-three sail of the line at Brest and twelve at Toulon, there were five at Cadiz, two of which got back to Toulon,

<small>demo-
lished at
Quiberon.</small>

seven caught in a sort of trap in the Vilaine, and seven at Rochefort ; while the English had more than made good such losses as they had sustained by the prizes taken. A blockade of the coast still had to be kept up, but in nothing like the same force as before ; while an immense amount of power was set free to act almost unmolested in the distant seas.

Flotillas had been prepared with a view to taking part in the invasion, at Havre, Dunkirk, and other Channel harbours. These ports, however, were efficiently blockaded by the Channel squadron, and considerable damage was done by a bombardment of Havre. Still, a small squadron commanded by Thurot succeeded in getting out of Dunkirk, and causing some annoyance on the Northern and Irish coasts, near which it was captured early next year.

While the fate of the French navy was being sealed by Boscawen and Hawke at sea, the fate of her power in **Wolfe in Canada.** Canada was being sealed on land by Wolfe. Cape Breton had been captured in 1758. Now that the whole French seaboard was in a state of blockade, Montcalm, the commander in Canada, could hope for no more reinforcements ; but England was free to act. According to the plan of campaign for 1759, one body of troops at the west was to advance to Niagara, which was regarded as the gate for the French in the direction of the Ohio Valley. The main body of the troops sent out in the previous year under Amherst and Wolfe were to proceed, under the former general, to retrieve Abercrombie's failure, capture Ticonderoga, and descend by Lake Champlain to Quebec, where a junction was to be effected with Wolfe ; who commanded a fresh armament, supported by Admiral Saunders, and was to ascend the St. Lawrence when navigation was practicable.

The western army captured Niagara, but found that no further progress could be made. Amherst captured Ticonderoga, but was checked on Lake Champlain. But Wolfe captured Quebec, and thereby decided the future of Canada.

Even as it was, the taking of Quebec was a brilliant feat. That it was possible at all is due, again, to the naval conditions. The French could get no supports; the English commanded the St. Lawrence without fear of molestation; and the admiral could co-operate with the general to make feints at whatever points were desirable.

Quebec is situated on the north bank of the St. Lawrence. On the west it is defended by the heights of Abraham; on the south is the river; on the east a bay formed by the junction of the river St. Charles with the St. Lawrence; while the course of the St. Charles protects it on the north also. The French were encamped for some

Defence of Quebec.

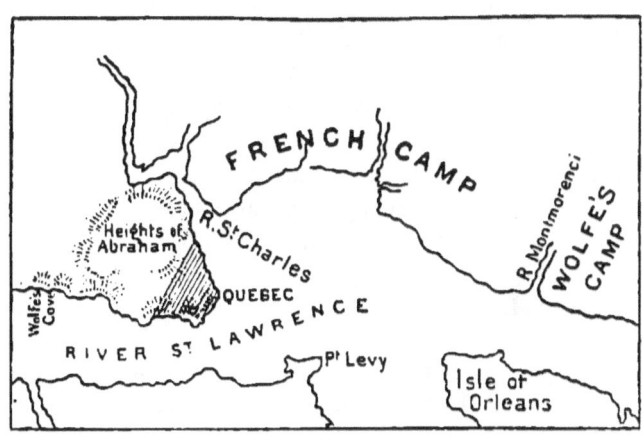

SKETCH MAP FOR SIEGE OF QUEBEC.

distance along the northern shore of the St. Lawrence, east of the St. Charles, in a very strong position; the defences of the town itself on this side not being strong enough. Thus the city could not be invested, and Montcalm was too strongly posted to be attacked. Wolfe, having established himself on the Isle of Orleans and at Point Levy on the southern bank of the St. Lawrence opposite Quebec, sent a squadron under Admiral Holmes higher up the river, to prevent any communications from arriving. Then he tried, vainly, to inveigle the French from their entrenchments by various feints; while the frequent attempts made by the enemy to damage the English vessels by means of fire-ships were foiled in their turn. Then an attempt to storm the French camp was successfully beaten off; there was no sign of the expected arrival of Amherst; Wolfe fell ill, and the English troops began to lose heart.

A movement was made up the river, as if to land troops there, but this did not entice Montcalm from his entrenchments. He did, however, send a detachment of 1500 men to watch the operations.

Wolfe now conceived the daring idea of scaling the heights of Abraham—a task of immense difficulty in any case, and possible only by means of a complete surprise. This was effected by means of the fleet. Up the river, a demonstration was made by Admiral Holmes; below, another was made on the lower part of the French camp by Admiral Saunders. Attention was drawn off to these two points. Under cover of night, Wolfe landed half his army below the heights, and started to climb, sending back for the rest of his troops. So unexpected and so audacious was the attempt that, when the small French guard at the top found the Englishmen scrambling up, they were seized with a panic. The first troops gained a footing on the summit unmolested, and, after that, it was comparatively easy for the rest to follow. Montcalm, hearing what had happened, brought up his troops from the camp, and faced the English. Thus the battle was fought and the victory won. Wolfe, and Montcalm both received their death-wound; their seconds in command were both killed also: but Quebec was taken. In five days the city capitulated (September 18, 1759).

Wolfe takes Quebec.

During the same year, the rich island of Guadaloupe was captured without difficulty by an expedition sent to the West Indies—an additional instance of the naval supremacy.

1760 was principally occupied in completing the conquest of Canada. There was still a considerable French force, at Montreal; and, in winter, Quebec was left merely with its English garrison, the river becoming unnavigable. Early in spring the commander at Montreal thought an attempt might be made to recover Quebec; and, owing to the fact that Murray, who remained in command, thought fit to come out and fight him in the open with inferior forces, the attempt very nearly succeeded. After a sharp fight, in which the defeated troops did more execution than did their opponents, the English were driven back into Quebec, but the French did not enter along with them. Entrenchments were promptly opened; but the river was becoming clear, and a few days later an English frigate appeared, followed, three days later, by others. There was no prospect of a French fleet appearing, and the siege was broken up.

Completion of the conquest of Canada.

Montreal now became the point of attack. Amherst came down against it from Oswego, Colonel Haviland from Lake Champlain, and Murray from Quebec. The advance of the three columns was skilfully planned, and so accurately timed that Amherst and Murray reached the Isle of Montreal on the same day, and Haviland the day after. Resistance under the circumstances was futile; Montreal capitulated: and now the only foothold retained by the French in America was at the mouth of the Mississippi. An expedition which succeeded in leaving France, having in view the conveyance of stores to Montreal, fell an easy prey to the English squadron at Louisburg.

Apart from the completion of the conquest of Canada, which had already become practically certain in the previous year, 1760 witnessed no striking events, naval or military. What we had been fighting for was in effect won, and a good deal more. But the death of George II., and the accession of his grandson to the throne would have been fraught with disaster had they

Accession of George III.

befallen a little earlier. As it was, the new king's favourite, Lord Bute, began at once to exercise a very dangerous influence on the royal counsels. 1761 was comparatively inactive, except for the capture of Belle Isle, off Brittany,— a barren enough conquest in itself, but one for the recovery of which France was likely to consent to a heavy price.

Danger from Spain. Negotiations, in fact, were going on for peace throughout the earlier part of the year. These might have been carried through in spite of the uncompromising character of Pitt's demands, but for the fact that France was also negotiating for a Spanish alliance, with a view to continuing the war. She had good ground for her expectations in the rancour of the new king, Charles (the Don Carlos who had been King of Naples when Captain Martin gave him an hour to accept his terms or be bombarded, and had never forgiven the insult). The old stock causes of quarrel, too, had never been settled, and Pitt soon became quite certain that Spain and France were going to form an offensive alliance. He urged the advantage, under the circumstances, of taking the initiative and declaring war against Spain, especially as the French began openly to claim concessions to Spain as part of the price of peace. Moreover, France wished to have Prussia left out of the **Fall of Pitt.** peace, and that was a condition which Pitt utterly refused to take into consideration. It became quite evident to every one that the negotiations must be broken off. But the Bute interest was now strong in the Cabinet, the Spanish war was flatly negatived, and Pitt thereupon resigned.

CHAPTER IV.

INDIA BEFORE THE STRUGGLE.

1707–1740.

Popular misconception of Indian history—India not a nation—The Mogul empire—Principal Indian states—Four main divisions—Conditions of a European conquest—Sea-power the controlling factor—The rival European powers—Chartered companies: the Dutch; the French; the English—Comparison of the French and English companies—French governors—La Bourdonnais—Ultimate certainty of English success.

WE have observed the course of events in the West during the great war, of which there were three main results—the establishment of Prussia in Europe, the expulsion of France from America, and the establishment of England in India.

The great factors in the conquest of India are fairly well appreciated by historians, though by no means always accurately set forth. But the ideas of ordinary Englishmen on the subject are nearly always hazy, and, very often, hopelessly misleading.

The popular notion seems to be that there was a great Indian nation with which England traded; that it occurred to the mind of a merchant's clerk, named Clive, that this nation could be conquered; that, at the head of a few Europeans and some few thousand native troops, he conquered India in a couple of pitched battles; that England then took possession, sent out governors-general, and organised a military administration; and that the whole conquest was due to the accident of Clive not having committed suicide at an early age. *Popular misconception of Indian history.*

Now, it is obviously true that, if the British race in India had not included men of capacity and courage, we should never have conquered the country. If many of them had not been somewhat exceptionally brilliant, the course of the conquest would have been much slower, and the establishment of our power much less stable. It is also true that the whole thing was so far an accident that it was not deliberately planned out by the English government, and the various steps in our progress were to a considerable extent forced upon us by circumstances. Nevertheless, the element of accident is not more prominent in the history of our conquest of India than in most other great movements. The causes at work are clear and distinct, and the results were, in fact, inevitable.

To understand the course of events, we must properly understand the conditions under which we began the contest that placed the whole of India eventually under British sway. Since our European relations and the earlier stages of our Indian connection acted on each other only in a very small degree, while it is of great importance, owing to the natural confusion produced by dealing with unaccustomed names, to view Indian affairs connectedly, I have deferred treating of Indian affairs in their chronological place by the side of European affairs; but inasmuch as the final struggle between France and England in India was contemporaneous with, and was, in fact, a part of that great contest with which this book deals, it is now time to treat consecutively of that struggle itself, and the events and conditions preceding it.

In the first place, then, we have to get a definite idea of the state of India when the fight began.

India was not a nation; it never had been a nation. It was a crowd of separate, loosely connected states and tribes. For centuries the peninsula had been the scene of a series of conquests by foreign invaders, who sometimes established themselves in the country, and

India not a nation.

INDIA BEFORE THE STRUGGLE. 113

sometimes merely ravaged and departed. Mohammedan marauders swept down through the passes of the Himalayas, established dynasties, made the native Hindu princes into tributaries, and were in their turn overthrown. For the most part the invaders did not displace the native populations, but dominated them; they made no attempt to organise a nation, but ruled as conquerors. But in the sixteenth century there appeared the great Mogul conqueror, Baber, whose grandson, the great Akbar, constructed a true empire over all the north of India—an empire with a system, in which the natural intolerance of Mohammedanism found no place. The last of the great Moguls was Aurungzebe, who reigned for fifty years and died in 1707. He extended the Mogul empire south over the Deccan, but, by his fanatical Mohammedanism and by the unwieldy expansion of his sway, prepared the complete disintegration of the empire. *The Mogul Empire.*

We can, however, arrive at a fair classification of the divisions of the Indian peninsula, at the end of the thirty years of disintegration following his death.

The headquarters of the Moguls were at Delhi, in the north—a Mohammedan dynasty. Their empire extended over the provinces of the Ganges basin, of which the chief were Oudh and Bengal, with Behar and Orissa; and further south over the great central district known as the Deccan, and the Carnatic. *Principal Indian states.*

In proportion to their distance from Delhi, the provinces of the empire, ruled by Mohammedan viziers, were more or less independent of the central authority. The governor of the Deccan, known as the Nizam-ul-Mulk, or Subadhar of the Deccan, nominally owned the suzerainty of the Mogul, and appointed the Nawab of Arcot, who ruled the Carnatic. South of the Nizam's dominions and west of the Carnatic was Mysore, also under a Mohammedan dynasty; and south of the Carnatic were the Hindu kingdoms of Tanjore and Trichinopoly. On the north-west

I

of the Mogul empire in the Punjab, was the Hindu confederacy of the Sikhs; south of them, the Hindu states of Rajputana. Further south, again, was the Hindu confederacy of the Mahrattas, spreading west and north of the Deccan, and running out between the Deccan and the imperial provinces of the Ganges basin.

Thus, from the Punjab down to Mysore, all Western India was essentially Hindu, and had thrown off the Mogul allegiance. The basin of the Ganges, the central provinces, and all the east coast were in the hands nominally of the Moguls, actually of Mohammedan dynasties practically independent of them and of each other. Moreover, while the Mogul empire was thus hopelessly disintegrated, the Hindu power of the Mahrattas was growing; and it is not improbable that, if no European power had intervened, the Mahrattas would have ultimately effaced the Mahommedan powers.

So, before we came into direct conflict, as an independent power ourselves, with the native races, we find **Four main divisions.** India divided practically into four sections: the Mogul empire in the Ganges basin, in the Deccan and Carnatic, and, on the east, between Bengal and the Deccan proper; in the north-west, the Sikhs and Rajputs, with whom we were not for a long time to come into collision; cutting in between the Deccan and Upper Bengal, and spreading down the north-west of the Deccan, the Mahrattas; and in the south, Mysore. In the earlier stages of the conflict, seeing that our advance was from the east, we shall find that the rulers with whom we have first to deal are the Nizam, with the Nawab of Arcot; the Mahrattas appearing as auxiliaries. Next appear the Nawabs of Bengal and Oudh; then Hyder Ali in Mysore, and the Mahrattas, as rival conquerors. The contest with the last was a contest for supremacy in India: the previous contests were with the states already breaking to pieces. But both the final Mysore war and the great Mahratta war fall later than the scheme of this volume ; and the struggle with the Sikhs later still. What we shall have to follow out is the practical institution of a solid English administration over the disorganised and separated states of the Mogul empire.

The foregoing considerations make it tolerably clear why it was no extravagantly difficult task for a foreign invader to upset the native dynasties, and to practically establish itself in their place over the greater part of India ; that is to say, they show that there was no great power of resistance in the native states, when we take also into our view the absence, not of soldiers, but of military organisation, and the inherent instability of Oriental despotisms, the uncertainty of Oriental alliances, and the anarchy which regularly succeeds the death of an Oriental ruler and the intrigues of would-be successors. *Conditions of a European conquest.*

Hitherto the invader had always come from the north by the passes of the Himalayas. He came again in the first half of the eighteenth century in the persons of Nadir Shah and of Ahmed Khan ; but neither of them attempted permanent establishment. In effect, they were not organising conquerors, but marauders. They ransacked Delhi, but they did not upset dynasties. And from the Afghan frontiers there was no fear of a different type of conqueror. Nor was there any fear of a descent from China or Thibet. The true source of danger—the quarter from which a subduing conqueror might come—was the sea.

On the other hand, for such a conqueror two things were needed—first, that his communications with his base should be kept open ; second, that he should have no one else competing with him on equal terms. Thus, if there came from the sea two rival powers, each able to maintain its supplies from home, each with adequate supplies at home to draw upon, each bent on remaining the equal of the other, India might have been divided between them ; while it is equally possible that some native power, such as that of the Mahrattas, would have held the balance.

But, if two rival powers appeared, one of which could maintain its home communications and secure supplies, and the other could not, it was absolutely certain that, whatever temporary successes the latter might gain, the former must in the end prevail. In plain terms, if a foreign power which had control of the sea chose to compete for supremacy in India, that power was absolutely certain to win in the long run, whatever temporary reverses it might sustain. And this is precisely what happened. Two rival European powers had a footing on Indian soil. As long as the other was there as a rival, neither could advance far in the direction of conquest. But one of the two held control of the sea. That fact made it impossible for the other to expel it, or ultimately even to resist it. The ability, the policy, the resources of the French in India were at times superior to those of the English. But when they achieved successes on the mainland, the successes of England by sea in other quarters of the globe compelled restitution of what had been won. During the rivalry, the English in India were not materially aided by supplies from home, but France could not send supplies even if she wished it. Once, the French superiority drove the English out of their most important settlement, but the peace of Aix-la-Chapelle compelled its restoration. And, in the end, the French fleet, which should have supported the French ashore, was driven from the Indian seas, while the English fleet remained to secure the success of the English arms in the struggle. Stated in the simplest terms there was only one European nation for which the ultimate conquest of India was possible, because the way to India lay over the sea, and England was mistress of the sea. Provided she maintained that supremacy, conquest was possible for her. It was feasible, indeed, for any other Power which should oust her

Sea-power the controlling factor.

from that supremacy; but she maintained it, and in consequence won India. Since no European Power could attack India except from the sea, to no European Power was the conquest practicable unless she held the supremacy of the seas.

We have now to examine the position of the Europeans in India, that we may understand how it was that the idea of a European predominance was initiated by a Frenchman, by whom also the means to secure it, as far as India was concerned, were definitely formulated; and how not he, but his English rivals, inevitably reaped the fruit of his labours. It is likely enough that the English would in no very long time have found the way for themselves, if Dupleix had not shown it to them. It is certain that, having been shown the way, they, and only they, could have reaped the full benefits unless France had beaten England from the seas, or at least proved her match upon them.

The early European trade with the East had been conducted through the Levantine merchants, and had been in the hands of the great sea-going states of the Mediterranean. The Portuguese discovery of the Cape of Good Hope opened a new route to the Indies, and substituted the ocean-going races of Western Europe for the Mediterranean states. Portugal led the way, Holland and England followed, and, long after them, France. But the Portuguese power was short-lived; the Dutch devoted their attention to the islands rather than to India; and, in the eighteenth century, English and French merchants were the principal Indian traders. *European powers in India.*

The conditions of distant commerce in the seventeenth century were curious. Trading companies made war on foreign trading companies, and endeavoured to secure a monopoly for themselves, without much considering whether the home governments were at war or not, and the home governments acquiesced in the *Chartered companies:*

arrangement. Companies held charters from their respective governments, practically giving them monopolies of trade in particular regions, with a free hand to make war, or peace, or alliances, very much as they might think fit ; the home governments having a mutual understanding that in the ordinary course their own relations were not to be compromised by misunderstandings between the companies. On the other hand, when the home governments went to war with each other, each usually endeavoured to make use of the war to get comparative monopolies for its own companies. Thus, for instance, the formation of the Ostend Company in 1722 was taken seriously to heart by the British government, and its suppression strongly insisted on.

It is to be observed that the conditions above described practically set the private enterprise of single individuals on one side. They would have been liable to perpetual attacks from rivals. But a strong company, with plenty of money, thorough organisation, and a possible appeal to the home government, necessarily became very nearly equivalent to an armed state, existing indeed primarily for purposes of commerce, but capable of armed action, either defensive or aggressive, on its own account.

The Portuguese, as serious rivals, disappeared at an early stage. By the middle of the seventeenth century the great competitors for the trade with the Indies were the two leading maritime powers, Holland and England, or, more accurately, the East India Companies chartered by those two Powers. There were constant collisions, but, generally speaking, the Dutch settled on and traded with the Spice Islands mainly ; the English with India, where they had factories at Surat on the west coast, Fort St. George (Madras) on the south-east, and, a little later, Fort William on the Hooghly. Towards the end of the century, however, France had, in the person of Colbert, a great minister who realised that the commercial ascendency of the future must rest with a power

the Dutch;

the French;

which could hold its own on the seas, and establish colonies in distant lands. In pursuance of the idea of maritime expansion, Colbert encouraged the formation of a French East India Company. The ambitious continental policy of Louis XIV. prevented Colbert's schemes from being properly carried out, and the navy was never developed to nearly the extent required for their adequate fulfilment. Still, the result was that, at the beginning of the eighteenth century, there were trading companies of three nations actively competing in the east; but the tremendous strain of her long wars had so weakened Holland, that she gradually withdrew from real competition on the Indian littoral, leaving the already established English and the newly arrived French to face each other's rivalry.

England had not been trading in those seas for a century without learning some lessons. The threatening disintegration of the Mogul empire, and the outbreaks of the Mahrattas into the Deccan, made it comparatively easy to put those lessons in practice; and the settlements had been turned into forts capable of defence, and, if need were, of being made the base of operations for advance. There were not wanting shrewd observers who saw, in the future, possibilities of the company being established as a territorial power; but the present object of the company was simply to increase their trade in the most profitable manner possible, while making sure of the security of their settlements. On the west coast, their main factory was transferred from Surat to Bombay, and a second fort, St. David, was established in the Carnatic. Thus the headquarters of the three future presidencies were already established at Bombay, Madras, and Fort William (Calcutta), each having its own affairs managed by a governor, each having its own forts and a few European troops.

The French had no important settlement on the west; but they had on the Hooghly Chandernagore, in the Carnatic Pondicherry; and what might have proved invaluable to them, but did not, the Isles of France and Bourbon (the Mauritius) in the Indian Ocean, commanding the route between India and the Cape of Good Hope.

It is important to observe, further, certain differences between the two great companies. The English one was the direct outcome of the action of traders; men of wealth who acted in concert and obtained necessary powers from their government, but resting financially on their own trade profits, and trading so successfully that they were able to lend government vast sums of money, in return for which they received powers which enabled them to act with a free hand. The French company was a creation of the French government. It was supported largely by government subsidies, and the freedom of action of its directors at home was hampered by the perpetual interference of state authorities.

The French and English companies.

Down to the time when Dupleix became Governor of Pondicherry, in 1741, the governors of the French company, Lenoir and Dumas, men of great ability, had, like the English, made the development of trade their first object. They had, indeed, taken more active steps than the English to secure the positive good will and support of native rulers, their rivals being content with the security of their settlements and an open market; but they had not plunged directly into the turmoil of native intrigues.

One more factor in the contest that was commenced by Dupleix and terminated at Wandewash is to be noted. In 1735 the Governor of the Isle of France was La Bourdonnais, and it was he who realised the vital importance of the presence of a strong French fleet in Indian waters. He saw that if there was to be a struggle for the East Indian trade, the victory must fall to the party which could best maintain its communications with Europe—to the party which could control the seas. He made every effort to obtain an adequate fleet from the French government, only to find that, if French and English went to war,

La Bourdonnais.

that fleet would be needed elsewhere. But to him belongs the credit of being the only Frenchman who recognized the true key to the situation. France, however, failed to supply it, and the result, let it be once more repeated, was not an accident, but a certainty.   *Certainty of British success.*

The East India trade was of such vital importance to England, so much of her wealth came from it, it was of such consequence to government to be able to borrow from the company, that if the French company had beaten the English company out of India, the English government would have been forced to make every effort to restore it. It could not have acquiesced, so long as it had the power to act. It is true that, while the contest was going on, it interfered as little as might be, and allowed the issue at one time to appear doubtful. But the difference was that England, if driven out by France, would have had no choice but to return to the charge, as her overwhelming sea-power would have enabled her to do; whereas when the English actually beat the French, France, with her shattered navy, had no means of attempting to recover her position, even if she would. Wandewash was a great victory, but it was at Quiberon that the destinies of India were decided.

CHAPTER V.

INDIA: DUPLEIX.

1741-1754.

Dupleix's scheme—Position of the rival companies—1743: Effect of the declaration of war between France and England—1746: Dupleix and La Bourdonnais—Capture of Madras—1747: Rupture between Dupleix and the Nawab—French military successes—1748: Pondicherry threatened by Boscawen—Effects of the peace of Aix-la-Chapelle—Influence of sea-power—New phase of the contest—1749: Rival claimants to native thrones—Plan of Dupleix—The English join in—Success of Dupleix—1751: Robert Clive—1752: Successes of Clive and Lawrence—Dupleix at bay—1754: His recall—The situation in 1754.

It was not till the outbreak of the war of 1744 between England and France in Europe, that the rivalry of the two countries in India took the form of active hostilities.

In 1741 Dupleix became governor of Pondicherry, having for ten years previously been in charge of the French settle-

The scheme of Dupleix.

ment in Bengal at Chandernagore. Neither the French nor the English company had as yet formed the idea of developing territorial dominion. Both were simply trading companies, with some military organisation for defensive purposes, and the governors of both were responsible to their directors at home. But in the service of both companies there were men to whose minds the possibility of territorial aggrandisement had presented itself, and the man who formulated the idea was Dupleix.

His scheme had two main objects—the practical expulsion of the English, and the assertion of a paramount influence in the native courts. For these purposes he discovered the requisite military machinery. He found, in the first place, that a handful of drilled Europeans were a match for a host of miscellaneous native levies ; and, in the second place, that natives drilled on the European system, and officered by Europeans, were nearly as efficient as European troops. He also made a point of placing himself in a certain official relation to the native princes, by parading the honours and titles which had been bestowed on his predecessor in the governorship by the nominal suzerain at Delhi, laying claim thereby to be accepted as an officer of the Mogul empire.

The theatre of the contest between England and France was to be the Carnatic. There were situated Pondicherry, with the English settlements of Madras and Fort St. David, one to the north, the other to the south. The ruler of the Carnatic was the Nawab Anwar-ud-din, who, in turn, owned the supremacy of the Nizam of the Deccan at Hyderabad. Further, to understand the military and naval operations of the contest, it must be remembered that the harbours of Madras and Pondicherry were neither of them capable of serving as permanent stations for fleets, and that the monsoons at certain seasons made naval operations impossible. *Position of the rivals.*

The approach of a European war between Britain and France was the opportunity which Dupleix desired, but it revealed the fundamental weakness of his position. An English squadron was ordered to the Indian waters ; but the French squadron, which La Bourdonnais, at the Isle of France, had succeeded with much difficulty in extracting from the French Government, was ordered home. At the same time, the directors in France instructed Dupleix to agree with the English governor, Morse, that the hostilities between the two countries should not extend to their Indian settlements. These pacific ideas did not suit Dupleix, nor did Morse favour them. There was every prospect of *Effect of the declaration of war between France and England.*

inflicting a heavy blow on the French company, bereft as it was of a fleet; while the English squadron might be expected very shortly. On the other hand, while Dupleix was crippled for the moment, his whole scheme would be upset if he were forced to enter into pacific engagements with the rivals whom he wished to expel. The energy and capacity of La Bourdonnais were well known; if he were given time, he might yet find a way of turning the tables. Dupleix resolved to make time, and he therefore applied to to the nawab to forbid the English to make their projected attack on Pondicherry, appealing to him on the ground of the good-will shown by the French settlement on the occasion of Mahratta risings, and pointing out that the nawab ought not to allow the English, who were his tenants on his territory, to attack the French, whose governor was an officer of the Mogul.

The nawab responded to the appeal, and forbade the English to attack Pondicherry. In the mean time, La Bourdonnais had been doing what he could. He succeeded in fitting out nine vessels, and with these he arrived in the Indian waters in June, 1746, while the English squadron was virtually blockading Pondicherry on the sea side. An engagement took place, which resulted in the English fleet withdrawing to the west coast.

Dupleix and La Bourdonnais.

Thus, for the time being, the positions were reversed. Dupleix had the support of a squadron, and the English had not. But now a fresh weakness appeared. Dupleix was supreme on land, but La Bourdonnais was supreme on sea, and the two chiefs were not in agreement. La Bourdonnais's ships, though he had done all he could, were inefficient; Peyton might reappear with his fleet; in October the monsoons would be coming on. He maintained, therefore, that it was useless to attack Madras until the English fleet had been decisively dealt with; and he was not in a position to deal with it decisively. Besides which, his instructions forbade him to retain Madras, even if he took it.

Dupleix, however, was, on the whole, in the more authoritative position, and La Bourdonnais did proceed to capture Madras. The French force, including La Bourdonnais' reinforcements, amounted only to some two thousand land forces, of which eleven hundred were Europeans. Morse had only about two hundred efficient soldiers, and he, in turn, appealed to the nawab for protection, but without result. Madras, therefore, was obliged to surrender, on the terms that it should be restored on payment of a ransom. This, however, led to a serious breach with Dupleix, who had no intention whatever of restoring Madras, and declared that La Bourdonnais' powers did not extend to the making of any such terms, as he was a subordinate on land. Hence, for some time, the latter refused to hand the settlement over, and, when he did so, the condition of his fleet made it necessary for him to withdraw to the Mauritius. *Capture of Madras.*

Now ensued a farther complication. The nawab, although he had previously shielded the French, refused to protect the English, because Dupleix assured him that when Madras was taken it should be given over to him. But Dupleix no more intended to give up Madras to the nawab than to the English, being bent on making sure that it should not get back into the hands of the English at all. When the nawab began to suspect the French governor of duplicity, he became naturally indignant, and made up his mind to seize Madras himself. He sent an army to do so, and Dupleix instructed the commandant to resist at all hazards. The native army numbered ten thousand men, the garrison five hundred. A sally was ordered, and the nawab's troops fled. It was the first contest between drilled Europeans and native troops, and it was a revelation of their relative capacities as fighting forces. The lesson was *Rupture between Dupleix and the Nawab.* *French military successes.*

brought home by a second engagement. A contingent was advancing to relieve the garrison, consisting of two hundred and thirty Europeans and seven hundred sepoys —that is, drilled natives. They were met by ten thousand of the nawab's army, who were promptly scattered. These two skirmishes changed the whole situation, by proving once for all that European methods of fighting would counterbalance an enormous superiority of numbers.

The appearance on the scene shortly afterwards of a small French squadron, inclined the nawab to come to terms. The prestige of the French arms had been very greatly raised; it appeared that Dupleix was to be supported; on the whole, his friendship seemed likely to be worth having, and the nawab had no great consideration for the English; therefore, he assented to the retention of Madras by the French.

There was now an opportunity for Dupleix to complete his scheme of expelling the English by the capture of Fort St. David, before an English squadron—which might be expected shortly from the Hooghly—should arrive. But Major Lawrence was in command at Fort St. David; the French squadron withdrew, and an English one appeared; the attack was foiled completely; and, a few weeks later (July, 1748), Admiral Boscawen appeared with a large fleet and reinforcements, which threatened Pondicherry itself.

Pondicherry threatened.

The forces now collected show about the maximum armaments of the struggle. Dupleix had 1800 Europeans and 3000 sepoys; the English 3700 Europeans and 2000 sepoys. The defence was admirably conducted, and was continued till the approaching monsoon made it dangerous for the admiral to remain. The English fleet withdrew, the troops returned to Fort St. David, and Pondicherry was saved. At the beginning of the next year, 1749, Dupleix contemplated the renewal of operations against Fort St. David; but his plans were frustrated by the news of the peace of Aix-la-Chapelle, whereby Madras was restored to the English in India, in exchange for Louisburg restored to the French in America.

So far, then, the course of events shows substantially that success attended Dupleix or the English chiefly in accordance with the relative strength of French and English fleets on the Indian seas. The one distinct acquisition made by the French, that of Madras, was directly due to the temporary predominance of La Bourdonnais, and the operations of Dupleix were always liable to sudden checks and reverses on the appearance of English ships. When the war was closed by the peace of Aix-la-Chapelle, Dupleix's actual gains on Indian soil were rendered nugatory by that general naval superiority of Britain which secured a restitution of such conquests. England had not yet used her power efficiently; much more might have been done: but the total result was that, although Dupleix had been able to obtain the intervention of the nawab in his own favour, to avert a like intervention in favour of his rivals, and, by his victories over the nawab's troops, to gain an immense amount of prestige among the natives, yet the close of the struggle left the rival companies practically in the same condition as before the war began. This was due to the English sea-power—a power which had been utilised directly as little as possible, but even so had proved too much for the French sea-power. Briefly, it was not so much the positive activity of English fleets as the enforced inactivity of French fleets which spoiled the designs of Dupleix.
_{The peace of 1748. Effect of sea-power.}

The peace of Aix-la-Chapelle introduces us to the second phase of the struggle between the rival companies. They could no longer make war upon one another; they could no longer aim directly each at the extermination of the other; yet, while Dupleix was bent on exterminating the English, the English were inclined to exterminate Dupleix. As matters stood, therefore, they
_{New phase of the contest.}

could only bid against each other at the native courts; and if parties should arise at the native courts, it was inevitable that they should take opposite sides.

There was, moreover, a secondary consideration. When France and England were at war both required troops. Now that war was over, the troops they had procured were on their hands. Simply as a matter of pecuniary convenience, therefore, it was worth while for both to find opportunities for hiring out their troops, if not precisely as mercenaries, still for substantial advantages of one kind or another. Moreover, the battles between the troops of Dupleix and those of the nawab had shown that a high price might be put on the services both of Europeans and sepoys. But, for the present, the English had not taken up for themselves the idea of Dupleix's policy, which was the direct extension of political influence for its own sake. They were anxious for it only so far as they expected a direct commercial value to attach to it.

It so happened that the means for carrying on their rivalry lay directly to hand. In 1748 the Nizam of the Deccan had died. A new Nizam, his grandson, was appointed from Delhi; but another claimant, his son, was in the field. The latter, Nadir Jung, had the advantage of being on the spot; the former, Muzaffar Jung, was resolved to secure his own rights. Moreover, Muzaffar Jung was a friend of Chunda Sahib, who had a certain title to claim the nawabship of the Carnatic, against the reigning nawab, Anwar-ud-din. As an obvious consequence, Anwar-ud-din and Nadir Jung supported each other as against Chunda Sahib and Muzaffar Jung; the former being respectively *de facto* nawab and Nizam, the latter claiming those offices *de jure*. But there was a further complication. Chunda Sahib was a prisoner in the hands of the chief of the Mahratta confederacy, who was known as "the Peishwa," and his ransom was not yet paid.

Rival claimants of native thrones.

Now, at the moment, the prestige of Dupleix was high. Moreover, he had under his control a larger number both of Europeans and of sepoys than the British. Also Chunda Sahib had received sundry good offices at the hands of the French. These considerations induced the two claimants to appeal to Dupleix for assistance, while, as a natural result, the two *de facto* rulers called in the English.

Here was Dupleix's opportunity. By guaranteeing the peishwa the ransom due from Chunda Sahib, he could set the latter free, and be fairly secure of the Mahrattas as allies. As yet no steps had been taken to bring in the British. If, by Dupleix's assistance, the *de facto* rulers could be turned out, and Muzaffar Jung installed at Hyderabad as Nizam, while Chunda Sahib was established as nawab, French influence would necessarily be supreme at the allied courts of the two most powerful princes in Southern India. *[margin: Dupleix's plan.]*

Dupleix promptly and energetically threw himself into the contest. The dispute for the nawabship was to be settled first. Chunda Sahib and Muzaffar Jung collected a large army of some thirty-six thousand men; they were joined by Bussy, the best of Dupleix's officers, with two thousand sepoys and four hundred Frenchmen. They met the reigning nawab at Ambur, and inflicted a complete defeat upon him. Anwar-ud-din himself was killed; his son, Mohammed Ali, fled to Trichinopoly, but continued to maintain his claim to the nawabship.

So far the English had not joined in the contest. But they had caught at the idea of taking part in the intrigues of native courts, and, by lending a temporary support to a pretender to the throne of Tanjore, had obtained for themselves, from the reigning rajah, the fortress of Devikota. About the same time, Boscawen, who had remained on the coast with his fleet, took his departure.

Up to this point, Chunda Sahib had been afraid of the English joining in. Now, however, he proceeded to

K

march against Trichinopoly, where was the rival claimant, Mohammed Ali. But on the way he wasted his time by inadequate attempts to reduce Tanjore; and so allowed Nadir Jung, his ally Muzaffar Jung's rival, to advance southwards; and Nadir Jung's approach caused his army to retreat upon Pondicherry, instead of advancing on Trichinopoly. The English seized the opportunity to declare in favour of Mohammed Ali, and sent a body of six hundred English, under Lawrence, to support the advancing Nadir Jung.

The English take sides.

The position, therefore, now was this: Nadir Jung, the reigning Nizam, was in alliance with Mohammed Ali, the claimant to the nawabship of the Carnatic, and with the English. Muzaffar Jung, the claimant to the nizamship, was in alliance with Chunda Sahib, the reigning nawab, and with the French. Nadir Jung was now a few miles from Pondicherry. The rival allies marched out to meet him, but disaffection set in, and they retreated, leaving Muzaffar Jung a prisoner in Nadir Jung's hands.

Dupleix fell back on the policy of intriguing among the nobles round Nadir Jung. A night raid of three hundred French, under De la Touche, alarmed the Nizam, and made him fall back. Soon afterwards, the capture of the fort of Gingi by Bussy raised the prestige of the French still higher. But it was not till late in December that a decisive engagement took place. The intrigues of Dupleix with the native nobles bore fruit. At the decisive moment, most of them deserted; Nadir Jung was killed, and Muzaffar Jung acknowledged on all hands as Nizam.

Thus the French candidate was now Nizam of the Deccan; the French candidate was Nawab of the Carnatic; the English candidate for the latter post, Mohammed Ali, had escaped to Trichinopoly, but was practically unable to act; and the best English officer, Lawrence, had been obliged to return to England. Everything now pointed to the successful issue of Dupleix's plans.

Success of Dupleix.

Nor was this position affected by the death of Muzaffar Jung, on his way to Hyderabad. It had been arranged that Bussy, with a corps of French and a troop of sepoys, should be attached to the Nizam's court. Bussy, therefore, practically controlled the situation, and was able promptly to set his own nominee on the throne, when Muzaffar Jung fell in a skirmish. Thus, while Mohammed Ali was cooped up in Trichinopoly by Chunda Sahib, the Nizam of Hyderabad was completely controlled by Bussy, who, moreover, seized the opportunity to obtain for the French a cession of the district lying on the coast north of the Carnatic, known as the Northern Circars.

It was evident, then, in the spring of 1751, that if Mohammed Ali were once crushed, and Chunda Sahib without a rival in the Carnatic, French influence would be supreme throughout Southern India. It seems exceedingly probable that, in such an event, the home government would have been compelled to interfere ; in accordance with the general principle that, so long as there was a possibility of things righting themselves without interference, no steps should be taken ; but that, if the worst came to the worst, England could, after all, place forces at the disposal of the company which would regain all that was lost. In other words, England's sea-power gave the English company a reserve to draw on, if they were driven to it, which would counteract the successes of their rivals. But the reserve was only to be drawn upon in the last extremity ; and the last extremity did not arrive. The man who did most to avert it was Robert Clive.

But, in the spring of 1751, matters looked very much as if it was coming. However, Saunders, the British governor at Fort St. David, realised that every effort must be made to save Mohammed Ali and Trichinopoly, while Dupleix was equally bent on helping Chunda Sahib to triumph. But whereas, up to this time, the French military officers had, on the whole, proved themselves distinctly superior to the

English, we now begin to find the order of things inverted. It has also to be remembered, as a factor in the military arrangements, that France and England, being at peace, the French and English troops could not act avowedly and directly against each other; they could only act as auxiliaries of their native allies against their rivals.

After considerable delays and sundry ill-conducted skirmishes, Mohammed Ali was shut up in Trichinopoly, which was invested by the forces of Chunda Sahib and the French.

It was now that Clive came to the front. Though a civilian, a "writer" under the company, he had shown **Robert Clive.** capacity as a volunteer; and now conceived a very daring scheme, in which he was supported with remarkable courage and confidence by Saunders. He proposed to march, with practically the whole of the company's forces, British and native, which had not already joined Mohammed Ali, north, into the heart of Chunda Sahib's country, and seize Arcot. This he did, his troops consisting of two hundred English and three hundred sepoys. A large part of Chunda Sahib's army was, consequently, detached to besiege him in Arcot; but the defence was conducted with such brilliant obstinacy and valour that, **Successes of Clive and Lawrence.** after fifty days, the besiegers withdrew. Clive, not content with this repulse, marched out after them, attacked them at Arnee, and inflicted upon them a complete defeat. In the mean time, some reinforcements from Mysore had considerably strengthened Mohammed Ali at Trichinopoly. Clive returned to Fort St. David, was joined by some few reinforcements from Bengal, marched out again, met the nawab's forces at Kaveripak, and, by once more inflicting a crushing defeat on them, cleared the district of North Arcot of active enemies. Meanwhile, Lawrence had returned to India, and he and Clive were free to march together to the relief of Trichinopoly, which was successfully accomplished. The result was, that the investing army in its turn was cooped up, the whole French force compelled to surrender, and Chunda Sahib slain, in June, 1752. The temporary incapacitation of Lawrence and Clive from illness, and dissensions among the native allies, enabled Dupleix to recover some of the ground he had lost; but, in September, Lawrence took the field again, and won a very hotly contested fight at Bahur.

Nevertheless, throughout the next year, the extraordinary courage, diplomatic skill, and pertinacity of Dupleix enabled him to maintain the struggle, now and then even getting the upper hand, until, in December, 1753, his troops met with a disastrous repulse before Trichinopoly. But it was only the exceptional qualities of Dupleix which had made even this possible; and during 1753 the directors at home resolved on his recall. The struggle was involving the company in heavy debts; they did not believe in territorial aggrandisement as a commercial speculation; they were living on subsidies from the French government, and the government was afraid of being prematurely forced into an English war; so, in 1754, Dupleix was superseded by Godeheu, and the master spirit of the forward policy was removed from India. *Recall of Dupleix.*

We have sketched in this chapter two periods in the contest for supremacy between the two companies. In both, Dupleix had been the moving spirit of the French policy. The first was contemporaneous with that preliminary war between England and France which lasted from 1744 to 1749, and was terminated by the peace of Aix-la-Chapelle, whereby the relative positions of the two countries were left without material change. During this period, England and France were avowedly at war with each other in India as elsewhere, and the results were directly influenced by the action of the hostile navies. The second period lasted from the peace to the recall of Dupleix. During this time the rivals faced each other nominally as *Summary to 1754.*

allies of native rivals. Each was struggling directly for paramount influence, but indirectly for the extermination of the other ; while, the home governments being at peace, the fleets had no definite share in the result. At the close, France was apparently in rather the better position. Bussy was still at the court of the Nizam, though the English candidate was nawab of the Carnatic. But the military prestige of the English was now thoroughly on a level with that of the French ; the strain on the French company had left it far more exhausted than its rival ; England was thoroughly alive to the importance of maintaining her position decisively ; the one man whose extraordinary ability had hitherto enabled the French company to hold its own so successfully, was removed from the scene ; and, with England's great predominance on the seas, the issue of a fresh contest, in which the home government might be involved, was hardly doubtful.

CHAPTER VI.

INDIA : ESTABLISHMENT OF THE BRITISH.

1754-1761.

Renewal of hostilities—1758 : Lally—1759 : Siege of Madras—Colonel Ford—Isolation of Lally—1760 : Battle of Wandewash—The French power crushed—*Bengal*—1756 : The Black Hole—1757 : Clive and Watson at Calcutta—Intrigues against Suraj-ud-Daulah—Omichund—Battle of Plassey—1759 : Capture of Masulipatam—Clive's position—Shah Alum—The Dutch interposition—1760 : Clive's application of Dupleix's policy—The new conditions.

WITH the departure of Dupleix commences the last phase of the Anglo-French contest for Indian supremacy, and the initiation under Clive's leadership of the policy of British advance—a policy which it was impossible to set fairly on foot until the expulsion of European rivals had become practically certain. The fall of the French power, and the British advance in Bengal belong to the same period of time as the Seven Years' War and the great naval conflict ; they were the Eastern parallel to the expulsion of France from America ; and they were due to the same leading cause, the command of the sea.

The recall of Dupleix and the appointment of Godeheu as his successor put an end for the time to all active hostilities. But a fresh war between Britain and France was imminent, and in 1756 it began. Neither of the rival companies was in a position to take decisive measures ; but the French government resolved to adopt the designs of Dupleix so far as expelling the English was concerned. Fortunately, however, their action was

Renewal of war.

dilatory, and the English seized their opportunity, took advantage of the misconduct of the Nawab of Bengal, and practically captured that province, the richest in India, before the French reinforcements arrived. Hence, when Lally appeared, in April, 1758, with a considerable force and with D'Aché in command of a squadron, he found the English ready to resist him, with Bengal to draw upon for supplies, and a naval squadron sufficient to paralyse the action of D'Aché.

Lally was instructed not to march inland or interfere with native princes, but to concentrate his efforts on the expulsion of the English, and this he attempted to do. His forces were adequate, but his resources were not, and he had no understanding of the natives. Moreover, he was endowed with an exceptional capacity for causing irritation; he was at daggers drawn with D'Aché, and was violently unpopular with his officers; while his complete disregard of the deep-rooted caste prejudices and religious sentiments of the native population brought him promptly into very bad odour with them.

Lally.

Still, his first measures were successful. Clive was away in Bengal. The garrison of Fort St. David was in a bad state of discipline, and the fort was surrendered to him in June. But he was soon in difficulties over the want of supplies, and matters were hardly improved by the high-handed methods of collecting them which he adopted. In August there was an indecisive action between D'Aché and the English squadron under Pocock; which, however, caused the French commander to withdraw to the Mauritius, declaring that he could not hold the sea without a port where he could effect necessary repairs. Meantime, Lally succeeded in quarrelling with Bussy, who, in consequence, would do nothing to help him from the court of the Nizam; while, on his being actually summoned from thence to join his superior, the French control at Hyderabad was effectually removed.

Lally had captured Fort St. David, and he resolved to attack Madras. But the English fort was well garrisoned, and in good condition to resist, while the French officers detested their commander, and hindered rather than helped him in carrying out his designs. The siege was progressing unfavourably enough when the English squadron hove in sight. D'Aché was away, and there was no choice left. The siege of Madras was raised. *Siege of Madras.*

The failure before Madras was a serious blow to the French power, and during 1759 it suffered an important reverse elsewhere. The district known as the Northern Circars, lying north of the Carnatic, had been granted to the French for the maintenance of Bussy's force at Hyderabad; and from this they were driven by an expedition under Colonel Forde, sent for that purpose by Clive from Bengal. Thus Lally had now only the French settlements in the Carnatic to depend on; there was no financial support from the Northern Circars; he was in want of money; the Nizam, now that Bussy had left him, was less than ever inclined to take active steps in the way of help; the natives were estranged, and inclined to regard the English as the better fighters; his own troops were on the verge of mutiny. The personal unsuitability of Lally for the position in which he was placed was accountable for much of this. Dupleix would, no doubt, have utilised his relations with the native princes after a very different fashion. But the main matter was beyond the control of the French commander. He was isolated in the Carnatic, and the slippery good will of nawabs and nizams would not have reversed the position; whereas the English could send in supplies and men from Bengal, and had ports to refit their ships, money to procure what they required, ships to guard the coast. When Lally was before Madras, an English squadron raised the siege; when D'Aché, later in the year, reappeared to fight another indecisive action, the practical victory still lay with the *Isolation of Lally.*

English, because D'Aché could not face them again without refitting, and to do that he had to retire again to the Mauritius—and this time his departure was final.

During the months which intervened between the time when the siege of Madras was raised in February (1759) and D'Aché and Pocock's last engagement, there had been little change in the situation. But the prospects of the French were now exceedingly unpromising, and the arrival of Eyre Coote with reinforcements in October turned the scale decisively.

Coote began operations by capturing the fort of Wandewash; and Lally felt that unless the loss were retrieved, French prestige would be hopelessly lost. The opposing armies met in January, 1760, before Wandewash. The French had something over two thousand European troops, the English rather fewer: the latter had a large supply of sepoys, but the former were supported by a considerable body of Mahrattas. The battle, however, was fought out almost entirely by the Europeans, under the admiring gaze of the natives. It was hotly contested, but resulted in a complete and decisive victory for the English, Bussy himself being taken prisoner.

Battle of Wandewash.

Coote pushed forward by degrees, capturing one fort after another. The French, despite certain futile attempts to induce Hyder Ali of Mysore to espouse their cause, were driven into Pondicherry. They fought stubbornly, but were hopelessly cut off from relief; and on January 16, 1761, Pondicherry surrendered. The fortifications were razed to the ground, and France was now finally without a foothold in India—just two years after Clive had prophesied, in a letter to Pitt, that her position would soon turn out to be hopeless, owing to the ample supplies now obtainable from Bengal, and the superiority of the English squadron.

The way was now cleared. The British had no European rivals to compete with, and, for the future, the only opponents of our advance in India were native states. The

INDIA: ESTABLISHMENT OF THE BRITISH.

first great collision between the English company and a native prince, with its immediate results, will occupy the remainder of this chapter.

The head-quarters of the padishah (or mogul) were at Delhi. Lower down the Ganges lay the province of Oudh, and lower again, including the whole delta of the Ganges, Bengal. Both provinces, like the Deccan, nominally owned the suzerainty of the padishah; both were practically independent. In Bengal, with which we have to deal, there were English, French, and Dutch settlements, the principal positions of the respective companies being at Fort William (Calcutta), Chandernagore, and Chinsurah. They were under their own governors, and had taken no part in the struggle waged in the Carnatic in the time of Dupleix. The Nawab of Bengal was then Aliverdi Khan, the Afghan, a Mohammedan. He had been a soldier of fortune, and was a ruler of considerable vigour and ability. But in 1756 he died, and was succeeded by his adopted son, Suraj-nd-daulah (the Surajah Dowlah of Macaulay)— a young man, wanting in ability and courage, but of a singularly ferocious disposition.

It was certain at this time that war would break out between Britain and France; and just as Suraj-ud-daulah came to the throne, Drake, the English governor at Fort William, began to place his settlement in a condition for defence, in case of French attack. The new nawab considered that the preparations were being made against him, and sent peremptory orders that they should be stopped. Drake protested that they were only being made for fear of the French taking the offensive. The nawab took this as implying that his European tenants in general cared very little for his authority, and in great wrath he marched forthwith on Fort William. The place was in no condition for defence; the garrison, such as it was, with the governor, fled down the river. Suraj-ud-daulah marched in, and took prisoners such of the English

Bengal.

The Black Hole.

as had remained behind. The story is well known. His officers thrust these prisoners, to the number of 145, into a room known as the Black Hole, where it would have been cruel enough to put a single European. When the doors were opened in the morning, of the 145 no less than 122 were corpses, and the survivors were in a frightful condition.

This was on August 16th. When the news reached Madras, the indignation there knew no bounds. Although it was expected that an outbreak of hostilities with the French could not be postponed for any great length of time, Clive was despatched to take the supreme control ashore, with Admiral Watson in command of a squadron ; but it was not till late in December that they reached the Hooghly.

Clive and Watson at Calcutta.

The nawab sent no answer to the peremptory British demand for redress. Clive and Watson attacked and captured Baj-Baj, a fort near Calcutta, and on January 2, 1757, the nawab's troops surrendered Calcutta. Troubles of various kinds arose from dissensions between Clive, as the company's representative, and the admiral, as an officer of the crown ; but the public spirit of both men prevented any disastrous consequences.

About this time it was reported that war had been declared between England and France. It seemed probable that the French at Chandernagore would join the nawab. Clive considered the prospect grave enough to necessitate an attempt to reopen negotiations with Suraj-ud-daulah. But the latter advanced on Fort William, with troops to the number of forty thousand. Clive and Watson, with a joint force of 1350 Europeans and eight hundred sepoys, attacked by night ; and, though they were not altogether successful, the nawab was frightened. He had recourse to the plan of proposing an alliance with the English and secretly corresponding with the French.

The position was difficult. It was important to have the

Bengal business settled and be free to return to Madras before French reinforcements arrived there; but then, either the French must first be beaten in Bengal, or a treaty of neutrality there must be concluded with them. The official news of the declaration of war between France and England decided the question: it was settled that Chandernagore should be attacked; and, on March 23rd, it was captured.

But this was not enough. Nothing was more certain than that Suraj-ud-daulah was not to be trusted, and the chances were that, the moment an opportunity occurred, he would try to crush the English. Before the English forces could be withdrawn, it was evident that the nawab must either be attacked and beaten, or removed from the throne and an English nominee substituted for him.

The condition of affairs at Suraj-ud-daulah's court made Clive decide on the latter course, and a systematic and complex intrigue was set on foot.

The nawab's chief captain was Meer Jaffier. His finances were practically in the hands of Roydullub and Jugget Seit. If these could be involved in a conspiracy against their master, the English were certain of getting the upper hand. Clive knew that the nawab was generally hated, and that there was wide-spread dissatisfaction amongst the native nobles; and when these chiefs made overtures on their own account, it seemed very much better to secure their alliance. **Intrigues against Suraj-ud-daulah.**

In carrying on the intrigue, great use was made of a native named Omichund, and Omichund's fidelity was exceedingly doubtful. Moreover, the stipulations he made for rewards to himself were very extravagant. Under these circumstances, Clive perpetrated the most inexcusable act of his career. He had two copies of a treaty prepared: one on red paper, containing the stipulations in favour of Omichund; one on white, omitting them. It was necessary, in order to satisfy Omichund, that **Omichund.**

the English signatures should be attached so that he might believe the "red" treaty to be genuine; while the "white" treaty was to be the real one. Admiral Watson refused to be a party to the deception, and Clive had his signature forged. When the thing was done, the admiral accepted the situation, and it was said that he had been told by Clive of his intention, and had raised no remonstrance. In any case, it is impossible to pretend that the action was anything but grossly dishonourable. Clive, who was thoroughly honourable and straightforward in all dealings with Europeans, and, apart from this occasion, with natives, argued that such a man as Omichund must be met with his own weapons. Still, there is no doubt that the advantage we have habitually gained by absolutely refusing to stoop to such methods, the credit obtained by consistent integrity, has proved over and over again the wisdom of honesty—entirely apart from the ethical question.

But whatever benefits might have resulted from a more scrupulous method of action, in this particular case the fraud succeeded. The negotiations were carried through. Meer Jaffier was to be placed on the throne of the nawab, the English were to receive heavy compensation, and the French were to be turned out of Bengal.

The arrangements being completed, war was, in effect, declared in June. Meer Jaffier was to join the English, the plot having been successfully kept from Suraj-uddaulah.

Clive advanced with his whole force—1,100 Europeans, 2,100 sepoys. The nawab had 50,000 men, but their value as fighting forces—if Meer Jaffier kept faith with the English—was small. Nevertheless, Clive's responsibility was enormous. Defeat would mean annihilation; delay, the possible failure of the conspiracy and the arrival of Bussy from the Deccan. All these events, it must be remembered, were taking place during 1757, before the Anglo-French conflict had been renewed

Battle of Plassey.

INDIA : ESTABLISHMENT OF THE BRITISH. 143

in Madras. Clive for once wavered : he held a council of war—the only one he ever did hold—and expressed himself in favour of delay. A minority of the council, including Eyre Coote, afterwards the victor of Wandewash, urged immediate advance ; but the majority decided against them. Clive withdrew, reconsidered the situation, resolved to take the daring step from which he had shrunk, and, in spite of the decision of the council of war, marched upon Plassey.

The event justified him. Meer Jaffier deserted at the right moment, and Suraj-ud-daulah's army was completely defeated (June 23, 1757). The nawab fled; when he found that there was no chance of collecting his forces again, he attempted to escape from his capital, Moorshedabad, by night, disguised : but he fell into the hands of enemies, and was murdered. On June 29th, Clive proclaimed Meer Jaffier the new nawab, and, with this proclamation, the company was practically established as the paramount force in Bengal.

There was, however, a lingering chance of a recrudescence of French power coming from the Deccan, until, at the beginning of 1759, Clive sent the force under Colonel Forde into the Northern Circars. The expedition resulted in the capture of Masulipatam, and the total loss of that district to the French. By this campaign, a considerable French force was prevented from joining Lally ; the French lost a country which was, at the time, their principal source of military revenue ; and, though it is in any case most improbable that they would have attempted to invade Bengal, the possibility of their doing so was now finally destroyed.

This expedition had been the most effective method of helping the English and crippling the French in the Carnatic ; but it had been undertaken in circum- Clive's stances involving no small risk to the company's position. position in Bengal. Clive, without any formal status, had still no choice but to be virtual ruler ; to make the nawab and the subordinate princes and the Hindu merchants all feel that he could promise what he would, and that promises made were certain to be fulfilled. But nawab, princes, and merchants were all jealous—all aiming at mastery, all apt at intrigue. Nevertheless, Clive took the risk, and almost denuded Bengal of European troops. At the same time, he resolutely adopted an attitude of uncompromising confidence in his own strength, and urgently impressed on Warren Hastings, who was at Meer Jaffier's court as British resident, the importance of maintaining the like attitude : taking precisely the tone that he might have done with twenty thousand British troops at his back.

The result was that Meer Jaffier, though discontented, was thoroughly afraid. The Englishman's courage and resources, and his power of accomplishing unexpected things with very small means, were thoroughly recognized. Nor was his reputation confined to Bengal itself. An opportunity for testing, and, at the same time, doubling his prestige, occurred at the moment when Forde departed for the Circars.

The padishah at Delhi was practically a prisoner in the hands of his own vizier. But his son, Shah Alum, escaped, Shah Alum. and proposed to himself something like a revolution. Joining the Nawab of Oudh, he intended to assert himself, and recover empire by invading Bengal. Meer Jaffier was thoroughly alarmed, but Clive seized his opportunity. He announced that the English never deserted those whom they had promised to help. Shah Alum besieged Patna : Clive collected all the little European force at his disposal, and marched four hundred miles in twenty-three days to its relief. His approach was enough. Shah Alum's army melted away, and the siege was raised. Meer Jaffier felt that for the second time he owed his throne to Clive.

Thus in 1759, the English were supreme in Bengal. The

INDIA: ESTABLISHMENT OF THE BRITISH. 145

French had lost there such footing as they ever had; they had been driven from the Circars, and their influence with the Nizam at Hyderabad was broken down by the withdrawal of Bussy: while in the Carnatic itself they were at bay. Yet there was one more brief but decisive conflict with another Western power, before the British were finally and conclusively freed from any possible rivalry with a European nation.

Holland was not involved in the Anglo-French war, and was at peace with England; but Dutch traders found the growing ascendency of the English in India injurious to their trade. The new Nawab of Bengal had hoped to make a cat's-paw of his English allies, and was very ill-pleased at finding himself their puppet instead. It occurred to him to use the Dutch to counteract his masters; and the Dutch were inclined to favour the experiment. In October, 1759, they sent ships, and troops to the Hooghly, ostensibly merely to protect their own interests. Clive understood the situation, and barred their passage up the river. The Dutch seized some English vessels; Clive felt that he was justified in taking active steps. The Dutch landed a force to march up to their settlement at Chinsurah, and their ships dropped down the river. Forde, who had returned from his successful campaign in the Circars, was sent against Chinsurah: three East Indiamen were sent down from Fort William to demand reparation from the Dutch, and, if it was refused, to attack them. Wilson, their commander, fought a completely successful battle, and the Dutch fleet was captured. Forde was no less successful on shore, demolished their land forces, and Chinsurah was taken. The Dutch owned themselves the aggressors, agreed to pay costs and damages, and so, within two months of the appearance of the Dutch ships, the episode finally terminated. A few weeks later the fate of the French in the south was sealed at Wandewash. The British power had now no

The Dutch interposition.

L

European rival to reckon with or to fear a reckoning with, except during a very short period, twenty-one years later, when the best of French admirals, Suffren, appeared on the Indian coast.

It will be observed that, up to this point, the operations in Bengal might be said almost as well to have been a part of the struggle with France, as of the struggle with native powers. Nevertheless, the part played directly by the French in that province was very small; they were never in a position there to take up an aggressive policy: and the episode of Suraj-ud-daulah derives its greatest importance from being the first decisive application by Clive of the native policy devised by Dupleix. It was based absolutely on the theory of establishing on native thrones princes wholly dependent on the good will of the foreigners—of the company securing recognition as king-makers.

Clive's adoption of Dupleix's policy.

For, hitherto, in the Carnatic, there had been rival king-makers, French and English; and if a prince found himself too dependent on one, he could turn to the other. Whereas, it was not so in Bengal. There, from the moment that Clive took the aggressive, there was no longer any real doubt that the English could turn the scale as they liked, and there was no appeal from their decision. In the south, the Nawab of the Carnatic was an English nominee, under the control of the English: the Nizam at Hyderabad was a French nominee, under the control of the French. But the moment Bussy was summoned from the Nizam's court, that prince was open to English influence: whereas, in Bengal, the nawab was bound either to annihilate the English or submit to their dictation. When Suraj-ud-daulah began the conflict, it still appeared as if there might be an appeal from one European power to another, though it was in fact certain that that state of things was only temporary. Plassey put Bengal decisively in the hands of the English: the fall of Pondicherry put

The new conditions.

the Deccan also finally under their control. But whereas, up to that time, the conflict in the south had been distinctly between two European powers, in the north the French interest in it had been only incidental. It was, in fact, the commencement of the struggle for mastery in India between Britain and Oriental dynasties.

CHAPTER VII.

THE WINDING UP OF THE WAR.

1761-1763.

Position of the combatants—1762 : Withdrawal of Russia—Catharine of Russia—Recovery of Silesia—1761 : Second Family Compact—1762 : The West Indies—Portugal—Bute's desire for peace—He alienates Prussia—1763 : Peace of Paris—Triumphant position of Britain—William Pitt—Features of the war—British naval policy—Its effect—England's debt to Pitt.

AT the close of the year, 1761, England was the only one of the belligerent powers which had materially and decisively profited by the war. The position of France in India and in America was demolished, and British fleets swept the seas, going where they would. France had, however, found an ally who might indeed have proved useful at an earlier stage, but now seemed to be merely a fresh object on which England might exercise her navy; yet Pitt had fallen, and though the work he had already accomplished could hardly be undone, his successor did his best to prevent any further advantages resulting from his policy.

On the continent, Frederick had kept up the struggle, and was still a long way from being beaten : but his enemies were closing in; and his prospects, with the support of England now at best half-hearted owing to Pitt's fall, were very gloomy. At this moment, however, came one of those turns of the wheel of fortune which so greatly affected the Seven Years' War.

Frederick was being slowly crushed by numbers. The

Position of the combatants.

combination of Russia on the east, France and the Empire states on the west, and Austria on the south, was overwhelming him: when suddenly Russia was converted from a bitter enemy to an enthusiastic supporter. The czarina, whose personal rancour against the Prussian king was the main cause of Russian interference, died (January, 1762); she was succeeded by Peter III., who had erected Frederick into an ideal hero, and was as wildly devoted to him as Elizabeth had been fierce against him. The troops, which had been acting in consort with the Austrians in the east, received orders to act with Frederick instead, whereby the situation was completely and surprisingly reversed. It was time for Austria to give up all idea of aggression, and devote herself to the preservation of what she had gained.

Withdrawal of Russia.

Accordingly Daun entrenched himself to cover Schweidnitz; there was no chance of inducing him to come out of his position, and a long time was spent in preparing to attack him. The arrangements were almost complete, when Russian policy again veered round. The new czar was deposed by his wife, Catharine. Fortunately enough for Frederick, she found that he had not, as she suspected, been responsible for certain insults the czar had put upon her—insults which had driven her to his deposition,—but had endeavoured to check him. Still, though this discovery prevented her from taking active steps towards the renewal of Elizabeth's policy, she did not choose to carry on the war on Frederick's behalf, and the Russian commander, Czernicheff, was instructed to withdraw. The operations, however, had reached a critical point, and, at Frederick's entreaty, Czernicheff kept his instructions secret, and allowed the Austrians to believe that his troops—now turned into mere spectators—were effectives. On the third day (July 21, 1762), Frederick stormed the key of Daun's position at Burkersdorf; the Austrians were obliged to retreat. The Russians departed, but the

Catharine of Russia.

Recovery of Silesia.

way to Schweidnitz was open. When that fortress fell in October, Frederick was able to return to Saxony, where the second allied army had been held in check by Prince Henry. Here, however, there was no time for aggressive measures, and the year closed with Prussia once more in full possession of Silesia, the Austrians in Dresden, and the Russians withdrawn from the contest.

Pitt had become thoroughly aware, in 1761, of the *rapprochement* between the French and Spanish courts. The actual treaty between them—the Second Family Compact, forming a close alliance, for mutual defence and attack on England, between the Bourbon princes of France, Spain, and Italy—was kept secret, though it was actually signed in August of that year; but information was obtained as to its general purport, and had weighed very greatly with the English minister in forming his design of taking the initiative and declaring war against Spain. The rejection of this plan by his cabinet had led to his immediate resignation. The intentions of the Spanish court had, indeed, been hardly veiled by its desire to wait for the arrival, before the actual declaration of hostilities, of treasure-ships which otherwise were almost certain to fall a prey to the English fleet. Bute, however, was blind to everything, beyond the desire to put an end to the war and get rid of Pitt. In the latter object he succeeded ; but no sooner had the treasure-ships arrived than Spain threw off the mask ; and even Bute, by the beginning of 1762, found that his first object was still out of reach, and was forced to declare war upon Spain.

The Second Family Compact.

He profited by the successes of Pitt's policy and the perfection of organisation he had left behind. Already there was one fleet in the West Indies operating against the French possessions there ; Martinique was captured in February, and one after another the French islands were falling into our hands. On the declaration of war against Spain, an expedition against Havanna, planned

The West Indies.

by Pitt as the first blow, was sent out under Admiral Pocock. Had it been despatched at the time Pitt intended, the conquest would have been effected with comparative ease; as it was, the delay till an inclement season made it a laborious operation accompanied with much sickness and loss of life. But although there was a stubborn resistance, there was no fleet to interfere with the operations, and Havanna was captured on August 13th. The great emporium of the Spanish trade, the naval key to her possessions, was in our hands. At the same time, our fleet in the East Indies captured Manilla, the capital of the Philippine Islands.

The Bourbons were also foiled in an attempt to force Portugal into alliance with them against "the tyrant of the seas." She had ground of complaint against us, because her neutrality had been violated in 1759, when Boscawen destroyed the section of De la Clue's Toulon fleet which had fled to the Portuguese coast near Cape St. Vincent. But Portugal regarded England with good will, partly because she was not in any case friendly to Spain, partly because of the generous aid which had been forthcoming at the time of her terrible national disaster seven years before, when Lisbon had been wrecked by the great earthquake. Moreover, she was aware that the hostility of Spain was of much smaller account than the hostility of England. Accordingly she declined the proposals from Madrid and Versailles, and appealed to England for protection. The needful assistance was promptly sent, and a Spanish army of invasion driven over the borders. *Portugal.*

Thus the continuation of the war through 1762 had resulted only in a series of losses to France and Spain, and the recovery of Silesia by Frederick. But the strain on Prussia had been so tremendous that she had no desire to go on fighting; Austria, deserted by Russia, had very little prospect of improving her position; the possessions of France and Spain lay practically at the feet of England; the Bourbon powers *Bute's desire for peace.*

alone had been responsible for the last phase of the contest, and England might have made what terms she chose, with the certainty that if they were declined she had only to go on a little longer and raise her price. Yet, so anxious for peace was Bute, that, in order to secure it at once, he deliberately threw away most of the fruits of this last year, and accepted a clause which required the restoration of all conquests not known at home on the day of the signing of the treaty, thereby losing the Philippines. But for the intervention of his colleagues he would even have handed over Havanna without compensation. With the same object of getting peace at any price, he had already made overtures to Austria (which were rejected), hoping by an alliance with her to hasten the assent of the Bourbons to a cessation of hostilities, and intending, at the same time, by this huge act of treachery, to induce Frederick to give up the struggle as hopeless. This remarkable proceeding on the part of Pitt's successor had its well-deserved effect afterwards, in losing England the one ally she had on the continent, while at the time it failed completely in its purpose.

He alienates Prussia.

Preliminaries of peace were signed in November, and on February 10, 1763, the treaty known as the Peace of Paris was signed. Such concessions as were not impossible even to Bute's pusillanimity were made, but he could hardly give away what had already been won before he came into power. The main results may be thus summarised : The whole of Canada remained in our possession ; the French claims on the valley of the Ohio were withdrawn ; while our dominions in America were completed by the cession by Spain of Florida, in exchange for which she was given back Havanna, an incomparably more valuable possession. Martinique, Guadaloupe, and other islands in the West Indies, were restored to France, the Philippines in the East Indies to Spain. In India, Pondicherry was given back, but no fortifications were to be raised ; and, as

The peace of Paris.

far as concerned our position in India, its restitution was harmless. Belle Isle, off Brittany, taken in 1761, was exchanged for Minorca. In Africa, England retained Senegal, but restored Goree.

Spain sacrificed Florida, but had Havanna and the Philippines restored. She conceded to England the original points in dispute, and received from France Louisiana in compensation for the loss of Florida.

England and France agreed to withdraw together from the Prussian war. At the same date (February 5th) Frederick concluded with Austria the peace of Hubertsburg, restoring Saxony, and leaving to Prussia and Austria exactly what each possessed before the commencement of hostilities.

So ended the contest which had in fact first broken out in 1739; which had been inevitable ever since the Family Compact of 1733, and was marked in its last phase by a renewal of that compact in 1761. When it began, Walpole had thought us incapable of resisting the combined might of France and Spain; when it ended, we might, had we so willed, have left France without a colony, and Spain without a defence for her trade routes; while we did actually leave them in such a condition that no conceivable naval combination against us could have excited the smallest anxiety. In North America our colonies were free to expand without a check; in India there was no possibility of the revival of a European competitor. So far as we did not take advantage of what we had won, not in a course of wanton aggression, but in acceptance of a deliberate challenge, Bute was responsible. That we won what we did, we owe to Pitt. He had breathed a new spirit into the nation, initiated a colonial policy, developed the navy. By him administrative energy had been aroused in subordinates, personal interest and jobbery in appointments had been suppressed, while his skill in selecting the right men for the right posts was never at fault.

Triumphant position of Britain.

The question whether Pitt's career was consistent, whether his attacks on ministers when he was kept out of high office were altogether honourable, whether in fact his sincerity in opposition was beyond cavil, is of more interest to the biographer than to the historian of national events. It may, however, be remarked that few statesmen, if any, can be named who have not found themselves compelled when in office to adopt measures which they reprobated in opposition. It is easier for most men to discover a moral justification for what is expedient for themselves, than to recognize one for what is expedient for their rivals. If Pitt was capable of playing the bully, he was also capable of a rare magnanimity. He could espouse Byng's cause when that unfortunate commander was the object of universal execration; and he was the only man who countenanced the Duke of Cumberland when the Convention of Kloster Seven had made him the most unpopular man in the country, in spite of the fact that the duke had exerted his utmost influence with King George against him earlier in the year. No doubt he had used language about Newcastle and Fox which made the subsequent coalition a surprising spectacle, but for the sake of the country the coalition was an absolute necessity. In the earlier war he had inveighed fiercely against subsidies, and when he came into office the subsidies he gave were enormous. But it was one thing to pay large sums for German princes to carry on a war which was serving Hanoverian rather than English interests, and another to support a valuable ally who must have been crushed without such assistance, and to defend Hanover when the electorate was exposed to attack solely on the ground of its connection with England. In brief, the situation when Pitt came actually into office was so far different that the change of principle in his attitude towards his colleagues, towards Hanover, and towards the method of subsidies appears in each case to be much greater than it really was—more especially if allowance be made for the tendency to theatrical and exaggerated expression common to most politicians out of office, and at all times somewhat characteristic of William Pitt.

Certain features of the war which ended thus deserve especial note.

Frederick had been fighting a defensive war against enormous odds. But in most of his battles it will be found that he fought to win, his enemies to avoid defeat.

The same principle marks the method of the English fleet. If we except the action of Byng at Minorca and of Holbourne at Louisburg, English ships always sought for battle unless clearly outnumbered and overweighed: French ships avoided battle unless they had an overwhelming preponderance. England and Prussia made it their object to force battles: France and Austria made it their object to avoid them. The same policy was pursued by the leader of the small battalions on land, and the chiefs of the larger fleets by sea; and by both alike with success. *The war: considerations thereon.*

What Frederick realised and the French did not was, that a sound defence does not consist necessarily, or solely, in eluding attack.

With Frederick this was a matter of necessity. Whenever he was facing an army in one quarter of his dominions, another was entering them in a different quarter. He could keep a detachment in the distant quarter to serve as a check, but no more. His main army had to do the work first in one place and then in the other. He could not assume the defensive and wait for attack; he must always disable the army he was fronting as quickly as possible, and then hurry away to disable the other. And the experience of Hochkirsch and Kunersdorf taught him that, if he was defeated, his enemies would give him time to recover before they took advantage of their success.

The English principle of action rested on the theory that the object of a fleet is to secure the mastery of the sea; the opposite theory treats it mainly as an auxiliary to operations on land. In this war the principle was carried out on a fully developed system. The first business of the English navy was to make the whole French navy wholly inoperative; its employment against stations was secondary. For this purpose, the complete blockade of French ports was the first step. The next was to reduce the French navy, so that more of our own ships might be free for the secondary object; so to cripple it that only a comparatively small portion of our own navy would be required to keep it inoperative. It was, therefore, always desirable to fight, unless there was a distinct presumption that, if we did, our fleet would be diminished and the enemy's augmented by capture. The mere war on merchant shipping was a wholly minor consideration. We commenced the war in 1756 with a very considerable preponderance in our favour, but, until the System was established by Pitt, France was able to assist her colonists in America. The moment it was established, the Canadians were left entirely to their own resources, while we were still able to spare a sufficient number of war-ships to convey supplies and troops without interruption. After 1757, the French navy only served to keep our squadrons guarding the French coasts; and, after 1759, even that purpose was served only to a very limited extent; while any attempt on the part of French ships to get out of port merely resulted in their being destroyed or added to the growing numbers of the hostile navy.

British naval policy:

This point can hardly be over-emphasised. For nine years, from 1739, we were at war, and at the end of that war the relative positions of France and England were almost unchanged. Eight years later the war was renewed, and for eighteen months it was France, not England, that was gaining ground. It was at this point that Pitt came into power, and systematised the naval policy. In twelve months France was held in check; in another year she was completely paralysed; and after two

Its effects.

years more it is no exaggeration to say that England could send any force she liked to any point she liked, at any time she liked, and appropriate whatever she chose. We fought for nine years, and made nothing of it ; for eighteen months, and made worse than nothing of it. The system was then put in force, and in four years the world was at our feet.

If at the outset of the war France had adopted a different line of conduct, Pitt's accession to power might have been too late to do more than save us, and leave the fight a drawn one. France failed, till it was too late, to recognise that victory in the colonies was the great thing to be aimed at ; that the only means of attaining it was by maintaining an equality or something like an equality with England on the seas, while Austria and Prussia might be left to exhaust each other. Had she perceived the truth in time, she would have devoted herself to the strengthening of her fleets, instead of wasting her energies on large armies under incompetent commanders in North Germany ; she would have allowed free play to the popular impulse which followed the capture of Minorca, at the same time utilising the jealousy of the other maritime powers, especially Spain, while England was still the scene of administrative anarchy. As it was, her rival only required to have a sound system applied to the war in order to paralyse France ; and then it was too late for her to counteract the early blunder. Moreover, if France had thrown her whole energies at once into the maritime war,—if, also, Pitt had never come to terms with Newcastle, nor his naval policy been enforced,—if France, in short, had possessed a Pitt and we had not, the termination of the war would, in all probability, have found the English colonists cooped up between the Alleghanies and the sea, with a certain renewal of the struggle at a later date in store, England expelled from India, and a fleet in the French ports which could hold its own against the English.

But when the war broke out, no one among those at the

head of affairs, whether in England or France, realised the true nature of the issues at stake; they did not see either the end to be aimed at or the means to its attainment. Pitt did see both the end—the empire of East and West; and the means—naval supremacy. He saw that this necessitated immense expenditure, and he spent money with a lavishness which made financiers stand aghast. It was, indeed, a vast capital outlay, but it was far more than compensated by the wealth that accrued from it; it was an immense investment, but a sound one. In the result, we held America and India without a European rival, and we held the seas without a rival at all. Our merchant shipping had multiplied and our commerce increased. But the war had one consequence which Pitt had not foreseen, though Montcalm had. The English colonists in America, freed from the dependence on the mother country which the presence of rival colonies, backed up by France, entailed, could now afford to air their grievances against England. If France had remained in America, there would have been no War of Independence. The developments in the American situation, which resulted in the loss of half a continent, and of the Indian situation, which turned a controlling influence in Madras and Bengal into complete supremacy all over the peninsula, have still to be related.

England's debt to Pitt.

BOOK III.
SURVEY OF THE WHIG SUPREMACY.

CHAPTER I.

THE CONSTITUTION.

1714–1760.

George I.—1716: The Septennial Act—1719: The Peerage Bill—Walpole—*George II.* and Queen Caroline—From Walpole to the coalition—Ministerial responsibility—*George III.*—Attack on the Whig oligarchy; by Pitt; by George III.; by the democrats.

THE expulsion of the Stuarts had been effected by the personal unpopularity of James II., fear of a Popish revival, and organised action on the part of a few great families. The revolution was oligarchical, but was supported by popular favour. Government became at first an alliance between the oligarchical group and the foreign monarch who was introduced. In the next reign, there was a considerable popular reaction; the Whigs were less sure of each other, less sure of their monarch, and less sure of themselves. It was not fear of a despot, but fear of a Papist, which secured the accession of the House of Hanover. There was nothing in the theory of the constitution to prevent the crown from exercising as much power as it had done under William III.

But circumstances combined to develop by degrees what was, in fact, a new theory of the constitution. The new king was the creature of the political organisation which had placed him on the throne. He could only remain on the throne as long as he had the unqualified support of the Whigs; the Whigs could at first only retain office and the emoluments of office by holding fast together, and at the same time securing the support of the commercial community. The king, therefore, was obliged to obey the dictation of the Whig party, and the Whig party could not afford to adopt a purely aristocratic scheme of government. At the same time, the great Whig families, with the support of the commercial classes, could command complete control of parliament. Hence the policy of the monarch was necessarily completely under the control of parliament. Within the bounds of the party he could exercise some choice in the selection of ministers; but the broad lines of ministerial policy would remain practically unaffected. Thus, to begin with, it would have been desperately impolitic for the king to attempt to impose his will on ministers; and from being impolitic, it rapidly became "unconstitutional."

George I.

This consummation was very materially aided by the personality of George 1. Expediency and inclination pointed to the same course of action. Expediency, because the only possible alternative to dependence on the Whigs was dependence on popular enthusiasm, and there was no conceivable possibility of his arousing popular enthusiasm. He was an elderly foreigner, of bad manners and bad taste, without a single quality which could attract the sympathies or smooth away the insular prejudices of his subjects. He made no pretence of affection for the people to whom he was given as a king; his thoughts were always in Hanover, and he escaped thither in the body whenever he could. He was almost ignorant of the English language, and transacted business with his ministers in Latin. There was no glamour of sanctity about the kingship of a German prince selected by parliament as the least inconvenient alternative to the legitimate heir. And inclination supported expediency, because he neither knew nor cared anything about English domestic affairs, while, as concerned the continent, his interests and those of the Whigs were nearly identical.

The constitutional powers of the various estates of the realm depend partly on custom, and partly on legislative enactments. The accession of the House of Hanover resulted in the limitation by custom of the powers of the crown. But in the early years of the reign of George II. two bills were brought in, of which one, which was passed, strengthened the House of Commons; and the other, which was thrown out, was intended to secure permanent political control to an aristocratic clique.

At the time of the accession of George I. the life of a parliament was limited to three years. With the immediate fear of facing the constituencies before them, the members were forced to be in touch with the gusts of popular feeling, and a ministry might be upset by some unexpected sidewind. *The Septennial Act.* With the modern advance of democracy, a strong body of opinion favours a return to this system, on the ground that parliament is, under such circumstances, much more truly representative of the actual desires of the electorate. The answer is, that the moment's caprices, not the settled wishes of the electorate, are so represented. The parliament elected on George's accession took the latter view. There was a strong settled wish among the body of the people to accept the Hanoverian dynasty; yet it was very difficult to be sure whether some momentary irritation might not suddenly replace the Whig ministry by a Tory one. At the beginning of 1714 there had been a large Tory majority, and the Whigs could only insure that it should not be renewed, by remaining in office long enough to tide over the unsettlement of the public mind, consequent on the accession of a new dynasty and an armed insurrection in favour of the exiled house. For this reason, the parliament in 1716 prolonged its own life and that of its successors to seven years, by the Septennial Act. An Act of a similar nature now would be regarded as unconstitutional, because the theory of the function of parliament is changed. Parliament is now generally considered not to be justified in passing any grave measure of constitutional importance until the principle has been submitted to the constituencies. But according to the Whig theory, when the parliament was once elected, it had a free hand to do whatever the majority willed, as occasion might arise. The theory was not democratic, but then in the last century the government was oligarchical. The bill was passed without any outcry, and with the obvious result of strengthening parliament in resistance to any outbreaks of popular sentiment of a temporary character. From the point of view of modern democratic theory, the measure was indefensible; from the practical point of view, when the settlement of the succession was a matter of vital importance, it was essential.

The second measure, by the failure of which an attempt to crystallise an oligarchy was frustrated, was the Peerage Bill of Sunderland. The abortive rising of 1715, by weakening the Jacobites, had made it possible for the Whig party to survive a schism. The causes of that schism lay in the different view of foreign policy advocated by Townshend and Walpole in England, and by George and Stanhope on the continent—differences accentuated by the jealousy with which the king abroad regarded the supposed influence of his son at home. Townshend and Walpole were driven into opposition, and consequently, when the Sunderland Whigs brought in the Peerage Bill, the displaced ministers resisted it strenuously, and prevented its passage; whereas it is by no means unlikely that, if they had been in office, they would have remained comparatively blind to its dangers.

Sunderland's Peerage Bill.

The Bill proposed to limit the number of peers to six more than there were at that time; to limit new peerages to heirs male: and to substitute, for the sixteen peers elected by the body of Scottish peers, twenty-five appointed by the crown. The professed purpose was merely to prevent a majority in the Upper House from being swamped by new creations—from a repetition of the use of the royal prerogative for the manipulation of majorities. But the measure was in effect purely oligarchical. It would have turned the House of Peers into a close hereditary corporation ; it would have given them complete control of legislation, or, at least, have enabled them permanently to prevent any legislation not entirely in accord with their own class interests. The honours which are the recognized reward of great services, would have become the privilege of an entirely hereditary aristocracy, between whom and the rest of the country a permanent and impassable barrier would have been erected. In short, it was a measure which, under the guise of limiting the royal power, was intended to place the real power of the state in the hands of a few Whig families, who would have been turned into a permanent caste. The bill was rejected, mainly owing to the vigorous opposition of Walpole, and to the indignation of the Scots, who threatened to attack the Union if it were passed.

When George I. began his reign, government was conducted by a Whig clique. When his son succeeded him, it was controlled by a great minister who was virtually dictator of his party. There was a Tory Opposition of little force, and a strong Whig Opposition : but the latter lacked homogeneity, and was practically hampered by the impossibility of combining with the Tories ; for Toryism was identified with Jacobitism, and Jacobitism was an impracticable policy for any Whig to support. Moreover, although Walpole drove one after another of the ablest men—Carteret, Pulteney, and Chesterfield—into opposition, they were not the men who controlled votes, and he retained the support of the commercial classes, and of a large proportion of the county gentlemen. He also secured the favour of the court, and, with it, the interests

Walpole.

of those Whigs who had no great ambition to control or to
interfere with policy, provided they were treated as persons
of importance. That is to say, Walpole kept the mass of
the Whig votes on his side, partly by corruption, partly by
court influence, partly by the convincing result of material
prosperity, which attended his administration; and partly
because there was no prospect of any alternative which
would not endanger the Whig supremacy.

As circumstances combined to make George I. set an
example of non-intervention, so they combined to produce
the like practical effect on his son. Not that George II.
was quite so ready to let things alone, though, like his
father, he took little interest in domestic affairs. But
Queen Caroline. Walpole and the queen were allies of the closest
description. He had won her heart, because every
one of his rivals had sought to obtain the ear of the new
king on his accession by currying favour with one of his
mistresses; whereas Walpole had the shrewdness to perceive
that the queen's influence was far stronger than that of any
favourite. From that moment her personal loyalty to the
great minister never wavered. She might on occasion
believe Walpole's policy to be wrong, and use every effort
to persuade him to change it, but she never allowed her
influence to weigh against the minister's. To the king,
her judgment was Walpole's judgment: those two commanded his confidence as no one else could command it;
and, whenever he did disagree, however strongly, it was he
who gave way. If he had not done so, he would have been
isolated, because all the intelligence and power of the
Opposition had combined to make a figure-head of the
Prince of Wales; and the Prince of Wales, after the manner
of the House of Hanover, was at daggers drawn with his
father. The nett result was that, while the king did seek
to influence foreign policy, he made no attempt to control
it, learning to accept the position that ministers must have
their way.

Queen Caroline died. Walpole stood alone in resisting a war which he hated ; his mismanagement of it, when it had been forced upon him, lost him public support, and he was attacked with daily increasing fury. The brilliant and sometimes quite unscrupulous free-lances of the Whig Opposition succeeded in effecting a temporary combination against him ; he was driven from power, but there was no individual to take his place. Pulteney lost his chance, extinguishing himself with a peerage ; Carteret, brilliant as he was, commanded no confidence, because he treated European politics as an exciting game which excluded all other interests. The *régime* of Walpole was followed, after a brief interval of confusion, by the *régime* of the Pelhams—that is to say, of party organisation. Pelham conciliated dangerous people, and Newcastle bribed useful ones. There was no cleavage of policy within the Whig party ; people who, when Walpole excluded them from office, had thundered against Hanoverian measures, were quieted by getting places ; the Pelhams could even use a crisis like the 'Forty-five to thrust Pitt upon the unwilling king. His power of resistance had by this time become strictly limited ; and though the administration was conducted with exceeding inefficiency, there was no alternative possible to the strict rule of party, and nothing like an active Opposition was practicable.

<small>From Walpole to the Coalition.</small>

A certain change was introduced by the death of Pelham. Newcastle now wanted to have everything his own way, with the result that, though he could command votes, he could not command the support either of the ablest men or of popular feeling. Pitt, whose extraordinary powers were by this time fully acknowledged, was unable to command the House ; Newcastle was unable to conduct a policy. The only possible solution of the difficulty was for them to combine. The combination was something of a triumph for popular as opposed to family power ; but it kept the crown as completely subservient to ministers as before.

Throughout these two reigns the great controlling factor of the relations between crown and ministers was this—that the king could not afford to have a strong party against him, lest the Hanoverian succession should be endangered.

Ministers having the real control, it followed that responsibility rested upon them; and, as they were no longer the nominees of the crown, but existed by mutual support, the collective character of that responsibility became gradually more marked. A man might remain in a ministry, and subsequently attack his leader for its acts as though no responsibility for them had rested on himself; but, though such a course of action was scarcely felt to be as discreditable then as it is now, it had begun to convey a certain stigma. It was still possible for the elder Pitt and Fox, sitting on the government benches, to constantly attack their nominal chief. It was still possible, under George III., for George Grenville to defend the Stamp Act on the ground that the extravagance of the war—during which he had been serving, under Pitt, as Treasurer of the Navy—had forced it upon him. Still, a degree of loyalty was expected; it is only sheer animosity which can reproach Walpole for having seized the first opportunity to eject Chesterfield from office after the latter had exerted himself to the utmost to wreck the excise bill, though Chesterfield's action found frequent parallels. In short, the idea of collective responsibility was slowly becoming a reality, though it had not yet been formulated as a principle of government.

Ministerial responsibility.

The system of government by party organisation, the system which made every statesman impossible unless he conciliated the interests of the Whig managers, was, under George III., to be attacked from three quarters, from three different points of view.

Attack on the Whig oligarchy:

Pitt hated the system. By it he had been kept, not indeed out of office, but out of effective power, till the state of public affairs had reached such a crisis that patriotism compelled him to swallow a compromise. By it, any man of vigorous and independent judgment was forced either to go into opposition, or to submit to the wire-pullers. By it, corruption had been developed into a fine art, which threatened to destroy any kind of political purity beyond recovery. By it, a premium was placed upon mediocrity, and the favour of Whig nobles was made the passport to office. For the brief and splendid period during which Newcastle was forced to give him a free hand, Pitt was able to disregard "party" claims. But his theory of parliamentary government was hopelessly unworkable. He wanted to choose ministers without distinction of party: the only result must have been divergencies in the cabinet. He wanted to exclude the jobbers and wire-pullers from office: the result must have been an Opposition with a permanent majority. A time came when he tried to form a ministry on his own principles; illness took the control out of his hands, and, in two years, government was in a state of chaos, while nearly everything ministers had done was precisely that which their chief would have himself most vehemently resisted.

<small>by Pitt;</small>

The second attack was made by George III. The position of the young king, on mounting the throne, was in every way different from that of his two predecessors. Their title to the throne had been obviously open to question: he was the heir of a dynasty now established for forty-six years. They were Germans in tastes, habits, language: he was a Briton by birth and breeding. They were unattractive and boorish: he was sufficiently good-looking, and of not unpleasing address. Their morals were low, and not condoned by the style of their favourites: the young king was of a blameless life. They were regarded by no small proportion of their subjects as usurpers: when he came to the throne, there was not so much as a flicker of Jacobitism to cause alarm. With the alternative of the

<small>by George the Third;</small>

Stuarts being reinstated if the new dynasty misbehaved, the two first Georges could not have afforded to try experiments, if they had wished to : but the only alternative to George III. was a republic, and nobody wanted a republic. The old idea of loyalty to the crown could now be revived where it was almost dead, and transferred, where it had survived in full or comparatively full force, from the now impossible king "over the water," to a monarch with many most popular qualities.

Thus the new king's position was, in many respects, exceedingly strong. The Tory section, which had always opposed the great Whig families had hitherto always been, at the same time, a menace to the reigning family ; but they would now rally to the king against the Whigs. For the first time since the Revolution, a king's party against the Whig chiefs had become a possibility.

If George had set about making the king's party a popular one, it is difficult to guess what the results might have been. As a matter of fact, neither the king on the one side, nor Pitt on the other, attempted to form a popular party. Pitt was essentially a popular minister—one whose power rested, not on influential connection, but on the favour in which he was held by the nation at large, the admiration commanded by his personality, the enthusiasm awakened by his acts. But he made no attempt to form a party, because he was opposed in principle to the recognition of party ties or obligations. The king, on the other hand, while he was anxious to curb the Whig nobility, was as little inclined as any one to pay heed to popular feeling. His plan was purely monarchical. He was too honest to profess views he did not hold, too courageous to yield to clamour, too obstinate to listen to argument. Hence he countenanced the most flagrant attacks on the liberty of the subject, struck at Pitt before he attacked Newcastle, and, while he succeeded in breaking up the great Whig connection, could only carry out his own policy by a precarious reliance on the temporary adhesion of some fragment of the party he had done his best to wreck.

The great constitutional struggle under the Stuarts had been the result of the crown's attempt to override parliament. George attempted, not so much to override, as to capture parliament. But alongside of this struggle a new one was rising, forming the third line of attack against the oligarchical system—the struggle to democratise parliament itself,—an end as little consonant with the ideas of the king as with those of the great houses who controlled so large a proportion of the constituencies. The question was coming to be whether the king, the families, or the people were to have the control of parliament. The broad dividing lines were not yet fixed; and the settlement of the question was thrown back for many years by the complications which the French Revolution produced. The democratic theory had not yet found a constitutional formula: while the name of Whig was claimed with equal fervour by representatives of every section of party—alike by Chatham, by the Rockinghams, by the Bedfords, by the king's Friends, and by the demagogues. *by the Democrats.*

The broad lines of constitutional movement during the reigns of the first two Georges were towards making parliament supreme, while keeping the control of it in the hands of a few families. With the reign of George III. a new constitutional contest set in, in the form of a treble but disunited attack on the oligarchy by reactionary monarchists, patriotic idealists, and revolutionary democrats; and, for the time, the monarchists carried the day.

CHAPTER II.

ENGLAND.

1714-1760.

Whigs and Tories—1720: The South Sea Bubble—Townshend and Walpole—Walpole's finance—1733: His excise scheme—His opportunism—His attitude to the Nonconformists—Causes of his power—His opponents—System of corruption—Results of his rule—1743: The Pelhams—Influence of Pitt.

THE England to whose throne George I. succeeded was sick of embroilments and domestic strife. The mass of the country favoured the new dynasty, but would have been ready enough to recall the Stuarts had that policy been accompanied by a better prospect of steady settled government. Hence the bulk of the population viewed the dynastic question with considerable apathy, and, when insurrections arose, for the most part looked on, and declined to take any compromising action in the quarrel.

But the failure of the Jacobites secured the Whigs in power for nearly half a century: and the Whigs, as a body, were bound to the interests of religious toleration and commercial expansion—if for no other reason, because the Nonconformists were the strongest opponents of Jacobitism, and were largely represented among the mercantile classes; while the position of the great mercantile corporations was too intimately connected with the established government for them to be otherwise than vigorously Hanoverian. Toryism, as distinct from Jacobitism, practically disappeared; and the competition for

Whigs and Tories.

office lay between politicians who were separated almost entirely by personal interests and personal rivalries, not at all by vital questions of principle,—since in matters of government they appealed alike to the "Glorious Revolution," and to Locke's "Principles of Civil Government" as their text-book. So that after one section of Whigs had been governing for a few years and were driven out by the great financial disaster known as the South Sea Bubble, they were replaced, not by a new party with new aims, but by another section of their own party, guided by the same broad principles as the fallen ministers.

The South Sea Company had been instituted by Harley on the analogy of the East India Company and the Bank of England, which owed their origin to the Whigs. A number of merchants combined to form a company wealthy enough to be able to purchase privileges and monopolies in return for advances made to government, or for taking over a portion of the National Debt. The chief privilege of the South Sea Company was the monopoly of the South Sea trade, which was expected to prove highly remunerative. Up to 1719, the trading had amounted to little more than the sending of a single ship to the South Seas. But the directors had ambitious schemes. Not England only, but Europe in general was, at the time possessed with a sort of mania for gambling on a large scale. The company had a huge capital; they thought they saw their way to double it. They offered to relieve government by converting a large portion of the National Debt into South Sea Stock. The Bank of England was jealous, and began bidding against them; but the company outbid it. Amazing rumours were put about of the wonderful things that were going to be done, the vast profits that would accrue to shareholders. The project could not conceivably have ended otherwise than ruinously; the capital required a gigantic trade to be employed with any profit at all, and the trade was not

The South Sea Bubble.

gigantic. But the inventions that started no one knew where, and changed and swelled and accumulated no one knew how, passed from mouth to mouth and were believed. A madness came upon the people. The shares were bought eagerly, furiously. A few reasonable persons made an effort to check the frenzy; Walpole openly attacked the scheme, though privately he dabbled in it a little with some success: but prominent members of the ministry had a far from innocent share in increasing the madness. In April, 1720, the government bill accepting the company's scheme was passed. The shares went up to an unheard-of premium; and then the bubble burst. Thousands were ruined; it was the most overwhelming financial disaster upon record; and when the public found how they had been duped, their rage knew no bounds. When it appeared that some among the ministers had profited by the disaster for which the government was in part responsible, their political fate was sealed. Stanhope was fully and honourably cleared; so was Sunderland—but in his case public opinion did not endorse the acquittal; Aislabie, Chancellor of the Exchequer, and other members of the ministry were hopelessly involved. It was now that the good fortune which had driven Townshend and Walpole out of office became apparent. The popular indignation was such that no member of the fallen ministry could have commanded confidence, and, but for the schism, a Jacobite government would almost certainly have come in. But Walpole was the ablest financier in the country; apart from the disaster, a Whig was preferable to a Jacobite; and since Walpole had been in opposition, he escaped all charge of complicity in the crash. The country turned to him to tide over its misfortune. Townshend succeeded Stanhope as Secretary of State, and Walpole became First Lord of the Treasury and Chancellor of the Exchequer.

At first, indeed, Walpole was not at the head of the government, Townshend being chief minister; and for some time they worked together. But, by degrees, it became evident that Walpole meant himself to be first and Townshend second. There were rivals — Pulteney, Carteret, Chesterfield; but they were fighting for their own hand, and had no sufficient backing. Townshend and Walpole were in general agreement; their differences were personal. By degrees their friendship became strained, till it developed into positive animosity; and at length Townshend, with a rare magnanimity, perceiving that a continual struggle between them would jeopardise the interests which both had at heart, and feeling that neither could serve peaceably under the other, resolved in 1730 to retire from public life, and leave the field free to his rival. {*margin:* Townshend and Walpole.}

In effect, however, it was when he succeeded Aislabie at the Exchequer, that Walpole really commenced that long-continued sway which has been so highly belauded and so angrily condemned. His policy, so far as foreign affairs are concerned, has already been discussed; it has now to be considered as it affected domestic affairs.

Walpole is the first English minister of the front rank who is great primarily in virtue of his finance. It was a financial disaster of the first magnitude that brought him into power; and he raised the country to an unparalleled pitch of commercial prosperity. He devoted his energies to the removal of all restrictions on trade which it was practicable to touch. In Opposition, no doubt, he posed as the advocate of the "mercantile theory," and strenuously attacked Bolingbroke's commercial treaty; but, in power, he applied the principle whenever possible. Such taxes as he could, he reduced. English merchants insisted on the most rigorous protection against colonial competition, but otherwise colonial commerce was carefully fostered. He propounded an excise scheme which anticipated the financial reforms of Huskisson, and would have been—as later generations have fully recognized—an immense boon to the nation; and he only dropped it {*margin:* Walpole's finance.}

because he regarded domestic order as of higher importance than economic reform.

The history of the excise scheme is very significant. The plan itself was tolerably simple, and its advantages great. *His excise scheme.* Owing to the heavy customs' dues on tobacco and spirits, a very large amount of smuggling was carried on which was of course injurious to legitimate trade, while the revenue was defrauded. Walpole's plan was to transfer tobacco from customs to excise, so that it might be landed and warehoused without paying duty until it was withdrawn for consumption. At the same time, the trader who wished not to sell his tobacco for English consumption, but to export it, could have it re-embarked without paying duty. A great encouragement was therefore afforded to legitimate trading, and the difficulty of collecting the revenue was materially diminished.

But the measure was hopelessly misunderstood and misrepresented. Excise was, at all times, an intensely unpopular method of raising revenue. The scheme was declared to be nothing better than a conspiracy to flood the country with a new army of officials who would manage elections in the interest of government; who would form a standing army (one of the popular bugbears then, and for many years longer); who would act as inquisitors, invading and examining private households on specious pretexts. Argument was useless; it was vain to point out that some six or seven score of new officials could meet the requirements of the whole country, and that they could not enter private households without a search-warrant, which would only be given when strong evidence in justification was adduced. The country was possessed with a wild panic. Walpole knew that he could carry the House with him; court and ministers were fully prepared to support him; but he saw that the process of compelling the public to accept a boon which they regarded with such horror, was by no means unlikely to produce a revolution, and he withdrew the measure.

The whole episode is particularly characteristic of Walpole's attitude towards popular sentiment. The intrinsic merits of a measure or a policy might commend themselves to his judgment: but he had learnt from the Sacheverell trial how disastrously effective a wave of unreasoning popular feeling might become. Moreover, he considered it essential that he should himself remain at the helm of the State. If a man changes his policy rather than resign office, he is open to the charge of placing himself above his country; and Walpole has been freely reproached for his love of office. To a man who has partaken largely of the fruits of power, retirement is apt to be bitter; and the purely personal feeling can hardly fail to influence him. But though he clings to office, motives more patriotic than these may influence him as well. In Walpole's case, it must be remembered that the dominant fact in the political situation was always the existence of the Pretender. The country must be kept steady. Measures, good in themselves, which would upset the equilibrium must be discarded. The task of management required a very skilful hand, and it was difficult to believe that any hand but his own could be adequate to the task.

His opportunism.

In this particular instance there can be no doubt that Walpole acted rightly. The excise scheme, received peaceably, would have been of immense economic advantage, but there was no moral principle involved in it. By yielding to the popular feeling, Walpole saved the situation.

His attitude towards the Dissenters is another instance of the same characteristic. Stanhope had been particularly anxious to relieve the Nonconformists of their disabilities: the justice of doing so was obvious, and Walpole always professed himself in favour of it. But he would not legislate. So far as it was possible in practice to disregard the letter of existing anti-Nonconformist law, every encouragement was given to do so.

Walpole and the Nonconformists.

But to legislate would have set the High-church clergy, and the High-church and Sacheverell mobs, in motion. "Quieta non movere" was the one indispensable rule. No relief measures were introduced by Walpole. Here, again, there was ample justification; for a cry of "The Church in danger!" was of all others the most to be dreaded, the most threatening to the stability of the Hanoverian dynasty. The most that could safely be done was to encourage a liberal interpretation of the law, liberal laxity in its enforcement, and a liberal practice in the matter of ecclesiastical preferments.

It was, in short, only when Walpole's peace policy was overthrown, and a war which he detested was declared,— when affairs reached a condition in which he knew he was incompetent to manage them, for he was quite aware of own unfitness for the ministerial conduct of a war,—when by retaining office he was unable to carry out either his own policy or the only efficient alternative one—that he can be charged fairly with clinging to power at the expense of patriotism.

Walpole secured the support of the commercial classes by a financial policy which led them to identify prosperity with the rule of Hanover. He retained the Nonconformists by practically minimising their disabilities, while he conciliated the Church by refusing to remove those disabilities by legislation. He conciliated the country gentry, among whom the old Toryism naturally found its stronghold, by making it a primary object of his financial schemes to reduce the land-tax; while circumstances combined to make him personally peculiarly acceptable to them as a minister. He was a country gentleman himself, and devoted to the sports beloved of his class. His opposition to the Sunderland Peerage Bill had greatly added to his popularity with them, because the large landowners were the class most keenly interested in keeping the entry to the Upper House open. There never was a less "academic" politician at the head of an administration; and country

Causes of his power.

gentlemen as a rule have a stronger distrust than any other section of the community for academic politicians. He kept himself secure of the steady support of the crown against all rivals, because he compelled both the Georges to recognise his capacity, and to respect his plain dealing; while he avoided the *rôle* of bully which has brought about the fall of many ministers who have been proud of being plain-spoken. And for many years his position was greatly strengthened by the unswerving support of Queen Caroline, secured by his astute policy at the moment of the accession of George II.

By the systematic conciliation of large bodies of public opinion, Walpole retained his control of the country, and established the Hanoverian dynasty. By his personal relation to Queen Caroline, he retained his influence with the crown. The control of parliament he retained by a rigorous autocracy in the cabinet and an extensive system of corruption. To the extent to which he carried the former, he in great measure owed his fall, while the latter has remained the most enduring blot upon his reputation. He would have no rival in the cabinet; and he did, in fact, turn out of it very nearly every man of real ability; supplying their places with official mediocrities and party managers, never with new talent. Hence there grew up a strong body of politicians who, without having any united policy of their own, were prepared to find a ground of attack wherever the smallest opportunity occurred. These included all those able men whom he had displaced, and the younger men who felt themselves permanently excluded from efficient control of public affairs, so long as Walpole continued minister. A time came when their combination proved strong enough to overthrow him, while from lack of coherence they could not themselves work together in office. Pitt, in those early days, had obtained no ascendency: Carteret, Pulteney, and Chesterfield were united only in the desire to crush the man who had so

His opponents.

long dominated the political field. On the occasions which Walpole seized for getting rid of his formidable colleagues his action was undoubtedly justifiable, as they had been devoting their energies, notably in the case of the Excise Bill, to frustrating his policy; yet, when we consider the quantity of talent among the informal opposition and nominal parliamentary supporters of the Whig government, and compare it with the agglomeration of mediocrities with which Walpole had surrounded himself in the later years of his administration, it is impossible to believe that a man with Walpole's capacity for managing men would have failed to avail himself of some of that excluded talent but for an undue thirst for personal supremacy.

With regard to the charge of corruption, it is easy to exaggerate the real enormity of Walpole's conduct. He was not the author of the saying that all men have their price, though doubtless he believed it of most men. Nor could he be accused of appropriating large sums of public money for himself and his friends. Bribery was not an institution dating from his tenure of office; and the expenditure under the head of "secret service" was often exceeded by other administrators. But the public morality was at a very low ebb during the period when Walpole was in power. Most men were willing to be bought, with gold or office, and a good many were willing to be bought several times over. Walpole took the situation as he found it, and bought the support which his enemies would have bid for if they could. The picture is quite sufficiently shameless, but at least it is unfair to the memory of a man who, with all his faults, was on the whole not less honest than most of his contemporaries, to speak of him as if he had introduced a new and degrading factor into politics. He did not invent the habit; but, finding it there, he developed it into a system, which he used rather more cynically and a good deal more economically than half the politicians of the day could have done in his place.

[margin: System of corruption.]

The means by which Walpole pursued his ends were in part thoroughly bad, resting on the doctrine that human nature was corrupt, and the wise man is he who turns the corruption to his own advantage. But he achieved his purposes with extraordinary skill. He kept the country out of war. He kept the Jacobites quiet. He established the Hanoverian succession. He increased the material prosperity of the country beyond all precedent. And, while doing these things, his government told steadily in favour of liberty, civil, religious, and commercial. Those who came after him were free from none of his political vices. Administrative corruption increased rather than diminished; timidity and vacillation took the place of resolution. Walpole, indeed, is not without his share of the blame. It was he who had systematised and avowed the methods which his opponents would have practised if they could; and his successors took these things from him as his most valuable legacy. It was he who had alienated men of ability till the predominance of mediocrity had become the only alternative to his own control. It was he who had taught England to rate public spirit so low that, for the first time in history, she distrusted, not only her own strength, but her own courage. In his horror of disturbance, he had encouraged the political apathy which, south of the Tweed, presents so pitiable a spectacle during the 'Forty-five. To Walpole's influence is largely, though by no means entirely, due the low state of political morality, of departmental efficiency, of *morale*,—the absence of all enthusiasm, of all political insight extending beyond the merest opportunism of party management,—which prevailed until the brief but splendid period of Pitt's ascendency. But the worst period did not come till Walpole himself had fallen. Against these evils, too, must be set those great material gains for which the country had to thank him almost exclusively. Under him the nation accumulated a reserve of strength without which the daring policy of Pitt would have actually been

Results of his rule.

the madness that it appeared at first to pessimistic onlookers.

The Pelhams carried on the same system, but with its good features less strongly characterised, and with all its defects and demoralising tendencies more marked than ever. When Henry Pelham died, and Newcastle was left alone at the head of affairs, the nadir of degradation was attained. The spirit of the nation had fallen low enough when Charles Stuart's march to Derby, with nothing but untrained Highlanders at his back, could throw London into a panic, and it was generally believed that some of the present ministers were meditating a transfer of allegiance. But a lower deep was reached when England came to view the idea of a war with France, not with moral repulsion, or grave apprehension, but with sheer terror,—and that at a moment when she was capable, not merely of offering vigorous resistance, but of showing overwhelming superiority. To the Pelhams, and to the political methods they had learnt from Walpole, England owed that degradation: to the policy to which he had applied those methods, she owed her power of recuperation.

The Pelhams.

From that depth of demoralisation England was rescued by Pitt. After his brief period of power, ministers might be guilty of corruption, of levity, of pedantry, of paltry meannesses enough: but her days of mere pusillanimity were over. Her leaders might be incompetent, misguided, selfish: but there were never again wanting some few who could strike the heroic note, some who would answer to their appeal. The country might still be wrong-headed: it could scarcely again become contemptible.

Influence of Pitt.

CHAPTER III.

SCOTLAND.

1707–1760.

Scotland at the Union—The clans—The Lowlands—Scots and English—Religious and educational legislation—The Union—Effects of the 'Fifteen—Discontent with the Union—Effects of the 'Forty-five—Heritable jurisdictions: in the Lowlands; in the Highlands—Break up of the clan system; result—Progress made possible—Scots in England.

IN the domestic history of England, the first half of the eighteenth century is a comparatively unimportant period. The country settled down to a career of commercial prosperity ; no important changes were initiated. The England of George III. differed from the England of William III., chiefly because, in the interval, she had become the head of an empire. From a prosperous and wealthy country she had grown to be more prosperous and more wealthy ; but the conditions of her progress had not radically altered.

But it was otherwise with Scotland.

At the close of the seventeenth century, the northern country was in very evil plight. She was desperately poor, and lacked means for recuperation. She had no commerce worth mentioning ; her shipping was annihilated by the Navigation Act, which excluded her from English colonial commerce ; the Highlands were barren ; in the Lowlands enterprise was choked by want of means, and by the protective system of her powerful neighbour.

Scotland at the Union.

Moreover, good government had been a thing almost

unknown. Even in the Lowlands, the feudal system had never been destroyed; in the Highlands, the clan system was wholly inconsistent with the preservation of order, or the encouragement of any peaceful arts. Beyond the Pentlands, the chief reigned supreme in his own clan, and raided his neighbours, especially his Lowland neighbours, very much at his own will. There the arm of the central government was powerless. Elsewhere, the central government can usually enforce its decrees by sending troops; but it was vain to send troops to the Highlands. For every clan was an effective fighting force, eminently skilled in hill warfare, and desperately daring: whereas government troops were made very ineffective by the total absence of military roads, and the constant peril in that wild country of being entrapped into an ambush. Of the chiefs themselves, some few were well trained in southern civilisation; several had some superficial tincture of it, and could play their part in cities with other gentlemen. But in their own fortresses, they followed the traditions of the race, surrounded by clansmen to whom their word was law in the fullest sense, and whose theory of their moral obligations beyond the limits of the clan itself was extremely rudimentary. The traveller who was not suspected of evil designs was for the most part treated with elaborate courtesy, and his property was perfectly safe. But in the Highlander's decalogue, cattle were excluded from the operation of the eighth commandment. He lived by the sword and by the chase: tillage and manufactures—except for women's work—were non-existent. The only trade held reputable was that of the smith. Speaking a tongue of their own, wearing a dress of their own, heeding no law but the custom of the clan and the bidding of its chief, the Highlanders to all intents and purposes were a separate nation from the folk of the Lowlands, whom they regarded for the most part as their legitimate prey.

In the Lowlands, the poverty of high and low alike was

extreme, since external commerce, even with England herself, was practically crushed for the convenience of English merchants. Nor did agriculture prosper under feudal tenures, while capital for effecting improvements was not forthcoming. When we consider that the entire population of the country was probably under two millions, and that, according to an estimate of the time, no less than two hundred thousand of these lived by begging from door to door,—" begging " is doubtless a euphemistic way of putting it,—a tolerably vivid impression of extreme poverty is obtained. To add to the grimness of the picture, we have to bear in mind that the population had long been harried with religious persecutions; that the persecuted were only too ready to turn persecutors in their turn; that the prevalent doctrines were those of the harshest of all schools, and were propounded with the fiercest fanaticism. We have also to remark that the administration of the law was for the most part held as an hereditary right by landowners with immense powers of summary jurisdiction, which might manifestly be exercised with a very limited regard to justice.

<small>State of the Lowlands.</small>

Moreover, if the Highlander had not amalgamated with the Lowlander, neither had the latter amalgamated with the Englishman. The sense of Scotch nationality was extremely keen; for centuries the English and the Scots had been perpetually at war, and the union of the crowns had not been accompanied or followed by any sort of attempt at national unification. Trade barriers were kept up always to the injury of the poorer country. The Episcopal system of the Anglican Church was anathema to the fierce Presbyterianism of the Scottish Covenanter. To England, the ill will of Scotland mattered little so long as the two countries were under one crown, and hostile feeling could not take the form of armed attack. It was not till the northern kingdom threatened formally to part the crowns and to choose a king for itself, when a Protestant

<small>Scots and English.</small>

successor to Anne should be required, that England realised the possible advantages she might gain in the long run by a Union which should make progress possible for Scotland.

At the end of the seventeenth century, legislation secured a general religious toleration which prevented the worst results of theological animosities among a singularly disputatious people. It established also, among the population at large, an educational system which gave to the poorest classes throughout the country an intellectual training infinitely superior to that of the corresponding sections of the community in England. These were the first steps towards setting the people free to follow their own bent, and giving their energies full play, when the bonds and barriers which held them back should be loosened and cast down.

Religious and educational legislation.

But the legislative Union with England, in 1707, may fairly be regarded as the turning-point in the fortunes of the Scottish people; and the reason of this is mainly to be found in the commercial arrangements between the two countries. Scotland was placed on the same footing as England, free trade was established between the two countries, customs and excise duties were equalised, all restrictions on colonial commerce were removed, and with them those imposed by the Navigation Act on Scottish shipping. These concessions were of vital consequence to Scotland; the existing conditions were intolerable, and the only alternative was complete separation with all its attendant evils. To England this would have meant the presence on her northern border of a perpetually hostile state. For Scotland, unless she had been able to extort commercial concessions by the threat of war, it would have effected little relief from poverty, and would very possibly have tended to anarchy. But Scotland was prepared to maintain the union of the crowns, if the commercial concessions were granted; England was prepared

The Union.

to make the concessions, if a legislative union were substituted for the personal union of the crowns.

The Union gave Scotland commercial freedom. Scotchmen were naturally endowed with a high average of commercial capacity. When prosperity became attainable, the country turned its attention energetically to attaining it. Externally, indeed, progress was not rapid for many years. The organisation of trade and agriculture took half a century to accomplish. The foundations had to be laid, and laying foundations is a process which occupies a great deal of time before the superficial results are very evident. Scotland made no sudden leap from dire poverty to marked wealth. But the Union removed those barriers to material progress which had hitherto proved insurmountable. In fifty years the extremity of poverty had disappeared. Manufactures were organised, and were spreading; commerce was increasing, slowly as yet, but surely; and education, of a kind which gave an intellectual flavour to the life of the working classes, was prevalent to a degree which might well have been envied in England.

The Act of Union freed the Lowlands of Scotland from the fetters which had held all material progress in check. The various Acts enforcing religious toleration removed or minimised one of the most fruitful sources of civil discord. The educational system produced a population as much above the average in intelligence as in physical hardiness. The pacification of the Highlanders, Scotland owed to the two rebellions and the measures which resulted from them.

The direct results of the 'Fifteen were comparatively small. But it brought home to the government the hopelessness of dealing with mountaineers in their own country without military roads. The Highlands were practically without roads at all : there were merely trodden tracks and paths, where regular troops were at the most complete disadvantage. Hence, not only

Effects of the 'Fifteen.

military communication, but communication of every kind, was very restricted. The clansmen dwelt apart from the Lowlanders, and at constant feud with each other. The will to extend intercourse and to produce exchangeable commodities was wanting. Had it been present, it would yet have had no scope, owing to the want of means of communication. One indirect result of the 'Fifteen was the building by General Wade of the great military roads through the Highlands; an enterprise which was not attended at the time by any very striking consequences, but which subsequently made the real opening up of the Highlands possible; while it at once enabled additional fortresses to be established, which were at least available as some check on the extremes of lawlessness, and were not altogether without influence in increasing the risk that must attach to actual insurrection. The means were thus provided for a largely extended intercourse between different parts of the Highlands, and between the Highlands and the south, while the power of the central government to apply the sanction of physical force to its decrees was greatly increased.

Yet little or no effort was made at the time to deal with the real causes which made the condition of the Highlands a constant menace to the more peaceful Lowlands. The clansmen were ordered to surrender their arms, with the natural result that those clans which favoured the existing *régime* obeyed, while the disaffected merely made a show of obedience. The power of the chiefs was not touched. They might be attainted, but the clansmen remained loyal to them. Every chief who was a Jacobite had his whole clan in arms as a fighting force, to bring into the field the moment the word was given. The disarmament failed entirely of its purpose. The men were trained as they had always been trained, and they lived in the constant expectation of the call to arms. There was not even the commencement of a tendency to start industries, or to recognize the validity of any law or any command other than that of the chief.

Practically, therefore, between the 'Fifteen and the 'Forty-five, the state of the Highlands remained unchanged. The building of General Wade's roads had been an important step, but it was followed up by nothing more.

Moreover, we have observed that in the south the effect of the Union had been, not to produce immediate and visible progress, but to establish part of those conditions without which progress was impossible. Hence the bulk of the population had not realised the enormous gain that it brought to the country, while it did realise, not without exaggeration, how much had been given up. Instead of being a semi-independent nation, Scotland appeared to have become only a small section of a large nation, which controlled its legislation, and whose policy was guided by that of the smaller incorporated country simply in proportion to the representation of the latter in the united parliament. Consequently, the Union was generally extremely unpopular. Scottish pride was frequently and bitterly offended by the tone adopted towards Scotland in the south. Tory pamphleteers, in the last days of Queen Anne, had done much to stir up ill-feeling. Sunderland's Peerage Bill had been felt as an attack upon the Scottish representation in the Upper House, which had also refused to recognise peerages of Great Britain conferred upon Scottish peers. Later, on the occasion of the Porteous riots in Edinburgh, it was believed in the north that the action of government had been dictated by contempt for the Scottish capital. In fine, the Union for very many years failed entirely to act as a measure of conciliation between the two peoples; and in the north its beneficial effects were only in part recognized, while the loss of independence was felt almost as a stain on the national honour.

Hence the Union was emphatically unpopular in Scotland, and not only among the politicians on one side. A considerable number of persons were consequently led to look forward to a Stuart restoration as a means to sever the

[sidenote: Discontent with the Union.]

Union, an expectation which actually brought Charles Edward not a few adherents in the 'Forty-five.

Effects of the 'Forty-five. The 'Forty-five, and the legislation which followed, completed the work of the Union. When the rebellion was crushed, there was little prospect left of any serious renewal of the attempt which had ended so disastrously, and consequently the Union itself was confirmed decisively, and its repeal ceased to be a factor in any political speculations. This of itself did something towards preparing the way for a better feeling between north and south. When it was at length realised that Scotland could not escape from the Union, and so must make the best of it, she set about doing so to more purpose. Thus the effect of Charles Edward's failure was to finally ratify the Union, and thereby to give an additional impulse to the tendencies which the Union naturally tended to foster.

But the rebellion had a further result. Partisanship in Scotland went much farther than it did in England. Jacobitism was much more widespread and much more enthusiastic. It would be an error to suppose that all, or nearly all, the Highlands rose in favour of the prince; but probably of those chiefs who did not rise, at least half were well-wishers to the cause, who refrained chiefly because Duncan Forbes had succeeded in convincing them that the enterprise was entirely hopeless. Many others would have followed their example, but for the magic of Charles's own personality. Yet the mere fact that he did find so many supporters in an attempt on the face of it so desperate, shows the intensity of Jacobite feeling. That feeling was very largely hereditary. The political partisanship had served as a line of division; clan animosities and divisions were kept alive and embittered by it: so that, with the disappearance of the last chance of a Stuart restoration, a principal source of tribal hostilities was also removed.

Again, the final fall of the Stuarts was probably more

felt in Scotland than in England as a conclusive removal of all risk of civil war. In the southern country the chance of a rising was always less than in the northern. Those which took place were effective as insurrections in Scotland, but only in a very minor degree in England. This chance, then, acted as a drag on enterprise in Scotland. Its disappearance brought more marked relief there, and of itself helped on the hitherto slow apparent advance of material progress.

But of all the consequences of the 'Forty-five, none was of such importance as the step to which the government was impelled by it, of abolishing heritable jurisdictions. In the Lowlands, the measure was of great effect, inasmuch as it placed the administration of justice in the hands of persons who were trained lawyers without local interests, instead of in the hands of local landowners. But the most dangerous effects of hereditary or heritable jurisdiction lay not so much in maladministration as in the enormous power it gave to landowners, when coupled with a feudal system of land tenure. It gave the landowner a regular body of retainers, over whom he had the fullest powers, in many cases even of life and death. The political danger of this system had been lessened in the Lowlands by enactments securing tenants against their landlords, when ordered to aid in breaking the peace ; so that practically the feudal relation had been materially weakened. The personal or family bond had already given way. Nevertheless, the mere possession of the power of summary jurisdiction on the part of the landlord had obviously made it much harder than it need have been for the tenant to act in opposition ; and thus, even in the Lowlands, the change in the law was beneficial. *The heritable jurisdictions: in the Lowlands;*

But in the Highlands, the bond between the chief and his clan had been one of extraordinary strength. Loyalty to the chief overruled literally every other consideration of law, morals, or interests ; and the law actually sanctioned this state of things by the powers of *in the Highlands.*

hereditary jurisdiction, coupled with practical non-interference from the centre. The result was, that not only had the chief an entirely devoted following, but the whole of his surroundings within his own district consisted of his own clansmen. No one from outside wished to settle among them, or, if they did, they soon found it advisable to withdraw, for they had no sort of means of appeal to a superior power. The chief's will was carried out, and no questions were asked.

The abolition of the jurisdictions was accompanied by improvements in the modes of communication, a rigorous disarmament, and the expulsion from the country of many chieftains, so that the arm of the law was greatly strengthened. For a time, custom enabled the chief to rule his own clan very much as he had done before, but those outside his clan to whom he did injury now had the law to appeal to. Hence it became possible to plant within the clan borders outsiders who were protected by the law; and the conception of a paramount power too strong to be resisted began to grow. In many cases, the chief's place was taken by some government nominee who could be nothing more than a landlord, so that the sentiment of chieftainship was undermined at the same time that its legal sanction had been withdrawn. The country could no longer be mapped out into clan districts, because new blood was brought in, and the aggrieved clansman no longer appealed to his chief for vengeance, but to the law for protection. Thus the cohesion of the clans was broken; the practical power of insurrection was removed; and the king's peace, enforced by the king's law, backed by the king's soldiers, began to extend to the Highlands as elsewhere.

Break-up of the clan system.

Customs prevailing over an extended area, but not outside it, necessarily tend to keep up the sense of separation between its inhabitants and those of the outside world. The Highlanders had counted themselves an entirely separate people, holding aloof from their Lowland neighbours. The possession of a national tongue and a national costume had materially helped to foster this feeling, which had still, perhaps, rested most of all on the clan system. The Gaelic tongue could not be abolished, but the principle of spreading the English language was carried out, and the wearing of the kilt became a legal offence. A little later, William Pitt took a step which largely helped to make the Highlanders feel themselves to be in reality an integral part of the larger nation, and to earn for them immense credit and respect. This measure was the raising of purely Highland regiments, whose value in the English army was immediately recognized. It may be remarked that the scheme had been mooted before, but it was only under the changed conditions introduced by the 'Forty-five that it became really practicable.

One other consequence of the insurrection is to be observed. With the loss of the chiefs' powers, a strong incentive which kept the clansmen together was removed. Moreover, cattle-lifting rapidly ceased to be a profitable occupation. Hence the pressure of over-population in comparison with the products of the soil was more seriously felt. A tendency to emigration set in, sometimes set in motion by extensive evictions, and the isolation of the Highlands was gradually destroyed.

Thus it is from the middle of the eighteenth century that the real prosperity of Scotland dates. It was during the earlier half of that century that one after another **The way** of the barriers to her progress were removed. The **of progress** institution of the educational system belongs, in- **opened.** deed, mainly to the last decade of William's reign ; the Toleration Acts, to that of Queen Anne. The Union of 1707 made it possible to lay the foundations of commercial advancement : the 'Fifteen prepared the way for the opening up of the Highlands : the 'Forty-five put an end to the clan system, and led to the unification of the country.

In the relations between Scotland as a whole and England,

no very great friendliness had as yet been induced, but at any rate the danger of active hostilities was gone. In the parliament of Great Britain, Scotland, in spite of her small representation, was fairly well defended, by the fact that, whatever party the members might belong to, on purely Scottish questions they formed a compact phalanx. Apart from such questions, their tendency to act as a single body whenever the question became one of supporting a Scotchman, and their reputed venality—a not unnatural consequence of their extreme comparative poverty, when most politicians were venal without that excuse—often rendered them an unsatisfactory element in English politics. The dislike of the Scots also became a useful weapon in the hands of demagogues in the earlier years of George III., though Chatham characteristically scorned to use it, and boldly condemned it in others. But the fundamental sources of anarchy in Scotland herself, and of division between Scotland and England, were all cleared away: and that the Union should be turned into Unity was only a question of time.

Scots in England.

CHAPTER IV.

IRELAND.

1714-1760.

Scotland and Ireland compared—The Catholic population—Commercial repression—Landlords and tenants—Representation—Education—Catholic inaction—English control—1724: Wood's halfpence—Signs of revival.

THE history of Ireland during this period offers a marked contrast to that of Scotland. In the northern country the whole influence of legislation was progressive. Trade was set free, and industry found consequent encouragement. The religion of the vast bulk of the population was recognized and established. Education was carefully and earnestly fostered. There were plentiful abuses in parliamentary representation, but the voice of the Scottish members generally controlled Scottish legislation, and the people at large had something to say in the election of their members. There was a reasonable system of land tenure; the abolition of heritable jurisdictions gradually carried the king's law into remote districts, and the law in general was recognized as beneficial. *[margin: Scotland and Ireland compared.]*

In Ireland, on the other hand, the entire system was calculated to destroy every prospect of progress. Industry was crushed at every turn. The religion of three-fourths of the people was proscribed. Education was almost unattainable by Roman Catholics. The Irish parliament represented practically a single class; the laws it passed could be amended at will by the British Privy Council:

O

the parliament at Westminster could legislate for Ireland independently; while practically every post of importance was invariably bestowed on an Englishman. The result was that the people of Ireland in general regarded law, not as the instrument of order, but as an engine of oppression.

Of the whole population of Ireland, at least three-fourths were Roman Catholic. Of the land of the country, at least three-fourths was owned by Protestant landlords, and of these the majority were English or Scotch settlers. The Roman Catholics—of whom I shall speak, for the sake of convenience, as the Catholics—could hold land only by inheritance; and their property became rapidly broken up, because for them each man's estate was divided up amongst his children, instead of going to the eldest son. No Catholic could buy land, or hold it on a long lease. Protestants, since the same law of succession did not apply to them, could accumulate land by purchase, while their estates were not divided on the owner's decease. Hence all the large landowners were Protestants, while the immense majority of the tenants were Catholics. Seeing that the general intention of the law was to make the most possible of differences in religious belief, thereby creating strong religious animosities, it followed that a very sharp incentive was given to animosity between landlord and tenant.

The Catholic population.

In a country where there is a great industrial population it is possible for agrarian difficulties to be of minor importance. But in Ireland there was no such population, for the very good reason that, in the interests of British merchants, no Irish industries, with the exception of the linen manufacture, were allowed to progress. This was the recognized commercial policy of the age. The British merchants sought to crush competition. They only conceded commercial equality to Scotland as the price of the Act of Union. America was lost because the same policy was pursued with regard to the colonies. But Ireland could not rebel, she could only writhe, and the

Commercial repression.

policy was carried out with deadly effect for her. Large parts of the country were eminently adapted for wool-growing : but the manufacture was killed, and even the export of the raw material practically prohibited, by the levying of crushing duties. Her western ports were eminently adapted for colonial trade : but she was precluded from all share in it by the Navigation Acts. All other natural wealth-producing capacities being choked, the soil only was left : and on the soil the population was obliged to live.

Even so, the normal incentives to industry were wanting. The tenant had no possibility of acquiring his holding, and no interest in improving it. Rack-renting, the application of the purely competitive method, was practically universal ; and the competition was altogether one-sided, since the alternative to accepting any rent that might be fixed was starvation. In England, if a man found that he could not live decently at the rent demanded, he sought other employment ; but in Ireland there was no other employment for him to seek. In England, landlord and tenant stood in a relation which commonly involved a degree of personal intercourse, so that the economic doctrine of making the best bargain attainable was modified by human sentiments of mutual good-will : in Ireland, most of the landlords were absentees, with a series of agents and middlemen standing between them and the cultivators, and there was no margin for the operation of sentimental considerations. The result was that the cottier paid all he could make above a bare subsistence to the middleman, who paid most of that to the next middleman, and so on up the scale. If a tenant did improve his holding, the middleman promptly raised the rent. The destructiveness of this absentee system is obvious. The landlord who sees the straits to which his tenants are brought, in a bad year, through no fault of their own, will probably remit a portion of the rent. But he will not be equally ready to

Landlords and tenants.

listen to the representations of an agent, and the agent is bound to support the landlord's interests. The fixing of rent by competition where labour is not easily and promptly transferable from agriculture to some other industry can only be tolerable when the landlord is both able and willing to distinguish between his just claims and his legal rights, which an absentee cannot do. In Ireland, the worst features of the system were further exaggerated by the hostility, fostered in many other ways, between the Catholic peasantry and their Protestant masters.

Moreover, the sense of injustice in the law was greatly increased by the fact that it had been imposed on a conquered by a conquering nation. The old proprietors had been dispossessed in favour of British immigrants, and the old land-law had been abolished for an alien system. The justice and policy of the change have been upheld by brilliant writers, whose chief complaint is that it did not go far enough. Whether they or their opponents are right, the fact remains that the new system, already established at the commencement of our period, was felt as a rankling grievance, bringing not only the specific law but all law into odium. Classes were set against each other, because government represented a single class interest, trampling on the interests of the rest—and the rest comprised the mass of the population.

If popular representation was inadequate and corrupt in England and Scotland, it was still more so in Ireland. **Representation.** None but Protestants might sit in the Irish House of Commons. Catholics were not expressly precluded from voting at first; but at the best of times those of them who had the franchise were few, and, in 1727, even they were formally deprived of it. The parliament therefore was entirely representative of the Protestant minority alone; while more than one-half of its members sat for rotten boroughs, and were mere nominees of a few patrons.

Three-fourths of the population were Catholics; but

Protestants owned nearly all the land, and consequently the wealth, of the country. Protestants alone were represented in parliament; Protestants alone were eligible for corporations, for the magistracy, for the bar, and for the bench. The established Church, supported by the tithe, was Protestant; and the Catholics were all but entirely debarred from education. *Education.*

No Catholic was allowed to keep a school or to act as a teacher, under severe penalties. A system of Charter schools was established, by which poor parents were enabled to have their children taken entirely off their hands, fed, clothed, and educated for nothing—provided that they were allowed no communication with their families, and were brought up as Protestants. To sincere Catholics, heresy was an evil which more than counterbalanced the mental and bodily gains promised. The schools were, in effect, a machine for manufacturing Protestants : this was the light in which the people regarded them ; consequently education in this form was generally refused, while it was not available in any other.

The whole system, in short, aimed directly at the destruction of Catholicism by the degradation and oppression of those who professed it ; and these formed, not a small minority, but a large majority of the whole nation. It was simply inevitable, under such conditions, that the Catholics as a body should hold the government in detestation. They were deprived of every incentive to good citizenship ; their sole inducement to obey the law lay in the power of the lawgivers to enforce their own decrees and exact a merciless penalty for disobedience. Their only defence was found in the readiness of some of the ruling class to connive at evasions. Thus, by one law, if a Catholic died, his children, if minors, were transferred to a Protestant guardian ; who, occasionally, might facilitate their education in the Catholic religion, if he could do so without detection.

It is remarkable that Ireland took no part in the rebellions of 1715, and 1745. The true reason appears to be that there was neither the temper nor the capacity to rebel among the downtrodden population. Emigration had removed the bolder spirits, who were winning fame for the fighting qualities of the Irish on the continent—in high military posts, like Browne and Lacy of the Austrian army, or in the ranks, like the Irish regiment at Fontenoy. The capable men had left the country, while those left behind lacked leaders and were devoid of organisation. The age of secret combinations had not set in in force : the Catholics had no means to organise a rising, and they knew it. Their tone, so far as their voices were heard, was loyal. In the time of the 'Forty-five, it was not only their broken state which accounted for this. In that year, Chesterfield was viceroy, and his term of office forms a memorable exception to the dreary record of men who accepted the post while disregarding its responsibilities. In England, Chesterfield was known in his own day as a brilliant speaker, and as one of the three or four men who hoped, not unreasonably, to challenge the predominance of Walpole ; to later generations, he is best known as the author of the famous "Letters." But, for Ireland, he was the one statesman of his day who displayed the powers of a ruler with equal justice and firmness. He refused to be the instrument of a section ; exercising his patronage with unwonted impartiality, while he allowed it to be thoroughly understood that the government was strong enough to compel obedience, and that justice was not a sign of weakness.

Catholic inaction.

The religious oppression, of which only a few leading points have here been set forth, would be quite sufficient to account for a very strong antagonism between the Catholic population and the government. The educational conditions fully explain the intellectual degradation of the poorer classes. The land system and the system of commercial repression made poverty inevitable, and intensified class animosities. But even among the ruling class, the political vitality which arouses the sense of citizenship and its responsibilities was deadened by the complete subordination of Dublin to Westminster.

At the time of the Scottish Union there appears to have been a considerable feeling in favour of a similar step for Ireland in that country. But the inducement for England was not the same. England and Scotland were two independent countries, in the sense that neither had any legal control over the other. England was the richer and more powerful, but Scotland had shown, through centuries of constant war, that she was not to be conquered, and was by no means to be despised as an enemy. In the last resort she could defy England, and, by recalling the Stuarts to her throne, could reduce the southern country to a state of perpetual ferment. The situation was so dangerous that it was worth while for England, in spite of her mercantile theory, to concede free trade as the price of security. But Ireland had nothing to offer. She was controlled by English regiments, and could not throw off the yoke. The predominant class might be dissatisfied, but for them Irish independence would have meant internal revolution as well, and the return of the Catholics to power. Ireland could not threaten England, seeing that, in effect, she was a subject province; whereas Scotland was an independent nation. The benefits that would have accrued to her from the Union are obvious, but England only saw the disadvantage of giving commercial freedom. The idea, therefore, had found no favour.

English control.

Consequently the political powers of those who possessed the franchise in Ireland were miserably limited. They had no voice in imperial concerns, and the scope of their domestic legislation was bounded by the right of the English Privy Council to amend or reject their measures. A bill could not be passed by the Irish parliament until it had been approved by the English Privy Council, and any amendments that body might insert the Irish parliament was obliged to accept, with the alternative of dropping the bill entirely. On the other hand, the English parliament claimed the right of legislating independently for Ireland, and even of introducing money bills; while the English House of Lords usurped the right of overruling the judicial decisions of the Irish House of Lords. That the right of amendment was in certain cases wisely exercised, does not alter the fact that it was incompatible with the freedom of the Irish parliament. It can only be defended on the ground that the Irish were not fit for freedom, and that it was best for them to lose the advantages while avoiding the dangers that free institutions would have provided.

Out of this subordination of the Irish arose the excited controversy of Wood's Halfpence, in which the "Drapier's Letters" of Swift played so large a part. The matter itself was one of which the importance was immensely exaggerated. In so poor a country many payments were necessarily made in small coin. To meet the demand, an Englishman named Wood was granted, in 1724, a patent for coining copper to the nominal value of £108,000, the amount of metal employed being worth only some £40,000. The coins were of little less value than the corresponding coins in England; but, the country being so poor, and the amount proposed to be coined relatively so considerable, it was believed that most of the silver and gold would pass to England, leaving only the debased copper coinage. The excitement ran high, and, in the course of time, Walpole, with his usual inclination to avoid popular ferments even in a good cause, withdrew the patent. But the proposal owed half its unpopularity to the fact that the coinage was to be thrust upon the Irish by the English, while the very patent itself was granted, not to an Irishman, but to an Englishman. Swift was not the man to hesitate at exaggeration if it suited his ends, and his treatment of the actual financial question was out of all real relation to the dangers involved; but he used the

Wood's halfpence.

halfpence as a peg on which to hang a very powerful indictment of the whole system of subordination.

Nevertheless, of political movement throughout the reigns of the first two Georges there was very little. It was only in the closing decade of the period that signs of something like organisation appeared, and the existence of a genuine parliamentary opposition, as against the government which took its mandates from Westminster, began to be evident. Bad as the whole system was, there had been no violent upheavals, no sweeping confiscations, no new intolerable burdens imposed on the community, and the spirit of the people, Protestant and Catholic alike, was gradually beginning to revive.

Signs of revival.

CHAPTER V.

GREATER BRITAIN.

1714-1763.

The American colonies—Colonial constitutions—The colonial theory—Dangers from the French—Results of the great war—Restrictions on trade—Attitude of Walpole—Change in the situation—*India*—Break-up of the Mogul Empire—Disorganisation of native powers—Rivalry between French and English—Three stages of the contest—The British advance inevitable—The new order.

IT is in America and in India that the real interests of the first twenty years of George III.'s reign are centred.

After the Treaty of Utrecht, the English possessions in America embraced Newfoundland, Nova Scotia, and the thirteen colonies which were subsequently formed into the United States.

These thirteen colonies form four groups. Commencing at the north, the first contains the four New England colonies, namely, New Hampshire, Massachusetts, Connecticut, and Rhode Island. The traditions of all these were entirely Puritanical in religion, and democratic in government. Next to these came New York and New Jersey, where there was a strong admixture of Dutch. Next, Pennsylvania and Delaware, closely akin to the New England group, Pennsylvania being Quaker in origin. Maryland, Virginia, North and South Carolina, and Georgia form the fourth group, all five being specially characterised by the predominance of a body of large land-

[margin: The American colonies.]

holders, marked by very much the same qualities as those possessed by the corresponding class in England.

The constitution of these colonies gave them all a liberty of self-government such as no other state had allowed to her dependencies over-seas. In each there was an elected Assembly, an Upper House or Council either elected or nominated, and a nominated governor. For all ordinary purposes they governed themselves very much as England governed herself, under forms sometimes rather more, sometimes rather less, democratic: but in one respect, that of religious liberty, they were all in advance of the mother country; since religious opinions did not constitute political qualification or disqualification. Colonial constitutions.

The colonial theory of the day was that colonies existed for the benefit of the parent state. They were to be allowed to do very much as they pleased themselves, provided that their interests were not permitted to interfere with those of the mother country; but, where her own prosperity was concerned, the mother country maintained in practice, as well as in theory, a right of extensive interference. On the other hand, the claim of the colonists to some assistance in disputes with foreign aggressors was also recognized. For it was at least clear that the ultimate use of the colonies to the mother country must greatly depend on their capacity for expansion, and as a simple matter of policy England was bound to see that their expansion was not unduly checked. The colonial theory.

Now, throughout the reigns of the two first Georges there was a constant danger of foreign encroachment. France was in possession of Canada on the north, and of Louisiana on the south; and the French colonists wished to unite their territories. The union could only be effected by cutting off the English colonies from all extension westwards beyond the Alleghanies. And, since the French could rely on some support from France, it was clear that, so long as they retained their Dangers from the French.

footing on the American continent in such force as to be capable of challenging the British settlers, these would necessarily desire the power of appealing to the mother country for help. In other words, however much they might kick at interference from England, and protest against British control, they were bound in their own interest to accept that minimum of supervision and regulation which were required to make England feel it worth while to give help when called upon.

But the situation was changed by the great war. No foreign power worth considering had a footing on the continent any more. There was no interference to dread. The English colonists could expand westward as much as they pleased, with no one to say them nay but ill-organised though cruel Indian tribes, against whom they would neither expect nor ask assistance from England. With the disappearance of the French power, the need of English help vanished; and with the need of help, the need of submission. Not that the idea of resistance had presented itself in a very tangible form; while the idea of actual separation had probably occurred only to the minds of occasional speculators in the realms of political possibilities. But the prime motive for submission had been removed; and if the alternatives should come to be subordination or separation, there was every probability that a people trained in democratic habits, springing in great part from the sturdiest opponents of oppression, self-reliant, energetic, and adventurous, would choose the second of the two.

Results of the great war.

The great advantage derived by the colonies from their union with the mother country had not been fully counterbalanced by the attendant disadvantages.

The supremacy of the British parliament in the last resort was a matter of minor consequence, because practically it was never exerted. But the standing grievance of the colonies was the interference of parliament in regulating trade.

England meant to have the full benefit of everything produced in America. Therefore, by the "Navigation Acts," all American imports must be from Great Britain; and all exports, to Great Britain; and must be carried in British ships manned by British sailors. *Restrictions on trade.* Hence the market for American goods was limited, and such goods as the colonists did not produce themselves they could only obtain from England, or at best from English colonies. Further, if the trade in the natural products of a colony interfered with any British industry, the colonists were liable to find the export of such goods or even the intercolonial trade in them absolutely prohibited. So it was with wool and woollen goods. More than that, an attempt was actually made to prohibit the manufacture of any sort of iron goods, even for home use; and though the attempt failed in its completeness, such manufactures were very seriously restricted. When the export of such goods as might affect British industries was not absolutely prohibited, duties were laid on them of sufficient severity to prevent their coming into serious competition with British manufactures. So with imports. To encourage the English colonies where sugar was made, heavy duties were laid on sugar and molasses imported from any other source.

The policy of Walpole and of the Pelhams tended to make the least of these restrictions. When British merchants demanded anti-colonial legislation, Walpole gave it them—precisely as he maintained anti-Nonconformist legislation in England, and on the same principles. *Walpole and the colonies.* He satisfied one party by giving and maintaining the laws they demanded: he avoided irritating the other, by looking the other way when the laws were broken. The expansion of the colonial trade was entirely in accordance with his financial theories, but he never tried to force his financial theories on the country. He was content with omitting to enforce in practice the doctrines which his legislation pretended to recognize; and so, without any open contest, his own principles were to a great extent given practical effect. Newcastle, after him, did very much the same—not because there were any theories to which he wished to give effect, but because the easiest course was to acquiesce in what was demanded of him, and, in act, to do nothing which could be left undone without raising a clamour at home.

Hence the trade regulations did not press upon the American colonists severely, because an enormous amount of systematic smuggling was allowed to go on unchecked. The restrictions, indeed, were quite sufficient to be a burden ; sternly enforced, they would have been a very serious burden. But the colonial policy under the two first Georges amounted to this : the colonists were to be let alone as far as possible, and when British mercantile opinion demanded interference, that interference was to be as far as possible nominal.

In view of the coming contest, this is the first point to be noted with regard to the trade relations between mother country and colonies—the legal restrictions had not been rigorously enforced. The second point is—that, so far as they were enforced, it was strictly with a commercial object. The avowed purpose was to benefit English commerce, not to increase the revenue of the state. It is an open question whether the purpose of taxation could affect the constitutional right to levy it ; there is no doubt at all that it could and would affect the willingness of the taxed to submit to it. This Walpole had recognized, and entirely refused to use the colonies directly as a source of revenue.

Thus we find that, when the Peace of Paris was signed, the main motive which had heretofore led the colonists to

Change in the situation. submit to control and interference had disappeared. At the same time, though the constitutional right of England to control and interference had not been denied, practice, if not law, had limited its scope, and enforced it with laxity. Under these circumstances, it should have been evident that, the moment these limitations were abandoned or this laxity gave place to rigour, the colonists, freed from the necessity for English help, would turn restive, and begin to call the whole system in question. It was time for the home government to realise that, by expelling the French, they had placed the colonies in a new relation to themselves, and that the Americans could afford to demand greater freedom and less interference. Instead of that, ministers only bethought them how they might get more out of the colonies than they had done hitherto. The result was, first irritation, then defiance, and finally decisive rupture.

In the islands of Great Britain and Ireland, and on the American continent, the changes which had already taken place or were in progress when George III. ascended the throne have nothing startling about them. They came about in the course of the natural and ordinary political movements.

With India, however, it was different. One is apt to feel as if the commencement and advance of the British dominion there had about them something of the miraculous—as if they were to be counted among the inexplicable mysteries of the magic East. Nevertheless, if we pay due attention to the facts, we find that there as elsewhere the course of events was, in the absence of unlooked-for disturbing factors, necessary and inevitable. *India.*

The death of Aurungzebe was immediately followed by the disintegration of his empire. That empire had itself been won by the sword and held by the sword. The race who reigned at Delhi were foreign Moslem invaders; they were maintained primarily by Moslem troops under Moslem captains; their distant provinces were ruled by viceroys of the same type. The native races who owned their sway were for the most part unwarlike Hindus; different in religion, different in manners, different in thought. So soon as the sceptre of the Moguls fell into a weak hand, each one of the viceroys was ready forthwith to set up for himself; while the Hindu *Break-up of the Mogul empire.*

races of the west—Sikh, Rajput, and Mahratta—who had never been dominated by the Mogul yoke after the manner of the people of the plain of the Ganges, were prepared to assert their independence, and, in their turn, it might be to claim actual ascendency.

Now, if a handful of Englishmen, in the interests of a trading company, had taken upon themselves to attack a mighty empire and had overthrown it, they would have accomplished a feat which would have been more than marvellous. But what actually happened was something quite different. To conquer a nation in arms, and to upset a series of unstable despots, are by no means the same.

Before any conflict arose between the empire and the traders from the West, the empire itself had broken up into a congeries of practically independent kingdoms, not one of which possessed a tolerable capacity for resistance to anything in the shape of an organised attack. In each one, the rulers belonged to a dominant section, alien in race and religion from the mass of the population they ruled, and maintained by mercenary troops. The populations owed no loyalty to their governors; they lacked alike the power and the will to stand up as free peoples, but it was of very little account to them who their rulers might happen to be. The rulers themselves owed their position to their own or their father's or grandfather's skill in managing mercenaries. No dynasty was sure of its seat; no man held his sceptre securely while he had a kinsman or an ambitious soldier in his service. His troops gave him their allegiance until it should seem more convenient to give their allegiance to somebody else, and no longer. They were without the two most elementary qualities required to convert an armed rabble into a fighting force; fidelity to their leaders, and courage to fight a losing battle. They were never prepared to face a bold attack, or to overcome a sturdy resistance. They were capable of training, but they had none.

The power of resistance, therefore, possessed by any one

of the native states which professed allegiance to the padishah was exceedingly small. None of them was in any sense a nation ; none had any idea of unity or loyalty ; none had an army, though all had large numbers of professional fighting men ; none had a ruler of real ability, though, before the collision with the English, there were capable governors in Oudh and in Bengal. A handful of Europeans could disperse twenty times their own numbers of such rabble as Eastern potentates could bring into the field against them—more especially when they had acquired prestige enough to make half the opposing army uncertain whether the other half might not desert at a critical moment.

The rivalry between the French and English traders suggested to Dupleix the idea that the one which could obtain most influence over the native princes would be able to completely get the better of the other. The end was the expulsion of rivals ; the means, influence at the native courts. But the first experiments led to an inversion ; control of the native princes became the end, and the expulsion of European rivals the means. How far even the leaders themselves consciously recognized that this was the case is doubtful. But, as the commercial advantages that would accrue from practical dominion became evident, and the possibility of obtaining it grew clear, the real meaning of Indian policy changed. The expulsion of the rival was to be a step to something more. *French and English.*

We can now trace the steps by which the change was brought about. The first stage was a direct collision between the two companies, in which the friendliness of the Nawab of the Carnatic to the French, carefully fostered by Dupleix, hampered the English. Incidentally Dupleix turned the Nawab against him, and the lesson of the immense superiority of European troops, or of natives trained on the European model, was brought home at once. *Three stages of the contest.*

P

The policy of the second stage was decided thereby. It assured the power of the Europeans, even with their small resources, to turn the scale decisively in an internal contest in a native state. But as there were rival Europeans, neither could afford to let the other gain control ; therefore, if one took a side, the other, perforce, took a side also.

Hence came the third stage. Neither French nor English could get lasting control while the other was present as a counteracting force ; but either without the other could get, not merely influence, but practical dominion. And then Suraj-ud-daulah, by the outrage at Fort William, demonstrated very clearly that mere considerations of safety might demand practical dominion. Thus the first direct blow for actual dominion was struck in Bengal, where the French rivalry did not count ; while in the Deccan, where it did still count, it was being annihilated.

Once dominion began, there was no choice but to extend it. To stand still was impossible. The alternative, each time we took a step forward, was expulsion. In the sense that we did not definitely purpose the conquest of India, the conquest was accidental ; in the sense that each step was designed generally with the knowledge that another step would have to follow, and that the whole chain of events is traceable as link after link of cause and effect, it was not accidental.

The British advance inevitable.

The collision, then, between French and British was the necessary result of their rivalry. Once the collision had taken place, there was no longer room for the two side by side, and the British rule of the ocean assured their ultimate victory. Once the English were without a European rival, with their military prestige established, their native neighbours felt their presence to be a perpetual menace : fresh collisions were inevitable, and the result of each collision, in the long run, certain. What is really remarkable is the good fortune which placed the control of British interests, time after time, in the hands of men who were exceptionally capable and daring, so that they accomplished swiftly and with small means what would otherwise have been done only after frequent reverses, and with a great strain on the national resources. Clive at Arcot and Plassey, Lawrence at Trichinopoly, Forde at Masulipatam, Coote at Wandewash, dared where weaker men would have shrunk, and completed in sixteen years that which with different leaders might not have been done in half a century. For more than a century the English company had remained a trading company, and nothing more: between 1745 and 1761 they turned themselves into the strongest Power in India.

When George I. ascended the English throne, the greater part of India was still under the sway of the Mogul empire, of which the disintegration was only commencing. An English company held settlements and factories here and there on the coast as tenants of the padishah for purposes of trade. When George III. became king, the seal was being set to a new order of things. India was divided up among a collection of despots and confederacies. The Mogul empire existed only in name, and the English trading company was the strongest military power in the peninsula. The Nizam of the Deccan and the Nawab of Bengal were the potentates who held sway over all the East, from the Ganges to Mysore, and each was under the control and practically at the mercy of the Englishmen. What the English Resident willed, that had to be done; and the Resident represented the interests of the company. There was no appeal. Before the name of Clive, armies melted; before the attack of his Englishmen or his Sepoys, native troops became as chaff. The change was sudden, but it was complete. But the new order of things required a new organisation, and it was some little time before the new organisation took a settled form. All over the world, the old order had been upset by a great war. A new order had begun, but it had not yet taken its definite shape.

The new order.

CHAPTER VI.

EUROPE.

1714-1775.

The Anglo-French alliance—The Bourbon union—Fleury and Walpole—The French error—Walpole's error—Tangles of French policy—From Walpole to Pitt—Fleury's successors—Pitt and Choiseul—Subsequent isolation of England—Development of French naval policy—Difficulties and opportunities of France.

THE accession of the House of Hanover in England, and the death of Louis XIV. in France, had placed those two powers

The Anglo-French alliance. in a new relation to each other. In England the reigning dynasty was threatened by an exiled house. In France, the regent was prospective heir to the throne, but his claim was not likely to pass unchallenged, and Spain was the probable challenger. Hence the two courts naturally looked to each other for support. At the same time, England was bound to Austria by her previous alliance, and by the loyalty to the empire of a prince who was Elector of Hanover as well as King of England. Hence the new combination was favourable, on the whole, to Austria, and hostile to Spain, which was left in isolation. Under these circumstances, England and France combined as a fighting force at its maximum strength by the concentration of the first on her navy and of the second on her continental resources.

Thus, when the regency in France terminated, and Walpole's rise to power in England was very shortly followed by Fleury's rise to power in France, Spain's attempts to renovate her navy had failed, and France had taken no heed of her own, so that the British predominance was extremely marked.

At the same time, the principal cause which had brought about the Anglo-French alliance ceased to operate in France; for the possibility of rivalry between the French regent and the Spanish monarch, as claimants to the French throne, vanished when the continuity of the line of Louis XV. became practically assured: and France and Spain began to draw together.

The presumption was that the power which would primarily suffer from such a combination would be Austria, because of the rivalry between Austria and Spain in Italy and Sicily, where each wanted to oust the other. Italy was the great bone of contention, and, **The Bourbon alliance.** from Walpole's point of view, everything was to be gained by preserving the friendship of France, to avoid her granting support to the exiled Stuarts. At the same time, if the Bourbon powers advanced too much at the expense of Austria, England would find herself isolated should the allies subsequently turn upon her. And this prospect was by no means improbable. Between Spain and England there were perpetual causes of irritation. Our possession of Gibraltar and Minorca was a constant insult to Spanish pride, and our illicit commerce with her South American colonies was a recurrent source of heart-burnings. Moreover, though the fact was not clearly recognized, the rivalry of English and French colonies in North America and of English and French companies in India was certain sooner or later to endanger the friendliness of the two countries. Walpole's method, therefore, was to remain on friendly terms with France, but to use all available influence in a pacific support of Austria.

Failing the recognition of the important issues at stake in North America and India, it was clear that France had no present cause for hostility to England, and that Spain had more pressing objects in quarrelling with Austria than with us. Hence, in spite of the warning given by the first secret "family compact," neither Fleury nor Walpole made preparations for a war which, sooner or later, was inevitable. Fleury, like the great majority of French statesmen, never appreciated the enormous importance that would attach to the navy in such an event. Probably, too, he imagined that Walpole's strong pacific tendencies, in combination with the fear of a Jacobite rising, would suffice to make England submissive if the two Bourbon courts became peremptory. Walpole, on the other hand, relied on his own diplomacy and Fleury's love of peace, as well as on his personal regard, to prevent a real crisis ever arising.

Fleury and Walpole.

In the event, the temper of the Spaniards and the English upset the calculations of the statesmen. England and Spain went to war, neither party having at the helm a man who understood the situation. England managed the war badly: under adequate control it might have been brought quickly to a triumphant conclusion. Fortunately, Spain managed no better, while France was quite unable to take an adequate share in a naval war.

In the total inability of France to understand the conditions of a war with England lay our salvation. If France meant to seriously injure England, it was imperative that she should concentrate her energies on matching her opponent on the seas. But she left her navy uncared for, and threw away her energies on continental quarrels. She failed to give efficient aid to Spain; she failed to make use of the Jacobite rising of 1745; while her soldiers were devoting their lives to the war of the Austrian succession, and the establishment of Prussia as a first-class power.

The French blunder.

The want of capacity shown alike by France, England, and Spain in this war is, perhaps, its most remarkable feature. But it appeared tolerably clear that, as long as the incapacity of England was equalled by the incapacity of her foes, she was strong enough to hold her own, and, perhaps, a little more.

The early foreign policy of the Whigs was thoroughly sound. The French alliance was entirely advantageous to England, because it left Spain the only really hostile power on the continent. Austria being also hostile to Spain, an active foreign policy was practicable, for the simple reason that, whenever England and France together chose to interfere, that interference was certain to be decisive : whereas at least one great reason for non-interference is usually the possibility that action will not be decisive. Then, as soon as France and Spain began to draw together, non-intervention, except by friendly and pacific pressure, became the true policy, very ably carried out by Walpole. But with the drawing together of the two Bourbon Powers, the inevitable struggle with France for America and India was also approaching. Walpole was almost certainly right in putting off that struggle as long as possible, but he was wrong in not foreseeing that it was inevitable, and making the necessary preparations ; and wrong, when war was forced upon him for entirely inadequate reasons, in not carrying it to a decisive conclusion. Nevertheless, when it was ended by the peace of Aix-la-Chapelle, England had profited much more than Spain or France, though much less than she should have done. For she was freed from the Jacobite bugbear, while Spain was too much crippled to be formidable again for a long time to come.

Walpole's error.

The inadequacy of the French foreign policy, however, was far more marked. It left the coming strife for the colonies out of count altogether. For the purposes of that contest, it was necessary that France should strengthen her own navy, and aid in the resuscitation of Spain. But at the beginning, the regent, moved by dynastic instead of national considerations, in effect helped to prevent the resuscitation of Spain, in order

Tangles of French policy.

to secure his own succession to the French crown. The Anglo-French alliance secured the position of the French regent, but did nothing to strengthen France; while it did strengthen England and weaken Spain, the one nation in whom France might have found a useful ally in the colonial struggle. And, for the purposes of that struggle, Fleury's policy was not very much better than his predecessors', since he continued to neglect the navy and to devote his attention to furthering the power of the Bourbons in Europe, thus weakening France rather than strengthening her for a duel with England. Hence, at the conclusion of the war, France was left with a quite incompetent fleet to face England alone. She had lost her opportunity, not only of shielding Spain, but also of striking a heavy blow at England's weakest point by supporting the Stuarts; for the reason that her navy was not strong enough for purposes of invasion, while she was devoting her energies to the continental war.

Thus the total result, when the first war had closed, was that Prussia had been established in central Europe as a counterpoise to Austria, while neither of those two powers had any real direct interest in the coming contest between France and England.

The two great statesmen who were at the head of affairs when the war had begun both really lost the control almost From Walpole to Pitt. immediately, and they both died before it had been long in progress. Before the outbreak, each had achieved for his government great diplomatic success; each had displayed much skill in domestic administration. Each was forced to enter on a war which he wished to avoid: neither, with war on his hands, knew how to conduct it; neither saw the issues at stake in the coming war, of which this was only the prelude. But, where they had been wise, their successors were unwise; where they had been blind, their successors were blinder. In England, there were three courses to follow: the best, under the circumstances, a vigorous prosecution of the naval attack, with a minimum of interference on the continent. The next alternative was adopted by Granville (Carteret), with the favour of the king—activity in the continental struggle. The policy was natural and attractive to a Hanoverian prince; but, for a naval power with an immense naval conflict before her, it was thoroughly unsound. But Granville's power was short-lived, and the Pelhams followed the third policy, of doing as little as possible anywhere.

France, on the other hand, was still less fortunate in her new advisers. The favourites of Madame Pompadour plunged headlong down the wrong line of activity, and wasted their energies on a continental war, the results of which were very unlikely to affect France herself materially; while her resources were drained, and her capacity for preparing for a real duel with England was disappearing. Thus, when the great war really broke out, in 1756, England, with all the means for a triumph in her hands, was crippled by the control of a group of oscillating and incapable administrators. She had a great navy, but it was badly officered, badly manned, badly equipped; and ministers knew neither what they intended to do, nor how they were going to do it. The French fleet was as badly off as the English, besides being about half its size; and the French government, though it had the advantage of the English in having made up its mind as to what it meant to do, had resolved to follow the worst method it could adopt under the circumstances. *Fleury's successors.*

At last, not a moment too soon, the one capable Englishman came to the head. William Pitt knew the thing that had to be done, he knew the way in which it must be done, and he selected the right men to do it. And then, when it was already too late, Choiseul came to power in France. He was committed to the wrong, or continental, policy; but he endeavoured to join to that the right, or naval, policy. He spent the rest of the war in learning the unpleasant lesson that it was too late; the *Pitt and Choiseul.*

British mastery had become too overwhelming to be gainsaid. Quebec was taken, Pondicherry dismantled, and no French fleet could put to sea.

Between England and France, the battle for empire overseas was virtually ended, and England had won. England's foot was in India and America: France's was there no longer. England's fleet swept the seas; that of France was powerless. But, in 1763, Choiseul was still at the head of affairs in France, and, in England, Pitt had given place to Bute.

Hence the peace of Paris gave France the opportunity of recuperation; whereas it made England heedless, and, at the same time, isolated her completely. Frederick of Prussia was not over-trustworthy as an ally at the best of times, but he liked his allies to be trustworthy, and his confidence in England had been entirely destroyed by Bute's treatment of him. It was certain that, the next time England had a great war on her hands, she would stand alone. England had humiliated France, and it was certain that, if France got a fair opportunity for revenge, she would take it.

Subsequent isolation of England.

Yet before revenge could be regarded as anything but a dream, it was imperative for France to be properly equipped in the first place, and to have an efficient ally in the second. But England's direct interest in continental alliances, save in view of a prospective French war, practically terminated with the collapse of the last effort of the Stuarts in the 'Forty-five; and no one but Pitt was sufficiently far-sighted to look forward to fresh dangers from France. On the other hand, if England was not moved to make foreign alliances, neither was she moved to make enemies on the continent. It may be very much doubted whether Pitt's purpose of a northern alliance would have been sound policy, because it is at least probable that, in the process of obtaining allies for ourselves, we should have driven some continental power into the arms of France. As matters stood,

France and Spain were alone, as England was alone, and there was certainly no present prospect of a fresh duel. France and Spain in combination were far from being a match for England on the seas.

Pitt, however, never really regained power, and France was able to make a considerable advance towards fitting herself to cope with her enemy once more. There was something in the nature of a national movement for the revival of the French sea power; ships were built, and French sailors learnt again to manage them. She was allowed to strengthen her position in the Mediterranean by taking possession of Corsica, an episode of considerable consequence. Corsica was subject to Genoa. The Corsicans resisted the Genoese, and would probably have offered themselves to England. But England was engrossed with American and domestic affairs, and allowed France to buy the Genoese out, and add Corsica to her own dominions, a few months before Napoleon Bonaparte was born. Whence it befell that Napoleon might have been a British subject, but was, in fact, born a French one: with large results—larger than the mere acquisition of an island in the Mediterranean by one power or the other, though that was important enough. *New naval policy of France.*

But while Choiseul encouraged French naval development, he was seriously hampered by the miserable condition of the national finances. His tenure of power lasted only down to 1769, and the policy of the court became anarchical. The last years of Louis XV. saw France so sunk in European prestige that Russia, Prussia, and Austria deliberately dismembered Poland, and appropriated its portions without so much as pretending to consult her; and when France, feeling the insult deeply, prepared to send a fleet to make a demonstration against Russia, England's threat of sending another counter-demonstration was sufficient to compel her to abandon the design. Nevertheless, despite the flagrant inadequacy of the administration, the naval reconstruction continued; and when Louis XVI. succeeded his grandfather, France, disorganised as were her finances, and, indeed, the whole of her internal affairs, was equipped with a respectable fleet. Her opportunity was not far off.

England, under a series of administrations which committed one blunder after another, had had her time thoroughly occupied with party contests and insubordinate colonists. She was on the verge of a war with these, which would of itself tax her powers severely; and in an alliance with America in revolt lay France's chance for recovering her lost laurels.

BOOK IV.
GEORGE THE THIRD.

CHAPTER I.
BUTE TO NORTH.
1760-1770.

Bute—His antagonism to Pitt—1761 : Fall of Pitt—1762 : Fall of Newcastle—Bute's triumph—1763 : His fall—The Triumvirate—The Bedford ministry—Wilkes—1765 : The Stamp Act—The Regency Bill—The King and the Bedfords—The Rockingham ministry—1766 : Pitt takes office—Pitt becomes Earl of Chatham—His plans—His illness—1767 : Charles Townshend—1768 : Chatham's resignation—Anti-colonial ministry—1769 : Re-appearance of Chatham—1770 : North's ministry.

UNTIL the accession of George III., Pitt, from the moment of his coalition with Newcastle, had been virtually dictator. There was no one to oppose him. He might have colleagues who murmured under the yoke, but they murmured secretly and obeyed orders. Now, however, the brief period of his personal ascendancy was coming to an end.

The general attitude of the new king to the Whig party has been already discussed. For it, the persons most responsible, after the king himself, were his mother, and the favourite, Lord Bute. In season and out of season, the former had always importuned him to " be a king " when he came to the throne; and to make him a king was the object that Bute set before himself.

Without any sort of political or parliamentary knowledge

Bute.

or experience, Bute's deficiencies in these respects had no effect on George's confidence in him. He was sworn of the Privy Council without delay, and at once took care that it should be recognized that he was the king's mouthpiece to ministers and counsellors in the closet; and that any one who wished to find favour with the king must begin by conciliating the favourite. At first, things went smoothly enough. There was a fair appearance of general peace and good will. Newcastle was more than polite to Bute; and Pitt—letting patronage alone—had no immediate cause of collision with him.

But the new *régime* was to commence its attack upon the great commoner. Bute meant to take an active and leading political part, and his chief idea was directly opposed to Pitt's schemes. His theory was that Britain ought not to be mixed up in continental affairs—an excellent theory so long as continental nations pay no attention to British affairs, but rather difficult of realisation in the face of an anti-British coalition. It is true that by this time the aim of Pitt's war policy was in a fair way to be secured; but a part of the scheme by which this purpose had been gained was the support given to Prussia. Year after year Frederick had fought on against odds which were always on the point of overwhelming him. He had fought, encouraged and sustained by England; in doing so, he had been fighting our battles as well as his own; and we were bound by every obligation of honour and good faith not to withdraw our support. Moreover, Pitt believed —and the event proved him entirely right—that France had no intention whatever of retiring on terms at all corresponding to the completeness of her defeat. As things stood, Pitt held that the terms of any peace made should secure us what we had conquered, and leave Prussia as she was before the war. Bute, on the other hand, wanted to have done with the war on such terms as we could get.

His opposition to Pitt.

In the end of March (1761) Parliament was dissolved.

Legge, Chancellor of the Exchequer and a follower of Pitt, was removed; Barrington and Charles Townshend, followers of Bute, were promoted; and Bute himself became Secretary of State, Holderness really resigning to make room for him. It was evident, in the first place, that Bute meant to take a prominent part in the control of the ministerial policy, and, in the second, that he and Pitt would not sit for long in the same cabinet.

The occasion of a trial of strength was not long delayed. As previously narrated, Pitt ascertained that France was preparing a fresh combination with Spain, and, for the sake of delay, was playing at negotiating by offering such terms as he would never accept. *Fall of Pitt.* Pitt insisted that there was only one course—to require immediate acceptance of his own terms, and meanwhile to take time by the forelock and declare war on Spain. Wise as that step certainly would have been, he could not carry so audacious a scheme through a divided cabinet: the colleagues who had supported him before, saw their way to get rid of an ascendency which galled them by taking sides with Bute; and Pitt, with his brother-in-law, Lord Temple, and his few personal adherents, resigned.

Newcastle was the next to go. He resigned when it became certain, in the following year, that Bute did not intend to renew the Prussian subsidy. Bute promptly assumed the Treasurership. But while *Fall of Newcastle.* Pitt, with an unusual magnanimity and remarkable self-restraint, refrained from any such active opposition as would embarrass ministers, Newcastle's anxiety to return to favour held him also back at first, and for a time Bute was supreme; though he was obliged to submit to George Grenville's threat of resignation, and insist on receiving compensation for giving up Havanna, in the treaty which was by this time in full progress.

The Opposition did not continue inactive. Pitt had abstained from embarrassing the government, but he could not allow the peace of Paris to pass without inveighing fiercely against its inadequacy. And Newcastle, finding that his overtures for a reconciliation with Bute were not progressing, became active against him. Nevertheless, the ministers remained unshaken.

It has been observed that a coalition of Pitt with Newcastle was before irresistible; yet it was now possible for government to command sweeping majorities in the teeth of both of them. The explanation, however, is not far to seek. Bute was applying Newcastle's own methods of organisation. He started with the support of the Tories, and of all who held high monarchical principles: for the king was at one with him. He commanded the votes of the Scotch members, because he was a Scot himself, and his influence was rapidly introducing Scotchmen into lucrative posts. He secured Fox by giving him the lead of the House of Commons, and, with his assistance, bribery and corruption were practised on an immense scale. Offices large and small were cleared of opponents, or *protégés* and connections of opponents: the system of the "spoils to the victors" was carried out with unparalleled virulence and pettiness of detail. The king made opposition a personal matter. Places were filled with men who, as a matter of policy, or, in a few cases, of conscience, were prepared to give unqualified support to the king; or who, like Fox and George Grenville, from jealousy or other motives, could be relied on not to combine with the Opposition chiefs. Thus, for the time being, the court had matters its own way.

<small>Bute triumphant.</small>

But this could not last. Though Bute might command votes in parliament, outside the House his measures provoked such a storm of unpopularity as he could not face. It was bad enough for a minister with neither experience nor knowledge to have ejected the popular hero and other statesmen of reputation. The vehemence of the animosity he displayed did not improve his position; and the taunts against him as the princess dowager's favourite, and as a

Scot who was filling his countrymen's pockets at the expense of Englishmen, appealed to the baser feelings of the multitude. In April, 1763, he resigned, and with him Fox (who retired in dudgeon to the Upper House as Lord Holland), and his Chancellor of the Exchequer Dashwood—author of the cider tax, one of the most detested measures of the administration. *His fall.*

Bute had no intention of withdrawing his hand from the manipulation of the political strings, when he resigned. His purpose was to avoid public responsibility and the odium attaching to his policy, by putting up other ministers to carry it out. The leaders he selected were George Grenville, a man of forms and precedents and of considerable administrative experience; Lord Halifax; and Lord Egremont, the son of that Sir William Wyndham who had for a long time been recognized by the Tories as their leader. But the "Triumvirate," as this ministry was called, was by no means inclined to give Bute all he wanted. *The Triumvirate.*

The Triumvirate was broken up by the death of Lord Egremont, in August; in the mean time, Bute had found that his own scheme for managing affairs was unworkable. The conflict with Wilkes had commenced, and although in this matter ministers had acted with the favourite, he felt that he could not control them. Under these circumstances he wished to be rid of them, and it is remarkable that the only means he could find were to advise the king to send for Pitt.

Pitt's terms, however, involved the return to office of the principal Whigs who had been driven out, and the complete subordination of the court party. This was more than the king could submit to, and the result was the formation of the Bedford ministry—a combination of Whigs who had broken with the party, and court nominees; but marked by the complete withdrawal of Bute in fact, though not, according to popular impressions, from active interference. *The Bedford ministry.*

Q

Yet ministers seemed fated to seize every available opportunity to make themselves unpopular. Their attack on Wilkes, **Wilkes.** ending in his expulsion from parliament by a vote of the House of Commons, for publishing a virulent comment on the King's Speech, in the famous "Number 45" of his newspaper the *North Briton*, made a martyr of him. Grenville, among his expedients for raising money, devised the plan of laying the Stamp Act on the American **The Stamp Act.** colonies, and thereby kindling a flame not to be quenched until the British empire was shorn of half a continent. The king fell ill; it became necessary to introduce a Regency Bill to secure the proper nomination of a regent in case of necessity; and the course ministers pursued produced a breach between them and the king, which made any real reconciliation impossible.

The questions involved in the affairs of Wilkes and of the American colonies require separate and consecutive treatment to be dealt with fully. The personal question had hardly less to do with the fate of ministers. The point of it was this—the Bill required the selection of the regent from **The Regency Bill.** among "members of the royal family." Was this to be taken as including or excluding the Dowager Princess of Wales? Ministers were bent on her exclusion, for they believed that, if she were named, Bute must recover his ascendancy. They proposed to define the words as including the queen and the descendants of the late king; and they obtained the royal assent by declaring that otherwise the Commons were certain to take the step of giving effect to the same view by the much more insulting method of excluding the princess by name. When the Commons proceeded instead to deliberately add her name to the list, by an overwhelming majority, the king was naturally furious with the ministers who had deluded him into assenting to her exclusion.

Thus, in 1765, the burden of Grenville was becoming intolerable. Hitherto, the court party had proved a failure except in so far as it had destroyed the general cohesion of the Whigs. The Bedford party was violently unpopular alike in the country and at court. In his perplexity, the king consulted the Duke of Cumberland, and, in consequence, sent again for Pitt. It was a golden opportunity, but Pitt's evil angel destroyed it. Lord Temple at this time became reconciled to his brother, George Grenville, and refused to enter a ministry except on the basis of a Grenville combination. Pitt would not form a ministry without Temple, or with Grenville. *Strength of the Bedfords.*

To his intense mortification, the king was compelled to recall Grenville and Bedford on their own terms. Those terms were, the cessation of all communication with Bute, the dismissal of Bute's brother, and the appointment of Lord Granby as Commander-in-Chief—probably as an attack on the Duke of Cumberland. The king gave way, but did not attempt to conceal his ill-feeling or his readiness for a reconciliation with the Whig nobility. When Bedford, fancying that the king was completely beaten, and had no choice but submission, proceeded to read him a private lecture couched in decidedly insolent terms, George felt that the yoke must be thrown off at any cost.

Once more he sent for Pitt. Once more Pitt was ready, but the scheme was wrecked by Temple's refusal. The king was driven to try the Whig houses without the great commoner: and the Rockingham administration was formed.

Lord Rockingham was selected as leader mainly because he bore a high personal character and was possessed of much tact. He had no gifts for debate, and could scarcely be called a statesman, though endowed with the ordinary share of common sense. But he had for his private secretary a man who possessed the brilliant talents which he lacked himself. Edmund Burke was hardly a man who could ever have led a party—he lived too much above the intellectual level of parliament, and "thought of convincing while they thought of dining." But Burke was the sole *The Rockingham ministry.*

ministerialist of transcendent ability, and he was only a private secretary. The leader of the party in the Commons was Conway—a man whose honour and integrity were beyond cavil, while his abilities as a leader were of the smallest. Very much the same thing might be said of every prominent member of the administration, with the additional disadvantage that nearly all were in the Upper House.

Nevertheless, this weak administration, receiving only a qualified support from Pitt, and much opposition from the court party, who, about this time, came to be known as "the King's Friends," is distinguished for having passed excellent measures during its brief term of office. The use of general warrants was declared to be illegal. The cider tax was repealed ; so was the American Stamp Act : while the right of parliament in law to tax the colonies was affirmed by a Declaratory Act. It was on this latter point that Pitt differed from ministers : and, in point of law, there is no doubt that they were right and he was wrong ; for, though taxation of the colonies by the British parliament was a violation of the spirit of the constitution, it was in strict accordance with the letter of the charters. Pitt approved of the repeal of the Stamp Act, but protested against the Declaratory Act. The king and the King's Friends protested against the repeal of the Stamp Act, as well as against the declaration that general warrants were illegal.

In spite of the good work accomplished, the ministry was too weak to last. The unqualified accession of Pitt would have rendered it powerful, but Pitt would not join. He was now resolved to have nothing to do with Newcastle, who was still in office ; and was, in fact, bent on his scheme of doing without party. Rockingham again and again begged for his support, and let it be clearly understood that the party desired him as their leader, and would defer to him in that capacity, though they could hardly assent to a wholesale redistribution of offices. However, they could not go on as they were, with no one of sufficient weight in the cabinet to control it. In July, 1766, the king sent for Pitt.

Once more Temple declined to join the ministry on any practicable terms. He demanded to be on an equality with Pitt, and Pitt would not have such divided power. The result was a complete estrangement, and Pitt composed his ministry according to his own ideas. Grafton, Conway, and one or two others of the Rockinghams remained; and various posts were given to personal followers of Pitt, or to the "King's Friends." *Pitt takes office.*

But the great commoner's return to power had come too late. He was wracked with disease, and his nerves were so desperately shaken, that he can scarcely at this time be regarded as of really sane mind. It was evident that he was physically incapable of steady attention to business, or of properly fulfilling the functions of Leader of the House. He resolved therefore to take a peerage. But, whatever might have been the result if he had remained in the Commons, retaining the nominal leadership while leaving the practical work to subordinates, this step meant ruin. Apart from the peculiar conditions, no doubt it would have been in every way a reasonable and natural proceeding : if any man could claim to have deserved the recognized reward for great services rendered, he could do so; his physical incapacity for the perpetual warfare of the Commons justified it ; no one could say that the desire for a peerage had influenced his political conduct. But there were two reasons which rendered the step a fatal one—his power rested on his popularity outside parliament, and on the peculiar character of his eloquence inside. However unreasonably, his acceptance of the peerage shattered this popularity ; while his eloquence was utterly unsuited to the atmosphere of the Upper House. It is quite possible that it would have been wholly impracticable for him to remain in the Commons at the head of a party ; it is quite certain *The earldom of Chatham.*

that, within England, though not on the continent, all the prestige and all the practical strength of a Pitt administration vanished when its chief became the Earl of Chatham.

The policy which Chatham intended to initiate, whether altogether wise or not, shows at least how immensely larger the view of national interests which he took was than that of the crowd of politicians around him. A more efficient government for India, the better government of Ireland, a more liberal treatment of the colonies, a bold foreign policy,—these were the subjects which occupied his mind. The transference of the Indian government from the East India Company to the State was one design over which he was brooding. A great alliance of the northern powers, which should paralyse the aggressive aims of the Family Compact between France and Spain, was a second. He desired for the colonies the utmost expansion, and the largest recognition of the rights of the colonials as fellow-citizens on equal terms with the parent stock. His theory of our trade relations was economically unsound, being based on the doctrine of giving preference to the colonial markets ; but it is difficult to prove that what is unsound economy may not, under special circumstances, be good statesmanship. The good will of the colonies might be worth paying for ; and, at the crisis which was approaching, worth paying a considerable price.

Chatham's policy, however, was destined never to take effect. The ministry, to begin with, were not welded together by any strong bonds. The minor offices were filled from very heterogeneous groups. The Prime Minister's dictatorial tone made individuals and groups alike restive. The strain of prerogative involved when, to prevent a threatened famine, an embargo was laid on the export of corn by an order in council before parliament met, gave a handle to the Opposition. When Christmas came, Chatham's name was great enough to keep the government still strong, but the elements of disintegration were there. In January, 1767,

Chatham himself was prostrated, and utterly incapable of
taking any part whatever in business ; while the *Chatham*
ablest orator on the Treasury bench, Charles *incapaci-*
Townshend, now Chancellor of the Exchequer, in *tated.*
the teeth of the Prime Minister's known views as to the
colonies, proceeded to lay certain minor import duties upon
them which were absolutely certain to produce violent irritation. Chatham remained utterly incapable even of discussion
in private ; and practically the Duke of Grafton became
the head of a singularly unmanageable ministry.

In September Townshend died, and Lord North was
received into the ministry as Chancellor of the Exchequer ;
while the retirement of Conway and Worthington made
room for a batch of the Bedford following.

A general election, remarkable for extraordinary venality,
took place early in the following year (1768). Personal dissensions in the cabinet resulted in the removal of *Chatham*
Shelburne from office, and in October Chatham *resigns.*
himself resigned, partly, at least, as a consequence. The
reappearance of Wilkes, his return at the head of the poll as
member for Middlesex, and the determined refusal of the
parliamentary majority to let him take his seat, absorbed
much of the attention of the government ; while, thanks to
Chatham's forced seclusion from public affairs, France was
allowed without active protest to acquire Corsica from the
Genoese.

Meantime, in America, Townshend's import duties had
revived the ill-feeling which, created by the Stamp Act, had
been only in part allayed by the repeal of that
measure. In Boston especially feeling ran very *America.*
high, partly owing to the unpopularity of the governor ;
and it seemed by no means unlikely that there would be
armed resistance offered to the officials of the government.
Bedford's proposal to transfer the trial of rioters from
America to England was a fresh incitement to anger. In
May, 1769, Grafton proposed to the cabinet that Townshend's

obnoxious measure should be repealed. He was strongly opposed by Lord North; and the cabinet, by a majority of one, decided on a merely partial withdrawal.

In July of this year, Chatham reappeared on the political scene. A violent attack of gout had served to relieve his disease, and his intellectual prostration was over. He returned, to find that his plans for Ireland had been dropped; that, in place of his scheme for Indian administration, government had arranged to accept a tribute from the company; that no progress had been made on the continent in the direction of alliances, while France had been allowed to strengthen her hands by the acquisition of Corsica; that America had been roused to fresh bitterness by measures as irritating as the Stamp Act and of even less pecuniary value; that, at home, the House of Commons was overriding the constitutional rights of electors in the matter of Wilkes; and that his chief personal adherents were no longer in office. His own position was, at the same time, somewhat altered by a reconciliation with the Grenvilles.

Reappearance of Chatham.

Parliament met in the beginning of 1770. Chatham forthwith attacked the action of ministers, more particularly in regard to Wilkes. Camden's strong support of him made his removal from the chancellorship necessary: within the ministry Lord Granby continued to stand by him; Rockingham joined in the attack, and Grafton resigned.

In regard to the colonies, and in regard to Wilkes, the king was entirely on the side of the ministers. To form an administration with Chatham or Rockingham at its head would have been to own himself finally beaten in the attempt to recover the political influence of the crown. This was more than he would do, and Lord North, reluctantly, and with the worst prospects of holding the Government together, became Prime Minister.

North's ministry.

CHAPTER II.

KING, PARLIAMENT, AND PEOPLE.

1760-1774.

Ministerial fluctuations—Break-up of the Whigs—Corruption—The king and his ministers—Parliamentary representation—Wilkes and liberty—1763: *The North Briton*—Number 45—Arrest of Wilkes on a general warrant—His release—He is expelled from the House—Attitude of the king—1768-69: The Middlesex elections—Effects of the contest—1771: Attitude of the City of London—Restriction of privileges—The press and the law of libel—Increasing power of the press—Junius.

THE early years of George III.'s reign are so crowded with brief administrations; new names flicker in and out and in again in such unexpected combinations; serious problems of statesmanship turn on measures or on personalities of a character so contemptible in themselves—that the whole period is puzzling and confusing, and it is only by first mastering those irritating details that we can clear our minds for the consideration of the important questions which were in course of solution. {Ministerial fluctuations.}

Briefly, the period falls into these divisions: First, the fall of Pitt under the attack of the court party led by Bute, and the ascendancy of the favourite. Then, the fall of the Favourite and the ascendancy of the Grenville and Bedford combination. Next, the sensible but weak administration of Rockingham. Finally the Grafton administration formed by Pitt, but rendered amorphous by the loss of its head within a few months of its formation, resulting in a sort of hand-to-mouth ministry, until the resignation of Grafton and the formation of North's government.

Throughout this time there were so many sections which were incapable of cordial co-operation that no stability was possible. The very mal-administration of these years gives them their importance. The close association of Chatham with the Rockinghams, or his active control of the Grafton government, would have averted the blunders that were committed, and perhaps have had far-reaching results of a positive kind. As it turned out, the blunders themselves were responsible for very far-reaching results indeed. Pitt was still, as he had been when he came into power in the last reign, the one man who could save the country ; but partly from ill-health, partly from the dictatorial manner which prevented co-operation, partly from the adverse influence of Temple, the interval during which he really held the reins was too brief for him to effect anything, and nearly everything which should have been done was left undone or made impossible, while most of the things that were done were thoroughly injurious.

At home, the features of the period are : the attempt of the crown to assert itself against the dominion of parties or individuals ; the disruption of the Whigs ; and the attempts of parliament to override popular rights in the interest of parliamentary privilege.

The disruption of the Whigs requires little elucidation. Chatham and his personal followers formed one section ; the

Disruption of the Whigs. Rockinghams, representing the theory of party government, another ; the Grenvilles and Bedfords, another,—the section of privilege and precedent.

By fostering this disruption, the king endeavoured to make the court party the controlling power in the State, and the court party meant those who were prepared to support the king under all circumstances. If they had set about the task of breaking up the established party system

with a view to the reform of the abuses which attended it,
the king might have become a popular champion. Unfortunately for the prospects of reform—fortunately, perhaps,
for the safety of the constitution—they did nothing of the
kind, endeavouring instead, by an extension and adaptation
of the existing abuses, to increase the power of the crown.
Bute himself was practically expelled from the royal counsels
by Grenville and Bedford, but we cannot wonder at the
popular conviction that he was continuing to influence the
king behind the scenes ; for the methods and doctrines which
Bute had instilled remained the methods and doctrines of
his pupil when the instructor was no longer there.

Walpole is commonly, though not altogether justly,
credited with having reduced parliamentary corruption to
an organised system. Newcastle had carried it
to even greater lengths than Walpole. But when   *Corruption.*
Bute attacked the Whigs, he used their own weapons with a
shamelessness which they had never matched. Twenty-five
thousand pounds were said to have passed in bribes in the
course of a single day. Places were not merely jobbed—
they were emptied and refilled wholesale, without pretence
of any motive other than political or personal animus, and
the expectation of votes to be gained. Political venality
was encouraged, instead of being checked. The court
having the means for corruption, and for the control and
manipulation of votes, was entirely in favour of the system
under which those means could be freely employed. The
greater the body of really free and independent electors in
any constituency, the harder it would be to manipulate.
The greater the proportion of rotten boroughs to constituencies with a genuine representation, the easier would be
the control of parliamentary majorities.

Thus the immediate consequence of Bute's ascendancy
was a largely increased corruption. Constituencies were
bought ; votes were bought ; the judicious voter received
his reward ; the independent expression of opinion was

punished, and the innocent friends, connections, and dependents of the recalcitrant were dismissed from their posts.

After Bute's fall matters were never carried to quite the same point of extravagance in this respect. But some examples of the prevalent condition of affairs are worth noting. General Conway was dismissed from his command on purely political grounds, though he was reinstated by the Rockingham ministry ; and Grafton and Rockingham were similarly deprived of the lord-lieutenancies of their counties. A little later, Chesterfield wanted to find a borough for a connection of his own, but was informed that the current price was from four to five thousand pounds. The Corporation of Oxford offered to re-elect the member for that city if he would pay off a corporation debt : they were compelled to apologise at the bar of the House, and were committed to prison ; they passed the time of their confinement in arranging another satisfactory bargain.

This condition of affairs shows how the organisation of a court party without popular support was practicable. It was not till the formation of North's government that that party really occupied a position of decisive control ; but the Rockingham ministry was the only one whose measures were not, on the whole, in accordance with the king's political views. The antagonism between the Bedfords and the king was entirely personal. Grenville and the king were at one on the questions of general warrants and American taxation. As soon as Chatham sank into temporary seclusion, the king found the Grafton cabinet carrying out his own views. The fact was, that, although there was no one among the King's Friends of sufficient weight or ability to be a moderately efficient minister, they were strong enough as a body to force the hand of each successive government.

The king and his ministers.

The House of Commons being constituted, and its members elected, on the principles described above, it is evident that it was not an assembly for the expression of the will of the people. It expressed the will of the owners of pocket boroughs, of the purchasers of rotten boroughs, and of the independent electors in the remaining constituencies. It was consequently to the interest of the crown, of most of the Whig nobility, and of people generally who were wealthy enough to buy seats, to support the existing system; and it was equally to the interest of all their nominees to do so. The man who owed his seat to the favour of the court or of a duke, was not anxious to find himself reduced to a precarious reliance on popular votes. Hence it followed that, within the House itself, as well as among the most powerful sections of society, there was a preponderant resolution to make members as much as possible a close body: to make them insist on their privileges, and press to the utmost the power of the House to control admissions to membership, to place members above the law, and to claim for itself as a body the power of overriding the law. It followed also that, both in the House and out of it, all the same sections were flatly opposed to any sort of reform in the constitution of the House itself. At the same time, constituencies like the City, which really elected representative members, and could not be put up to auction by boroughmongers, were by no means in favour of the existing condition of affairs. *Parliamentary representation.*

The whole of the struggle between Wilkes on the one side, and the king and ministers on the other, turns on two points affecting the privileges of the House as opposed to the rights of the people. In the first part of the contest, ministers endeavoured to silence comments; in the second, they endeavoured to establish the practical right of the House to annul the free election of a member obnoxious to the parliamentary majority. The chief actor, Wilkes himself, was an unprincipled adventurer, clever, but wholly unscrupulous in his scurrility, and without any sort of pretence to statesmanship, or title to respect on account of either abilities or character. But whereas, when *Wilkes and liberty.*

the struggle began, the debates in the House were secret in so far as they were not allowed to be published ; when it ended, they were so no longer. When it began, election petitions were tried by the House, and decided in favour of the candidate who was on the side of the majority : when it ended, they were tried by a reasonably impartial committee. When it began, comment on the action of ministers was liable to be punished by distorting the law, or even overriding it by a resolution of the House : when it ended, comment was practically free. Finally, at the close of the struggle an agitation had been set on foot for reforming the constitution of the House, which was countenanced by Chatham, and would fairly have taken effect under the younger Pitt, had not the events connected with the French Revolution intervened to defer the whole question till the fight of the great Reform Bill. Throughout the contest, the king and the court party were against Wilkes : so, in the earlier stages, were Grenville and the party of privilege ; though, at the end of his career, Grenville, being in opposition, resisted ministers, and was himself the author of the measure transferring election petitions from the House to a committee. Throughout, Chatham and the Rockinghams supported the position of Wilkes, regarding the persecution of him as an infringement on the liberty of the subject and the rights of electors ; though much of the force of their support was weakened by the impossibility of feeling any personal sympathy for an individual so offensive.

The whole story is so vividly illustrative of the parliamentary conditions of the time, and of the personal characters of many leading persons, to which, in great part, the blunders of successive administrations were due,—it goes so far towards rendering intelligible the pettiness and the general absence of broad political principles which were responsible for the disasters of the reign,—that it is worth detailing with more fulness than the intrinsic importance of the contest would justify. The principles involved were of great moment, but the issue was never really doubtful. It is the history of an attempt at reaction which was doomed to failure, but was possible because of a political disintegration which had other and disastrous results.

John Wilkes had become member for Aylesbury in 1757, but he had made no mark as a debater, being chiefly known for the extreme profligacy of his character, and more particularly for his connection with the "Medmenham Brotherhood," an association of kindred spirits, which included Dashwood (Bute's Chancellor of the Exchequer), and other persons of more notoriety than note. Failing to obtain a lucrative post under government, and attributing the failure to Bute, Wilkes resolved to attack that nobleman in the *rôle* of patriot. Accordingly, in 1762, he started a periodical entitled *The North Briton*, chiefly devoted to abuse of Bute and the Scotch in general. He was encouraged by Temple, but openly denounced by Pitt, who never hesitated to espouse an unpopular cause, and constantly spoke in the highest terms of the services rendered by the Scotch regiments. *<small>The North Briton.</small>*

The North Briton was more open in its criticisms than had hitherto been deemed advisable, ministers being attacked by name without the formal veil of dashes and stars. But the crisis was brought on by the forty-fifth number.

Bute's resignation, in 1763, was followed promptly by the closing of the parliamentary session. The king's speech, on this occasion, was the object of Wilkes's attack. It was by no means a particularly able attack, but it was exceedingly virulent, and it had what the writer no doubt chiefly desired, an intensely exasperating effect. Grenville, now at the head of the ministry, and not as yet estranged from Bute, resolved to punish Wilkes. The resolve was foolish; the measures taken to carry it out were perhaps illegal, and certainly calculated to enlist the whole force of popular sympathy on the side of *The North Briton*. A general warrant was issued for the seizure of the authors, *<small>General warrant.</small>*

printers, and publishers of the obnoxious pamphlet, without specifying names. Wilkes was arrested, and his papers seized and examined, before any official proof existed that he was the author of the pamphlet in question. Moreover, at the commencement of his confinement, he was not allowed the use of pen and ink, or to receive visits.

This stringency was promptly relaxed, and, within a week, Wilkes was liberated by order of Chief Justice Pratt (afterwards Lord Camden), on the ground that, as a member of parliament, he was exempt from arrest, except for treason, felony, or a breach of the peace—under none of which heads could the pamphlet be brought. Grenville had given Wilkes a magnificent advertisement; had himself appeared as a representative of tyranny, and made nothing of his motion; but had given his opponent a fresh popularity, while his own unpopularity and that of Bute were much increased.

Instead of taking the lesson to heart, Grenville resolved to crush Wilkes; and the campaign opened in November, when the new session began. Ministers moved in the Commons that "Number Forty-five" was a "false, scandalous, and seditious libel, tending to traitorous insurrections," and should be burned by the common hangman. In the House of Lords a certain profane and obscene production of Wilkes's pen (the " Essay on Woman," a parody of Pope's " Essay on Man "), which had never been published at all, was produced by his quondam friend, Lord Sandwich, to whom it was dedicated, and an address praying for the prosecution of its author was carried. Wilkes, owing to the results of a duel, betook himself to Paris, and the House of Commons voted his expulsion. Not long after, he was outlawed for not appearing to answer the indictment against him; but, in the interval, the riots attending the attempt to burn " Number Forty-five " publicly attested the odium ministers had incurred; and the award of heavy damages for false imprisonment was received with popular rejoicings. Ministers, however, took the opportunity to pass, in both

Expulsion of Wilkes.

Houses, a resolution contravening the decision of the Chief Justice, and affirming that privilege did not protect a member in the case of writing and publishing seditious libels. And they maintained their doctrine of general warrants being legal; though a subsequent resolution, passed by the Rockingham ministry, established the opposite view.

Wilkes was beaten for the time being. The sentence of outlawry kept him out of the country; and it was not till the dissolution of parliament in 1768 that the fight was renewed, under different conditions. George Grenville was now in opposition, and the struggle was really between the court and the demagogue; for, from the very beginning, the king himself was as thoroughly bent as any of his ministers on crushing the author of "Number Forty-five." It seems impossible to attribute George's attitude to anything but personal animus. He appears to have regarded the expressions used about the king's speech as personal reflections on himself, in spite of the fact that the speech from the throne was constitutionally recognized as being the utterance, not of the monarch, but of his ministers, and was distinctly so treated in the comment. Considering the relations between the king and Bute, Wilkes's violent animosity against the favourite would doubtless have justified very strong resentment on the king's part, and this personal animus was George's chief motive. It is impossible to defend his line of action on the score of Wilkes's character, seeing that Sandwich was notoriously at least his equal in infamy, and yet was treated by George with some favour. *The king's attitude.*

The dissolution decided Wilkes to return to public activity. Although still an outlaw, he stood for the City, where he was defeated, and then for Middlesex, where he was returned at the head of the poll. The question immediately arose whether, being an outlaw, he could be elected. The point was set aside by Lord Mansfield declaring the outlawry itself null and void *The Middlesex elections.*

R

on a purely technical ground. But the verdicts previously given against him were confirmed, and he was sentenced to two years' imprisonment and a fine.

Wilkes had surrendered himself; but all these proceedings were accompanied by violent rioting, in the course of which some half-dozen persons were killed, and several more wounded by the soldiery. As the troops employed happened to be Scots, the popular indignation at the "massacre" was the greater.

Parliament met in November. Wilkes's friends at once raised the cry that his imprisonment was a breach of privilege, as he was already a member when arrested. His enemies were equally prepared to contest the validity of his election. To complicate the situation, Lord Weymouth, as Secretary of State, had written to the Surrey magistrates with regard to applying for military assistance in case of threatened riots; and Wilkes had published this letter with comments, and had further published certain comments on Lord Mansfield. The House of Commons proceeded to vote that the former publication was an "insolent libel," and the latter a "groundless aspersion." In February (1769), Barrington moved the expulsion of Wilkes, on the old grounds, and the motion was carried by a large majority.

To assert that Wilkes was legally incapable of representing a constituency was clearly impossible. Therefore the House had fallen back on the expedient of expelling him for acts which had not legally incapacitated him. There was no manner of logical justification for this course, which was equivalent to a claim on the part of the House of Commons to expel any member on the general ground that the majority wished to be rid of him. The constituency which had deliberately chosen Wilkes was furious, and re-elected him without delay. The House replied by declaring that an expelled member was incapable of re-election. No other candidate would come forward, and Wilkes was elected again, to be again ejected. Then the government found a candidate, Colonel Luttrell, to put up against him; and when Wilkes was returned, the House declared that the votes cast for him were void, and that Luttrell was duly elected.

Wilkes was excluded, and the court had its way; but it hardly benefited by the victory. Ministers had an extra vote in the House, and an obnoxious member had been removed; but at the cost of a wholly un- constitutional extension of the powers of the House of Commons, of overriding law, and of rousing the fiercest enmity. The House had claimed the right of the majority to exclude a legally elected member, who laboured under no incapacity, in defiance of the electors. Wilkes in parliament would have been harmless; as it was, he was elevated into a martyr of the cause of free election, as he had already been made a martyr of the cause of a free press. When the court party expelled the member for Middlesex, they practically left themselves no course but to maintain his exclusion at all costs; but, in doing so, they set at defiance the principles of liberty, by in effect setting a party vote in the Lower House above the law of the land. The Opposition was, indeed, far too strong, and the Court was too conscious of its own weakness, to allow any great danger of such reactionary principles being carried to great lengths; but the appearance of the danger immensely strengthened the hands of agitators and demagogues, besides giving a palpable and manifest basis to legitimate demands for reform. *Effects of the contest.*

The antagonism between the House and the people was marked, not only by the action of the Middlesex electors, but also by that of the City of London, which came forward as champion of Wilkes. He was made an alderman. The city was active in presenting petitions and resolutions against the action of ministers, showing small respect even for the king's person in the course of the agitation; and in 1771, after Wilkes was released, it came into violent collision with the House, over *The City of London.*

the question of an arrest ordered by the Commons, but prevented by Lord Mayor Crosby as a breach of the City charters. Crosby, with Alderman Oliver, who had supported him, was committed to the Tower, and the judges upheld the committal. But the proceedings were highly significant of the tendency on the part of the House to strain its privileges beyond endurance, and of the tension of feeling amongst those who were opposed to it.

Although Chatham was in favour of considerable parliamentary reform, by increasing the representation of the counties and of growing commercial centres, the hour for extensive changes had not arrived. At the same time, the feeling roused by the efforts of ministers to strain privilege resulted in sundry minor curtailments of privilege. The practice of assuming judicial functions, and punishing offences against ministers without recourse to the ordinary tribunals, ceased. The extension of the protection of privilege to the household of a member was abolished. Instead of the House deciding election petitions by a party vote, the decision of such cases was transferred to a committee sworn to give judgment in accordance with the evidence.

The second question of main importance in connection with Wilkes was the position of the press: and the result of the whole struggle was a very considerable extension of the freedom of the press and of its powers. When the fight began, the House conducted its debates in private, and the king and ministers alike were bent on restricting freedom of comment by every available means; and especially by the unsparing application of the law of libel. To this end, the resolution declaring that privilege did not extend to cases of libel was passed. Moreover it was laid down by Lord Mansfield, and had been held by Lord Hardwicke and the most eminent lawyers, with the almost sole exception of Lord Camden, that in a case of libel the jury could only decide on the fact of

publication, the motives and justification being entirely in
the decision of the judge. This view reduced the position
of the jury to futility; while it was hardly possible for a
judge's decision to be accepted as wholly free from bias. It
was considered that prosecutions were malevolently instituted
by government, and consequently juries did everything in
their power to prevent the prosecutions taking effect,
regarding the doctrine of the judge's powers in the matter
as a means for carrying out the wishes of ministers. Hence
they were prepared to acquit in defiance of evidence, and
prosecutions for libel failed which would otherwise have
taken effect. The result was that Lord Mansfield's legal
maxim really tended to protect libellers, and encourage
violent writing on the popular side, instead of checking it—
very much as excessive harshness in criminal law defeats its
own ends by leading juries to refuse to convict. It is
probable that the virulent attacks of Junius would have
been modified, and the damage done by him to the popular
estimation of the king, of Grafton, of Mansfield, of Bedford
and others, considerably diminished, but for the consciousness that in any prosecution the jury were certain to do their
utmost to shield the libeller.

Thus the practical effect of the attempt of ministers to
apply the law for the purpose of suppressing criticism
produced a belief that they were ready to strain the law to
curtail legitimate freedom of speech and comment. The
press was strong enough, and ministers weak enough, to
give the ultimate victory in the struggle to the former,
though the latter might now and then succeed in inflicting
some damage on an individual. And the practical outcome
was a considerable increase in the virulence, the ability, and
the influence of the press; of which the most marked
example is to be found in the letters of Junius.

CHAPTER III.

THE BREACH WITH AMERICA.

1763–1774.

The bond with colonies—Effects of the past war—Influence of distance —1765: George Grenville and the Stamp Act—Theory of Taxation—Mutual obligations—Claims and counter-claims— Action of the colonists—1766: Repeal of the Stamp Act—Difficulties of the problem—Logic *versus* compromise—Grenville's want of tact—The standing army—The Rockingham concessions —1767: Townshend's new taxes—Renewed irritation—Strength of the anti-colonial party—Disturbances at Boston—1773: The Whately correspondence—Repressive measures—The Quebec Act —Unanimity of the colonies—The Continental Congress—1774: Preparations for war—Action of the British Opposition—North's conciliatory bill—Its futility.

THE confusion of affairs in parliament, following on the accession of George III., has necessitated a more detailed treatment of them than their inherent importance would seem to warrant. The same thing can hardly be said of the subject which now comes before us—the relations of the mother country and her colonies during this period.

Politicians are disagreed in their theories of colonisation. Some hold that, as soon as a colony is capable of

Colonial union. autonomy, it should as a matter of expediency, and will as a matter of fact, set up for itself, severing all connection with the mother country. Others maintain that there is no natural bar to the maintenance of union, and that union may be, and ought to be, a source of strength to both colony and mother country. The course of events which led to the great disruption of the English-speaking peoples affords very insufficient data for proving either thesis. The disruption itself was precipitated by a series of blunders of an entirely wanton character: and these were due to the then universally prevalent theory, that colonies exist for the convenience of the parent state— not as partners, but as dependencies. Under the conditions, separation was inevitable ; but the circumstances afford no proof that it would have been so, had the theory of subordination given place in the minds of statesmen to that of partnership.

The British Empire had gained enormously by the French war, at the cost of tremendous expenditure ; and to no section of the Empire was the gain so palpable as to the American colonists. When the war began, there was a foreign power to their north and to their south, seeking to cut off completely their expansion westwards. At the close of the war, practically no European power but England had a footing on the continent. The colonists were free from the fear of any foe but the red man : and the red man was incapable of organisation. This gain had come to the colonists with the minimum of exertion and expenditure on their part. The armaments had been maintained out of the British treasury, and most of the fighting had been done by British soldiers. Consequently when the Peace of Paris was signed, the colonies were full of loyalty to the mother country, and of gratitude to Pitt, who had made their cause his own.

Effects of the war.

Protection, however, had in fact been given so efficiently that it was no longer in demand. Habit and gratitude in combination might have induced the colonies to go on paying for it : but, unfortunately, the British government now endeavoured to raise the price ; gratitude gave place to irritation, and habit is not very strong in a young country. Compromise became impossible, loyalty went the way of gratitude, and America was severed from Great Britain.

There are truths with which we are all perfectly familiar, which we nevertheless fail to realise as a matter of habit. *Effects of distance.* One such truth, of enormous consequence when we attempt to compare the course of events in the last century with present-day conditions, is the vast difference in the ease of communication. It is the merest commonplace, but it is perpetually though unconsciously overlooked. Popular ignorance of our Australasian colonies at the present day is as nothing compared with popular ignorance of the American colonies when George III. was king; and the difference between official knowledge then and now was far greater. The tendencies which develop a misunderstanding into a serious breach were incomparably stronger; the state of public feeling at a distance was much harder to ascertain, and very much harder to realise: irrevocable steps were taken on insufficient information; events passed while correspondence that would now be settled by a couple of telegrams was occupying months; before the reply to a dispatch was received, the conditions under which the dispatch had been written might be completely altered. American colonists had the smallest possible knowledge of English statesmen; English statesmen had the smallest possible knowledge of American colonists. Hence it was only the men of large imaginative powers, like Chatham and Burke, who successfully realised the nature of the struggle; while the men who conducted it were those to whom America was a coloured space on an unfamiliar map.

The colonists realised that they had reaped vast benefits from the war. English ministers knew it also, and, not unnaturally, were of opinion that the colonists should pay their share of the expenses. Accordingly, in 1765, George Grenville proposed the Stamp Act.

Now, the right of the home government to regulate *The Stamp Act.* colonial trade had never been questioned. Restrictions in favour of British industries were held to be perfectly legitimate; and it is undoubtedly true that such restrictions were all, economically speaking, taxes on the colonists, inasmuch as the price of goods was enhanced by them, or the market for American products limited. But they were not recognized as taxation, *Theory of* because they were intended, not for purposes of *taxation.* revenue, but for the benefit of the British merchant. The Stamp Act was, in fact, the application of an accepted principle ; but in a new field, where it was not recognized. The constitutional doctrine was at once enunciated in answer to it, that it was essential to freedom that taxation should only be with the assent of the taxed, given by himself or his representative. In practice, it is true that this is a very inaccurate account of the theory of taxation, even within the British Isles. Speaking broadly, the principle accepted was that no one should be taxed unless by the assent of a majority of representatives ; while there was a large body of taxpayers in Great Britain, in the rising manufacturing towns, who were formally altogether unrepresented under the existing parliamentary system. None the less these bodies of unrepresented opinion could make themselves actively felt under pressure, so that, roughly speaking, it may be said that within Great Britain taxation by representatives was the working rule.

To pretend that the American colonies were as effectively represented in the British parliament as the manufacturing towns of England, was absurd. On the broad principles traditional in the Whig party—the principles which had justified the Great Rebellion and the Revolution of 1688 —the taxation of a body of citizens who were totally unrepresented was an infringement of their rights as citizens. George Grenville answered with strict accuracy that, under the colonial charters, such taxation was legal ; but was met with the rejoinder that the violation of the rights of citizenship, merely on the ground that such violation is sanctioned by law, is not statesmanship, but tyranny.

The plain truth is that the constitutional relation between the colonies and the mother country could only be maintained by a readiness on both sides to make reasonable concessions, and to recognize moral obligations, instead of standing on the letter of the law. The government started with the perfectly legitimate proposition, that if Britain expended blood and money mainly in the interests of the colonies, the colonies ought to repay her part of the money. Their proper course, the course in accordance with precedent, would have been to invite the colonies to vote an adequate contribution. Moreover, in forming a just idea of what such a contribution should amount to, the fact that Great Britain did already benefit largely by her accepted powers of legislation in regard to trade, and that in effect she did already tax the colonies in time of peace—thereby incurring the obligation of defending them in time of war—ought to have been taken into consideration.

Mutual obligations.

The colonies, however, during the war, had shown a disposition to take all the help they could get, and give the least possible return. Those whose frontiers had not been actually threatened, had objected to sending native levies across their own borders. They raised statues to Pitt and King George; but they showed no anxiety to spend anything which they could induce the mother-country to spend instead. Ministers conceived that an invitation to contribute would receive an altogether inadequate response, and the attitude of the colonies gave colour to their expectation.

The position of ministers would have been very much stronger if they had first tried the effect of inviting the colonists to vote the money. But they were entirely unaware of the importance of the step they were taking. They committed themselves to a principle without in the least realising its far-reaching character. The Stamp Act in itself was not a large measure, entailing a heavy burden;

and they assumed that, though it might meet with opposition, the pockets of the colonists would not be so seriously affected as to make the opposition formidable. Moreover, Grenville made matters worse by his tactless procedure—he took the opinion of the colonies before bringing in the measure; and when that opinion was expressed very strongly, he disregarded it. Such treatment was irritating to the last degree, but Grenville never understood that it is rarely politic to irritate. The Act was passed; the opposition to it at home, though weighty, was numerically slight, and the whole affair excited little comment.

But in America a storm was roused. The Virginian assembly passed a series of resolutions, denying the right of parliament to tax them; other colonies followed suit. Boston took the lead in urging the various assemblies to send delegates to a general congress. Riots took place in Boston and elsewhere. The congress met at New York, and proved unanimous and determined. When the government stamps arrived, it became evident at once that to distribute them would be nearly impossible. At the same time, associations were everywhere formed for what we should now call boycotting British merchandise until the Act should be repealed. The irritation of the colonies was at the same time increased by the government measures for the reduction of smuggling, the ordinary customs resources being supplemented by ships of war. {American action.}

When the British parliament met in January, 1766, the Rockingham ministry had replaced that of Grenville. When it was found that Pitt utterly condemned the Stamp Act, the new ministry felt that they could safely follow their own desire and repeal it. They had the support of the whole mercantile class outside, who found themselves suffering severely from the loss of the American market. Two bills were brought in, one repealing the Stamp Act, the other declaring the supreme power of parliament in all matters of taxation {Repeal of the Stamp Act.}

or legislation. In the interests of future concord, it might have been well to avoid the latter Act; but it would have been practically impossible, if for no other reason, because the Bill for the repeal of the Stamp Act would then have been thrown out. The king and the court party were induced, as it was, to accept the repeal; but without the Declaratory Act, they would have thrown their whole weight into the other scale. On the other hand, the Declaratory Act did not trouble American sentiment at the time. It was regarded, rightly enough, as having been added without any practical intention, except to serve as a salve to the wounded dignity of the home parliament—a means to enable the government to retreat with a show of honour from an untenable position.

So closed the first chapter in the history of the quarrel. In justice, however, to the Grenville party, it must be observed that the constitutional problem with which they endeavoured to deal, with such ill success, was a serious one. If Great Britain was to be responsible for the defence of America, some means were necessary to compel the Americans to pay their share. On that ground, Benjamin Franklin admitted the right of the home government to impose customs duties, as the colonial payment for the services of Britain in guarding the seas and protecting colonial commerce. But if Britain was also called upon to guard the inland frontiers of the colonies, by the same argument she was entitled to claim pecuniary compensation as a right, not as a mere act of grace. In theory, the funds raised by taxing America were to be devoted to the maintenance of a sufficient army for purposes of protection on the American continent. The logic of admitting the right of levying customs while denying the right of excise is, under the circumstances, a little difficult to grasp. Moreover, the policy of leaving the colonies to settle their own contribution was complicated by the absence of any central colonial authority. Each one

Difficulty of the problem.

of the thirteen colonies would have to be left to arrange its own payment for itself.

But the levying of inland revenue was a new departure. It at once suggested opposition, because it was new. And it suggested a particular line of opposition, which was certain to end in a total repudiation of the right to tax at all; in the claims, which had always been admitted in practice, being questioned as opposed to the true theory of the British Constitution. Either inland taxation as well as customs duties was justifiable, or neither was. Both parties had been fairly content with the compromise allowing one and not allowing the other. But the British ministers tried the application of the principle in its logical fulness, and consequently the colonists began to dispute the principle altogether. So that the situation resolved itself ultimately into this: If Britain is to protect America, she must be able to tax America. But to tax America, is to tax the unrepresented; which is contrary to the first principles of the constitution. If the British ministers fall back on the colonial charters, the colonists can reply by appealing to the Bill of Rights. Therefore, unless the constitution is violated, either America must have full representation (a practical impossibility), or Britain is not to be called upon to protect her. Evidently the only way out of the difficulty was a working compromise based solely on the recognition on both sides of a moral obligation to give help when needed, and to pay for it when given. But states, like individuals, are very much disposed to become blind to the existence of moral obligations towards people who have irritated them; the recognition of such claims depends on carefully preserving mutual good will and mutual interests. The interest of the colonists in these mutual services having been enormously lessened by the expulsion of France from America, it behoved the home government to cultivate colonial good will the more vigorously and judiciously. Yet the home government

Logic v. compromise.

seized this inauspicious opportunity to attempt to extract the minimum of real profit out of the colonies at the cost of a maximum of irritation ; just at the moment when the services they had already rendered had made the colonies practically independent of the need of similar services in the future.

It must further be observed that George Grenville had not only applied the power of taxation in a new field, he had also gone out of his way to apply recognized rights in that irritating manner which caused them to be felt as a grievance. Duties were enforced which were known to be extremely vexatious ; new duties were introduced which were small in amount, but irritating out of all proportion to the revenues they produced ; and, though some duties were diminished, strong measures were taken to enforce them. Now imports, on which is laid a duty generally felt as a real burden, are certain to become the objects of extensive smuggling, and such smuggling never meets with very severe reprobation from the moral sense of the community. Popular sympathy is generally on the side of the smuggler rather than of the revenue officer, and the latter is likely to find his activity and his unpopularity increase or diminish together. A large number of highly respectable citizens were, in fact, in league with smugglers along the American coasts, and the revenue officers had avoided excessive activity. But when they were reinforced by the officers and men of the British fleet,—when smugglers found, not only that it was much harder to avoid discovery, but that detection was followed by increased severity of punishment,—when, moreover, it was felt that the smuggling was all in the interest of the colonists, while the duties were all in the interest of Britain, the existence of the duties, felt only as minor sources of annoyance while they were loosely enforced, developed into a serious ground of complaint against the whole system, and a fruitful subject for appeals to popular passion.

Grenville's want of tact.

One other point in Grenville's policy requires to be dwelt on, because it at once affords a certain justification for him, and an additional explanation of colonial opposition. The extra funds raised were to be applied to the maintenance of a small standing army: to be employed partly against the Indians, who sometimes became aggressive, and partly in case of another French war arising, when a French descent on the American coast might be confidently expected. But the colonists considered that the colonial militias could deal with any such invasion, and they regarded the standing army merely as an instrument of coercion in the hands of the home government. *The standing army.*

Still, for the time being, the repeal of the Stamp Act allayed irritation, and the storm seemed to have blown over. In fact, the wind had been sown; the whirlwind was still to reap. The colonists had discovered unexpected strength in themselves: the idea of resistance had taken shape, and the idea of colonial union had also begun to be realised at the New York congress.

Rockingham's ministry, however, went farther in the direction of concessions in the way of removing obnoxious duties. It is worth noting that, in the case of molasses, the duty was reduced from sixpence to one penny per gallon, with the result that the revenue from that source rose from £2,000 to £17,000—a striking comment on the unwisdom of the excessive duties which result in wholesale smuggling. Unfortunately, his tenure of power was brief; Chatham, who succeeded him, fell ill, and Charles Townshend became the strongest man in the cabinet. In the mean time, American satisfaction at the repeal of the Stamp Act was taking the form, not of gratitude for an act of reparation, but of triumph for a victory. The colonists felt encouraged, by their success, to attack other grievances. Patriots began to hold forth against all British interference. The assembly at Boston and the *The Rockingham concessions.* *Charles Townshend.*

Governor Bernard were in open opposition to each other. Boston vehemently resisted the clauses in the Mutiny Act requiring the colonies to provide certain necessaries for the troops; New York refused point blank to submit to them.

With regard to the Stamp Act, public feeling in England had been generally on the side of the colonies. Their conduct after its repeal induced a reaction, as being factious and unreasonable. Hence, Townshend found plenty of support when he revived the doctrine that America should contribute more to the British revenue, which, indeed, was very much in need of contributions. He did not propose a renewal of inland taxation, but he imposed new customs duties, and established a Board of Commissioners of Customs to secure the more drastic execution of the law. The whole estimated addition to the revenue amounted to only about £40,000, and the most important of the new taxes was a duty on tea.

The soothing effects of the repeal of the Stamp Act were at once destroyed by these new measures. Moreover, it at once became evident that the whole of the revenue collected would be absorbed in the additional expense involved in the attempt to collect it at all. Bernard declared that the only means of keeping a semblance of order in Boston was by quartering additional troops there. Yet, while there was absolutely nothing to be gained by the new measures, it was practically impossible for parliament to recede a second time, if any pretence of respect for its authority was to be preserved. The Assembly of one colony after another declared the new laws to be illegal: and one after another they were dissolved in consequence. Practically all the colonies were engaged in defying their governors and every official sent out by the home government, openly setting the Customs at nought, and forming associations for the exclusion of British goods. Riots were frequent, and, here and there, custom-house officers were tarred and feathered.

Renewed irritation.

At home, changes in the ministry were all in the direction of introducing anti-colonials. North, who succeeded Townshend, was entirely in favour of his policy, which was energetically supported by the king, and the "king's friends." Hillsborough, as Secretary for the Colonies, was determined to suppress resistance. Shelburne and Chatham resigned; and Bedford made the preposterous proposal that the trial of rioters should be transferred from the colonial courts to England, by reviving an obsolete statute of Henry VIII. The cabinet, in spite of Grafton and Camden, while repealing the other new duties, insisted on retaining that on tea, by way of maintaining a principle. The resignation of Grafton resulted in the formation of a purely anti-colonial ministry under Lord North (1770). *Strength of the anti-colonial party.*

In March, 1770, there was a serious affray in Boston. There was a collision between a mob and a few soldiers, for which the mob were entirely responsible: but the soldiers fired on them, and three were killed and six wounded. The "Boston massacre" became the text of the agitators, although the Bostonians themselves honestly acquitted the soldiers of real blame when they were put on trial. On the night of June 9, 1772, the royal schooner *Gaspee*, which was engaged in the prosecution of smuggling, was boarded and burnt. On December 16, 1773, three tea-ships in Boston harbour were boarded in the presence of an immense assembly, and their contents emptied into the water. *The "Boston massacre," & Boston tea.*

The insubordinate spirit, of which these are the leading examples, was encouraged by a step of Benjamin Franklin's, taken during 1773. Franklin was, at this time, agent in London for four of the colonies. Hutchinson, who had in 1769 succeeded Bernard as Governor of Massachusetts, and Oliver, the Chief Justice, were naturally both strong supporters of law and order, though often disapproving of the British legislation. *The Whately correspondence.*

s

They had carried on a private correspondence with a Mr. Whately in London, who had an important official connection, in which they had expressed their personal opinion with the natural freedom of confidential letters. Whately died, and Franklin, by means which have never been cleared up, came into possession of the whole correspondence. He forwarded the letters to Boston, and, once there, it was no long time before they were copied, printed, and circulated, and the writers violently denounced. The Massachusetts assembly passed a resolution petitioning for the removal of the offenders. In England, on the other hand, Franklin was denounced for having made a most dishonourable use of documents which were never intended for the public eye, and which he knew to have been in effect stolen.

Retreat was now impossible for either side. Accordingly, a series of repressive measures followed in 1774. **Repressive measures.** The first was the Boston Port Act, prohibiting the use of the port of Boston until the re-establishment of order, and the payment by the town to the East India Company of the value of the tea destroyed. The second was a revision of the Massachusetts charter, placing the constitution of the colony on a less democratic basis. A third permitted the trial of any officers of the crown accused of any breach of law to be transferred to some other colony or to Great Britain. A fourth quartered the British troops on the colonists.

In addition to these, great offence was caused throughout the Puritan and democratic colonies by the Quebec Act. **The Quebec Act.** This Act was, indeed, justified by the peculiar circumstances of Canada. Canada was a province which had been won by war; the population was mainly French and Roman Catholic; and the Quebec Act sought, very rightly, to establish a system adapted to those peculiar conditions. But the practical establishment of the Roman Catholic religion there excited Protestant feeling elsewhere, and the large powers retained by the crown were feared as a handle for applying a like interference with democratic institutions in other colonies.

Boston was the town which had taken the lead in resistance throughout ; Massachusetts was the state against which the repressive acts were directly aimed. But the other states did not desert them. The idea of colonial unity had been steadily gaining ground throughout the conflict, and had been fostered by the establishment of correspondence committees, as well as by the general congress at New York. The Virginian House of Burgesses showed their sympathy by setting apart June 1, 1774—the day when the Boston Port Act was to come into operation —as a day of fasting ; meetings were held all over the country ; and a new general congress was summoned to meet at Philadelphia in September. *Colonial unanimity.*

It is to be noted, however, that the colonies still absolutely denied any desire of independence. There were agitators who had started the notion, but it met with no general acceptance. The colonists felt that they might have to fight for their rights, but it is clear that the great bulk of them believed that separation might be avoided, and was not to be desired.

The "Continental Congress" in effect declared all the new measures since 1763 to be violations of the rights of the colonies. It admitted the claims put forward by the British government before that date. It admitted the British right of regulating trade for the benefit of the British merchant, but denied the right of taxation for the purpose of raising revenue. It denied the right to maintain a standing army without the consent of the colony ; of transferring trials from one colony to another ; of legislation by a nominated council, as under the Massachusetts revised charter. It renewed an agreement for non-importation of British goods ; it promised Massachusetts the support of the other states in resisting the new Acts ; and, finally, it flatly repudiated *The Continental Congress.*

the desire for independence. With the exception of New York, the voice of the states was unanimous.

Massachusetts naturally took the lead on its own account. The members of the new Council refused nomination; the writs for the Assembly were cancelled by the governor (now General Gage), but the Assembly met as a "provincial congress," and its edicts were obeyed as if they had legal force. It organised a militia of twelve thousand men, who being ready to answer a call to arms at a minute's notice were known as minute-men, collected stores, appointed a committee of safety and a committee of supplies, opened correspondence with Canada, and sent delegates to the other states; whose exertions resulted in the formation of corps in Virginia, Carolina, and Rhode Island.

Warlike measures.

Everything, therefore, pointed to war, unless the British parliament was prepared to accede to the colonial demands, and repeal the obnoxious Acts; for only by arms could the Acts be now enforced. It remains to consider the attempts of the Opposition in England to advocate the cause of the Americans, and their hopeless failure. Chatham and Burke both practically endorsed the attitude of the American "Continental Congress," and called for the repeal of the whole of the obnoxious Acts; but their supporters, though able, were hopelessly out-voted. And the government proceeded farther to refuse even to receive a remonstrance sent by New York, in which that state separated itself from the rest, and went so far as to declare its readiness to bear its full share of aids to the public service. It extended what was practically the blockade of Boston, to other sea-ports; it answered the non-importation agreements by Acts restraining first the New England colonies, and then others, from all trade with Great Britain, Ireland, and the West Indies; and resolved to raise the British troops in Boston to ten thousand.

The British Opposition.

One attempt Lord North made, in the direction of conciliation. It was probably well meant: it was certainly impracticable; and it increased the violence of the anti-American party, who thought they had been betrayed, though the announcement that the king was in favour of it rallied his supporters. This was a proposal to exempt from taxation for the purposes of revenue any colony which was prepared on its own account to raise, for imperial defence, such a fixed contribution as should satisfy parliament. *North's conciliatory bill;*

Had the proposal come earlier, there would have been something to be said for it. But its weakness as a working scheme was clear. If the colonies and the British parliament differed as to what constituted an adequate contribution, the old troubles would revive. It was regarded on one side as a scandalous concession to colonial claims, which, whatever justice there might originally have been about them, had lost all title to consideration by the manner in which they had been put forward by Boston mobs. On the other, it was viewed as an insidious attempt to break up the newly developed union of the colonies, and master them in detail; as a measure neither honest in intention, nor practicable in execution. *its futility.*

The summoning of the Continental Congress at Philadelphia had been something not far short of a declaration of revolt. It had resulted in a sort of ultimatum from America, declared by Chatham and by Burke to be essentially just. One remarkable measure of conciliation, and several measures of repression had been the reply; and the inevitable consequences followed.

CHAPTER IV.

INDIA.

1761-1773.

Clive's work—1761 : Paniput—British misrule in Bengal –1765 : Clive returns to India—His reforms—The Diwanee—Foreign policy—1767 : Clive leaves India—Madras and the native powers—Need of a new constitution—Parliamentary inquiry—1773 : Lord North's regulating Act.

EARLY in 1760, Clive had found it necessary to leave India with his work uncompleted. During the three years he had **Clive's work.** spent in Bengal, he had annihilated the French and Dutch as political forces ; he had effectively put an end to all present danger of encroachments from the other native states ; and he had established on the throne of Bengal a nawab so entirely dependent on British influence and support that he could not choose but be obedient. Moreover, he had obtained for the East India Company immense sums down, and a permanent revenue to be drawn from specified districts, as well as the monopoly of the salt-tax. Further, he had thoroughly established the prestige of the British, not merely as a fighting force incomparably superior to that of any native state, but also as consistent and trustworthy, and determined to stand by those to whom they had once promised support. The Hindus, from whom Meer Jaffier, hard pressed for money, attempted to extort what he wanted, found a protector in the Englishman, who was virtually dictator. The one instance in which Clive had stooped to fraud, that of Omichund, was much more than counterbalanced by his habitual straightforward dealing.

He had, indeed, been guilty of one error in policy, for which it is scarcely possible to blame him. He accepted for himself a large sum of money, and a permanent revenue. There was no sort of irregularity in his doing so, nor could his action be regarded as in any way dishonourable; and he might, had he chosen, have taken a far larger reward. But he set a dangerous example, which, as others were not slow to profit by it, resulted in systematic extortion. At the same time, brilliant as his conduct of affairs had been, it was impossible for him to establish, during the brief period of his control, a satisfactory system of administration. Hence the years which followed his temporary retirement were evil years in the history of British rule.

The period during which French and English were struggling for mastery was marked also by important events among the more westerly native states which had thrown off allegiance to the padishah. The power of the Mahrattas had been steadily increasing. The recognized head of the confederacy was the Peishwa at Poona. The great chiefs were the Gaikwar at Baroda, Holkar at Indore, Sindhia at Gwalior, and the Bhonsla at Nagpore. They had been a constant thorn in the side of the Nizam of the Deccan, to which we owe it that he was unable to take an active part in the Anglo-French conflict, despite Bussy's presence at his court; and they had even raided Bengal and Oudh.

Paniput.

Meanwhile, the Afghan Ahmed Shah had appeared as conqueror of Upper India—all those provinces which had not yet practically thrown off the Mogul allegiance. The padishah was, in fact, under the control of Ahmed Shah's minister. While English and French were settling their rivalry in the south and east, in the west the Hindu Mahrattas were challenging the Mohammedan Afghans. The contest was terminated for the time by the great battle of Paniput (January, 1761), in which the Hindu power was defeated and its power of aggression checked ; the Afghan conqueror, however, did not take the opportunity to consolidate a new empire, as perhaps he might have done. Upper India was left to follow its natural course of disintegration. But while the victor of Paniput omitted to create a new power in the north-west, he effectually drove back the wave of Mahratta expansion ; so that, in the long run, it was the English who reaped the fruits of his victory. The collision between English and Mahrattas was deferred, while the divided condition of the north-west made our later progress there inevitable.

Clive's departure from Bengal was followed by a period of the gravest misrule. Neither Council nor civil servants there had undergone the stern training of the long struggle in the Carnatic ; a swift and sudden triumph had placed them in a position of immense power, and they abused it for their personal ends. The directors in London had always paid their servants badly, and allowed them to indemnify themselves by private trading. They now devoted themselves to private trading, and disregarded the interests of the company. Clive and others had received large presents as rewards for their services to Meer Jaffier ; the company's servants took to extracting presents in return for no services at all. Meer Jaffier was in straits to pay them what he had undertaken to pay. They made matters worse, by compelling him to allow them to trade free of duty, thereby heavily curtailing his finances ; and followed this up by removing him from the nawabship, and substituting his finance minister, Meer Cossim. But Meer Cossim was not a puppet, and made vigorous efforts to resist the tyrannical conduct of the Council. The governor-general, Vansittart, opposed the overbearing proceedings of his Council, and was supported by Warren Hastings ; but they were overruled by the rest. The finances of the company were in grave disorder ; the

British reputation for justice and honesty was fast vanishing. The ill-feeling between Meer Cossim and the English was growing. At last Mr. Ellis, the head of the English factory at Patna, attacked and captured the city, which was promptly retaken; Ellis himself and many others being made prisoners and subsequently murdered.

The consequence of the capture of Patna was, that the Council reinstated Meer Jaffier as nawab, extracting an immense price from him for so doing. Meer Cossim took refuge with Shujah Daulah, the Nawab of Oudh, who considered the opportunity a favourable one for making a descent on Bengal. He was, however, thoroughly defeated by Munro at Buxar, a collision which brought the British into direct contact with the Upper Provinces.

In the mean time, Clive had been engaged in a prolonged contest with the directors in England. Pitt was out of power, and the influences against him were strong. At last, however, Clive got the upper hand; it was evident that his firm and experienced control was needed on the spot, to put an end to the anarchy which had overtaken the company's management in Bengal. And, in 1765, he re-appeared on the scenes as governor-general and virtual dictator, with a committee of four named by himself. *Clive returns to India.*

The prime source of the troubles in Bengal had been due to the fact that, while the company insisted on the nawab paying them money, and granting them quite unjustifiable trade advantages and monopolies, they had refused to be responsible for administration themselves. Hence there was no adequate check on the immense abuses of power by the company's servants, who practically set themselves above the law, and used their position for their own personal enrichment. Thus the first fruit of Clive's recovered predominance was an order forbidding the acceptance of gifts without leave from head-quarters. And Clive on his arrival proceeded at once to *His reforms.*

accept for the company the business of the financial administration (called the Diwanee) of the province, making it in effect the responsible ruler, and turning the nawab into a mere pensioner. This was accompanied by the prohibition of private trading, and the appropriation of the salt-tax to the payment of the company's servants as compensation for the loss so inflicted upon them.

The Diwanee.

Thus Clive's first measure was the prohibition of those practices which had led to the private interests of individuals entirely overriding those of the company, and to various gross abuses of power. The second was the establishment of the company as the responsible ruler of Bengal, no longer managing a puppet nawab, but openly conducting the administration itself. The third was to put a stop to any present policy of expansion by a treaty with the Nawab of Oudh, whereby that province was established as a buffer state between Upper India and the provinces of Bengal, Behar, and Orissa, now definitely recognized as under British rule.

Foreign policy.

Clive, in fact, perceived clearly that, if our conquests were carried farther, we should have to undertake more than we were in a position to manage. The company might consolidate its administration in Bengal; but if it went on, it would have no choice but the entire conquest of the Mogul Empire, and that was a task beyond its existing powers. It might have been practicable for the English nation: it was not practicable for the company. The conquest itself would not, indeed, have been difficult; but the organisation and consolidation would have been too much.

The result of this policy was that we were left with a free hand in Bengal, without present fear of a collision with the Upper Provinces. It was understood that we had no intention of attacking them, while they were sufficiently occupied with securing themselves against the advance of Hindu powers from the south and west.

It was Clive who conquered Bengal; it was Clive who laid the foundations of an administration based on sound principles; it was Clive who conceived the still larger plan, which was not carried out till another century had passed, of transferring the sovereignty of the East India Company to the nation. When in England, he had suggested the scheme to Pitt; and when Pitt took office and became Lord Chatham it was undoubtedly his intention to carry it out, though his plan never took definite form. But it is clear that Clive had no expectation of any such scheme being really effected, and his energies were devoted to establishing a working system under the company.

Unfortunately he was not able to remain long enough in India to perfect the machinery; he could only construct the basis of a constitution with the materials at hand. The nawab was still nominally sovereign; the nawab's officials collected the revenue: the nawab's officials administered justice, though the system was controlled by the British, and the entire military organisation was in their hands. Moreover, the three presidencies were still independent of each other; Clive had made himself a host of enemies; and there were numbers of Englishmen in India who were still ready to avail themselves of any opportunities for the abuse of their position, though nothing like the license which prevailed between 1760 and 1765 was again possible. Consequently, when Clive finally departed from India in 1767, he left behind a far from perfect government, while at home there were strong influences freely brought to bear to discredit him and the work he had done. *Clive leaves India.*

The events in the Madras Presidency at this time were unfortunate. An adventurer of exceptional ability, named Hyder Ali, had made himself master of Mysore, and had erected that country into a very formidable military state, and constantly threatened the Nizam of the Deccan. The Mahrattas' invasion of *Affairs in the Madras Presidency.*

the north had been beaten back, but they had extended their sway practically across the whole central district from east to west, and they also were a permanent danger to the Nizam. On the other hand, the English were the Nizam's tenants, and policy required that they should retain his good will.

Now, it was possible that any of these three native Powers might at any moment be fighting against any other of the three. And the Nizam was jealous of the English, because his nominal suzerain, the padishah, had granted them the Cirkars (which they already held) as a free gift, without consulting him, though they formed a portion of his province. To calm him, the Madras government promised to assist him if he were involved in a war; and, almost immediately after, he was attacked by Hyder Ali, with whom the English were thus forced into collision—though that very able potentate showed more than once that he would have preferred entering upon a genuine alliance with them. The British troops marched to the assistance of the Nizam, and a band of Mahrattas was also invoked to attack Hyder Ali. But these latter, having secured a quantity of plunder, preferred to withdraw before they were called upon to share it with their allies. The Nizam then intrigued with Hyder, and turned on the British; and, although he was severely defeated by them, it was not till 1769 that Hyder Ali himself chose to come to terms—and then it was not because he was beaten, but because he wanted an alliance with the British until he should feel strong enough to turn upon them.

These proceedings were somewhat inglorious. They did not advance British prestige. We were in no better position at the end than at the beginning of the war; and the war itself had been carried on only by dint of large remittances from Bengal. Even in Bengal itself matters had not been going well, because the dual control there had interfered with administrative efficiency,

Need of a new constitution.

while the instructions sent out by the English directors had prevented the council from taking so active a part as they might otherwise have done. Accordingly, between the drain from Madras of prolonged and futile military operations, and inefficient administration in Bengal, the finances of the country suffered severely. The situation was made more pointed when, in 1770, Bengal was swept by a devastating famine which the company's officers were powerless to alleviate. They were even charged, on the contrary, with having turned the sufferings of the population to their own private advantage, by making what we now call "corners" in rice.

The reports of maladministration ; the quarrels of the different parties among the directors at home ; and, finally, the announcement that the company could not pay their £400,000 to the government, but wanted a treasury loan instead ; brought matters to a crisis, which led to a parliamentary enquiry. {Parliamentary enquiry.} Such an enquiry had already been instituted when Chatham took office ; but after his retirement, owing to illness, its object had been reduced merely to seeing how much the company could pay the government for their privileges.

Now, however, it was clear that a much more searching investigation must be made, and that much more drastic measures of reform in the whole Indian system were required. It was declared that conquests by force of arms belonged to the state. Clive was virulently attacked ; but though it was impossible to avoid a formal condemnation of particular acts, such as the affair of Omichund, the House added a resolution, carried almost unanimously, to the effect that he had rendered great and honourable services to the nation. Shortly afterwards, he died by his own hand.

The enquiry resulted in two Acts which revolutionised the system of Indian administration (1773).

The first dealing with the finances of the company, arranged for an advance from the government and regulated their dividends so as to prevent a recurrence of the awkward position in which they had recently been placed. The second, Lord North's "Regulating Act" reorganised the Courts of Proprietors and Directors in London, and reconstructed the system in India.

Lord North's Regulating Act.

Although, under the new arrangement, the crown did not take over the administration from the company, the supremacy of parliament was asserted in general terms, while certain of the principal appointments were to be made, not by the company, but by parliament. Instead of three independent presidencies, the Governor of Bengal was to be Governor-General of all the English dominions in India. He was to rule with the assistance of a council, whom he could not override, and at whose deliberations he had only an ordinary and a casting vote. The governor-general and council were, in the first instance, to be appointed by parliament. Further, side by side with this authority, a Supreme Court of Justice was set up, though the precise relations between this court of justice and the Indian government, and the relations of both to parliament, were very inadequately defined. The measure was altogether incomplete, leaving boundless opportunities for contention as to the powers of the governor-general, the council, and the supreme court, and as to their dependence on a parliament which could not be communicated with in less than six months: but it involved a more definite assumption of responsibility than had existed heretofore; it placed the company in a more direct relation to parliament; i concentrated control at Calcutta; and, finally, it nominated as the first governor-general the man who was best fitted to accomplish the work of consolidation—Warren Hastings.

CHAPTER V.

IRELAND: THE POLITICAL REVIVAL.

1760-1776.

The Catholics—The Whiteboys—The Irish constitution—Short parliaments— Habeas Corpus — The Judges — Corruption— Summary of grievances—The Undertakers—1767: Lord Townshend viceroy —1768: The Octennial Bill—1772: Harcourt viceroy —1773: The absentee tax—Commercial relaxations—Attitude of Parliament—Effects of the colonial quarrel.

FOR eighteen years from the accession of George III., the legal status of the Catholics in Ireland remained substantially unchanged. During that period, however, the Catholic question never becomes prominent. Merciless as the penal code was; harshly as its provisions with regard to land, to education, and to political life weighed upon the Catholics; its most cruel powers were rarely put in force, and many of the restrictions it imposed were habitually evaded with the more or less open connivance of the government. The division between class and class was indeed gravely accentuated by the stress laid on religious differences, and the population was vehemently hostile to the representatives of Protestant ascendancy; but the attitude of the Catholics generally towards Britain was decidedly loyal. Some of the reasons for this have been noted in a previous chapter; to these may be added the conviction that the Protestant rulers of Ireland were not in perfect harmony with the parliament at Westminster. This feeling naturally biassed the Catholics in favour of that body, the more so as it was the less vividly responsible for unjust administration.

Accordingly, the Catholics throughout Ireland showed no disposition to rebel against the British connection, and gave clear signs of their loyalty during the great war. Nor did they attempt to organise themselves in opposition to the existing order of things. It is to be noted however, that the extreme poverty of the peasantry, aggravated by the general conversion of farms into pasture as well as by the grinding exactions of the middlemen, gave rise about this period to those secret agrarian organisations which, under one name or another, have continued to this day, often scotched but never entirely killed. The Whiteboy movement persisted with varying activity for many years, until it was merged in movements of a more insurrectionary type; but at its initiation it was neither political nor religious, but purely agrarian. Bands of masked marauders houghed cattle, meted out vengeance on obnoxious persons, and committed innumerable outrages in defiance of law and authority, sometimes even in broad day. They claimed to be the representatives of that justice which was denied by the law, but they enforced the claim by the vilest cruelties. Where the law is universally regarded as an instrument not of justice but of tyranny, the moral sense of the population is inevitably blunted; and the most odious practices were condoned in the minds of the peasantry by the oppression of the system against which the movement was directed.

The real interest, however, of these years lies in the history of what may be called, not very accurately, the National movement; the movement, that is, of constitutional progress in that section of the nation which already had a voice in political affairs—the movement to obtain for the Protestants of Ireland that political freedom which the English people had secured for themselves at the Revolution of 1688. In England, the fight had been between the people and the king ; in Ireland, it was between a section of the people and the British domination.

Under the existing constitution, the British Parliament claimed the right of legislating independently for Ireland, but this was rarely exercised. According to the normal procedure, there were three bodies concerned in Irish legislation ; the Irish houses of Parliament, the Irish Privy Council, and the British Privy Council. The Irish Privy Council prepared bills which were then submitted to the British Privy Council. This body suppressed them or amended them as it thought fit. The amended bills were returned to the Irish Parliament, which might either reject them or pass them *in toto,* but had no power of amending them. In practice, however, the bills sent over from Ireland had not taken their rise in the Privy Council there, but had been sent up to that body, under the form of "Heads of Bills," as recommendations from the parliament. The first desire, therefore, of the National party was to have the parliamentary right of originating bills recognized and emphasized by the admission of the doctrine that money bills could originate nowhere else. *[sidenote: The Irish constitution.]*

Secondly, the only limit to the continuity of a single parliament was the king's life. One parliament sat without any fresh general election from the first to the last year of George II. There was no provision whereby it could be ensured that the members in any sense represented the views of their constituencies. In England, many politicians held that seven years is too long a life for a really representative House of Commons ; but in Ireland they had one sitting for thirty-three years. A septennial parliament was the second popular demand. *[sidenote: Other grievances.]*

The Habeas Corpus Act had for a long time been regarded in England as fundamental to the liberty of the subject. So had the Bill of William III., which made the judges irremovable save by the direct censure of parliament. But

T

neither of the rights—as they were held to be in England—conceded by these Acts, was extended to Ireland.

Farther, the methods of political corruption prevalent in England were exercised with equal freedom in the sister island. Parliamentary majorities depended on control of rotten boroughs; that control depended largely on the extent to which the government of the day satisfied their owners. In both countries, therefore, places were bestowed and pensions provided out of the public funds for the political purposes of the party in power; and in Ireland, as in England, the system was the cause of much popular irritation, and was hotly attacked.

In Ireland, then, there were two main sets of grievances: those of the Catholic majority, who had no political existence, no voice either in the making or the administration of the law; and those of the Protestant minority, who had political being, but still lacked those privileges which English citizens had claimed and won for themselves as manifest rights, at the cost of a civil war, the head of one king, and the crown of another, in the course of the previous century. In addition to these there were the grievances shared by the English people, which led to the demands for economic and parliamentary reform; and the grievance of commercial repression, shared with the American colonies.

As in England parliament was very largely under the control of a group of Whig families, so in Ireland a few great proprietors commanded a majority of votes. The Undertakers, as they were called, were useful to the British government so long as their steady support could be secured; but when they began to take a line of resistance, it became a matter of some importance to break their power. The analogy between the attitude of the king to the Whig chiefs in England, and that of the government to the Undertakers is very close; and the confusion of Irish parties on particular questions finds its parallel in the division of the Grenvilles, the Chathams,

The Undertakers.

the Rockinghams, and the King's Friends. The Undertakers wished to resist British domination, and this was popular. But they wished to retain their own ascendency, and in this were opposed to the popular party. The government made bids for the support of the chiefs, by promising measures or pensions according to circumstances; and the general corruption was universally reprobated, yet steadily taken advantage of by the majority of those who came in the way of it.

During the first years of the reign, the Irish demands for the Habeas Corpus Act, for a Septennial Bill, and for similar legislation, were rejected in England; while the English Privy Council sent over money bills, which were promptly rejected, but for which new money bills arising in the Irish parliament were substituted. Still, the force of the Irish claims became steadily more evident; and with the appointment of Lord Townshend as Viceroy, in 1767, it appeared probable that the movement for Irish liberty would begin to take effect.

The first intention of the ministry was to inaugurate a new *régime*, under which the Viceroy was to remain constantly in Ireland, instead of for a period of six months out of every two years. Two objects would thereby be effected: the feeling of habitual neglect produced by the old system would be removed; and the power of the Undertakers, who practically controlled the whole administration in the Lord Lieutenant's absence, would be diminished. Further, the king was set on getting a specific measure carried—the augmentation of the Irish standing army, involving an additional strain on Irish resources, without any additional benefit to the country, The object was simply to have additional troops at command, while throwing the burden of maintaining them upon Ireland instead of Great Britain. It was obvious that in order to get this measure carried, concessions would have to be made.

Townshend.

Townshend began by promising a measure for the security of the judges' tenure in office. A bill to this end was promptly initiated in Ireland, with a proviso that they should be removable on an address from both Houses, as in England. The English Privy Council required that the address should be endorsed by the Irish Privy Council, but the bill as amended was at once rejected by the Irish parliament, the good faith of the British ministers being, not unnaturally, called in question.

To allay the irritation, and to secure the passing of the augmentation scheme, Townshend was instructed to hold out hopes of a Septennial Act; while a tax upon absentee pension and place-holders was granted, and a promise made to limit the granting of further pensions.

Accordingly, early in 1768, an Octennial Bill was introduced, greatly to the popular satisfaction. Eight years was **The Octennial Bill.** substituted for seven, because parliament was in session only in alternate years. The passage of the bill did not, however, immediately secure that of the augmentation scheme: but though this was for the time defeated, it was only by a small majority; the general election which followed strengthened the hands of the government; and Townshend felt himself in a position to attack the Undertakers. Nevertheless, a Habeas Corpus Bill had just been once more refused by England, and the first step of the new parliament was to reject a money bill sent over from Westminster, on the ground that it had not taken its rise in the Irish Commons. But the supplies were as usual voted for the next two years, and the augmentation scheme passed; whereupon, to the general indignation, Townshend prorogued the parliament (December, 1769).

A period of much agitation followed. Townshend ejected the Undertakers who headed the Opposition, and strained every nerve to secure supporters in parliament by the bestowal of honours, places, and pensions, in spite of promises made; and when the House again met in February,

1771, he had a majority. The remainder of his viceroyalty was mainly occupied in extending opportunities for corruption, with a view to securing the maximum of support for the government: including a grant for re-imbursing the tax on some of the more important absentee place-holders. In 1772, Townshend was recalled, and his place was taken by Harcourt.

The financial strain upon Ireland, poor as the country was, was very severe. Parliament did not meet again till the autumn of 1773, and in the mean time the new Viceroy had been enabled to ascertain the views and opinions of leading public men. He proposed, therefore, to meet the financial difficulty by imposing a tax upon absentee landlords, who, it must be remembered, owned a very large proportion of the land, while the money drawn from it was spent elsewhere. The measure, however, met with strenuous opposition in England. Several great Whig peers, including the Rockingham connection, were among the absentees, and they represented the tax as a punishment on them for residing in England where their principal estates were. It seems a fair retort that, however good their own reasons for absenteeism might be, their action was injurious to Ireland, and that she might reasonably claim compensation. But the vital question was not whether the tax was wise or just, but whether the decision as to this should lie with England or Ireland. On this point Chatham was emphatic, and his argument convinced Shelburne, who had been inclined to take the other side. Chatham applied to Ireland precisely the same constitutional principle which he applied to America—that the elected representatives of a country were the only people who ought to control its taxation. The Opposition, however, was too strong; but Harcourt, perceiving that the rejection of the measure in England would arouse intense ill feeling, adopted the course of openly supporting it, while actually intriguing for its rejection by the Irish parliament itself. This plan was successful.

The strength of the feeling in Ireland, that money bills ought to emanate from the Commons and from nowhere else, was by no means diminishing, and the usual rejection of the Habeas Corpus Bill was followed by the usual rejection of the amended Supply Bill sent back from England. A slight relaxation of the restrictions upon Irish commerce was, on the other hand, hailed with much satisfaction; a bounty upon the export of corn was permitted, which did not indeed bring the produce of Ireland into serious competition with that of England, where the bounties were higher, yet did something to improve the market. Harcourt himself deserves much credit for the conciliatory influence which he brought to bear upon English opposition. But, throughout this period, the name which is most honourably associated with the Irish cause is that of Henry Flood, the real parliamentary leader.

The first fourteen years of George III., in fact, marked a great change in the political aspect of Ireland. After a long period of acquiescence in British domination, that portion of the population which was allowed a voice in the government had roused itself to claim the rights and privileges for which the English parliament had fought long before. The movement was not a national one in the proper sense, since three-fourths of the people were outside it. But within the limits of the ascendant classes a strenuous political life, a demand for the same political liberty which existed in England, had grown up. It is difficult to write of Ireland without a suspicion of a present day partisan intention; but, simply to prevent the drawing of misleading inferences, certain primary differences between the demands of the Nationalist of to-day and of a hundred years ago must be pointed out. Now, however we may regard the substance, there is at least the form of a united legislature for Great

Attitude of parliament.

Britain and Ireland ; in which each part has a voice, apportioned approximately to its population, in legislation alike for itself and for the other parts of the whole. A century ago, Ireland had no voice in the counsels of the United Kingdom ; it was not admitted that what was just for one member was just for the other ; she was directly subordinate to the will and pleasure of England, and whatever of her demands was granted came as a concession by favour, not as of right, though the English people had been ready to assert their own claims to similar concessions, not as favours, but as rights, at the cost of civil war.

The movement received a very strong impulse from the colonial complications of the period. It was obvious that Britain was now formally asserting her right to overrule the interests of dependencies in her own favour. The colonists, on the other hand, were asserting their counter-claim to the rights of citizenship—to the applicability to themselves of the same principles of liberty which were axioms of citizenship in the mother country. The Irish were fighting identically the same battle for themselves. They, too, were claiming the right of legislation for themselves, of commercial liberty, of taxation by representatives. And although, when the American war broke out, the government control of votes secured a parliamentary majority which condemned the colonies, and supported the ministerial policy, the feeling of the country was actively favourable to America. There the contest was carried on between armies and fleets ; in Ireland it was fought by constitutional methods : but the American war had no small share in establishing the principles which carried the day in Ireland as in the colonies. It can hardly be questioned that if the issue of the war had been different, the principles of the anti-colonial party would have triumphed in Ireland as well.

Effect of the colonial breach.

BOOK V.
THE BRITISH AT BAY.

CHAPTER I.

THE OUTBREAK OF WAR.

1775-1777.

The colonial theory—Separation not desired—Eve of war—Battle of Lexington—The war commenced—George Washington—Battle of Bunker Hill—The "Olive Branch"—Washington before Boston—American expedition to Canada—Washington's difficulties—1776: Evacuation of Boston—The Southern States—Slackness of the British—Widening of the breach—Washington at New York—Lord Howe's arrival—Declaration of Independence—The armies before New York—Failure of negotiations—Washington driven back—British success—1777: Recovery of Washington—British plan of campaign—Burgoyne's expedition—Surrender of Saratoga—Capture of Philadelphia—Importance of Saratoga.

The colonial theory.

THE common statement that the separation of Britain from her colonies over seas was inevitable, may be held to have been proved true in one sense; in another it may fairly be maintained that the facts are inadequate to prove either its truth or its falsity. When the quarrel broke out, the doctrine that colonies exist primarily for the advantage of the mother country, and only secondarily for the benefit of the colonists, was not only prevalent, but was practically undisputed. Yet it was entirely irreconcilable with the necessary aspirations of a very energetic race, growing up in a country which seemed to offer almost unlimited opportunities for development. So long as that theory ruled, a quarrel sooner or later was certain ; certain, also, to be renewed, even though it might have been temporarily healed by the exercise of tact and forbearance ; certain, in the long run, to lead to war. And thereafter, no victories of the British arms could have re-established any real unity ; while any attempt to hold the colonies in perpetual subjection by military control would have been manifestly impossible. Given the old colonial theory on the one hand, and on the other the colonies freed from the need of protection against French rivalry, the tactless blunders of successive administrations under George III. merely precipitated the inevitable disruption.

But if the colonial theory had been displaced by a more rational doctrine, if hampering restrictions had been steadily removed instead of being multiplied, if the thirteen colonies had been allowed to attain to the practical autonomy of our colonies at the present day,—the history of the disruption affords no data for forming a decisive judgment as to the probable results. Every clearly ascertainable cause of friction, every act which tended to make the breach wider, is directly traceable to the old colonial theory. It is particularly to be noted that there was no spontaneous desire for a severance of the bond between the colonies and the mother country. The idea was only forced gradually on the minds of the bulk of Americans. For a long time it was earnestly, almost passionately repudiated. It was only accepted at last, when the conviction could no longer be resisted, that the action of the home government had rendered any other solution of the difficulty hopelessly impossible. Even after the outbreak of the war, the majority of Americans were anxious for a reconciliation on terms of a return to the conditions prevailing before 1763. To the very last, there was a great body of loyalists who refused to be reconciled

Separation not desired.

to the separation at all. Prior to the Declaration of Independence, the number of persons who would have actually preferred separation to reconciliation on just terms was very small, though the ablest men had long been aware that to look for such reconciliation was vain. Throughout the war a very large section of the population, known as "Tories," stood by the Union, rendering very considerable assistance to the British, and incurring the fiercest animosity of the party of revolt.

In the spring of 1775, even those Americans who still nursed a lingering hope that the British ministry might be brought to see the justice of the colonial demands, and amity be restored, were for the most part prepared to resist to the uttermost rather than withdraw those demands; and though they were anxious to avert collision, their hope of doing so was very faint. Moreover, they had been irritated up to a point at which the desire for peace might easily be converted into a desire for war. The first active hostilities were certain to be followed by a general conflagration.

The eve of war.

General Gage, Governor of Massachusetts, the commander-in-chief of the British troops, held four regiments, in America. There were small bodies of men in various forts, but the bulk of the soldiers were massed in Boston. The governors of the provinces farther south depended for support, in case of conflict, on the British ships which commanded the sea. Similarly, it was in Massachusetts that the most active preparations for resistance had been made. A considerable body of militia had been raised, supported by contingents from Connecticut and Rhode Island, and great efforts were being made to collect stores and ammunition. The colonists had established a depot for these purposes at Concord, eighteen miles from Boston. On the night of April 18, 1775, Gage sent a body of soldiers to destroy these stores. They were met on the march by some of the militia. Shots were exchanged.

Battle of Lexington.

Concord was reached, and some damage was done. Then the British troops fell back, the skirmish lasting until they were reinforced by a fresh party. This fight, which fairly opened the war, is known as the battle of Lexington ; and though the British had succeeded to some extent in the specific object of the moment, they suffered more than their opponents, who meanwhile had learned the encouraging lesson that the militia were quite capable of standing up to the regulars. The Provincial Congress of Massachusetts openly defied the governor. The numbers of their army increased rapidly, and cut off the British garrison of Boston on the land side.

Farther north, the fortress of Ticonderoga, on Lake Champlain, was surprised and captured, without resistance, a few days later, by Ethan Allen, and with the fort a considerable supply of stores fell into the hands of the colonists. At the same time, the Continental Congress met again at Philadelphia, voted the raising of an army of fifteen thousand men as a " Continental Army," and issued bills for two million dollars. On the other hand, on May 25th, a fleet carrying two thousand troops from England reached Boston, with generals Burgoyne and Clinton. Thus reinforced, Gage proclaimed martial law, while offering pardon to all who should come in, except Samuel Adams and John Hancock, two leading spirits in the party of resistance. Congress replied by unanimously voting the office of commander-in-chief to George Washington of Virginia. *War begins.* *George Washington.*

The appointment of Washington gave the hostilities a more formal shape. But before he was able actually to take up his command, occurred the famous battle of Bunker Hill.

Boston lies on the south side of the mouth of the river Charles. On the north side is Charlestown, and near Charlestown two heights, known respectively as Bunker Hill and Breed's Hill, the former being more to the north. It was known that Gage *Battle of Bunker Hill.*

intended to occupy Bunker Hill. On June 17th a colonial contingent under Prescott, sent to anticipate the British movement, occupied Breed's Hill—apparently by mistake—and intrenched themselves; being thereby enabled, if they could plant batteries, to make the British camp on the Boston side of the river untenable, and so to compel the evacuation of the city. On discovering this, a body of three thousand regulars was sent to dislodge them. These troops, covered by the guns of the fleet, were landed, marched straight up the hill, and were driven back twice; but, being reinforced, succeeded the third time in carrying the intrenchments, and forcing the Colonials to retire, their ammunition being exhausted. The British loss, however, was naturally considerably greater than that of their opponents, on whom the fight, though actually a defeat, had a like encouraging effect to the battle of Lexington. Moreover, the indignation of the Bostonians was farther aroused by the burning of Charlestown, a step which the British commander justified, on the ground that his troops were fired on from the town. The act, however, was scarcely politic, even if justified by the rules of war.

Even after Bunker Hill, the colonists desired reconciliation. Once more a petition, known as the "Olive Branch," was voted by congress. There is no doubt that the great majority were still in favour of reconciliation, if it could be had on reasonable terms; and would have been satisfied with a return to the regulations in force prior to 1763, or with the abolition of all trade restrictions on condition of contributing at a fixed rate to the imperial exchequer. But the king and the ministry, and even the bulk of the population in England, were now bent on simply enforcing obedience, and when Penn arrived with the "Olive Branch," he was not even granted an audience, or allowed to present the petition. In August a royal proclamation for the suppression of rebellion was issued, and the King of England

The "Olive Branch."

bargained with German principalities for troops to help in crushing his recalcitrant but still reasonably loyal subjects in America. General Howe took the command of the troops in place of General Gage, while his brother, Lord Howe, commanded the fleet. When Parliament met in the autumn, an Act was promptly passed, prohibiting trade with the thirteen colonies. Nevertheless, though these proceedings drove Congress to increased activity, and more open hostility, the representatives of some states, headed by Pennsylvania, still held out against the idea of separation.

In the mean time, military affairs moved slowly. It was all that Washington could do to keep up a show of efficiency in his army, which was most inadequately supplied with war materials, ill disciplined, and constantly, as it seemed, on the verge of breaking up. Yet he held his lines round Boston, where the British remained inactive; while in the south the governors of the revolted colonies had taken refuge on board the British ships, which were practically unassailable. *Washington before Boston.*

As the year drew to an end, the Americans made a disastrous attempt to carry the war into Canada, with a view to uniting that province with the thirteen colonies. Their expedition proved fairly successful at first. The French and the Indians were disposed to be friendly, and Montreal was captured without any long resistance. But the troops began to melt away the moment their term of enlistment was up. A second expedition, under the command of Benedict Arnold, detached by Washington, arrived before Quebec in December, barefoot, ragged, exhausted, and considerably short of its original numbers. The whole body, when joined by the force from Montreal, amounted to little more than a thousand men. An attempt to storm Quebec naturally failed, with heavy loss; but there the besiegers remained, their commander being obstinately determined to achieve his end, although without the means or any chance of obtaining them. Reinforcements arrived *American expedition to Canada.*

in March (1776), supplemented by farther detachments from Washington's army. But in the interval the feeling of the Canadian population had turned against the invaders, whose ranks were thinned by desertion and disease. Their position was more and more evidently hopeless. At last the siege was raised, and the broken remnants of the besiegers fell back across the Canadian border.

Thus, as far as concerned Canada, the winter of 1775-6 was disastrous for the Americans. The attempt to draw the Dominion into the colonial revolt proved a signal failure. In the mean time, Washington held his army together before Boston, in spite of insubordination, dissensions, and jealousies, which must have broken it up altogether under any leader less firm, less judicious, or less single-hearted. The task was a dreary and thankless one, bringing the general much unpopularity, with no chance of distinction or credit for his efforts at all proportionate to the difficulties which required to be surmounted. Washington, however, held his ground, and, as the spring advanced, prepared to make an attack on the city. General Howe was himself anxious to quit Boston, from whence he could see no prospect of conducting an offensive campaign. The place could, moreover, be evacuated without difficulty, as the British ships could move where they liked, although the anarchy reigning in all the government departments at home caused the provision to be very bad in this as in other respects. Howe intended to strike some sort of blow before leaving, and when Washington began to throw up works on Dorchester heights—the completion of which would leave the evacuation no longer a matter of choice—he attempted an attack ; but a storm frustrated his design, and before it could be renewed the opposing lines had been too much strengthened to make the attempt worth while. Accordingly he embarked his troops, though many of his stores had to be destroyed owing to the inadequacy of his fleet.

Washington's difficulties.

Howe evacuates Boston.

Ten days later, on March 17, 1776, he sailed out of Boston Harbour, and, for the time being, made Halifax in Nova Scotia his headquarters. In the south, the British had no effective hold on the continent, yet the methods adopted by Dunmore, the Governor of Virginia, had greatly embittered public feeling. He proclaimed martial law, offered pardon to all servants and slaves who would come in, and cannonaded and burnt Norfolk. *The Southern States.*

The first year of the war is a study in mismanagement. The thirteen colonies were in revolt, but they had not reached the stage of homogeneity. Their professions of unanimity were attended by innumerable petty jealousies, sometimes merely personal, sometimes inter-colonial. *Laxity of the British.* The seat of authority was by no means stable; and in the continental army neither officers nor men had had the training which would have made them formidable opponents for a strong force vigorously handled. Britain, on the other hand, with all her resources, had absolutely free water-way; she was entangled in no other war; she had ridiculed the idea of any termination to the contest other than the complete and unqualified submission of the insurgents; yet, at the end of twelve months, her army had been compelled to evacuate Boston, her governors could not set foot in the southern provinces, and no single effective step had been taken for the suppression of the revolt.

This laxity may have been in part due to the conviction that there was not enough coherence or vigorous purpose in the colonies to carry the matter through; but much more it was the consequence of the administrative anarchy from which England had never been really free since King George had actively interfered in politics. Still it would hardly be just to lay too much stress on the personal element. The British habit of underrating the effort required to carry a war through until some imminent peril or some grave disaster brings the truth home has been too frequently displayed. The same characteristics were hardly less prominent in Walpole's war, and in the Seven Years' War before Pitt attained the practical dictatorship. The plain truth of the matter was that, after the war had once begun, the chance of reconciliation was over, except on terms of the unconditional surrender of the king's party. Conquest could only have been temporary. But conquest was the policy deliberately chosen by Britain; and conquest of a sort was practicable. Howe, adequately reinforced, could have broken through Washington's lines, and shattered his army; and if that was regarded as an end worth achieving, the sooner it was done the better. Ministers, short-sightedly enough, believed that it was worth doing, but they failed to make the effort requisite to do it. To allow matters merely to drag along was sheer stupidity.

Moreover, every month that passed was making the breach more hopelessly irreparable. The idea of separation was steadily gaining in popularity. The incidents of the war were constantly embittering public feeling. The utterances in favour of independence were becoming less guarded and more confident. Most significant of all, the proposal to invoke foreign aid began to be seriously mooted.

Widening of the breach.

After the evacuation of Boston, the disastrous Canadian expedition was still to drag on for a few months; but otherwise military affairs moved slowly. Washington transferred his headquarters to New York, which the British were expected to select as their next point of attack, the supporters of the Union being more numerous and influential in that part of the country. In June Lord Howe at length arrived with his fleet. The Americans were much encouraged by the successful defence of Fort Moultrie against a British squadron at the end of the month, but, a day or

Washington at New York.

Arrival of Lord Howe.

two later, some forty-five ships, conveying the reinforced army from Halifax, appeared off Sandy Hook.

In the mean while, the movement in favour of independence had been advancing rapidly. The demand of a few individuals had become the desire of the bulk of the colonies, though they were not yet unanimous. Early in June the proposal was formally brought before Congress, by Lee of Virginia and John Adams; coupled with resolutions in favour of seeking foreign alliance, and of framing a plan of confederation. These two resolutions were unanimously adopted; the first was postponed, but a committee was appointed to formulate a declaration.

Three weeks later, on July 4, 1776, the Declaration of Independence was adopted, and signed by the representatives of twelve colonies, New York alone abstaining. The document itself is rather a piece of rhetorical defiance than a statement of political principles; but it expresses with more than sufficient vigour the leading fact of the situation—that the American colonies, as a whole, had definitely made up their minds at last that compromise was out of the question, and that they themselves held the King of England responsible. As a statement of the whole case, it is naturally of an extravagantly partisan character; but its value lies, not in the form it takes, but in the truth which it expresses.

Declaration of Independence.

The Declaration of Independence, in short, threw away the scabbard, and altered the whole character of the situation. There was no possible drawing back from it. Hitherto the war had been avowedly waged merely to obtain justice; it was now openly a war of separation. Hitherto there had been more than a profession of readiness to return to the conditions prevailing before 1763. Now the states demanded recognition of their complete severance from Great Britain. The accompanying resolutions of

Congress in favour of forming foreign alliances and of confederation, were simply additional expressions of the same fact. The Americans were no longer loyal subjects forced to revolt by tyranny, ready to return to their allegiance on receiving a due measure of liberty : they avowed themselves a free nation, battling against foreign subjugation.

Almost simultaneously with the adoption by Congress and the states at large, of the Declaration, the opposing armies again came face to face with one another. The British troops, under General Howe, were landed on Staten Island, in front of New York ; the British fleet, under Lord Howe, the general's brother, was in the bay. New York stands at the south end of a long strip of land, cutting the channel of the river Hudson in two. Across the eastern channel lies Brooklyn, on a corner of Long Island ; south, facing New York, is Staten Island. New York is the southern point of New York State. On the mainland southward is the State of New Jersey, divided on the west from Pennsylvania by the Delaware River ; on which, some ninety miles south-west of New York, stands Philadelphia, where Congress was sitting. When the engagement was about to recommence, the Colonial army held New York and Brooklyn ; the British army was on Staten Island, with the British fleet in the bay, ready to co-operate.

The armies at New York.

The fight, however, did not commence at once. Lord Howe and his brother held a commission, though with very limited powers, to make terms with the Colonists ; and some fruitless efforts at reconciliation followed, Lord Howe issuing a proclamation granting pardon to all who should come in, and endeavouring to negotiate with Washington personally. The latter attempt failed, because the British commissioners could not recognize Washington's official position ; while he, on his side, refused to receive any communications, unless it was recognized. The proclamation was met by a counter-invitation to the

Failure of negotiations.

foreigners in the British service—there were large bodies of hired German troops—to enroll themselves as American citizens, in consideration of grants of land.

On August 22nd the contest was reopened. General Clinton crossed from Staten Island to Long Island, and marched on the American camp at Brooklyn. The American commander, Greene, was prostrated by a fever at the time, and Putnam, who took his place, did not know the ground. *Washington driven back.* The British drove their opponents into the Brooklyn fort with heavy loss ; and it was all that Washington could do to cross the river, and rescue the remnant of the army, carrying it back to his own camp at New York.

That city soon became untenable. There was a brief but futile conference between three commissioners from Congress—Franklin, John Adams, and Rutledge of Carolina—and Lord Howe, who consented to meet them simply as a private gentleman. Two days later, Howe sailed up the Hudson, and attacked ; the American troops showed that they were desperately demoralised, and Washington felt that he must abandon the city. On September 15th he withdrew to the north end of New York Island, and intrenched himself at Haarlem Heights and Fort Washington on the western bank of the Hudson. General Howe soon after forced him to abandon his position, first cutting off his communications by sending a couple of ships up the Hudson. The English then falling back, Washington was enabled to take up his position at Fort Lee, Fort Washington being also occupied, with a view to covering Philadelphia ; but, on November 16th, the latter fort was captured with great loss, and three days later the advance of Cornwallis made the evacuation of Fort Lee also necessary. Washington escaped with his army over the Delaware, and the English did not press him farther. In the mean time, the New England states were threatened by a detachment under Clinton, which recovered Rhode Island, while Carleton in the north advanced from Canada, and occupied Crown Point, near Ticonderoga.

So far, then, the renewal of hostilities had told decidedly in favour of the British. They had met with practically unvarying success; they had secured New York, driven Washington into Pennsylvania, were threatening the northern states, and held undisputed control of the sea. The American army was in a state of demoralisation; confidence in a commander, whose abilities were perforce displayed, not in achieving successes, but in averting ruin, was on the wane; matters were not improved by the jealousy of others, who thought that they or their friends should take his place; while money and supplies were badly wanted, as well as men—although an attempt was made to meet this last requirement, when Congress, after repeated representations from Washington, voted the enlistment of troops for the term of the war, instead of only for short specified periods.

Success of the British.

But the British commander was satisfied with his success, and allowed the Americans to rally their forces and recover their *morale*, instead of pressing on to crush them. Congress at least had the credit of backing up Washington; instead of listening to the murmurs of malcontents, it endowed him with a temporary dictatorship in all matters relating to the war. The British remained inactive, and in midwinter Washington suddenly made a highly successful raid into New Jersey, crossing the Delaware on the ice; surprised Trenton, captured a large number of prisoners and a quantity of stores; defeated, in January, a British brigade sent against him under Cornwallis; and established himself in New Jersey: thus substantially improving on the position at the end of November. Here he remained throughout the spring and the early summer (1777), during which time no important movement or engagement took place.

Washington recovers ground.

The British, however, intended to open a vigorous

campaign in July. According to this plan, an attack was to be made on the north from Canada, under General Burgoyne. Descending the Hudson from the lakes, he was to be met by General Clinton with a detachment from New York, so that the New England states would be completely cut off. In the mean time, Howe proposed to deal with Washington, and to capture Philadelphia. *British plan of campaign, 1777.*

Burgoyne started on July 1st, with a considerable force; and at the outset was successful enough, the states militia seeming unable to cope with the regular troops. Before long, however, Gates, the commander of the northern army of the Colonists, was considerably strengthened by detachments hardly spared to him by Washington. Burgoyne was repulsed in an attack on Barrington; his troops began to desert, while Gates's forces were steadily increasing: the British were worsted, or barely held their ground in a series of engagements. Clinton's expedition up the Hudson from New York, planned with intent to form a junction with Burgoyne, was still too far off to afford any hope of assistance. On October 16th, Burgoyne was forced to surrender with all his troops and stores, at Saratoga. *Burgoyne's expedition. Surrender of Saratoga.*

In the mean time, Howe had been more successful in the south, though to no great purpose. He was bent on the capture of Philadelphia, but failed to draw Washington, whom he could not pass, into a general engagement. At last, leaving Clinton—who ought to have commenced his northward march long before—in New York, Howe, with the bulk of his troops departed by sea, sailed round the coast, and landed at the head of the Chesapeake Bay. Washington had been moving south, and was still able to cover Philadelphia with part of his army, but was now forced to an engagement at Brandywine Creek. Here he suffered a defeat on September *Capture of Philadelphia.*

11th, and, although reinforced soon after, he was unable in this part of the country, where the inhabitants were to a great extent loyalists, to maintain his position. A small force left to keep the British in check was defeated, and on the 26th Philadelphia was taken. About the same time, Clinton advanced up the Hudson from New York, and captured a couple of forts; but was too late to be of any assistance to Burgoyne.

The capture of Philadelphia was in itself worth but little. Congress had taken its departure from the threatened city, and the strategical value of the place was of the smallest. On the other hand, Burgoyne's surrender, destroying as it did, all chance of active operations in the north, was a real disaster to the British arms; Gates, moreover, had been immensely strengthened at the expense of the southern army. At the same time, since he now refused to part with any of his borrowed troops, Washington was left, as usual, in such a position that the most he could possibly do was to evade some crowning disaster. Accordingly he withdrew into winter quarters at Valley Forge, while the British settled down in like manner at Philadelphia.

Serious as was the position of the American chief, this winter was yet the turning-point of the war. For a long time past, the Colonists had been negotiating with the French court, which had been growing more and more favourably inclined to active interference. The news of Burgoyne's surrender was apparently decisive. During December the Americans received positive promises of support, and of recognition as an independent state; and this alteration in the international situation, which opened the second period of the war, completely changed the prospects of recovering British ascendency.

Effect of Saratoga in France.

CHAPTER II.

THE FRENCH INTERVENTION.

1776-1780.

Strength of the anti-colonials in England—Continental opinion—Attitude of France—Turgot—Vergennes—Spain—Strength of the Bourbon powers—French volunteers—Secret support of Americans by France—Effects of Saratoga—Colonial Confederation—1778: *France declares war*—North's conciliatory bills—Chatham's last speech—Congress rejects overtures—Changed conditions of the war—Evacuation of Philadelphia—Lord Howe and D'Estaing—Battle of Ushant—Clinton's embarrassments—Cornwallis in the south—1778-9: D'Estaing at Savannah——Position of the British in 1780—*The War in the West Indies*—1778: Santa Lucia captured—1779: D'Estaing and Byron—1780: Arrival of De Guichen and Rodney.

WHEN Lord North became Prime Minister, the effect was virtually to make the king dictator. The cabinet was the king's cabinet, and carried out the king's policy whatever might be the particular views of individual members. There was a majority of members who held office for the sake of office; there were others, like Barrington, who held it because they conceived it to be their duty to the king, to remain in his service and fulfil his bidding so long as he willed that they should do so. For a long time, North himself avowedly conducted a policy which in his heart he believed to be mistaken, simply because the king would not have him resign. Hence, the anti-colonial party in parliament was irresistibly superior in numbers to the Rockingham and Chatham section which opposed the war, while

Strength of the anti-colonials in England.

their best men were intensely desirous of maintaining the union. Unhappily, the country had come over to the king's side, partly because it altogether failed to realise the issue at stake, partly because it felt that the colonies had thrown down the gauntlet with insolence and must be chastised at any cost, partly because the belief was very generally prevalent that the resistance could not last. Indignation at the action of the Americans, and ignorance of its causes, were at the root of the popular favour in which the war was held. Moreover, this attitude was confirmed by the injudicious methods of the bulk of the Opposition, who tried the invariably unsuccessful plan of sulking in their tents, or else, like the younger Fox, who was now rapidly winning fame as an orator, espousing the cause of the insurgents with a heat and vigour which caused them to be regarded less as partisans of America than as enemies of England. Chatham and Burke were almost alone in fighting the colonial battle on patriotic lines; while the former was too frequently incapacitated by illness, and the later held too subordinate a position in the party, for either of them to exercise wide influence.

On the other hand, the set of continental opinion was thoroughly adverse to England. Her opponents in the great war were all thirsting to see her humbled; her ally Frederick had been turned into an enemy by Bute's treatment of him, although he had no intention of giving any sort of assistance to either side. But the matter of vital importance was the attitude of France and Spain.

Continental opinion.

The victory of the revolted colonies in the duel would mean the triumph of republican principles; but to the French court, supremely unconscious of the volcanic eruption in preparation, this was a small matter. Republican theories were very much in fashion where Republican practice was the last thing dreamed of. The rights of man—in the abstract—were in high favour,

Attitude of France.

and the concrete application of this theory on a distant continent at the expense of Great Britain was eminently attractive, while the possibility of its being applied at home was conveniently ignored. Nor was France much touched by the prospect of her colonies following suit and revolting from her control. The matter of primary importance was, that if the American colonies proved successful, Britain would suffer a very serious blow.

French sympathies, then, being altogether with the Americans, the question arose, whether the country should take any active part in supporting them. Turgot, the finance minister when the war began, was distinctly opposed to any participation. He held that, in the long run, the colonies must win; and that, in any case, the financial position of France would make it madness for her to become involved in war. Moreover, in his view, the colonies had become a source, not of strength, but of weakness to Great Britain; which would suffer more from victory than from defeat. On the other hand, Vergennes, who now occupied the position formerly held by Choiseul, was bent on interference; which should in the first place take the form of secret encouragement only, to be followed up by openly taking sides when action should be most effective. Vergennes, however, counted on the co-operation of Spain; and Spain could hardly adopt his attitude without serious misgivings. She had vast colonies from which nearly all her wealth was derived. If this revolt should prove successful, there was the strongest ground for supposing that her own colonies would follow suit. On the other hand, resentment against England and the craving to recover Gibraltar urged her to make any sacrifice which should injure the Power she hated. Thus, to both France and Spain, the revolt of the American colonies presented the prospect of an opening for an effective war of revenge; which could be accompanied by no large gains to the

Turgot.

Vergennes.

Spain.

Bourbons, and might very possibly end for Spain in the loss of her colonies ; but, undoubtedly, held out hopes of inflicting serious loss and humiliation on Great Britain.

In comparing the position of the Bourbons at this date with their position during the last great war, two vital differences may be observed. Then, France had been constantly hampered by a great war raging on the continent of Europe : now, she would be acting with no such drain on her resources ; she would be able to concentrate her energies on a purely English war. Then, by the application of a vigorous policy, England had been able in a very short time to establish a complete naval supremacy, which annihilated the prospect of French success : now, France had learnt her lesson, at least in part, and her navy was in all respects infinitely superior to what it had been. In short, England, with a navy which had been allowed to fall off in efficiency, would now be standing alone against the naval powers whose fleets had improved in the interval, her hands tied by a serious war in America, while her rivals would be unhampered.

Comparative strength of the Bourbons.

The policy of Vergennes prevailed. As early as the spring of 1776, the French court was arranging to support the insurgent colonists with money, and had persuaded the Spanish court to follow its example. In July of that year, Silas Deane arrived from America to negotiate. Publicly his position was not recognized ; privately he received the warmest assurances coupled with substantial contributions. Before long, energetic Frenchmen were flocking as volunteers to join Washington, all expecting and receiving high military posts—not a little to the embarrassment of the American general, who had no choice in the matter. Nevertheless, many jealousies and heartburnings arose, especially as not a few of these volunteers were by no means particularly competent. Some of them, however, notably the young Marquis de la

French volunteers.

Fayette, who were actuated by a genuine belief in a great cause, proved of great service. The reception in France and in Europe generally of the Declaration of Independence was very remarkable. The document spoke of the "inalienable rights" of man, and of the relations of peoples to governments, in a manner which would have justified revolt against nearly every government in Europe—as Mirabeau saw,—but the court was too much occupied in cheering on its *protégés* to the combat to realise the menace to its own position. Men, money, and stores were secretly shipped off to the insurgents (who, as we have seen, were badly in want of all the help they could get), while a considerable parade of neutrality was kept up—the more markedly as the moment for throwing off the mask appeared to be drawing nearer. It was impossible, however, to conceal the fashionable sentiment with regard to the war when Franklin, who arrived in Paris at the close of 1776, was rapidly elevated into a popular hero of the first rank. {Secret support given.}

Yet France was unwilling finally to compromise herself while there was any apparent chance of an early collapse on the part of the Americans. If the campaign of 1777, had been properly carried out, the war might have been ended for the time being. Had Clinton effected a junction with Burgoyne, while Howe pushed every advantage he gained, the close of the year might have seen Washington's army crushed, and the New England states helpless. Instead of this came the surrender at Saratoga; while Vergennes was enabled to realise from a distance, what Washington's countrymen close at hand saw far less clearly, the immense capacity of the American chief for dogged defence under the most disheartening conditions. Therefore, before the year ended, the minds of the American commissioners in Paris were relieved. The positive promise of recognition as an independent state, and of active support, was given; although the plans of the {Saratoga turns the scale.}

French government were still for a while concealed from the English ambassador.

A month earlier, Congress had taken the second step which was the necessary corollary to the Declaration of Independence. It adopted and submitted to the individual states, which as yet formed merely a loose congeries with no adequate authority for enforcing united action, a scheme of confederation. The articles, however, were not signed till July of the following year; and then only by eight states, North Carolina and Georgia following suit a month afterwards. It was only in March, 1781, that the last of the thirteen colonies gave in its adhesion.

Colonial confederation.

The Franco-American treaty, virtually a declaration of war against England by France, was not notified in London until March 17, 1778. It was at once recognized that the whole situation was changed. The suspicion had been prevalent for some little time that something of the kind was coming. North, aware of his own incompetence, was anxious to retire; the king himself was beginning to suspect that he might ultimately be forced to give way. When the treaty was announced as an accomplished fact, he is said to have contemplated the idea of dropping the American war, and concentrating the energies of the country against France. Ministers, however, had substantial knowledge of the treaty at an earlier date; and, on February 17th, North brought in fresh conciliatory bills, granting all that the colonies had originally claimed, and giving power to appoint two commissioners with full power to treat on those lines.

France declares war.

Attempts at conciliation.

But it was now too late. The bills could only be regarded as a sign of weakness. They emanated from the very men who were primarily responsible, at an earlier stage, for the rejection of all overtures. They only produced the impression that these men had lost hope of

ultimate victory; and the Americans had already gone a
step farther, and would accept nothing short of the recognition of complete independence. In England, on the other
hand, the country was being rudely awakened to the fact
that a tremendous national crisis was at hand. Instinctively
she turned to the man who had saved her before; but still
the king's obstinacy made him stubbornly refuse to accept
Chatham as minister is spite of North's entreaties. Nor was
Chatham himself fit for the post. On April 7th, **Chatham's**
the end came. The Duke of Richmond, on behalf **last**
of the Rockinghams, moved for the withdrawal of **speech.**
all fleets and armies from America. Chatham spoke, utterly
repudiating the idea of giving up the colonies, though he
had at all times declared that to conquer them was impossible. His speech was at times hardly audible, and his
extreme exhaustion and suffering were evident. Richmond
replied: Chatham attempted to rise, but fell back in a fit
of apoplexy. He lingered for another month; but his voice
was never heard again. On May 11th, the great statesman
died, leaving a more conspicuous blank than any Englishman
since the accession of the House of Hanover.

The news of Lord North's bills reached America before
the French treaty; and, for a short time, there was uncertainty as to their possible effects. Congress, **Congress**
however, was much more decided than was the **refuses to**
popular sentiment, which was not enthusiastic **treat.**
about the war. The answer was a refusal to treat unless the
fleets and armies were withdrawn, or independence definitely
recognized. The arrival and publication of the French
treaty a few days later (May 3rd) dissipated all doubt
whether the action of congress would be generally endorsed.
The day of conciliation was over. When the commissioners,
Lord Carlisle, Lord Auckland, and Governor Johnstone
arrived on June 4th, and attempted to open negotiations,
they were met with the response that judgment had already
been passed on the bills. The first condition of treating

must be the recognition of independence. Nor did the efforts of the commission prove more successful as time went on. Attempts were made to win over individuals, and Johnstone was charged with offering bribes. He denied the charge; but, in spite of his resignation, much fresh ill-feeling had been aroused, which culminated when at last, in October, conciliation was angrily discarded, and the Americans were threatened in terms which were taken to imply the intention of importing new and more savage methods into the strife.

From the time of the French intervention the war changes its character. Hitherto it had been carried on by land, the fleet being merely used as an adjunct to the army; although Lord Howe had urged throughout that the navy could be the more effectively employed of the two. Had it been properly utilised the chief ports might have been blockaded, and the line of the Hudson secured, in accordance with the scheme for cutting off the New England states so disastrously attempted by Burgoyne. But England had failed to use her fleet while she was free to do so; and from this time it became too fully occupied in coping with equal or superior rival fleets to render independent assistance in offensive operations of British armies. The interest of the war becomes primarily maritime, and the operations on the continent fall into the second place.

Changed conditions of the war.

Henceforth we shall have, at times, to watch operations carried on in four different regions: European waters; Indian waters and India, where a war was being waged with Hyder Ali of Mysore, to which we shall revert later; the West Indies; and the continent and coast of America—the two last being intimately connected. For France had not joined in the war with the simple intent of freeing the colonists from the yoke of tyranny; that object was only a part, though an important one, in the great design of breaking the power of England.

The winter of 1777-8 had been passed in inglorious ease, at Philadelphia, by the British army ; which had, moreover, succeeded in alienating, by misconduct of various sorts, the Quaker population of that city. Washington, at Valley Forge, had been all the time in an extremely precarious position, suffering as usual from want both of men and of supplies. With the completion of the French treaty, the British lost their power to strike, being thrown on the defensive by the expectation of a new attack from the sea, which they had hitherto controlled. The first order was for the evacuation of Philadelphia, and withdrawal to new York, Clinton now taking Sir William Howe's place in command of the land forces, while Lord Howe remained in command of the fleet. The evacuation was completed on June 17th. The retreat was effected with considerable skill, while Washington was doing all he could to harass the rear. A battle was fought at Monmouth on June 28th, in which the Americans were practically worsted, as they failed to check the retreat. The result was mainly due to the misconduct of General Lee, who, with his friends, believed that he was himself the proper person to hold Washington's position. His consequent suspension after a court-martial was doubtless a considerable relief to his chief. *Evacuation of Philadelphia.*

Clinton duly arrived at New York, though with diminished forces. Meanwhile, Lord Howe, by dint of great skill and energy, brought his fleet out of Delaware Bay with the transports, and reached New York Harbour ten days before the arrival of the French fleet, which had sailed from Toulon in April.

The treaty had not been announced till this squadron was almost ready to sail. The French admiral, D'Estaing, was not, however, sufficiently alive to the need of rapidity. His force was nearly double that of Lord Howe, and if he had succeeded in anticipating the British admiral at Delaware Bay or at Sandy Hook *Lord Howe and D'Estaing.*

outside New York, the opposing force would have been severed, and Clinton's position would have been rendered extremely precarious. Under these circumstances, the capture of New York would have been a crushing disaster. But Howe's skill had saved the position. The navigation of the bay was difficult, and D'Estaing, in spite of his superior armament, would not venture on an attack. He may, indeed, have been influenced more by political than strategic considerations, for the immediate termination of the war on the continent would have turned the contest into a simple duel between England and France, from which less advantage might be reaped in the end. But, whatever the reason, D'Estaing sailed for Rhode Island to co-operate with the Americans against the British there. Again, however, his plans were foiled. The Americans were not fully ready; before they were, Lord Howe had appeared. The French still had much the larger fleet, though the British had been reinforced; but the wind was in favour of the latter, and D'Estaing was afraid of being attacked. He put out to sea, but, before either he or his adversary felt in a position to make an attack successfully, a storm arose: so much damage was done that the French commander declared he must put into Boston harbour to refit; and, since the movement of the troops on shore was dependent on his co-operation, the Americans were obliged to retreat. In November, D'Estaing left the American coast, and sailed for the West Indies, on the same day when Commodore Hotham, with a division of the British fleet and five thousand troops, sailed from New York for Barbadoes.

In the meantime, the first actual naval battle of the war had taken place on July 27th off Ushant, when two large **Battle of Ushant.** fleets were engaged without any definite result, much to the indignation of the English. The French fleet from Brest and the British Channel fleet fought each other, and then returned to port. Coupled with

D'Estaing's unchecked voyage to America, this marks very clearly the different naval conditions prevailing in 1759 and in 1778. At the earlier date the British power was such that when the Toulon fleet had put to sea it was broken up by one British squadron, while a different British squadron was more than a match for the Brest fleet. Now, however, while Keppel at Ushant had under his command a fleet not markedly superior to that of his opponents, there was no adequate force to prevent D'Estaing from sailing out of the Mediterranean and crossing the Atlantic unpursued.

Although Clinton's strength was very considerably diminished by the departure of Hotham with five thousand men to Barbadoes, D'Estaing's withdrawal at the same time left him with an army substantially superior to Washington's, and a fleet sufficient to control the communications by sea. Instead, however, of concentrating and striking at Washington, Clinton was ordered to further reduce his force at New York in order to send an expedition to the south, for the recovery of Georgia and the Carolinas. The most that could result from such a plan was the securing of individual points along an extended line, with no force anywhere large enough to reduce any considerable portion of the country or to resist a regularly concentrated attack. Hence Washington passed the winter of 1778-9 at Middlebrook, in New Jersey, without that sense of being constantly on the verge of some irreparable disaster which had hitherto haunted him. Indeed, when the spring came, he found himself chiefly occupied in restraining the ardour of Congress, which was now anxious to take the offensive and send another expedition to Canada—committing the very blunder of their opponents in sending to the south. Washington, however, had more than military reasons for his opposition, though these alone were strong enough. He recognized that, since the French intervention, interference

Clinton's embarrassments.

x

with Canada was likely, so far as it proved successful, to result in the restoration there of French influence, and so to revive the very danger from which the British colonists, as they then were, had been saved twenty years before by Pitt and Wolfe.

On the other hand, the British expedition to the south had succeeded in its actual object. There were large numbers of loyalists in the southern states; the British troops got the best of the fighting, and Savannah was captured about the end of the year (1778), though an attempt upon Charleston had to be abandoned. Otherwise, beyond the injuries inflicted by ravaging expeditions on both sides — that of the Americans was directed against the Iroquois in revenge for a raid on Wyoming in 1778, — little was accomplished on either side until September, 1779; except the establishment of a British fort at Penobscot to protect Nova Scotia, and the disastrous failure of an American expedition against it.

Cornwallis in the south.

In September, the reappearance of D'Estaing's fleet — to whose operations since November, 1778, we shall revert very shortly — produced a brief effect. The British contingent at Newport, Rhode Island, expecting a renewal of the combined military and naval attack so ably frustrated by Lord Howe a year earlier, evacuated Newport hastily. D'Estaing, however, made little use of his opportunity. He wasted time before Savannah, where the British, in occupation, were being besieged: and then made a wholly inopportune though gallant attack, which was completely repulsed. After this, the French fleet once more withdrew, the admiral departed home, and those ships which did not accompany him returned to the West Indies. The antagonists on the continent were left very much as they were before; and the British pressed on their policy of recovering the southern states, the evacuation of Rhode Island supplying fresh troops for that purpose. By the end of the year large reinforcements from New York were on their way south by sea. In February, 1780, they arrived before Charleston, which capitulated in May. Thus, broadly speaking, the southern states were now so far in the hands of the British that there was little resistance offered to them, though, owing to their high-handed procedure, the feeling of the population was turning against them. In respect, however, of the future conduct of the war, the important feature of the situation on the American continent by the middle of 1780 was, that the British army was in two divisions, one at New York under Clinton, the other in the south under Cornwallis ; so that, since the intervening country was in revolt, their communication depended entirely on the control of the sea ; and if at any time a superior French fleet should appear in those waters, the British forces would be effectively cut in two.

We may now return to watch the course of naval events from November, 1778, when D'Estaing and Hotham left Boston and New York respectively for the West Indies ; where the fighting was mainly confined to the neighbourhood of the Windward Islands. Here we should observe that—taking the islands from north to south—France held Guadaloupe ; Dominica was an English possession, but was captured by the French in September, 1778 ; Martinique was French, as was also Saint Lucia ; Grenada, and farther east Barbadoes, were in the hands of the English. Now, inasmuch as any of these islands was practically at the mercy of the Power which happened at a given time to have the naval preponderance in the West Indian seas, the true policy to be pursued by either power was to secure such ports as were of definite and strategical value, and to aim at a general naval preponderance ; regarding the temporary occupation of other islands as of quite minor importance.

As Howe by his superior promptitude had been beforehand with D'Estaing at Delaware Bay and Sandy Hook, so

The war in the West Indies.

now Barrington, the British admiral at Barbadoes, forestalled the French commander. Two days after Hotham's arrival with the transports, Barrington put to sea and seized the island of Santa Lucia, which had an invaluable port; and was enabled so to dispose his ships that D'Estaing, arriving the next day, was unable to make a serious attack. Thus a thoroughly good position was secured for the British fleet in the immediate neighbourhood of the principal French port on Martinique; in spite of the fact that the French had the larger fleet, so that the British were prevented from acting farther on the offensive.

Capture of Santa Lucia.

Barrington had achieved success in an important operation by his superior capacity as a commander. For several months, nothing more was done on either side. Both the fleets were reinforced, Barrington being superseded by his senior, Admiral Byron; but the preponderance still lay with the French. In June, Byron sailed out with most of his vessels to convoy a party of merchant ships clear of the islands. D'Estaing took the opportunity to sail south, capture St. Vincent, and attack Grenada. Byron reappearing with his smaller fleet, and having an incorrect idea of D'Estaing's force, attacked him. On discovering the true position he was obliged to draw off; and in allowing him to do so, his adversary committed a very grave blunder. The explanation appears to be that, in D'Estaing's view, the important point was to secure the present capture of Grenada. Whereas if he had used his opportunity to inflict a serious blow on the weaker fleet, he would have so increased the naval preponderance as to make himself master of the West Indian Seas (July 6, 1779).

D'Estaing and Byron.

Twice it had been in the power of the French fleet to strike a crushing blow: in 1778, when D'Estaing was foiled by Howe's superior promptitude; in 1779, when he sacrificed naval supremacy for the sake of capturing Grenada. On either occasion, a decisive French victory would have brought the conclusion of the war within measurable distance ; on both occasions the French superiority in numbers was such that victory ought to have been secure. Both opportunities were lost, one by inferior seamanship, the other by short-sighted strategy.

D'Estaing's abortive attack on Savannah, already described, followed in September. In October he sailed for France, part of the fleet rejoining the West Indian squadron ; which was reinforced in the following spring (March 1780), by a new commander, De Guichen, shortly before the arrival of British reinforcements, also under a new admiral, Rodney. But before this time the difficulties of Great Britain, already enormously increased by the intervention of France, had been still farther enhanced by the addition of Spain to the belligerents.

De Guichen and Rodney.

CHAPTER III.

THE STRUGGLE FOR LIFE.

1779–1783.

Spain joins the allies—Naval superiority of the allies—1780: Rodney and the Spanish Fleet—Rodney and De Guichen in the West Indies—July, 1780: The situation—The Northern Army—1780-1: Cornwallis in the South—1781: Cornwallis retreats to Yorktown—1780: The armed neutrality—War with Holland—1781: Arrival of De Grasse in the West Indies—His failure to crush the British fleet—July: position of the British in America—The opposing fleets at the Chesapeake—Surrender of Yorktown—Change in British sentiment—Strength of the rival navies—1782: Siege of Gibraltar—The relief by Lord Howe—1781: Suffren sails for India—1782-3: Suffren and Hughes—1782: De Grasse and Hood at St. Kitt's—Arrival of Rodney—Battle of The Saints—Results of the struggle—Desire for peace—Preliminaries signed—1783: Final treaties.

SPAIN had for some time past been much under the influence of the French court; she had taken a similar line to her neighbour, though less vigorously, in sending secret assistance to the revolted colonies. She still, when France threw off the mask, carried on the pretence of endeavouring to mediate, and of good will to England. But the pressure of France, combined with the intense longing to recover Port Mahon and Gibraltar, proved too strong; and, in April, 1779, she signed a convention with France in which the restitution of these two places was made the prime object of the war. Two months later, war was declared between England and Spain.

Spain joins the allies, 1779.

Within the coasts of Great Britain, the effect of the new combination was to stiffen the resolution and courage of the people. The war with America never aroused enthusiasm; the war against the united Bourbons set the fighting spirit of the whole nation, Whig or Tory, ablaze. It was a battle in which the odds on paper were heavily against us, and the only chance of reversing them lay in the superior management of inferior fleets. Before war had been declared for a month, Gibraltar was invested. In August an allied fleet nearly double the size of the squadron for defence appeared in the Channel. But nothing resulted. There was no battle—for the disproportion made it impossible for the British to challenge,—the French and Spanish commanders quarrelled, and the two fleets went home having made an imposing demonstration but effected nothing whatever. Nevertheless it is clear that with these immense armaments threatening her shores, it was impossible for England to spare any adequate portion of her navy to obtain control in any one quarter. *Superiority of the allied fleets.*

In the winter, however, Rodney was dispatched, in the first place, to relieve Gibraltar by throwing in supplies, and, in the second, to act against the French in the West Indies. On January 8th he fell in with a smaller Spanish squadron, which he captured; and on the 16th he destroyed a second squadron, under the Admiral Langara. These two victories seriously crippled the Spanish navy. Gibraltar was relieved without interference; and the major part of the fleet, with the prizes, returned to England; while Rodney, with the remainder, departed for Barbadoes. *Rodney off Spain, January, 1780.*

The French, commanded by De Guichen, still retained a clear numerical superiority in the Antilles; but they nearly lost it in a battle on April 18th, when Rodney out-generalled his antagonist, and would, in all probability, have inflicted a crushing defeat on him, but for the misunderstanding of signals. As it was, the British had the better of the encounter, and De Guichen acquired a very wholesome *De Guichen and Rodney, April, 1780.*

respect for his opponent's skill and tenacity. Even the arrival of a Spanish squadron did not enable him to take the offensive; but Rodney, for his part, could strike no blow.

Thus, at midsummer, 1780, De Guichen and Rodney were watching each other in the West Indies, neither feeling strong enough to make the attack. On the American continent, Cornwallis had established himself in the southern states, where, for the time being, active resistance was over; although it was clear that, if any part of his force was withdrawn, the colonists were still ready to rise; while his communications with New York depended entirely on the sea. Meantime, Clinton, at New York, though in no danger, had been too much reduced in force by the support given to the southern army to be able to take the offensive.

The situation in July, 1780.

Washington, on the other hand, was materially strengthened in July by the arrival of a large body of French troops, under Rochambeau. These might, indeed, have become a cause of weakness, of jealousies, and of divided counsels, but the French government had very judiciously given instructions that their officers were to be treated as subordinate to those of the American army itself, while Washington was given rank in the French army, placing him above Rochambeau.

The northern army, July, 1780–1781.

Nevertheless, the position of the Colonial army was seriously endangered in September by the treason of Benedict Arnold. This very daring soldier, the same who had displayed such conspicuous courage in the conduct of the disastrous Canadian expedition, had laid himself open to a serious charge of peculation. A public reprimand filled him with such indignation that he entered upon a treasonable correspondence with Clinton. By the capture, within the American lines, of Major André, a British officer carrying Arnold's papers, the plot was disclosed. Major

André was hanged as a spy, but Arnold himself made good his escape, and with his flight the danger was ended.

The winter was passed by Washington very much in his chronic condition, of trying to hold together an army which was receiving little of its pay, was suffering from totally insufficient supplies, and was more than once on the verge of mutiny. The presence of Rochambeau's contingent, however, was, no doubt, of considerable assistance ; and the extremes of the discontent among the rank and file were somewhat diminished in the spring of 1781, by the exertions of Robert Morris, the newly appointed Superintendent of Finance, who succeeded in, at least, modifying some of the most crying grievances.

At the close of June, 1780, Cornwallis had announced that in Georgia and the south resistance was practically at an end. Before long, however, the Colonials made head again in Virginia, where Gates, the victor of Saratoga, was placed in command. At Camden, on August 16th, this new army was scattered ; but the British administration was so harsh that bitter popular feeling was aroused against them. The insurgents, under Sumpter and Marion, gathered in sufficient force to harass Cornwallis considerably, and force him to fall back ; while Greene, Washington's favourite subordinate, was sent to take the command in place of Gates. *Cornwallis in the south, 1780.*

Nevertheless, Cornwallis determined to carry out his design of marching through North Carolina and Virginia to the Chesapeake, and so effecting a conjunction with the northern army. In spite of a victory at Cowpens (January 17, 1781), Greene was obliged to retreat ; yet after another engagement, at Guilford Court House (March 15th), the British commander found it necessary to withdraw to Wilmington, on the coast, lest his communications should be cut off. But, although, at the end of April, he continued his northward march, the Carolinas had only been awaiting his departure to rise *1781.*

again ; so that Greene, leaving La Fayette to keep Cornwallis in check, was able, in spite of minor reverses, to drive in the English troops which had been left in the south, to Savannah, Charleston, and Wilmington.

In August, Cornwallis received orders from headquarters to send back three thousand troops to New York, and to retire himself to Yorktown at the mouth of the Chesapeake, where practically the last act of the war, as far as concerned America, was to take place. Thus the main force of the British on the continent was divided between New York and Yorktown, and it is clear that, if the allied enemies obtained control of the sea between these two points, they could entirely prevent efficient co-operation, and by skilful concentration might have half the British forces at a time practically at their mercy. At the moment, the main fleets on both sides were at the West Indies, while neither the French squadron under Du Barras at Newport, nor the British ships at New York under Graves, were strong enough to efficiently control the American waters. We have now to take up the narrative of the naval events during the twelve months, ending in the fall of Yorktown.

Cornwallis withdraws to Yorktown, August, 1781.

In August, 1780, De Guichen left the West Indies for France, with fifteen ships. Rodney, not knowing his destination, left half his fleet in the Antilles, and sailed with the other half for New York, fearing that the enemy had gone to co-operate in the American continental war. His arrival paralysed for the time the action of the French squadron, actually at Newport, but, in the absence of the more pressing danger, he felt it necessary to return to the West Indies, lest the fleet there should be overpowered.

The fleets, 1780.

The privateering exploits of the American Paul Jones, in British waters, about this time, may be mentioned ; but they did not influence the larger operations of the war.

In this year also (1780) a new European confederation

was formed, which was aimed against the British claims to naval supremacy.

The Baltic Powers combined to assert and defend the rights of neutral vessels in carrying the goods of belligerents, in a manner which would render the supremacy of one of them by sea very much less effective; and when, in December, Holland joined the "Armed Neutrality," as it was called, England forthwith—though America, France, Spain, and Hyder Ali and the Mahrattas in India, were already on her hands—declared war against Holland as well. Here, however, it must be remarked that she had little to lose, and possibly something to gain; as Holland was separated from the other belligerents, while England hoped that some of the Dutch possessions over seas might fall into her hands. *The armed neutrality. War with Holland, December 20, 1780.*

The immediate result of the declaration of war against Holland was the capture by Rodney—for the moment, in superior force—of two Dutch islands in the West Indies. But at the end of April (1781) the French admiral, De Grasse, arrived with twenty-one ships of the line, and a convoy. England, on the other hand, was unable to send reinforcements. A fleet had, indeed, sailed early in March, which should have intercepted the French admiral; but it was unable to pursue him, owing to the pressing necessity for succouring Gibraltar, where the garrison had been unrelieved since February, 1780, while it was now covered by a large Spanish squadron lying at Cadiz. *De Grasse arrives in the West Indies, April, 1781.*

De Grasse found Rodney in person absent, and Hood with eighteen ships blockading the port of Martinique. The English wished to prevent De Grasse, with his larger fleet, from cutting them off from Santa Lucia, or effecting a junction with the ships blockaded in Fort Royal. Hood, however, failed in his manœuvre, and the French effected their junction. Their forces were now so far superior, that

Hood, if brought to an engagement, could only have escaped a great disaster by showing immense superiority in seamanship and tactics. De Grasse, however, let him go, thereby missing the opportunity of securing great naval preponderance, instead of only a marked superiority.

In the month of July, then, the important divisions of the British army were disposed at New York and Yorktown, respectively. There was a small French squadron at Newport, and a small English squadron, under Graves, at New York. The main American army, under Washington, with the French reinforcements, under Rochambeau, were before New York; but since the Jerseys and Pennsylvania were in their hands, they were in a position, as Clinton was not, to transfer their operations by a land route to Yorktown. Neither the existing French nor British squadron was strong enough to take decisive action; but a superior fleet of sufficient size, acting in combination with the land forces against either New York or Yorktown, would make the position of the British exceedingly precarious.

<small>British position in America, July, 1781.</small>

Washington and Rochambeau decided to make the move against Yorktown. Accordingly, dispatches were sent to De Grasse, urging him to sail for the American coast, and unite in operating against one of the two great divisions of the British. Meanwhile the army crossed the Hudson, and was well on its way to the Chesapeake with too great a start for pursuit, before Clinton had realised that the attack was to be made, not on him, but on Cornwallis.

Meanwhile, De Grasse sailed in force from Hayti for the Chesapeake; taking an indirect route, in order to mislead the British. Three days before his arrival (August 27th), Du Barras sailed with the French Newport squadron, making a wide circuit to avoid the English fleet, also with the purpose of reaching the Chesapeake. Rodney himself was obliged to sail for England, but he detached Hood from

<small>De Grasse at the Chesa-peake, August, 1781.</small>

the West Indies with a considerable fleet, inferior, however, to that of De Grasse, to operate on the American coast. Hood, taking the direct route, found no enemy's ships at the Chesapeake ; and, not knowing De Grasse's destination, proceeded to New York to join Graves, who took the chief command : whence the combined fleet sailed on August 31st, to find De Grasse. On reaching the Chesapeake, with their nineteen ships of the line, they found De Grasse already there with twenty-four. Graves attacked, unsuccessfully ; De Grasse, according to the regular French habit, but with right for once on his side, considered that the chance of inflicting a heavy blow on the adversaries' fleet was not worth the risk of Cornwallis being relieved, and maintained the defensive ; holding the British in play till the squadron of Du Barras also had successfully cleared them, and found its way into the Chesapeake. The British were now hopelessly outnumbered by sea ; the prospect of naval assistance was destroyed, while Cornwallis was closely invested by land, with the whole force of the American army. By October 19th, the situation was absolutely hopeless, and on that day Cornwallis surrendered with the whole of his forces. *Surrender of Yorktown, October 19, 1781.*

This, as far as America was concerned, practically concluded the war. England, outnumbered in all quarters by the enemy's fleets, was fighting for life ; she had not the power to pour fresh armies into America, and she no longer had the will. For the country was now convinced that the conquest of the colonies was in itself neither possible nor really desirable. Even the king began to see, what Lord North had long realised, that the struggle was a vain one ; and the surrender of Yorktown in effect clinched the matter. No more offensive operations were attempted. The parliamentary support of ministers showed rapidly waning majorities ; by February 27, 1782, the majority had become a minority. Yet it was *Change in British sentiment.*

not till March 20th that North was able to induce the king to accept the resignation which had been proffered time after time ; and George, with the most intense chagrin, and not without first seriously proposing to withdraw from England to Hanover, was compelled to accept a new Rockingham ministry comprising all the steadiest and fiercest opponents of the war, from its inception to its close—Shelburne, Fox, Burke, and the rest.

But if the nation was weary of the American war, no relaxation was shown in the stubborn determination to fight the Bourbon Powers to the uttermost.

The superiority in numbers and weight of a combined French and Spanish fleet over the British in European waters has already been remarked upon. The principal effect, however, was chiefly the permanent threat of invasion which resulted and which prevented the English from appearing in superior force in any of the regions where fighting was going on. Thus, when De Grasse sailed for the West Indies in March, 1781, the British admiral, Derby, having failed to intercept him, was unable to pursue. Yet he passed south, threw supplies into Gibraltar and Port Mahon, which was also being besieged, and came home again without being assailed. Later in the year, the French and Spanish fleets formed a junction, and made a demonstration with fifty ships of the line while Derby had but thirty ; yet, owing mainly to the action of the Spanish commanders, no effort was made to force a battle. The demonstration did no more. Early in February, 1782, however, Port Mahon was forced to surrender.

<small>Naval force of the allies. 1781.</small>

This year, 1782, is of especial interest from a naval point of view, inasmuch as England was throughout engaged in fighting, not for empire or conquest, but for her hold on the seas ; while the war on the American continent no longer intervenes to withdraw attention from the naval issue.

<small>1782.</small>

In Europe, the central point is the siege of Gibraltar, on the retention of which—especially since Port Mahon had fallen—depended Britain's power in the Mediterranean. Gibraltar had endured a long siege with the utmost stubbornness. Twice she had been relieved, by Rodney and Derby, as already related. But this year the allies were resolved on the capture. Through the spring and summer their great combined fleet guarded the waterways; in September they gathered to co-operate with the besiegers on the land side in a crowning effort. From sea and land bombs and cannon balls were to be poured into the devoted fortress; and an assault in overwhelming force was finally to dispose of the exhausted garrison. For four days the bombardment went on; on the fifth, ten battering ships stood in and anchored, to make the storm more deadly. The plan was effective, until the automatic arrangements for extinguishing fire failed. One after another the battering ships took fire; and the flames spread. Nine of them blew up, and the tenth was boarded and burnt. The grand assault had failed, and now the hope of the besiegers lay in starving out the garrison.

Siege of Gibraltar.

But the British were alive to the need of a relief; moreover they had realised by this time that, when they had to deal with French and Spanish ships in combination, they might calculate on dissension among the enemy's commanders and superior seamanship in their own captains, to counteract very considerable apparent odds. Lord Howe, now in command of the fleet, appeared with transports and thirty-four ships of the line on October 11th; out-manœuvred the allies; passed the supply ships into the harbour; and sailed out of the Mediterranean on the 19th. Next day there was an engagement, but Howe, having only thirty-four sail of the line to his adversaries' forty-nine, could only take the defensive; the fleets never came to close quarters, and the battle itself was of no importance, since the whole purpose of Howe's

Relief of Gibraltar, October, 1782.

arrival had been thoroughly accomplished, and Gibraltar effectually saved.

When De Grasse had sailed for the West Indies in 1781, a small portion of his fleet was detached for India, under Suffren—an admiral who is remarkable as being the one instance of a Frenchman who habitually recognized that it was of primary importance to attack the enemy's fleet whenever there was a good chance of inflicting more injury than his own ships would suffer. His expedition, indeed, had little actual effect on the war, for two reasons: he received insufficient support from France; and, while he proved himself a more skilful commander than his adversary, Admiral Hughes, the latter was much better served by his captains, who fought their ships with a doggedness and a seamanship which was not displayed by the French officers.

Suffren sails for India, 1781.

Suffren had with him a convoy of troops for the Cape, which was threatened by a British expedition. This he found at Porto Praya, where he attacked and to some extent crippled the squadron; being thereby enabled to reach the Cape first, and land his troops. He then proceeded to the Isle of France, and joined his senior, d'Orvés (October 25, 1781); succeeding to the command on that admiral's death three months later, when nearing Madras.

The English at this time were at war with Hyder Ali; and there was no serviceable port in the hands of the French, who, however, had somewhat the superior numbers at sea. Hughes was lying at Madras; Suffren resolved to try and capture Trincomalee, in Ceylon, which the English had taken from the Dutch. By doing so he would secure a strong naval base; while, without it, he had no adequate port to retire to for refitting when repairs were needed.

Throughout the year there was a series of hot encounters between the two squadrons, which reflect the highest credit on Suffren's ability and on Hughes's stubbornness. The first battle was on February 17th (1782), when Suffren was foiled of his immediate purpose; though he was able to land troops to act in concert with Hyder. In April he was again at sea in search of Hughes, whom he forced to fight on the 12th. The French had the better of the encounter, but Hughes was the better able to refit, and Suffren's only gain was the forced temporary inaction of his opponents. They met again with similar results on July 6th, off Cuddalore, but the British ships this time were more seriously damaged; and Suffren, putting to sea again first, was able to capture Trincomalee on August 31st before Hughes could come to the rescue. On September 3rd was fought the fourth action, when once more the English squadron would have been thoroughly crippled but for the splendid conduct of its captains and the incompetence of the French officers. Once again the two admirals met, in June of the following year, 1783, and this time the British were obliged to retire; but it was too late to profit, since the success was immediately followed by the news of peace. The main point to note is, that, whereas in the previous war the British had carried the day decisively against the French and secured their own position in India by means of superior naval force, on this occasion their situation in the land war was made extremely precarious because the naval advantage lay on the whole with the French, though neither side could claim decisive predominance.

Hughes and Suffren in Indian waters, 1782.

1783.

When Cornwallis surrendered at Yorktown in October, 1781, the French and British fleets returned to the West Indies, where they remained under the command of De Grasse and Hood respectively. Both expected reinforcements early in the coming year; but, for the time, the French force was considerably the larger.

De Grasse and Hood in the West Indies.

In January, De Grasse—carrying out the usual policy of

capturing islands—proceeded to attack St. Kitts. Hood, conscious that in the existing circumstances audacity was needful, sailed from Barbadoes to cope with him. He found De Grasse at anchor, the French troops already landed, and the British garrison being besieged. The odds were twenty-two sail of the line against twenty-nine French, but Hood resolved to attack, the enemy not being in good position. His plan was, however, upset by an accident, and he had to withdraw. De Grasse put to sea with his superior fleet, but Hood outmanœuvred him, got by without a close engagement, and anchored in a strong position close to the French admiral's previous anchorage; so that he must lie between De Grasse and either Martinique or the French force on St. Kitts. On the following day (January 26th), another attack was made by the French, quite unsuccessfully; and for nearly three weeks Hood maintained his position.

January, 1782.

Both the fleets received news of the dispersal of the French squadron of reinforcements, out of which two vessels only reached De Grasse. Rodney, on the other hand, was known to be on his way. With his great superiority in ships, it was now clearly the French admiral's policy to force an engagement with Hood, and so cripple him that Rodney might be dealt with separately. Nevertheless, though St. Kitts was taken, Hood was allowed to cut his cables and escape by night. Joining Rodney, their united forces now barely outnumbered those of the enemy who retired to Fort Royal.

Arrival of Rodney, February, 1782.

The plan of the allies for the year was to unite the French and Spanish fleets and capture Jamaica: the success of the plan depended on their effecting a junction. Rodney lay at Santa Lucia on the watch for the French to sail out of Fort Royal.

On April 8th, De Grasse put to sea, and the British started in pursuit. As they were overtaking the enemy, on April 9th, the rear was becalmed, being under the lee of Dominica. Hence, for a long time, the whole of the French fleet had it in its power to attack the English van, and should have been able to crush it thoroughly before the rear caught a wind to bring it up to the rescue. An attack by the remnant of Rodney's fleet would then have been out of the question; De Grasse would have effected the desired junction, and the odds must have become altogether overwhelming. The French admiral, however, preferred to leave the English alone, and make for Cap Français, where he was to meet the Spaniards.

The French ships were the swifter, but they were delayed during the next two days by accidents to some of their number; so that on the 12th, Rodney overtook them close to the islands called "The Saints," forced a general engagement, and succeeded in breaking up the fleet, capturing several vessels including the flag-ship with De Grasse on board. The tables were thus completely turned; the French, now completely outnumbered, with their admiral a prisoner and their navy scattered, were no match for the superior seamanship of their opponents; all hope of a junction with the Spanish fleet was abandoned, and the projected attempt on Jamaica was dropped. Rodney's victory was a brilliant one, giving the British for the time undisputed mastery in the West Indian seas; though it has been held that, if he had followed up his success as he might have done, the defeat, decisive as it was, might have been developed into a quite overwhelming disaster for the French. *Battle of "The Saints," April 12, 1782.*

Apart from the isolated encounters going on in the Indian seas between Suffren and Hughes into the summer of 1783, the military interests of the war end on the American continent with the capture of Yorktown, in October, 1781; in the West Indies, with the battle of The Saints, in April, 1782; in Europe, *Results of the struggle.*

with the final relief of Gibraltar, in October of the same
year : while the brilliant efforts of Suffren failed to obtain
material advantage for the allies. Great Britain had entered
upon a vain war with America—vain because it aimed at a
conquest which, in the nature of things, would have had no
permanence. Ireland has sufficiently taught us the difficulty
of governing a disaffected country of comparatively small
extent, lying close at hand : America would have been a
gigantic Ireland cut off by the Atlantic. In that war, Great
Britain had deservedly failed. The result was precipitated
by the French intervention : without it, America might
have been for a time reduced to submission ; but from the
time that war became inevitable, the ultimate separation of
the colonies from the mother country became inevitable also.
The European belligerents, however, gained nothing. By
sheer hard fighting, England held her own against overwhelming odds ; with a fleet of inferior numbers, she
remained unvanquished on the seas, where, at the end of the
war, she was relatively stronger than at the commencement.
Her commerce had not suffered more than that of her
opponents, and it may be said that her one substantial loss,
apart from America, was Port Mahon, while she was at the
end in a better condition for carrying on the war than her
adversaries. The general direction of the struggle had not
been well carried out, and compares very unfavourably with
Pitt's management twenty years before : attention had not
been concentrated on the division of the enemy's fleets by
keeping guard on their chief ports—the method which had
been pursued so triumphantly in 1759 ; and England had
attempted in every quarter of the globe to face superior
armaments which should never have been allowed to combine.
Nevertheless, through the seamanship of her navy, and the
audacity of her admirals, she had held her own ; and stood
at the end of the war, not indeed in the paramount position
to which she had attained in 1762, but in a stronger
position relatively to France and Spain than she had occupied

in 1778. We have now to turn from the military to the political conditions which led up to the peace of 1783.

There was, in fact, no one of the belligerents who could look forward with any feeling but one of grave uneasiness to the prolongation of the war. France, Spain, and the States were all on the verge of bank- ruptcy; England would be threatened with ruin if anywhere she met with a serious disaster. It is especially curious to note that in America the condition of Washington's army was never more unmanageable, would never have been more desperate if any move could have been made against it, than during 1782. Congress was hopelessly unable to raise the pay of the troops or to carry out its pecuniary obligations. Washington still felt that any renewal of hostilities might produce disaster. So serious was the situation that, when Sir Guy Carleton arrived with instructions to supersede Clinton, and make overtures for peace, Congress and the commander-in-chief alike doubted the genuineness of the proposal; while the administration of Congress was so inefficient, that Washington received an address praying him to become literally king.

Desire for peace.

Thus all the Powers involved were anxious for peace. Great Britain was treating with each of her opponents separately, while each of them was concealing the course of her own negotiations from her allies, each being now distrustful of the others, though all were bound to act in concert only. Hence affairs moved slowly, until the Americans were alarmed by a recrudescence of loyalism in several of the states. Their commissioners in Paris—Franklin, Adams, and Jay—signed preliminaries of peace in November,—a proceeding for which Franklin had to apologize to Vergennes, but which did not actually cause a breach. In January, 1783, preliminaries of peace were signed between Great Britain, France, and Spain, and soon after with Holland. Shelburne was driven out of office in England, and a coalition ministry, including both Fox and

Preliminaries signed.

North, was formed, but without very substantial change being made in the peace proposals. The definitive treaties, however, were not signed till September 3, 1783.

Under these treaties, the independence of the United States was definitely acknowledged, and inadequate pro-

Final treaties, September, 1783.

vision was made for the dispossessed loyalists who had suffered extremely harsh treatment at the hands of the successful party. Congress was also invited to extend consideration to them; an invitation which was not acted upon. France and England each restored what she had taken from the other, except that France retained Tobago; Spain retained Minorca and Florida; Holland gave up Negapatam. The practical summary of the outcome of the whole war is, that Britain had been rent in two by the loss of America, as she would have been sooner or later, whether Europe had taken part in the struggle or not; but that otherwise she had held her own and perhaps a little more, fighting single-handed against her three greatest naval rivals in combination. She had fought with tremendous odds against her, but, despite an administration which never attained even to the level of mediocrity, she had not been beaten.

CHAPTER IV.

THE RETENTION OF INDIA BY WARREN HASTINGS.

1772-1785.

The northern provinces—The Mahrattas—The Nizam—Hyder Ali—The sea—Bengal—Hastings and Oudh—1773: the Rohillas—1774: Aspects of the Rohilla war—Policy of Hastings—1774: Bombay and the Mahrattas—Action of Hastings—1777: French overtures—Bombay blunders—Goddard and Popham—French declaration of war, 1778—Hyder Ali; his annoyance—1780: He falls on the Carnatic—1781: Eyre Coote—Critical position of the British—1782: Arrival of Suffren—The Mahratta pacification—Death of Hyder Ali—1783: Peace with France, and end of the crisis—Summary.

To most readers, India is so unfamiliar, and geographical divisions and racial distribution are so vaguely grasped, that it is necessary by a comparatively frequent repetition to recall with some degree of accuracy the precise position at given times. The events of the career of Warren Hastings are peculiarly confusing and complex, and it is therefore advisable on turning to them to make sure that the position of the British and of the various native states is rightly apprehended at the outset.

The British control, then, was firmly established in Bengal and Behar on the Ganges, forming the Bengal Presidency. We held, also, on the east coast, the Cirkars, and the Madras district with the forts of Cuddalore and Fort St. David; and on the west coast, Bombay. On the north-west frontier of the Bengal Presidency was Oudh, ruled by the Vizier Shujah Daulah. South of this, still on our western frontier, lay Benares, held

Northern states of India.

under Shujah Daulah by the Rajah Bulwunt Singh. Southwest of Oudh were Allahabad and Corah, where the titular mogul, Shah Alum, had been established by the British. North-west of Oudh was Rohilcund, where a Hindu population was ruled by the Mussulman Rohilla chiefs. The north-west provinces were nominally under the rule of Delhi; while beyond, in the Punjab, the Sikh confederacy had attained now to such strength as to be an efficient barrier against any further Afghan invasions; and south of them lay Rajputana, thus making up the northern division of the peninsula.

The whole of the central division was more or less in the hands of the Mahratta confederacy, with its five chiefs—
The Mahrattas. the Gaikwar at Baroda; Holkar; Sindhia; the Bhonsla at Nagpore; and the Peishwa, nominally head of the whole, at Poona in the south-west. The Mahrattas therefore lay on the north and west of the dominions of the Nizam of Hyderabad. South of these and west of the Carnatic was Hyder Ali of Mysore.

The great aggressive movement of the Mahrattas had been checked in 1761 by Ahmed Shah the Abdallee at Paniput; but they were far the strongest of the native Powers, and their weakness lay mainly in the mutual rivalries of the great chiefs, each of whom aspired to be recognized as head of the confederacy, so that they lacked the cohesion of a state directed by a single leader. The Mahrattas, then, were the race who alone might endanger us in northern India, since the Vizier of Oudh would not have ventured to turn on us, even if he had not needed our protection; consequently the prime purpose of the foreign policy of Bengal was to strengthen Oudh as a barrier against the Mahrattas.

In the south, however, Madras necessarily had diplomatic **The Nizam.** relations with three Powers—the nawab of the **Hyder Ali.** Carnatic not being reckoned. There were the Mahrattas again, the Nizam, and Hyder Ali of Mysore. With none of these were our relations satisfactory. Reference has been made in a previous chapter to the war which ended in 1769 with a peace vaguely binding all four to support each other in case any one of the parties adopted an aggressive policy. In the ensuing year Hyder Ali and the Mahrattas had come to blows, the British had refused to interfere, and each of the native states had considered itself seriously aggrieved, and, without prejudice to their desire to injure each other, sought primarily an opportunity of injuring the British.

To complete this sketch of the position, it must be added that the Mahrattas lay so that each of the three British presidencies was isolated by land; but, inasmuch as no native state possessed a fleet, the communication by sea for military or other purposes between Bengal, Madras, and Bombay was complete, and could only be interrupted by the appearance of a European fleet. Moreover, since the French had no good fort, the chance of their intervening with any sustained success was comparatively slight. When Suffren did arrive, in 1782, he found himself able to obstruct, but not to accomplish much; although, after Trincomalee, in Ceylon, fell into his hands, his increased power of activity might have made his presence a yet more serious danger than it proved, had the war been prolonged.

The sea.

The Mahrattas had restored Shah Alum to the throne of Delhi, and he found himself practically under their orders. They made him assign to them Allahabad and Corah, and proposed further to appropriate Rohilcund. The British, who had made over Allahabad and Corah to Shah Alum with the object of strengthening Oudh against Mahratta incursions, not of handing them to the most dangerous of the native Powers, proceeded to occupy them. The Rohillas appealed to Oudh for support, and since Oudh would at once be open to attack if the invaders conquered Rohilcund, the vizier readily obtained assistance from Bengal, and the Mahrattas withdrew.

Bengal.

North's Act, and the appointment of Hastings as governor-general, did not come into force until 1774.
Hastings and Oudh. Hastings in 1772 was governor of Bengal. The attitude of the Mahrattas was exceedingly threatening, and the company was very badly off. Hastings, maintaining the policy of strengthening Oudh, in 1773 transferred Allahabad and Corah to the vizier, for a large sum of money, accompanied by an agreement for a subsidy to be paid to the British for assisting in their defence. At the same time, a new project was mooted by the vizier.
The Rohillas. It appeared that the Rohillas might offer alliance to the Mahrattas, and make common cause against Oudh; but, whether he was seriously afraid of such a step or not, he felt that his province would be very much safer if he became possessed of Rohilcund. Alleging the untrustworthiness of the Rohillas as a sufficient reason, he invited Hastings to co-operate in the annexation of their territory. The advantages which would accrue were obvious, and very considerable. An act of deliberate aggression for the sake of cash payments and increased security is not easy to justify on moral grounds; but the greater the danger guarded against, the easier it is to find a justification therein. Moreover, the Rohilla chiefs were at best merely conquerors who had established themselves by the sword, and their right of possession was no more than a comparatively recent occupancy gave them. Hastings therefore acceded to the vizier's proposal, stipulating, however, for payment, and to this Shujah Daulah in turn agreed, in November, 1773. In January the joint forces marched against the Rohillas, and accomplished the purposes of the expedition; but, unhappily, the British had not stipulated for the control of operations, and the annexation was accompanied by cruelties common enough in Oriental warfare, against which the British commander could only protest in vain.
Aspects of the Rohilla war.
The military expediency of the war is unquestionable; its

moral justification is to be found only in the extremity of the danger threatening, and the very doubtful title of the Rohillas to their possessions. No Oriental would have thought twice about the justice of the measure; but, from the point of view of political expediency only, an act of injustice on the part of the British was certain to have an ill effect in impairing their moral ascendency. The arguments for and against the Rohilla war are fairly evenly balanced, and its marked success in securing the Oudh frontier goes far at any rate to excuse it; but there is no excuse for the omission of the British to retain in their own hands the control of operations, since they could not evade the moral responsibility for cruelty and violence which were disgraceful, and which the merest policy, quite apart from morals, required them to repress. Nevertheless, the picture of wholesale expulsion and destruction drawn by Macaulay is a very gross exaggeration, giving a wholly misleading idea of the actual facts.

However serious the blame attaching to Warren Hastings for these measures, they had the practical effect of making Oudh an efficient barrier against the Mahrattas, **Policy of** as far as Bengal was concerned; besides affording **Hastings.** considerable relief to the financial embarrassments of the administration. These were the ends, it must be borne in mind, which Hastings had chiefly in view. It was emphatically his policy not to extend our conquests beyond our power of efficient control, but to secure what we had already won against the aggression of native powers from without, so that strong administration might be established and consolidated within our own borders. But Bengal could not be managed independently, as though unconnected with Bombay and Madras, and it was no very long time before those two presidencies involved us in fresh wars and complications, with which we shall now deal, deferring the discussion of administration till a later chapter.

The first trouble arose from Bombay. The council there

were anxious to strengthen themselves, and desired to take possession of Salsette and Bassein, two ports which offered considerable advantages. Now, there came to Bombay a Mahratta named Ragonath Rao, commonly known as Ragoba, who was eager to assert his claim to the office of peishwa. The peishwa, it should be observed, was nominally not king, but minister; but the office was hereditary, and the titular monarch was a mere puppet, without even the semblance of power or influence. The present peishwa was a babe, represented at Poona by a council of regency. Ragoba persuaded the Bombay authorities that, if they would espouse his cause, he was secure of success; and as part of the price of support, he ceded Salsette and Bassein to them. So Governor Hornby, on his own responsibility, declared war on the regency, to whom Sindhia and Holkar, at first inclined to support Ragoba, had now given their adherence. Unfortunately, Ragoba's claims had no real supporters among the Mahrattas, so that, practically, this amounted to a declaration of war against the head of the Mahratta confederacy. By this time Lord North's Act was in force, and Hastings was governor-general. The Bombay council had exceeded their powers in entering on the treaty with Ragoba, and when their project was laid before the governor-general in council, it was promptly repudiated.

Bombay and the Mahrattas.

In the mean time, however, the Bombay authorities had committed themselves too deeply. Their troops had marched; they had occupied Salsette and Bassein; and they had suffered severely at the hands of the Mahrattas in an engagement at Arras (1775). However impolitic a Mahratta war might be, Hastings was fully alive to the fact, that to withdraw from one actually commenced, under such circumstances, would have a fatal effect on British prestige among fighting Oriental tribes. Therefore, when the news came, he resolved promptly to cancel the order for withdrawal, and

Consequent measures of Hastings.

take active measures to restore the reputation of the British arms; and accordingly he despatched across India reinforcements for Bombay. At the same time, under pressure from the council, an emissary was sent to Poona, with the object of negotiating a peace on the basis of the British retention of Salsette and Bassein.

These terms were by no means satisfactory to the Mahrattas, and, in 1777, a new factor was added to the conditions, in the person of a Frenchman, the Chevalier St. Lubin, who arrived at Poona with overtures from the French government to the Mahrattas, and a proposal for the cession to France of a port on the Malabar coast. The prospects of French assistance made the regents the less ready to accede to terms which they had already declared to be unsatisfactory, but which were still the most that the British thought they could in honour allow. Hastings, therefore, resolved to strike at once. He sent a body of troops, under Colonel Goddard, to assist in a fresh attempt to set up Ragoba as peishwa; but Goddard, on his arrival to take the supreme command, found the difficulties of his task greatly increased by the precipitate action of the Bombay authorities. They had sent their expedition out without waiting for him, under incompetent officers; it had signally failed, and the English had been forced to retreat ignominiously. The troops, indeed, had been completely hemmed in, and, instead of attempting to cut their way through against enormous odds, had entered upon a convention (known as the Convention of Wargum) under which they were allowed to retire on terms of the restoration of all that the British had taken from the Mahrattas during the war; and farther, of surrendering the person of Ragoba to Sindhia, who was to mediate between the British and his fellow Mahrattas. At the same time an attempt made by Hastings to detach the bhonsla from the confederacy, by playing on his hope of becoming head in place of the

French overtures.

Bombay blunders.

peishwa, had met with no practical success. The Mahratta chiefs might have their own rivalries, but they were fully alive to the danger of settling them by British intervention.

The Convention of Wargum was a severe blow to British prestige ; still, in 1780, something was done to restore it by Goddard, whose campaign, so far as it went, was successful. At the same time, Captain Popham was operating in Gohud, where the ruler, known as the Rana, was being attacked by Sindhia in the natural course of Mahratta aggression. Popham, by a brilliant feat of arms, captured the fortress of Gwalior, which had hitherto been reputed impregnable, cleared Gohud of the invaders, and took the city of Lahar.

<small>Goddard and Popham.</small>

After Popham's departure, Sindhia expected to turn the tables, but was surprised and routed by Captain Bruce, in the spring of 1781.

Before these latter events had taken place, news came to the governor-general of the declaration of war between England and France in 1778. Hastings acted with characteristic promptitude, seizing Chandernagore, and sending instructions to Madras for the immediate reduction of all French ports.

<small>The French declaration of war, 1778.</small>

Pondicherry and other stations were captured, though not without stubborn resistance. But out of the seizure of Mahé, a small French port on the Malabar coast, in 1779, fresh complications arose.

Hyder Ali of Mysore had been watching for ten years past for an opportunity of striking at the British. He had viewed with entire satisfaction their embroilment with the Mahrattas, the one other Power which was a source of danger to him. Being possessed, moreover, of unusual strategical capacity, he was thoroughly alive to the importance of control of the sea in a war ; and, with this in view, he intrigued actively with the French, whose naval station was at the Mauritius.

<small>Hyder Ali: his annoyance ;</small>

The capture of Mahé, therefore, by no means fell in with his plans; and he gave notice at Madras that the port was under his protection. His protest was disregarded, Mahé was taken, and troops were marched across his territories for that purpose. He was bitterly offended, and determined to take his revenge as soon as possible.

The British were already at war with the Mahrattas, though that Power was not actually threatening the southern presidency. In attempting to isolate themselves the more thoroughly, the Madras council offended the Nizam of Hyderabad, who, as yet, was standing neutral, though favouring the claims of the peishwa as against Ragoba. Hyder entered into a secret alliance with him. Rumbold, the president, left for England under the impression that peace reigned in the presidency, and the British were secure. He had hardly departed, when, in 1780, the storm burst. Hyder, with his vast hordes, swept down into the Carnatic, devastating the country, and driving the British in haste behind the walls of fortified places. *He falls on the Carnatic.*

Baillie, and Sir Hector Munro, were sent against him; but they did not act together: the Mysore Sultan fell upon the former separately, and cut his force to pieces; Munro was forced to retreat precipitately. This was that terrific invasion made so famous by the oratory of Burke.

Again Hastings rose to the occasion. Goddard and Popham had redeemed the honour of the British arms; he could now press negotiations with the Mahrattas, and concentrate the whole of his military energies on the war in the Carnatic, where our very existence was threatened. Sir Eyre Coote was now at once a member of the Calcutta council, and commander-in-chief. He was promptly despatched to Madras with all the troops and all the money that could be raised, and with practically full powers.

In January, 1781, Coote took the field. Hyder Ali was well aware that he now had to deal with a soldier—no longer, indeed, so brilliant as in the days when he urged Clive forward at Plassey and conquered the French at Wandewash—but still of a very different calibre from the recent captains of British armies. Hyder drew back, but in July there was a great battle at Porto Novo, where Coote routed the immense forces opposed to him. Hyder, however, was a great leader, by no means easily disposed of. He rallied his forces and again gave battle to Coote, in August, at Pollilore, where Baillie had fallen. He was defeated, but the fight was a hard one, and the defeat by no means crushing. At the end of 1781, the Mysore sovereign was still in force in the Carnatic; the Mahrattas were in no haste to come to terms; the bhousla, instead of allowing himself to be detached from the confederacy, was threatening the Bengal frontier; and the French fleet, under Suffren, was soon to appear in Indian waters. Already D'Orvés's squadron had shown itself, but not in sufficient force to materially affect the British communications, or to co-operate actively in Hyder Ali's campaign, as he had designed that it should do.

Eyre Coote in command.

Danger to the British power.

On the other hand, the declaration of war between England and Holland had been of some service to our interests in India, since Negapatam permanently, and Trincomalee in Ceylon—a valuable port—for the time being, fell into our hands.

The year 1782 opened badly, for a detachment of British and Sepoys, under Colonel Braithwaite, was surrounded and cut to pieces after a desperate defence. In February, Suffren arrived with his fleet, and the British had to face on the seas an antagonist who, if he failed to break their power, proved, at any rate, their match. Two thousand French troops were landed, and joined with Tippoo Sahib, the son of Hyder Ali, in an attack on Cuddalore, which was in no case to resist so formidable an armament, and was forced to surrender. The

Effects of Suffren's presence.

tale of Suffren's series of pitched battles with Hughes has been already told. The capture of Cuddalore is an instance of the immediate effect of equality on the seas between the two parties; for in the previous year a similar design had been abandoned because the French admiral had been unable to render the needful assistance to the Mysore troops.

Nevertheless, for the remainder of the year the British held their own. Peace was concluded with the Mahrattas, Sindhia using his influence to forward it. Salsette and Bassein remained with the British, but other cessions of territory were made to the Mahrattas. Sindhia got his price in the abandonment of Gohud, and the Poona government promised to assist in suppressing Mysore—a promise which it had no intention of performing, regarding the southern kingdom as an invaluable check on British aggression. Mahratta pacification.

By the capture of Trincomalee, however, Suffren secured the naval base which he wanted, though happily England's naval successes elsewhere prevented him from receiving reinforcements. It was fortunate, too, that Hyder himself died at the close of the year, though his son Tippoo was both capable and vigorous; while the British forces hitherto engaged against the peishwa were now free to act on the west of Mysore. Here they met with success at first, but were presently overwhelmed by Tippoo with superior forces (1783). Death of Hyder.

In the spring of 1783 Suffren was doing what he could to make full use of his naval superiority before further British reinforcements should arrive. The veteran Bussy landed and strengthened the garrison at Cuddalore. Sir Eyre Coote, who had withdrawn to Calcutta at the close of the previous year owing to ill health, returned to take the command at Madras, but died on landing. The British invested Cuddalore, but their chief showed more vigour than skill, and when Cuddalore saved by the peace.

Suffren, in his last encounter with Hughes, succeeded in forcing the latter to retire, the position of the forces before Cuddalore became critical. The probabilities, indeed, are that a signal disaster would have been suffered, though the effects might, in the long run, have been reversed by the appearance of a superior British fleet in the Indian waters; but at this juncture the news came of the preliminaries of peace between England and France, on the basis of a restoration of conquests. Suffren, aware that all he had accomplished or looked to accomplish would be lost again unless he received naval support, which he could not expect, was much relieved. The French troops were withdrawn from Cuddalore and from Tippoo's army; the French fleet departed, and Tippoo stood alone. The war dragged on for some months, but in 1784 he was ready to make peace.

For seven years the British had been fighting with one or both of the two greatest military native Powers in India.

Summary. For almost the whole of that time England had been occupied with war on the other side of the globe; for the greater part of it she had been at bay, outnumbered by the opposing fleets of the three greatest maritime Powers in Europe. Yet by sea she had held her own; in India she had held her own, relying almost entirely on the resources of Bengal for supplies. To what straits Hastings had been driven to produce those supplies we shall presently see; and whatever judgment is passed on him, it must be borne in mind that on their production depended our existence in India. Whether the means he adopted were justifiable or not, to him we owe it that our foothold in India was retained. India was but one of the fields where, from 1778 to 1783, we were fighting, not to extend our empire, but to preserve our existence, and in the light of that knowledge we must pass our judgment on the man who preserved it.

Here, also, let us once again recall the vital military

lesson of the Indian wars of the last century. If England had not overmatched France on the seas when we were fighting for empire in India, we should never have won it. If France had overmatched England on the seas when we were fighting for life there, we should have lost it.

CHAPTER V.

INDIAN ADMINISTRATION UNDER WARREN HASTINGS.
1772-1785.

Objects of North's Regulating Act; its provisions—The Supreme Court—Confusion of authority—1774: The new members of council —1775: The council and Oudh — Nuncomar —1777: Hastings becomes predominant—1780: Duel of Hastings and Francis—1778: The Madras council—Financial difficulties of Hastings—The council and the judges—The Rajah of Benares— 1783: The Oudh begums—1784—The work of Hastings; his retirement.

PRIOR to Lord North's Regulating Act, the position of the company in India had been exceedingly anomalous, and devoid of recognized system. The working of it had depended mainly on the personal vigour and authority of individuals like Clive. Now, this Act was the first attempt to relate the Indian system to the home government. There were no precedents to serve as guides, and as an experiment in constitution-making the attempt was a decided failure; the machinery devised was too grossly defective. Nevertheless, the intention of the experiment was sound, and the leading causes of its failure were so marked, its leading lessons so obvious, that the task of so amending matters as to reconstruct a fresh constitution, not perfect but competent, became practicable.

Objects of North's Regulating Act;

Under the new Act the three presidencies were no longer independent in India, and subordinate only to the courts of directors and proprietors at home : the two minor presidencies were subordinated to the central authority at Calcutta. The central authority was, on the

its provisions.

other hand, divided between the governor-general in council and a newly-established Supreme Court of Judicature. The governor-general himself was the responsible head; but his council consisted of four other members, so that three of these voting together could entirely paralyse him, since all decisions lay with the vote of the majority. Farther, the position of the Supreme Court was ill defined. It was avowedly appointed to check illegal proceedings on the part of the administration. It claimed the sole power of interpreting the law, and of defining the limits of its own jurisdiction; while the administration was in a perpetual condition of challenging its powers. The Supreme Court, in short, claimed that the sovereignty lay in Great Britain; that the court represented the sovereign; and that the Indian administration was subordinate to it. The administration claimed that the Nawab of Bengal was sovereign *de jure*, the Indian government consequently sovereign *de facto*, and that the court was subordinate to the government.

The judges.

Further, while the governor-general and council were, in the first instance, nominated by parliament, subsequent appointments reverted to the court of directors in London; who controlled patronage generally, and to whom the Indian officials were responsible for the policy they followed. The directors, again, might be overruled by the court of proprietors, consisting of all those who owned a certain amount of stock. The judges, on the other hand, were amenable, not to the company, but to the sovereign.

Confusion of authority.

Here, therefore, were the elements of violent and perpetual discord between a resolute governor-general, a council which overruled him, and a Supreme Court constantly interfering with administration. To increase the difficulties of the situation, the central government was liable to be embroiled in complications arising from the action of the minor presidencies; such as the blunders of

Bombay in dealing with the Mahrattas, and those of Madras in dealing with Hyder Ali.

Hastings, as we have seen, was appointed governor-general. In October, 1774, the Rohilla affair having been concluded, the new members of council arrived, and with them the new judges. The former were Sir Philip Francis, Monson, and General Clavering, the fourth member being Barwell, one of the company's servants in India. The chief justice was Sir Elijah Impey.

The new members of council.

The three new members had been appointed as representatives of ministers, really to control the officers of the company. Hence Hastings, though loyally supported by Barwell, found immediately that the majority of his council were prepared to oppose him at every turn, and out-vote him persistently. They acted not as a council, but as an inquisitorial board, making it, apparently, their direct object to discredit the governor-general in every way, hailing accusations against him, and discovering every conceivable evil motive at the back of all his acts in the past and his policy for the future.

In January, 1775, Shujah Daulah, the Nawab-Vizier of Oudh, died, and was succeeded by his son, Asaph-ud-Daulah. Hastings had pursued the policy of strengthening the vizier's hands in every possible way; if possible, for a consideration. The majority now made peremptory demands for the payment of the stipulated sums, threatening the new vizier at the moment when his position was necessarily unstable; required the cession of Ghazipur and Benares; and farther hampered him by insisting that certain rich districts should be retained as the appanage of his mother the Bhow Begum, who was notoriously at bitter feud with her son. It was, in fact, assumed that Hastings's administration had been thoroughly corrupt, and the council appear to have resolved to break it down first, and prove the corruption afterwards.

The council and Oudh.

They next insisted upon hearing personal charges against Hastings, brought forward by Nuncomar, a Brahmin holding a high official position, and by the Rani of Nun-Burdwan, and on having them laid before the board; while Hastings himself refused to sanction such proceedings, offering to have a committee of inquiry. Nuncomar was a man whom the governor-general mistrusted intensely, and who, in his turn, bore a grudge against the governor-general. Hastings turned to bay, and prosecuted Nuncomar for conspiracy; and at this opportune moment an enemy of Nuncomar's, named Mohun Persad, accused the Brahmin of forging a bond. Nuncomar was tried, convicted, and hanged. That the conviction was singularly convenient for Hastings is beyond doubt; that his execution was a shock to the native mind, which regarded forgery as a venial offence, is also clear. But there is no proof that Hastings was directly responsible for the charge being brought, or that there was any unfairness in the trial; the council refused to take any steps for Nuncomar's respite; the most competent judges hold, to-day, that the evidence against him was conclusive. The affair was so useful to Hastings that his enemies could hardly be blamed for suspecting foul play on the part of a man who was, in their estimation, capable of any iniquity; but the presumption is entirely in favour of his acquittal in this respect. The justice of Nuncomar's doom may not be conclusively established, but it is certainly inexcusable to affirm that he was judicially murdered for personal ends.

With the fall of Nuncomar the personal charges against Hastings collapsed. The council, however, continued to do what it could to upset his administrative policy. He had substituted regular provincial courts for the criminal jurisdiction of the native officers of the titular Nawab of Bengal; these the council abolished, restoring the old order. And matters were complicated by collision between the council and the courts, to which we shall revert presently.

With the prospect before him of being for ever outvoted, Hastings was for a while prepared to resign if he found the directors at home set against him. In September, 1776, however, Monson's death equalised matters on the council, and Hastings, having a casting vote, could take his own way. The court of proprietors stood by him, but his agent in England, misunderstanding the situation, sent in his resignation; it was accepted, and Clavering was appointed to act until the arrival of Wheler, whom the directors chose to succeed Hastings. The news reached Calcutta in June, 1777. Hastings refused to resign; Clavering claimed his place. The troops were with Hastings, who offered to let the court arbitrate. The Opposition could hardly refuse: the judges decided in favour of Hastings: and so he carried the day.

Hastings becomes predominant.

Clavering died soon after; Wheler, Monson's successor, was unimportant, and Sir Eyre Coote—who came out as military member—though not easy to manage, had no inclination to join a cabal against the governor-general: so that, for the remainder of his career in India, Hastings, although Francis worked hard against him, and used all available influence at home to injure him, succeeded in carrying matters generally in his own way.

For a time, however, in the thick of the Mahratta War, Francis was able to cause serious embarrassment. Barwell retired on leave of absence, Francis having promised generally not to upset the governor-general's policy. But when the treaty with the Rana of Gohud came up, Francis declared that this was a new political departure, and there was no breach of faith in his opposing Hastings. The result was a duel between the two, in which Francis was severely wounded. Soon after, he retired to England, where he prosecuted his feud against Hastings with zeal and bitterness; but his departure in 1781 left the ground free from further serious dissensions within the council.

Duel between Hastings and Francis.

The quarrels in the Calcutta council were reflected in at least one of the other presidencies. The Madras government, in defiance of the directors at home, ejected the Rajah of Tanjore, which they handed over to the Nawab of Arcot. The directors dismissed the governor, and sent Lord Pigot to take his place, and reinstate the Tanjore rajah. But certain influential Englishmen had been granted assignments of Tanjore revenue, in payment of debts, by the nawab. They objected to the restitution, and Pigot was outvoted, as Hastings was in Calcutta. Pigot, however, made a mistake which Hastings avoided—he transgressed his legal powers in order to assert his authority. The troops supported the council, and Pigot was himself imprisoned. He died a few months later. The members of council were all dismissed, and a new president and new council were appointed (1778), not much, if at all, better fitted for their posts than their predecessors. The whole incident illustrates forcibly the weakness of the existing system, since the conditions of our rule in India imperatively demanded that the central government above all, but the subordinate governments as well, should act decisively, consistently, and systematically; whereas the method of councils acting by a majority vote, often from purely personal motives, was destructive of all dignity, authority, and decision. *The Madras council.*

In 1777 the governor-general was at last supreme at Calcutta; though dependent on Coote's support, owing to the continued opposition of Francis and his supporter Wheler. It was fortunate that he was so far predominant, since, about this time, Bombay was seriously involved in the Mahratta difficulty; the French war was threatening; and it was of the utmost importance that the government policy should be definite and vigorous. Moreover, it was obvious that exceptional measures of one kind or another would have to be taken to make financial provision for the troubles accumulating. *Financial difficulties of Hastings.*

Whatever expenses the government might find itself plunged into, they would have to be met out of revenue. There was no prospect of pecuniary assistance from England, which found its own revenues sufficiently heavily taxed. The method of borrowing heavily to meet exceptional outlay, adopted by European governments on plunging into great wars, was out of the question in India, where the stability of the government itself was still uncertain. The extra expenses would have to be met mainly out of income; and all the time the directors at home would demand an adequate trade profit, which the normal expenses of administration and defence made it hard enough to meet out of normal resources. In this fact we shall find the explanation of many acts of the governor-general which are open to severe censure according to normal standards. There was no question of ambitious designs of annexation or extension of empire. The question was whether we could hold our own. If we were to do so, the sinews of war must come from somewhere, and the normal legitimate sources were insufficient. Hastings had to decide whether he was to draw upon illegitimate sources, or give up the struggle. Had he taken the latter course, he would have had his full share of obloquy, and India would have been lost. He preferred to save India, and got more than his share of obloquy in consequence. But his country, and, it may be added, India at large, reaped the benefit. For it will hardly be questioned that his harshest acts, painted in the blackest colours, would have been mere commonplaces to the native Powers with whom he was striving; or that the predominance of the Mahrattas in Central and Northern India, or of Hyder in the south, would have been fraught with far greater misery and far more anarchy, for the native states and populations in general, than British rule has been. Hastings dealt hard measure in certain quarters; harder measure over much larger districts would have been dealt out by his opponents if he had retired from the field.

And undoubtedly, in his view, there was no third course open.

Before turning, however, to the stories of Cheyte Singh and the Oudh begums, the disputes between the council and the Supreme Court demand our attention. The court, avowedly in the interest of the natives, claimed jurisdiction over all the company's officers, and especially constituted itself as a court to which all landowners could appeal against the revenue officials. The system was alien to the native conceptions; the people were accustomed to find judicial and administrative functions combined in the same hands: and the practical effect was paralysing, inasmuch as every official found himself liable to be summoned from up-country to Calcutta to answer charges, sometimes frivolous, sometimes deliberate concoctions, and sometimes no doubt just—but certain in any case to be decided under unaccustomed forms of procedure, and by wholly unfamiliar legal canons.

The council and the judges.

Consequently the council and the courts quarrelled violently. Hastings, always on the best of terms with Impey, found himself compelled to take the council's view of the matter, since the pretensions of the court were bringing administration to a standstill, and for a time there was a serious breach between him and the Chief Justice. The supervision of the Supreme Court was destroying the power of the district courts which were conducted by revenue officials. Hastings came to the conclusion that separate civil courts must be established, and these would require proper judicial control. It occurred to him, therefore, that affairs could be placed on a proper footing, and the breach with Impey be healed, by formally giving the Chief Justice the supervision of these courts, as an appointment from the governor-general in council. The proceeding was afterwards to be used to give colour to the charge of collusion between Hastings and Impey, and has been freely described as a bribe; but its merits as a practical scheme for regulating the administration of justice are undeniable, and the advantage of removing the causes of collision between the court and the council are equally clear. The last act of Francis, before his departure, was to protest against the measure.

With a manageable council, and at peace with the judges, Hastings was still in serious financial difficulties, in conse-
The Rajah of Benares. quence of the wars forced upon him. Benares, under the Rajah Cheyte Singh, son of Bulwunt Singh, had recently been transferred to the British by the Oudh vizier. The rajah was to hold it from the British, as he had before held it from Oudh: that is, he was to pay a fixed annual sum to the government, to maintain troops, and to be generally responsible for the prevalence of law and order.

Hastings, in much need of money, held that the limitation of the sum payable by the rajah did not secure him against extraordinary claims upon extraordinary occasions. Cheyte Singh became restive under these demands, repeated year after year, while the Mahratta war was in progress; he did not refuse to pay, but he abstained from paying. When news came of Hyder Ali's doings in the south, strong suspicions arose that the rajah was hoping to escape the British dominion altogether. The fact that he had personally offended Hastings at the time of the great dispute with Clavering, made the governor-general certainly not less ready to think his punishment a necessity. He was ordered to pay a fine amounting to about half a million for his contumacy; and Hastings went to Benares with a small escort to demand the payment, determined to eject him if he refused. As Cheyte Singh showed no disposition to accede, Hastings arrested him. The troops rose in his favour; a company of Sepoys was cut to pieces; and Hastings was obliged to retire in haste to Chunar, a small fortress thirty miles away. From thence he issued his orders ; the rising was promptly suppressed ; the rajah fled the country, and his estates were forfeited.

But the financial difficulties were not yet solved. The Nawab of Oudh was still heavily in the company's debt, and he was quite unable to pay. For this, the company had mainly to thank the council's action on his accession : action taken in the teeth of Hastings's judgment. As before narrated, a very rich district had been reserved on their demand for the begums, Asaph-ud-Daulah's mother and grandmother, who hated him, were themselves able and active, and were well served. The whole policy of the council had, moreover, tended to weaken in every way the power of the nawab himself, not a very capable ruler in any case. Asaph-ud-Daulah could get little out of his own subjects, and nothing out of the begums. Now, however, he pointed out to Hastings that, if he were enabled to forfeit their estates, reasonable allowances might be made to them, while he would in turn be able to pay his debt to the company. If the council had guaranteed these possessions to the begums, still, Hastings had himself opposed the guarantee ; it might be maintained that it was not in its nature permanent, and the very strong suspicion that the ladies in question had actively fomented the Benares rising might be taken as an adequate reason for now withdrawing the company's support.

The Oudh begums.

Unfortunately, the mere withdrawal of the guarantee and the permission to the nawab to appropriate the territories were insufficient. The begums were quite strong enough to offer adequate resistance to the attempts of Asaph-ud-Daulah. Hastings threw himself actively into the contest, on the ground that the begums were in rebellion, and had thereby forfeited their title, and that they had shared in the responsibility for the Benares insurrection. Naturally the resistance of the begums was quickly suppressed ; their estates and treasures were forfeited, though a good allowance was granted them ; and the nawab's debt was paid.

As usual, however, the suppression was accompanied by circumstances of severity, mild enough for Oriental potentates, but quite unjustifiable according to western ethics. As in the case of the Rohillas, the responsibility lay upon Hastings; though he gave no sanction to the severities, it was his duty to prevent them, and he abstained from doing so.

The year 1784 was occupied chiefly in the reorganisation of the Benares administration, and in introducing a sounder working system in Oudh, where Asaph-ud-Daulah was grateful enough for assistance. His hands were considerably strengthened, and restrictions were placed upon the English resident, who had recently taken upon himself to interfere arbitrarily in administrative arrangements, in a manner detrimental to the dignity of the nawab—a course quite opposed to the policy of Hastings; which was to make Oudh a strong state, while keeping it a secure supporter of British power in Bengal, and of British influence among the native states.

1784.

But the end of his governor-generalship was at hand. In the face of enormous difficulties, thwarted perpetually by his colleagues, embarrassed by the blunders of the minor presidencies, hampered by the financial demands of the company, Hastings had conducted the experiment of establishing a commercial company as a first-class territorial power, while England was doing battle for life with the three greatest navies in the world. We owe the survival of our power in India mainly to his resolution, his audacity, his organising capacity, and, in part, it must be owned, to his disregard of those scruples of conscience to which the onlooker is commonly more alive than the ruler, who feels that the end he has in view must be attained somehow. But personal enemies were at work against him at home; party dissensions and party rivalries more and more were finding in India material for abuse and recrimination. In February, 1775, Warren Hastings left India,

The work of Hastings;

and returned home to find himself almost unsupported and undefended, the object of the fiercest vilification by the most brilliant orators and debaters of the day. His retrial falls to the province of the biographer; but it stands also as a grim example of the distortion of vision which personal rancour produces even in men who honestly believe themselves, like Burke, to be actuated by the purest motives of patriotism and of justice.

his retirement.

CHAPTER VI.

IRELAND: THE VOLUNTEERS.

1776-1784.

1778: Relaxation of the penal code—Demand for free trade—Rise of the volunteers—Effect of the movement—1779: Demand for redress of grievances—Free trade granted—1780: Demand for legislative independence—Grattan—The Mutiny Bill—The Mutiny Act made perpetual—1781: Lord Carlisle viceroy—Reception of the news of Yorktown—The volunteers at Dungannon—1782: The Constitution of 1782—"Simple Repeal"—1783: the Renunciatory Act—Grattan and Flood—The Bishop of Derry—The volunteer convocation in Dublin—Demand for parliamentary reform—Rejection of the Reform Bill.

THE Catholic question, as previously explained, had to a considerable extent fallen into the background in Ireland; religious animosities were in some degree sunk in the antagonism of the Irish people to the British predominance. Some of the penal laws against Catholics had become practically obsolete, others were more and more habitually evaded. Although most of the leading men were not for a moment prepared to admit Catholics to a share in political power, a far more tolerant spirit was abroad than had prevailed at the beginning of the century; and this was greatly encouraged by the marked loyalty shown by the Catholic gentry, and the absence of political movement among the peasantry.

Relaxation of "penal code."

Hence the stringency of anti-Catholic regulations began to be relaxed. The army was no longer recruited exclusively from Protestants. Tentative movements were made to render their exclusion from all interest in land less vigorous, and in 1778 the first real measure of Catholic relief was carried. By this law, Catholics were allowed to hold leases for 999 years, though not to purchase the freehold; and the law of succession was assimilated to that applied to Protestants, so that the perpetual subdivision was put an end to. At the same time, the rule by which one son of a Catholic could inherit the whole property by turning Protestant was done away with. The peculiarly demoralising character of this rule needs little explanation. Wherever there was an unprincipled son, the temptation was placed before him of securing his own comfort at the cost of his family; the worse the man, the stronger was the chance of his availing himself of the opportunity; and thus much of the land which had remained in the hands of the Catholic gentry passed into the sole control of the worst members of the stock. It is to be noted that Henry Grattan, a young orator of brilliant attainments and the highest character, who had by this time come to the front in Irish politics, took the lead among his fellow Protestants in asserting the title of their Catholic fellow-countrymen to the same measure of justice which the Protestants claimed for themselves.

Strong as was the demand for legislative independence the pressure of those commercial restrictions which were intimately associated with that demand was at this time even more prominent. The financial difficulties during Harcourt's vice-royalty were serious enough, but when he retired, in 1776, the gravity of the situation was increasing. The American war had thrown an additional military burden on the country; the relations with France were strained, and the commerce with her was suffering in consequence. The necessity for free trade was urgently pressed upon the British government, and North, aware of the exigencies of the situation, was disposed to yield to it. But so vehement was the opposition

Demand for free trade.

2 A

in the great trading towns, with the partial exception of London; so resolute were the British manufacturers to resist the intrusion of a competitor into any of their markets; that North was obliged to give way. British interest in Irish affairs was strictly limited; but within the limits it was strong. No ministry was allowed to make concessions to Ireland which interfered with the privileges of British landlords (as shown in the Absentee Bill) or of British traders (as shown in the commercial measures). The relaxations granted in 1778 were whittled down to the extension to Ireland of the benefits of the Navigation Act, and the removal of the duty on cotton yarn home-spun.

But the outbreak of the French war in this year gave rise to a new movement wholly loyal in its origin, which was destined to play a very great part in the political questions of the time. The strain upon the military resources of Great Britain was tremendous, and all the available troops were withdrawn from Ireland, leaving in that country a wholly insufficient supply of soldiers, while the channel fleet was far too weak to protect the Irish coast. Expectations of an invasion were universally prevalent. Ireland, however, did not seize the moment of England's peril to wring concessions from her by threats of rebellion; on the contrary, the opportunity was taken for a very marked display of the most energetic loyalty. Headed by the Protestant gentry, aided by liberal subscriptions from the Catholics who were prevented by the code from raising troops themselves, the people rose to arms, formed associations for defence, and soon covered the country with troops of fairly efficient, enthusiastic, and well-drilled volunteers. It was evident that if this newly organised soldiery turned their arms against the British domination, there would be a very dangerous counterpart to the American war much nearer home, and the government viewed these measures with

The volunteer movement.

the gravest alarm. In fact, however, no more striking proof could have been given of the fundamental loyalty of the Irish people at that time than their conduct of the great volunteer movement, by which, when the troops paid for by Irish taxes to defend them were withdrawn, they by their own efforts placed the country in a state of defence.

At the same time, the mere fact that the people were in arms, though for the defence of the empire, gave their demands on their own behalf a new significance. To put down the movement and dismiss the volunteers without supplying other means of defence was out of the question; but while they were in arms, their claims could no longer be ignored. The men who were ready to lead their followers against the invader might follow the example of the American colonists—with whom, as already remarked, there was the strongest sympathy, owing to the similarity of the grievances to which both were subjected: they had long been bent on obtaining freedom of trade and legislative independence; and they in turn might head rebellion, if their legitimate demands were not conceded. When parliament met in October, 1779, the loyalty of the leaders to the crown, coupled with their determination to obtain redress, were decisively shown. Grattan moved an amendment to the address, in favour of free trade; Burgh supported him, severing himself from the government; Flood, though retaining the office of Vice-Treasurer, to which he had been appointed by Harcourt, went farther than Grattan; and the amendment, in the form which he had given to it, was carried without a division. Supply was granted only for a period of six months; and a bill to relieve Dissenters from the sacramental test, the principle of which had already been affirmed in Ireland only to be rejected in England, was again carried by a large majority.

Demand for redress of grievances.

The demand was too strong and too efficiently supported

to be resisted longer. The test was abolished, the commercial restrictions were withdrawn, and Irish trade, except *Free trade granted.* with Great Britain, was placed practically on the same footing as that of England and Scotland. Ireland was even allowed to retain the benefit of the bounty previously granted on linen imported to England—the linen trade, which did not interfere with British manufacturers, having hitherto been almost the sole exception to the policy of commercial repression (1779-80).

Free trade had been obtained under the influence of a sudden impulse ; but the question behind it was one of a more fundamental character. For the commercial concessions were granted by Britain, and in the existing relation of the two countries they might be recalled at the will of the stronger nation when opportunity should occur. Security even of what was already granted could be obtained only by a constitutional change, and this was the great desire of the volunteers. Their doctrine was, that the two kingdoms were necessarily, and for the good of both, united under one crown, but that one had no right to overrule the other in the conduct of her own legislation. It was claimed that the principles recognized in the English parliament applied in Ireland : that the king, lords, and commons of Ireland alone should legislate for her ; that the control alike by the Irish and the British privy council were opposed to constitutional principles ; and that, while the right of the English parliament to legislate directly for Ireland was based on a misinterpretation of the law, the Declaratory Act of George I., claiming that right, was actually contrary to the law. These were the views of the Irish leaders, and the victory they had already won encouraged them to hope for further success ; while the volunteer organisation, which had proved so useful a means to that victory, continued to advance steadily in effectiveness. On the other hand, North and the ministers who

Demands for legislative independence.

had staked their political being on the doctrine of Great Britain's right to overrule the will of her dependencies in America, were still in power. It was contrary to every principle they had professed to admit that British predominance was not a matter of right. Even the Rockinghams, while affirming the inexpediency of overriding the popular will in the colonies, had passed the Declaratory Act asserting the power of Great Britain to do so. Lord Hillsbrough, the Secretary of State in whose department Ireland lay, was inclining to the belief that a legislative union would prove the only way of reconciling the conflicting claims, but that view was not as yet publicly advocated, while the present difficulty was assuming very threatening proportions.

On April 19, 1780, Grattan introduced in Parliament a declaration of independence, embodying the principles above stated. The debate was indefinitely adjourned, but the unanimity of feeling was manifest. The government had not lost its control over the actual voting-power in the House, and succeeded in defeating a motion brought forward by Yelverton to deprive the Irish Privy Council of its power of amending bills. But the question was brought to a head by Bushe's Irish Mutiny bill. *Grattan.*

The English Mutiny Act, annually passed, was held to apply to the troops in Ireland. By calling in question the constitutional power of Great Britain to legislate for Ireland, the validity of the Mutiny Act was, of course, impugned. The Act could only be enforced by the co-operation of the magistrates: the magistrates were nearly all associated with the volunteers. To prevent the complete disintegration which would necessarily result if the magistrates declared that the Mutiny Act was not law in Ireland, Bushe introduced an Irish Mutiny Bill. If it were passed, the army could be controlled, but if England accepted it, the principle that British legislation *The Mutiny Bill.*

was valid in Ireland would be given up, as the invalidity of the English Mutiny Act would be implied in it.

Bushe's bill was passed by an immense majority. In England, the annual nature of the Mutiny Act made it a powerful instrument in the hands of parliament for the assertion of popular rights ; since, by a refusal to pass the bill, the organisation of the army would be forthwith destroyed. It was, of course, the intention of Bushe and Grattan to secure the same power to the Irish parliament, but when the bill was returned from England it was found to have been so amended as to be rendered perpetual. In the mean time, every effort had been made by the government to win votes ; several members were now alarmed at their own audacity : and, in spite of the strenuous opposition of Grattan, the bill as amended was carried.

For months past, the Viceroy Buckingham had been fighting the battle of the government in the teeth of the national sentiment, and very much against his will ; and he had been driven to the most extreme use of official corruption in the struggle. Peerages, pensions, and places were bestowed in profusion, and yet not so profusely as to fulfil all Buckingham's pledges. He was now succeeded by **Lord Carlisle.** Lord Carlisle, who soon discovered the strength of the popular sentiment in Ireland ; and the volunteer organisation, under stress of the unceasing danger of invasion (1780-1), was stronger and at the same time more indispensable than ever. Undoubtedly their unquestionable loyalty went far to strengthen the case of the leaders. On the other hand, while the government were fairly certain of a majority of votes when the House should meet in the autumn, outside parliament the determination to press for legislative independence was practically unanimous ; though a doubtful inclination at last to accept the Habeas Corpus Bill seemed to be the only concession the government was likely to grant.

This bill was passed by a large majority. But Grattan

and Flood were defeated when they moved a limitation of the perpetual Mutiny Act. It is remarkable, however, that the news (December 4th) of the surrender of Cornwallis was made the occasion of a very strong demonstration of loyalty by the Opposition in the House. Although Grattan and Flood desired to amend the address so as to include a demand for legislative independence, the majority against them was very large ; it being felt that the primary need of the moment was to give the strongest possible proof of the absence of faction— a course which compares very favourably with the proceedings in the British Parliament at the same date. *News of York town.*

The address itself had been moved by Yelverton, one of the most earnest supporters of the popular demand ; and he now took the lead again in pressing for the abolition of the Irish Privy Council's legislative powers. The government majority was too strong, but Carlisle was privately pressing the British ministers to withdraw their opposition. Proposals for the further relief of the Catholics were discouraged, chiefly on the ground of the violent riots which had so recently resulted from similar measures in England and Scotland ; but the Habeas Corpus Act was at length passed.

It was sufficiently evident that, so long as the government could control a mass of votes in parliament by the use of patronage, the voice of parliament itself could not be regarded as truly representative. In February, 1782, a great meeting was summoned at Dungannon, to which the Ulster volunteers were invited to send delegates ; and when they met, there could be no question of their genuinely representative character. The meeting affirmed the principle of legislative independence, of a limited Mutiny Bill, and of the rest of the associated measures ; it appointed a series of committees for perfecting the volunteer organisation ; and, finally, on the motion of Grattan, it expressly affirmed the *The volunteers at Dungannon.*

principle of religious toleration, and of the relaxation of the
Penal Code. The delegates at Dungannon stood for the
people of Ulster, but their pronouncement was promptly
followed by resolutions in support of it from every part
of the country. Carlisle was thoroughly alive to the
unanimity of feeling that prevailed, and strongly urged on
ministers the necessity of conceding the Irish demands.

In March, North resigned, and the Rockingham ministry
came in. The new administration, represented in Ireland
by Portland, would not immediately commit itself. The
address, moved by Grattan in the House, passed unanimously.
Portland found it to be the general belief that the fallen
ministry would have made all the concessions very shortly,
under Carlisle's advice; and he himself recognized their
necessity. He wished, however, to enter on negotiations
as to the limitations of legislative and commercial independence, while Grattan refused to admit that
limitations could be discussed. Fox accepted the
situation. The Declaratory Act was repealed.
The Mutiny Act was limited to two years. The legislative
powers of the two Privy Councils were abolished (1782).

The constitution of 1782.

The Irish victory was, in the main, due to Grattan, who,
throughout, had been thoroughly consistent and unwavering
in his claims, and had, at the same time, shown the frankest
readiness to rely upon the complete and unqualified good
faith of Great Britain. Flood, however, was less confident.
It was certain that there was a considerable party in England who were anxious to have the concessions revised and
limited; it was suspected that some of them would try to
take advantage of any technical loop-holes in the new constitution. Such a loop-hole was to be found in the "Simple
Repeal" of the Declaratory Act. It was said that the Act
affirmed a principle; and that its repeal did not amount
to an affirmation of the opposite principle, but left the
question open. Flood and his followers declared that a
further Renunciatory Act was needed; Grattan maintained

that to call for it would be casting a slur on the honour of the men whose intention in repealing the Declaratory Act was clear. The Viceroy Temple, who had succeeded Portland, seeing the divided state of public feeling, urged upon ministers the advisability of confirming the repeal by a Renunciatory Act, and his advice was promptly followed; so that in 1783 the legislative control of Great Britain was formally resigned.

With the formation of the coalition ministry of Fox and North in England (April, 1783), Temple retired, and was succeeded by Northington. But, in Ireland, fresh causes of uneasiness had now come to the front. Grattan had generously taken his stand on trusting to British honour. Flood had adopted the attitude of distrust, and by his action considerable ill feeling was naturally aroused, while Grattan could no longer work in accord with him. Charlemont, the most trusted of the volunteer chiefs, could go the whole way with neither Flood nor Grattan. Fresh disputes arose when Flood demanded a reduction of the army, a step which would inevitably increase the political power of the volunteers, and threatened to throw all real political control into the hands of a military organisation. Grattan, on the other hand, would have disbanded the volunteers, while Charlemont, anxious to restrain them from any excessive interference, still felt it necessary to keep them in reserve.

Grattan and Flood.

The volunteers, however, were bent on activity. A very remarkable man, the Bishop of Derry, headed the extreme section ; and a leading feature in his schemes of reform was the political emancipation of the Catholics—a plan, indeed, to which Grattan was far more favourably disposed than either Flood or Charlemont. The most serious matter, however, was that the bishop's prominence marked the rise of a turbulent section, which had hitherto been held in restraint to a very remarkable degree. The studied moderation, loyalty, and orderliness of the whole movement which had culminated in the Irish constitution of 1782 is very singular. The stage to which we are now coming has very different characteristics.

In July, 1783, an assembly of volunteer delegates met at Lisburn. It passed resolutions for the removal of grievances, for the reform of parliamentary representation, for short bills of supply until grievances were redressed; and it summoned a volunteer convention, to be held in Dublin in November.

The volunteer convention, 1783.

Charlemont, after hesitation, decided to take part in the convention, feeling that, since he could not prevent it—for he fully recognized the danger of having a species of armed parliament sitting as it were at the doors of the constitutional parliament—the best thing to be done was to bring into it as large an element of moderation as he could compass. His efforts met with considerable success, a large number of moderate delegates being returned. A bill for parliamentary reform was drawn up, chiefly by Flood, but the bishop's efforts to introduce the question of Catholic franchise were unavailing.

The reform of representation is a proposal to which any parliament is inclined to offer strong opposition; especially when, as in the Irish and English parliaments at that day, it involves the destruction of the very influences by which half the members hold their seats. Those who control political power are rarely inclined to give up any of their own share in it, on grounds of public justice or expediency. The Irish parliament was, in consequence, by no means inclined to accept the policy of the convention: and many members who were prepared to support its policy were resolute against yielding to its dictation. When Flood and other members of both parliament and convention appeared in the House in uniform, leave to bring in the bill was refused by a large majority. The defeat in parliament was followed by the victory of Charlemont and the moderate

Demand for parliamentary reforms.

party; for, although the plan of reform was adopted, and an address justifying the action of the volunteers was carried, the convention itself was dissolved.

In March, 1784, Flood brought in the bill again; but the Opposition to reform within the House was too strong, and it was defeated. The history of the Great Reform Bills, both in Ireland and England, shows that the personal interests of members and patrons alike were too deeply involved for them to yield their privileges, except under the imminent threat of revolution.

CHAPTER VII.

THE CONFLICT OF PARTIES.

1772–1784.

King George's rule, through North—Catholic emancipation—1780 : The Gordon riots—Strength of the ministry—Parliamentary corruption—Economic reform—1782 : North resigns—Second Rockingham administration—Fox and Shelburne—Measures of reform—The Shelburne ministry—1783 : Coalition of Fox and North—The ministry of Portland—Fox's Indian Bill; it arouses violent opposition—Intervention of the King—The Younger Pitt Prime Minister—1784 : Government in a minority—Pitt's increasing popularity—Dissolution—Pitt's triumph.

THE ministry formed by Lord North in 1770 developed an unexpected and surprising stability. The king had in fact at last succeeded in filling all posts with his own friends; whereas hitherto it had always been necessary to include some section of Whigs who refused to be entirely subservient, and occasionally took upon themselves to dictate. In North, George found a minister who was ready to suppress his own judgment, to follow the king's, and to pay more regard to subserviency than to capacity in the selection of colleagues. Ministers found they could count on the support of a solid majority in the Commons; the action of the colonists made the repressive American policy popular; Chatham's followers and the Rockingham party were not in thorough accord. The administration, in short, while marked by exceptional incapacity in almost every department, followed on the

King George's rule through North.

whole a popular though desperately misguided policy, and enjoyed all the advantages which a practical dictatorship on one side always gives in party contests. The country supported the king on the main question of the colonies: the excitement of the democratic movement had died down; and the king went his own way, his ministers and their majority steadily supporting him, though it might be in the teeth of their own convictions; while, even on the American question, the Opposition was weakened by divided councils. Chatham and his followers stubbornly declared against the claim for independence, even while they most warmly advocated the right of resistance to oppression; the Rockinghams inclined more and more to the conviction that independence was the sole possible solution of the problem. The secession to their ranks in 1774 of Charles James Fox, then a young man of only twenty-five, gave them the assistance of the most brilliant debater in the House, while they already possessed its most distinguished orator in the person of Edmund Burke; but he too failed to supply them with that coherence necessary to make their attacks on the government really formidable.

Year after year, therefore, North held unshaken sway. In view of the subsequent attitude of King George in regard to Ireland, it is somewhat curious to find this ministry responsible for an act of Catholic emancipation in England. It emanated indeed from the Whigs, but the resistance to it came also from the Whigs. The existing Acts against the Roman Catholics were flagrantly unjust, and rested on the hypothesis that the members of that Church were politically dangerous; such justification as there was for them vanished with the collapse of Jacobitism, and they had already ceased to be generally enforced. Nevertheless the popular dread of Popery was not yet eradicated; the Quebec Act, which established Roman Catholicism in Canada, was fiercely assailed in England, while in the Puritan states of New

Catholic emancipation.

England it had not been the least of the colonial grievances against the British parliament. The emancipating Act was passed in England in 1778, but the proposal to extend it to Scotland excited a fierce outburst of fanaticism, and had to be withdrawn; while in the southern country, a kind of panic of Protestantism gave rise to the celebrated Lord George Gordon riots in 1780, when for a moment London was at the mercy of an armed mob, and a very grave danger was averted mainly by the king's own undaunted personal courage and readiness under emergency.

Parliament had been dissolved early in 1774 without affecting the overwhelming majorities commanded by ministers in both Houses. Their refusal to listen to the overtures of the colonists, their farther repressive measures, their prosecution of the war generally, were endorsed by heavy votes. Grafton and such Whigs as had remained in the ministry in the hope of exercising a conciliatory influence, were obliged to resign, but they carried no supporters with them. As time went on, however, the current of opinion began to turn. The misconduct of the war, Burgoyne's surrender, the continued resistance of the colonies, the intervention of France, strengthened the conviction in some quarters that the American struggle could have no satisfactory termination. The policy of coercion was rapidly becoming unpopular, while the policy of submission remained distasteful. North was thoroughly alive to his own unfitness for conducting the tremendous struggle on which the country was embarked, and was ready, even eager, to resign his place to Chatham, to whom also the nation was turning with longing eyes. But George remained stubborn. He was determined to carry matters his own way, and that would be impossible with such a minister as Chatham. Then Chatham died in May, 1778, leaving no successor; the policy of the Rockinghams had not yet won general acceptance, and North struggled on.

The nation was becoming alive to the fact that the king

and the king's personal influence were responsible for the state of the administration, and for the persistence in a policy daily growing more discredited. Some of the supporters of the government were known to be wavering. It was evident that much of the king's power was derived from the immense opportunities of corruption he possessed. While an enormous war expenditure was draining the treasury, the civil list had attained immense proportions. Large sums were expended on secret service. There was a host of sinecure places which existed only for the purposes of corruption. Curtailment of expenditure is nearly always popular; and the Opposition seized upon Economic Reform as the cry whereby they would be enabled to strike hardest at the excessive power of the crown. When it came to details, no doubt the interests of too many influential persons would be touched for effective measures to be easily carried, but the cry gave the Opposition popularity.

Parliamentary corruption.

Economic reform.

In 1780 the agitation assumed large proportions. County after county passed resolutions against the expenditure in corruption. In the Commons, Dunning succeeded in carrying against ministers a resolution that "the power of the crown has increased, is increasing, and ought to be diminished." Burke brought in an Economic Reform Bill which passed the second reading, and was only smothered by the resistance of small majorities over details in committee. Ministers, however, began to recover their preponderance, partly no doubt because individuals began to realise that their private interests were being threatened, partly because the Gordon riots, with others, were bringing the methods of agitation into discredit. Parliament was dissolved in September, the king's friends strained every nerve, and when the new House met, North was on the whole a little stronger than he had been. The election, however, is notable, because the younger William Pitt now took his seat for the first time, at the age of twenty-one.

Through 1781 North remained in office. But at the end of November in that year came the news of the surrender of Yorktown. This was the blow that decided the war; it was the turning-point in parliament also. The ministerial majority diminished immediately; by March it had vanished, and Lord North resigned.

North resigns.

A Whig union was now the only possible government. Shelburne, the chief of Chatham's followers, was unable to form a ministry, and the king in great bitterness of spirit was forced to accept Rockingham as Prime Minister, with Shelburne and Fox as Secretaries of State, and other offices divided among the Rockinghams and the old supporters of Chatham. Thurlow, however, one of the few really able members of the last administration, remained as Chancellor, devoting himself strenuously to George's interests.

Second Rockingham ministry.

The new cabinet contained serious elements of dissension. Shelburne was a very able man, but possessed a quite exceptional capacity for earning the complete distrust of all his colleagues. Thurlow had a line of his own to take. Of the Whigs, Shelburne was the one on whom the king relied; Fox the one towards whom he was most bitterly hostile. Causes of dissension arose quickly between the two secretaries. The Foreign Department was Fox's, the Home and Colonial Shelburne's. American independence not being yet recognized, negotiations with the States fell to Shelburne, those with France to Fox. Each had his own representative in Paris, and the two did not work in concert, while an informal proposal of Franklin's that Canada should be handed over to the States by way of compensation for losses was never brought before Fox at all.

Fox and Shelburne.

Nevertheless, the second Rockingham ministry, like the

first, was the author of useful measures. The corrupt influencing of parliament was attacked by bills excluding contractors from the House, and disfranchising revenue officers; two very efficient sources of corruption being thereby removed. A bill for economic reform was again introduced by Burke, though in a shape somewhat modified by Shelburne and Thurlow acting on the king's behalf. Burke, who was at the time Paymaster-General—a position of great profit—took the opportunity to bring in a bill to curtail the emoluments of his own office.

Measures of reform.

Another measure aimed against undue parliamentary influence was introduced independently by Pitt, who, young as he was, had immediately made his mark, and had caused a good deal of surprise by refusing to join a ministry unless he held cabinet rank. Pitt moved for a committee to inquire into parliamentary representation, with a view to reform in two directions—the abolition of rotten boroughs and an increase in the number of county members. The government, however, was too much divided to take up the proposal, though Fox supported it; and the motion was lost.

At the end of June (1782), the dissensions in the cabinet came to a head. Rockingham died; Fox and some others of his party resigned on Shelburne becoming Prime Minister. His main task—the negotiation of peace—was made easier by the news of Rodney's victory, which had turned the scale in naval affairs, placing the superiority—though not an overwhelming one—once more in the hands of Great Britain. Up to this point, our opponents had had the better of the fight; now, America being relinquished, the victory off The Saints had changed the position at a stroke, and there seemed a good prospect of regaining ground steadily. So that France and Spain, already feeling somewhat distrustful of the attitude of the Americans, urged their claims against us

The Shelburne ministry.

2 B

with diminished confidence. The signal failure of the grand assault on Gibraltar in September, and Howe's relief of the fortress, farther strengthened the ministry in their negotiations.

Nevertheless, Shelburne could by no means obtain the confidence of his own colleagues. Pitt, who had become his Chancellor of the Exchequer, stood by him loyally, though even he found his relations with the Prime Minister so unsatisfactory that in after years he refused to give him office. Other ministers, like Richmond, were openly at variance with their chief. The public were discontented with the terms of the preliminaries of peace, though it is difficult to see how England could have claimed or her adversaries have conceded more in view of the fact that one signal naval reverse might still have proved sufficient to cripple her fleet, while even Rodney's victory had not sufficed to place such a disaster out of reach.

Thus at the beginning of 1783 there were three great parties—the followers of North, of Fox, and of the government. Any combination of two could overpower the third; and the amazement was universal when, instead of a combination between the two sections of Whigs, or between North and Shelburne's section, which would have best pleased the king, it was found that Fox and North had come to terms. The old coalition between the elder Pitt and Newcastle bore some points of resemblance, inasmuch as Pitt had used language about his colleague as unmeasured as Fox had indulged in about North. But in 1757 the coalition had obviously been the only possible chance of saving the country from impending ruin; in the present case a strong ministry might have been formed by the coalition of either Fox or North with Shelburne, without doing serious violence to any principles. The union of Fox and North was in fact a junction for the expulsion of Shelburne; while in theory it was a coalition for the establishment of a ministry

Coalition of Fox and North.

independent of the royal influence. The former coalition was justified by its supreme success; the later one stands condemned by its complete failure.

For the moment, however, the alliance triumphed. On February 24th, Shelburne resigned, on the passing of a vote of censure on the terms of the peace. The king was furious. He could not endure Fox, while he regarded North's action as shameless desertion. He struggled hard for five weeks to induce some member of the fallen administration to form a cabinet; but one and all recognized that the task was impracticable. On April 2nd, Portland, the chosen figure-head of the coalition, was appointed to the treasury. Pitt and Richmond went into Opposition with Shelburne, flatly refusing to join in any ministry with North, in spite of urgent appeals. *Ministry of Portland.*

The new cabinet had no very definite programme. It refused to commit itself to parliamentary reform, and a series of resolutions moved by Pitt to that end was rejected. The modifications introduced into the definitive peace signed in September were of no great importance, despite the terms that had been used about the preliminaries. The great struggle came over Fox's East India Bill.

The government of India was becoming a matter of pressing importance. It was obvious that the existing system was inefficient, nor was it enough to throw all responsibility for maladministration on the misconduct of Hastings. The public were aware of the actual misdeeds of the governor-general, which had been carefully painted in the blackest of colours. They were aware of the blunders which had plunged us into war with the Mahrattas and Hyder Ali, and their ignorance of the general situation led them to believe that Hastings was grievously to blame for not having prevented them. No one was inclined to follow the unpopular course of defending him. But besides this, the system was inadequate to the *Fox's India Bill.*

needs of the empire. The House had censured both Hastings and Impey; the court of directors had voted their recall: but the court of proprietors had set the House and the directors at defiance, and negatived the order, while the condition of parties in parliament was still uncertain. Such a state of affairs was too chaotic to be allowed to continue.

The question was opened by a bill brought in by Dundas, who had attached himself to Pitt. The remedies he proposed were the recall of Hastings, and the appointment, by the crown, of a practically absolute governor-general. Coming from the Opposition, the proposal was rejected; but the government brought in a bill of its own, chiefly the handiwork of Burke and Fox.

Fox proposed to replace the courts of directors and proprietors for purposes of government by a body of seven commissioners, appointed by the legislature, who should hold office for four years. The commissioners were to have absolute power of appointment to all offices in India, and absolute control of administration and policy. They were to be removable only on an address from either House. A body of nine assistant directors was to be chosen, also by the legislature, from among the proprietors; who were to manage commercial details. In the former body, vacancies were to be filled by the crown; in the latter, by the proprietors. The practicability of Indian policy being dictated by any body of men sitting in London is doubtful enough;

It arouses violent opposition. but the opposition to the bill was based on an appeal to popular sentiments more easily stirred —the interference with the East India Company's charter which would shake the basis of all chartered companies, and the vesting of the whole Indian patronage in the parliamentary majority.

With regard to the former of these two arguments, Burke and Fox could show that an interference with the company's political control was a positive necessity. The second argument was difficult to meet, except by remarking that, appointments being for four years only, there was no serious risk of patronage being grossly abused. According to the Opposition, however, the danger lay in this—that wealthy Indian officials exercised an enormous control over rotten boroughs; these would thus be under the control of the commissioners; these, in their turn, would be the instruments of the party now in power : in short, the whole scheme was simply a plot of that party to obtain a control over the elections which would place it permanently in office.

The king believed that the passing of the measure would be the death-blow to all royal authority ; the Opposition proclaimed that it would be the ruin of all electoral liberty. Public feeling was with the Opposition, but the coalition had a great majority in the Commons. The bill was passed in the Lower House by majorities of two to one.

But in the Lords there were many of North's old supporters, whose allegiance to him had been seriously shaken by the coalition with Fox. The Whig peers were divided. The attitude of the bishops was at best uncertain. When the bill came before the House the king allowed it to be known that he would treat the votes upon it as a personal matter. On December 17th the bill was thrown out. In the Commons, ministers supported and carried easily a virtual vote of censure on the king's unconstitutional interference. Ministers would not offer to resign, and George was driven to demand the seals from the Secretaries of State. On the 19th it was announced that William Pitt had accepted the post of First Lord of the Treasury.

George's intervention.

The ejected ministers had an almost overwhelming case in their favour. They had been defeated in the Lords, despite their vast majority in the Commons, by a flagrantly unconstitutional exercise of the royal influence. If they had demanded a dissolution, resistance would have been impossible. Instead, they made the

Pitt Prime Minister.

astonishing blunder of opposing a dissolution, and trying
to force Pitt to resign. By so doing they entirely lost the
moral advantage derived from the king's action. It was
the Opposition, not Pitt, who refused an appeal to the
country. The impression was produced that, in spite of
their numbers in the House, they expected to be beaten at
the polls. Moreover, their appeal ought to have been made
against the unconstitutional methods by which they had
been driven from office; they spoiled their own case by themselves adopting the technically unconstitutional position of
claiming the right to select the king's ministers for him,
when they demanded not a dissolution but resignation.
They lost the constitutional advantage which the king had
given them, and gave away a tactical advantage by showing
distrust in the result of a general election. And the blunder
was enormously intensified in its effect by the unique opportunity given to the young minister for the most effective
display of his exceptional powers under circumstances which
could not but evoke the enthusiasm of all who were already
well disposed towards him, and the sympathy of every
generous opponent.

Parliament met early in January after the Christmas
holiday. The Opposition had not yet developed their
scheme of resisting dissolution, and Pitt's position
looked hopeless. With hardly one good debater
behind him in the Commons except Dundas, and
a cabinet chiefly remarkable for the absence of tried men,
he had against him Fox, Burke, Sheridan, North, and a
majority of votes. Day by day his courage and skill in
fighting the unequal contest raised him in public estimation,
while the ungenerous demeanour of his opponents deprived
them of all sympathy. The means whereby the India Bill
had been defeated were forgotten in the growing unpopularity of the bill itself. The new challenge of the king's
prerogative of selecting his own ministers rallied not only
the king's friends, but the general conservative instinct

*Govern-
ment in a
minority.*

against the coalition; at the same time, Pitt's own attitude as to parliamentary reform made the reformers look to him more hopefully than to the Opposition. Moreover, his personal popularity was greatly increased by an act which finds a close parallel in his father's disinterested action when he was made Paymaster-General. Barré had received a pension from the very Government which had attacked the economic system of which pensions formed a part. The highly paid sinecure office of the Clerkship of the Pells now became vacant. Every one expected Pitt, a poor man, to nominate himself to it—a course which would have been in entire accordance with precedent. Instead, he nominated Barré, on condition of his resigning his pension. *Pitt's increasing popularity.*

An India Bill was a necessity, and Pitt introduced one. It was thrown out. Still he did not dissolve, knowing that the tide of opinion was now setting strongly in his favour, while the attitude of the Opposition made it impossible that they should denounce him for not dissolving. The majority wavered. Proposals for a compromise were made, but they broke down on Pitt's insisting that Thurlow should remain in any new cabinet—a course to which Fox refused to assent, his primary object being the exclusion of royal influence. In March, the Opposition were no longer secure of a majority even in the Commons. Pitt's time had come. On March 25, 1784, parliament was dissolved. King's friends and reformers, the mercantile classes, the Nonconformists, and that great mass of Englishmen who take a comparatively small interest in politics, but whose sporting instincts are aroused by such a contest as had been waged for the past three months, all combined. The Opposition was shattered, and Pitt returned to parliament at the head of an enthusiastic and overpowering majority. *Dissolution. Pitt triumphant.*

EPILOGUE.

BEFORE THE FRENCH REVOLUTION.

1784–1789.

William Pitt—Foreign affairs—The Commercial Treaty with France, 1786—Pitt's finance; taxation; loans; sinking fund—End of parliamentary reform, 1785—The Regency Bill, 1788—*Ireland:* reform—Progress—Commercial restrictions—Pitt's proposals; their failure, 1785—*India*—Pitt's India Bill, 1784—Concluding remarks.

THE career of William Pitt the younger is remarkable for many reasons, but most of all perhaps because the things **William Pitt.** he accomplished and the things he left undone were as nearly as possible the reverse of what might have been looked for. He came into office as a reformer, and reform was deferred for nearly half a century. He was an ardent advocate of the anti-slavery cause; but it was not he who abolished the slave-trade. His early endeavours to establish complete free-trade with Ireland were wrecked by the shortsightedness of the mercantile community. When he carried the Act of Union, it was at the cost of Catholic Emancipation to which he was most deeply pledged. He craved for peace, and his name is most intimately associated with the most tremendous of all wars.

The biographer must view his career as a whole; whereas only a small part of it falls to be dealt with in this volume. The French Revolution changed the whole course of European politics, and for the time produced a violent reaction against domestic changes in England, and in Ireland a widespread revolutionary sentiment; thereby breaking the continuity of development everywhere except in India. The Napoleonic wars were indeed the final phase of the great duel for empire with which this book mainly deals. But the problems connected with the French Revolution are too vast, the policy of Bonaparte is too comprehensive, the details of the history are too complicated, to be even outlined or suggested in the closing chapters of a work of this kind. I propose, therefore, now merely to pass in review the leading events which took place before the whole current of affairs was diverted by the cataclysm in France.

Hence foreign affairs call only for the briefest notice. Spain could only display the trappings of a great Power; the substance was gone from her. France was struggling with her ruined finances. In the East, Poland was the pivot on which turned the international relations of Austria, Prussia, and Russia. They had already accomplished the first partition of that unhappy country in 1772, each of the great Powers appropriating a large slice of her territories; and a further redistribution was shortly to be effected. In 1786 died Frederick the Great, leaving Prussia at the head of a confederacy of German states known as the Fürstenbund, whereby she was substantially strengthened as against Austria; but his successor was a man of very different calibre, wholly unfitted to maintain the country in that dominant position to which she had been raised by the genius alike for war and for organisation which had been united in the person of Frederick. *Foreign affairs.*

The tremendous blow dealt to Britain by the loss of her American colonies, and the exhaustion consequent on the war, would have made a policy of non-intervention imperative, even under a less peacefully disposed minister than Pitt. The necessities of the position only confirmed his natural inclination to avoid any embroilment in European affairs. In this field his main *Pitt's Commercial Treaty.*

achievement, the Commercial Treaty with France (1786), was an economic rather than a diplomatic triumph. It was a measure of free trade, closely akin to that which Bolingbroke had designed but had failed to carry in 1713. It is remarkable, however, that the economic theories which had served to wreck the earlier treaty now found few advocates, and the strength of the opposition lay mainly in the political argument that France was by nature and necessity hostile to England, and would utilise the treaty less to benefit herself than to injure her rival; while the mutual concessions would not only fail to remove mutual hostility, but would alienate from Britain other states which would be deprived of their exceptional commercial advantages by the new treaty. It is particularly curious to find this line being vigorously taken by Fox, who was afterwards so ardent a champion of France.

It is in the field of finance that Pitt's claims to success are chiefly to be found. A disciple of Adam Smith, as Shelburne had also been, he succeeded in carrying out the policy which Shelburne had failed to do. He recognized that excessive duties on articles of general consumption defeat their own purpose, by giving a great impetus to smuggling, since they make the illicit traffic extremely profitable ; and at the same time they raise the price of the goods to a point which seriously checks the demand. By the substitution of a great variety of light duties for a few heavy ones, the revenue was materially increased, while the temptation to smuggling was much diminished.

Pitt's finance.

Another measure of great importance was the change which Pitt introduced in the method of receiving tenders for public loans. Hitherto it had been the practice to conduct these arrangements by private contract—a system which was not only unnecessarily expensive in any case, but further opened a door for very extensive corruption, providing a means for secretly satisfying the claims of great numbers of people who could not be given rewards of a more obvious kind. This system Pitt abolished; accepting, instead, the lowest tender by public competition, and so sweeping away at a single blow one of the most fruitful sources of corruption, quite as effectively as would have been done by an avowed bill for economic reform.

By his efforts in the direction of free trade, by his altered scheme of taxation, and by the substitution of open competition for private contract in government loans, Pitt has established very high claims as a financier; but the financial measure which in his own day gained him the loudest applause was one which is now recognized as essentially unsound. This was his institution of a sinking fund, whereby a million was to be appropriated annually, accumulating at compound interest, for the reduction of the national debt. *The sinking fund.* The scheme was too complicated for examination here; but its practical outcome is generally held to have been that, in order to pay off loans contracted at a low rate of interest, larger loans had to be contracted at a higher rate of interest, the difference being supposed to be covered by a thoroughly misapprehended method of investment.

Parliamentary reform was the first object with which Pitt had identified himself on his entry into the House of Commons. However, although the interest in that subject had at one time run very high, and the opposition to it had been mainly due to a comparatively limited number of influential persons whose power would have been lessened by almost any improvements in the existing system, the strength of public sentiment had died down again. *Parliamentary reform.* The explanation is perhaps to be found in the fact that, when public opinion was sufficiently aroused, privilege and private interest had yielded to it. The popular triumph at the general election, when Pitt was returned to power, gave the impression that there was no such crying need for reform as had been supposed; while its opponents could remark how thoroughly the existing system was compatible with the carrying into effect of any strong popular demand. Hence, when Pitt brought in a Parliamentary Reform Bill, several of his own colleagues opposed him; he refused to make it a question of resignation, and the bill was rejected (1785). Nor did he repeat the experiment; and the whole subject was dropped, not to be revived again in a practical form till long after Pitt was in his grave.

In 1788 a curious question of constitutional law was raised, the king becoming for a second time incapacitated by mental disease. A regency seemed a necessity, but the method of appointing the regent involved serious difficulties. It was agreed that the Prince of Wales was obviously the proper person to assume the functions. Pitt, however, maintained that it was for parliament to confer the office upon him, with such restrictions as were deemed advisable. Fox and the prince's friends held that the prince became regent with all the royal powers necessarily, if the king were incapacitated, precisely as he would become king if the king died. In point of law the question seemed to resolve itself into a choice between assuming the authority of the prince, and assuming the power of parliament to legislate without the crown when the royal powers were practically suspended. The more actual present interest involved was, the extreme probability that the prince's favour would bring Fox into office in place of Pitt, since a large section of the Prime Minister's supporters were people who would be equally ready to support Fox if Fox was backed by the court. The contest is a mere episode, as the king recovered before the Regency Bill was through. The Irish had intentionally made a display of their independence of the British parliament in the matter; and, adopting Fox's theory, sent a deputation with an address recognizing the prince as regent,—whose arrival in London after the incident was already closed by the king's recovery, adds an irresistible touch of comedy to the whole affair.

The Regency Bill.

In Ireland, as shown in a previous chapter, the question of parliamentary reform met with much the same fate as in England. Members of parliament held their seats in virtue of the existing system, and were not disposed to vacate them for the sake of abstract justice. The borough-owners could control Parliament, and would not willingly resign their power. Moreover, the reformers were divided between those who desired to restrict the franchise to Protestants, keeping the government in the hands of the gentry and the well-to-do portion of the population; and the rising democratic faction, who desired a great extension of the franchise, involving practically the transfer of power to the Catholic majority. This party had to some extent captured the volunteers, among whom a number of Catholics from the lower classes were being enrolled; and an immense impetus was about to be given to their movement by the French Revolution. Pitt was ready to exert his influence at Westminster in favour of the moderate reformers; but the failure of his own English schemes, and the preponderance of the anti-reformers in the Dublin Parliament, effectually prevented him from taking any steps in the desired direction; and the continuance of the glaring evils in Irish representation helped to foment the revolutionary spirit which timely reforms might have checked at the outset. *[margin: Ireland: reform.]*

Even more serious than the unfortunate failure to lessen administrative corruption, and to improve representation, was the collapse of a great scheme which, if carried to a successful issue, would have enormously increased the material welfare of Ireland, and would have instilled a new feeling of loyalty and friendliness to Britain. Already the concessions granted, which had opened up foreign trade to the Irish, had greatly advanced their prosperity. Agriculture also had been revived by a system of bounties, which English economists invariably condemn, and less prosperous countries as *[margin: Irish prosperity.]*

invariably approve. It is evident that bounties are a tax upon the community for the benefit of a particular industry. It is also clear that where there is plenty of capital, the owners of which can afford to wait for their profits, an industry which requires extraneous support must be one unsuited to the conditions of production in that country, and the capital engaged in it would be more beneficially employed in other fields. But where immediate returns are a necessity, and capital cannot be sunk for the sake even of large profits in the remote future, an industry which is capable of becoming really profitable may never have the chance of starting, or, when started, may be hopelessly starved, unless some extraneous assistance is forthcoming; and it is at any rate disputable whether, in a poor or a "young" country, the application of bounties for a time to carefully chosen industries may not prove ultimately profitable.

Whatever conclusion we may come to on a survey of data gathered from sources sufficiently wide to allow of decisive generalisation, the evidence appears to show that, in Ireland at this particular time, the bounties by which agriculture was aided were accompanied by a general improvement : and the part of the population which lived on the soil—in Ireland a very large proportion of the community—was greatly benefited by the conversion of pasture into tillage.

Commercial checks. The great external check on Irish industry was now to be found in the restriction of her commerce with Britain. Linen was almost the only product which she could import into Britain free : and her goods were absolutely prohibited by the duties imposed from competing with those of English and Scotch merchants.

The material injury was serious, and that much ill feeling was aroused is sufficiently shown by the very prevalent sentiment in favour of retaliatory protection duties and non-importation agreements : an idea suggested by the action of the American colonies before the war. Grattan exerted himself strenuously to mitigate this feeling, as did those of his followers who were shrewd enough to see the weakness of a hostile policy, and wise enough to hope more from improved relations and strengthened confidence between Ireland and Britain, than from a system of retaliation from which the poorer country was certain to suffer far more than the richer one. But the feeling was there.

This state of things Pitt proposed to remedy by a commercial treaty instituting complete free trade between Great Britain and Ireland ; in return for which, the surplus of the hereditary revenue, whenever the finances showed a surplus, was to be handed over for the navy : Ireland thus recognizing the obligation to take her share in national defence. In Ireland, the proposed arrangement was welcomed by Grattan, and passed through parliament without much opposition, except from a few politicians who regarded the contribution to the navy as a sort of tribute, and a few merchants who objected to being deprived of the power of levying protectionist duties. In England, however, the mercantile classes were up in arms against the measure. Petitions poured in ; Fox thundered in opposition. Pitt was forced to modify his scheme, and when the proposals were brought before parliament in May, 1785, their whole character was changed. Restrictions were introduced, and it was made a part of the new plan that the British parliament should have the whole power of commercial legislation in the future. *[margin: Pitt's proposals.]*

The result was that, while British merchants would lose the monopoly to which they clung, the legislative independence, granted to Ireland by the constitution of 1782, was withdrawn in one most important particular. The British opposition was intense ; while, in Ireland, the commercial advantages offered seemed more than counterbalanced by the surrender of a part of that independence which had been so hardly won. Hence the whole scheme collapsed. The attempt had proved a *[margin: Their failure.]*

disastrous failure, and had only aroused increased animosities instead of the conciliatory effects intended.

It remains now to describe the new administrative machinery for India, which the difficulties, the dangers, and the misdeeds of Hastings's governor-generalship had proved to be an imperative necessity.

The Indian problem. The fundamental weakness of the position lay in the natural incapacity of a trading company to undertake imperial functions. Large dividends are too irresistible an object of desire, and officials whose policy subordinates dividends to other considerations are inevitably hampered at every step. Moreover, any effective administration must be in the hands of rulers who are, at any rate, in a position to carry their policy through consistently. Lord North's Regulating Act had left the ultimate control in the hands of the directors and proprietors of the East Indian Company in London; while the governor-general's powers had been so restricted that Warren Hastings had found himself thwarted at every turn by his colleagues.

Fox's bill had attempted to remedy this by substituting a board of commissioners appointed by parliament, for the India House, as the ultimate controlling body: and it had not made adequate provision for strengthening the governor-general. How and why that bill was defeated, we saw in a former chapter. Pitt, on his return to power in 1784, immediately took the question up; and the constitution constructed by him, or perhaps it should rather be said by Dundas, and modified at the instance of Lord Cornwallis, remained in force until the Indian Mutiny caused the whole machinery of government to be transferred to the crown in 1858.

By Pitt's bill, a board of control was established, which formed a part of the ministry, with a parliamentary head. This body had access to all the correspondence, and supervised the instructions of the board of directors, who still retained the effective guidance of affairs in their hands. The directors could take the initiative, and issue their instructions subject to the approval of the board of control, while they were also obliged to carry out positive instructions emanating from the board. [Pitt's India Bill, 1784.] Thus the directors were, in the main, allowed to take their own course; while the ministry of the day had a supervising power, which replaced the demand for Acts of parliament interfering with the policy of the directors. Patronage remained in the hands of the company; but it is easy to see that the board of control were practically enabled to have the benefit of it at will. As to the administration in India, each of the presidencies had its own governor, its own commander-in-chief, and two other members of council; but the other two governors were subordinate to the Bengal governor-general, whose commander-in-chief was also commander-in-chief for India. By the reduction of the members of the council, the prospect of the nominal head of the government being outvoted by his own colleagues was removed; and the additional powers secured by Cornwallis, of acting on emergency without the council, made the governor-general practically autocratic, though still responsible to the directors and the board of control at home. The obvious impossibility of waiting for instructions, and the necessity of allowing the ruler on the spot to judge of needful measures as occasion arose, made this ultimate responsibility play a comparatively small part in the politics of the future. The practice was at once commenced and maintained of appointing to the office of governor-general some one who had not been trained in the Eastern atmosphere, and of making his council consist of Oriental experts. These appointments, too, lay nominally with the directors, but the power of the board of control to exercise overwhelming influence is manifest. The first governor-general sent out under the new system was Lord Cornwallis.

Into the history of his governor-generalship we shall not

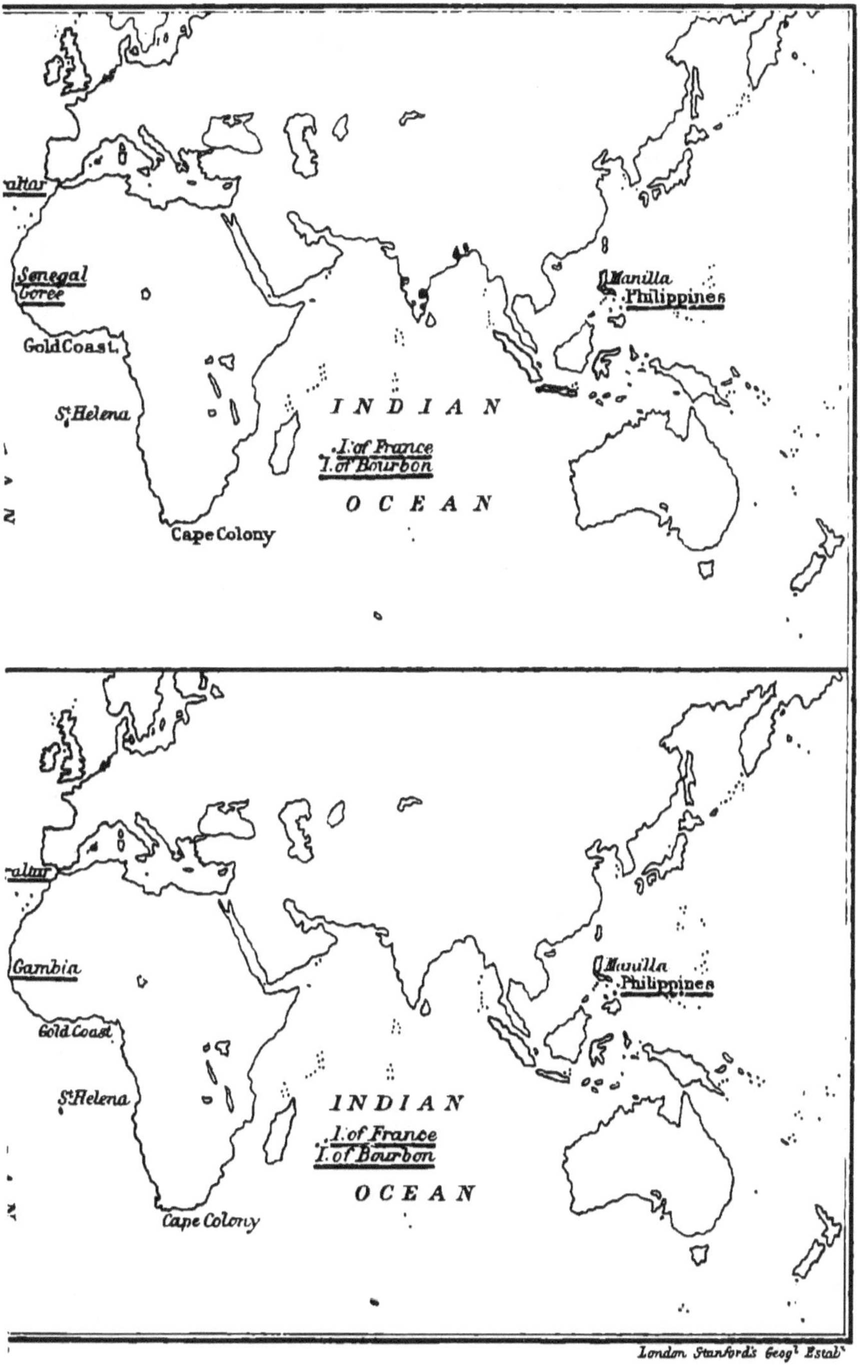
Senegal
Goree
Gold Coast
St. Helena
INDIAN
I. of France
I. of Bourbon
OCEAN
Cape Colony
Manilla
Philippines
Gambia
Gold Coast
St. Helena
INDIAN
I. of France
I. of Bourbon
OCEAN
Cape Colony
Manilla
Philippines

London Stanford's Geog[l] Estab[t]

INDEX.

Abercrombie, at Ticonderoga, 103, 106.
Abraham, the heights of, scaled by Wolfe, 108.
Absentee Tax, 277, 354.
Acadia, v. Nova Scotia.
Acts, v. Parliamentary Acts, etc.
Adams, John, with Lee of Virginia, brings proposal of American Independence before Congress, 289. American peace commissioner in Paris, 325.
Adams, Samuel, 283.
Afghan invasions of India, 115, 263, 328.
Africa, Senegal and Goree captured, 103. Goree restored to France. —Senegal retained, 153. Suffren at the Cape, 320.
Ahmed Khan invades India, 115.
Ahmed Shah, the Abdallee, 263. At Paniput, 328.
Aislabie, Chancellor of the Exchequer, involved in South Sea Bubble, 172.
Aix-la-Chapelle, Treaty of, 70. Condition of Europe after it, 70, 71, 74, 215. Effects in India, 127.
Akbar, grandson of Baber.— His empire over the north of India, 113.
Alberoni, the one statesman of insight in Spain, 8, 31. His able administration.—Hampered by the Queen's Italian schemes, 31. Want of time to reorganize the navy, 32, 33. His war, 32–37 (v. Wars). Fleet destroyed at Cape Passaro, 35; and in the Bay of Biscay, 36, 37. Failure of other schemes, 35,

36. Summary of his schemes, 36 End of his political career, 37.
Aliverdi Khan, nawab of Bengal, 139.
Allahabad, assigned to the Mahrattas, 328, 329. Transferred by Hastings to the vizier of Oudh, 330.
Alleghanies, The; western boundary of the English colonies, 76, 203.
Allen, Ethan, captures Ticonderoga, 283.
Aller, repulse of Richelieu behind, 89.
Ambur, battle of, 129.
America, North :—
British colonies, 202. Characterised, 203.
(1) Period of Anglo-French rivalry :—
Position of rival colonists, 3, 76, 77. Commencement of inter-colonial war, 96. Canadian campaign of 1768, 102, 103. Conquest of Canada, 106–109. Expulsion of French from America, 111, 135, 148 (v. Canada).
(2) From expulsion of the French to the rupture with Britain :—
The colonial theory, 203, 246. Effects of expulsion of French, 158, 203, 204. Trade restrictions, 205–207. Theory of taxation, 206, 249. Separation, in what sense inevitable, 247. Absence of representation, 249. Discontent with the Stamp

2 D

Act.—Its repeal, 251. Beginnings of opposition roused, 253. Suspicion of the standing army.— The Boston Assembly in opposition to Governor Bernard, 255. Irritation increased by Townshend's measures of taxation, 256. The Boston massacre, 257. The circulation of the Whately correspondence aggravates the situation, 257, 258. The Quebec Act, 258. The Continental Congress at Philadelphia, 259. Massachusetts takes the lead in warlike preparations, 260. The ultimatum from Philadelphia, 261.
(3) War of Independence: v. Wars.
America, Spanish, British illicit traffic with, 46, 213. English trading rights with, 5, 31, 50. Commercial quarrels with, 51 (v. Wars).
Amherst, Lord, replaces Loudoun in Canada, 102. Captures Ticonderoga, 106. Checked on Lake Champlain, 106. Descends on the Isle of Montreal, 109.
André, Major, 312, 313.
Anne, Queen, her dislike of Oxford.— Seized with apoplexy, 18. Death, 19.
Anson, Lord, 'commands expedition against Spain.—His voyage round the world, 54. Naval victory, 69.
Anti-Orleanist faction, 33.
—— plot, discovered by Dubois, 36.
Antilles (v. West Indies).
Anwar-ud-din, reigning nawab of the Carnatic, 128. Killed at Ambur, 129.
Arcot, capture and defence by Clive, 132.
Argyll, Duke of, with the Duke of Somerset, surprises the Tory Council, 18. Is sent north against the Jacobites, 22. At Sheriff-muir, 24. Suspected of complicity with the insurgents, 27.
Armed neutrality, 315.
Arnee, battle of, 132.
Arnold, Benedict, commands expedition to Quebec, 285. His treasonable correspondence with Clinton, 312.
Arras, battle of, 332.
Asaph-ud-Daulah, 342, 349, 350.
Austria, Hanoverian sympathy for, 9. Rivalry with Spain in Italy, 10, 213. Fresh arrangements in 1717 (the Duchies to Don Carlos, the Sicilies and Milanese to Austria), 32, 33. Confirmed in 1720, 38. Turkish war, 33, 34. Treaty of Vienna (with Spain), 38, 39; (with the allies), 41. Joins Russia in supporting Augustus of Saxony as candidate for Polish crown, 43. Treaty of 1737 (Sicilies to Don Carlos, Duchies to Austria), 44. Death of Charles VI., 56. The succession, 9, 38, 56 (v. Maria Theresa). War of (v. Wars). Peace of Aix-la-Chapelle, 70, 71. Schemes to crush Prussia; Kaunitz, 78, 79, 84. Seven Years' War (v. Wars). Peace of Hubertsburg, 153. Partition of Poland, 219, 399.
Aurung-zebe, the last of the great Moguls.—His fanatical Mohammedanism, 113. Disintegration of the Mogul Empire after his death, 113, 207.

Baber, Mogul conqueror of India, 113.
Bahur, battle of, Dupleix defeated by Lawrence, 133.
Baillie, defeated by Hyder Ali, 335.
Baj-Baj, captured by Clive and Watson, 140.
Baltic, English fleet in the, 35, 41.
Baltic Powers, and the Armed Neutrality, 315.
Bank of England, 171.
Barbadoes, Admiral Barrington at, 308.
Baroda, the Gaikwar of, one of five chiefs of the Mahratta confederacy, 236, 328.
Barré, nominated to Clerkship of the Pells, 375.
Barrington, his reasons for holding office, 295.
Barrington, Admiral, at Barbadoes. —Takes Santa Lucia, 308.
Barwell, member of the Bengal Council.—Supports Hastings, 342.

INDEX. 391

Bassein, ceded with Salsette to the Bombay authorities by Ragoba, 332; by the Mahrattas, 337.
Battles:—
Ambur, 129.
Arnee, 132.
Arras, 332.
Bahur, 133.
Bergen, 91.
Brandywine Creek, 293.
Brooklyn, 291.
Bunker Hill, 283, 284.
Buxar, 265.
Cowpens, 313.
Crefeld, 91.
Culloden, 67, 68.
Czeslau, 57.
Dettingen, 59.
Falkirk, 67.
Fontenoy, 60.
Great Meadows, 96.
Hochkirchen, 91.
Kaveripak, 132.
Kirch Denkern, 95.
Kolin, 85.
Kunersdorf, 94.
Leuthen, 88.
Lexington, 282, 284.
Liegnitz, 95.
Lobositz, 83.
Maxen, 94.
Minden, 91, 92, 103.
Mollwitz, 56.
Monmouth, 303.
Paniput, 264.
Plassey, 142.
Pollilore, 336.
Porto Novo, 336.
Prague, 85.
Preston, 23, 24.
Preston Pans, 65.
Quebec, 108.
Rossbach, 88.
Saratoga, 293.
Savannah, 306.
Sheriff-muir, 24.
Ticonderoga, 283.
Torgau, 95.
Trichinopoly, 133.
Wandewash, 138.
Zorndorf, 90.
———, Naval.
Cape Passaro, 34.
D'Aché and Pocock, 136.
De Grasse and Graves at the Chesapeake, 317.

De Grasse and Hood, at St. Kitts, 322.
De Guichen and Rodney, in the Antilles, 308.
Hughes and Suffren's five battles in Indian waters, 321.
Lagos, 104.
Langara and Rodney, 311.
Porto Praya, 320.
Quiberon, 105.
"The Saints," 323.
Ushant, 304.
Bavaria, the Elector of, rival of Maria Theresa.—France supports his claim, 56. Receives the imperial crown, 57. Death, 59.
Bedford, Duke of, prime minister, 225. Breach with the king, 226. Recalled.—Exasperates the king, 227. Excites the anger of the colonists, 231. Abused by Junius, 245.
Bedford Party, the, 225-227. Their extreme unpopularity, 227. Personal antagonism between them and the king, 236.
Begums, the Oudh, 342, 349; their territory forfeited, 349.
Begum, Bhow, 342.
Behar, under British rule, 266.
Belle Isle, captured by the English, 110. Exchanged for Minorca, 153.
Benares, subject to Oudh, 327. Its cession demanded by the Bengal Council, 342. Transferred to the British by the Vizier of Oudh, 348. Hastings and Cheyte Singh, 348, 349. Reorganisation, 350.
Bengal, a province of the Ganges, 113. Fall of the French, and advance of the British, 135. Its geographical limits.—Ruled by the Afghan Nawab Aliverdi Khan, 139. By Suraj-ud-daulah, 139, 140. English, French and Dutch settlements, 139. Clive establishes the British power, 141-144 (v. Clive). Attempt of the Dutch to check the British, 145. Clive adopts Dupleix's native policy.—Its relation to France.—Conditions in Bengal and the Carnatic compared, 146. Clive's work there, 262. British misrule in Clive's absence, 264, 265. Governor-General Vansittart and Warren Hastings, 265. Shujah Daulah's descent on the province,

and defeat at Buxar. Clive returns and institutes reforms, 265. The Diwanee transferred to the Company, 266. Evil results of dual control, 268. Famine, 269. Parliamentary inquiry, 269. North's Regulating Act, 270. Bengal under Warren Hastings, v. Hastings. New Constitution under Pitt's India Bill, 384, 385.

Berlin, the route to, left unguarded, 86. Austrian raid on, 87.

Berwick, commands French troops on the Pyrennean frontier, 37.

Bevern, 86, 87. Taken prisoner by the Austrians, 88.

Bhonsla, the Mahratta chief at Nagpore, 263, 335, 436.

Bills, v. Parliamentary Acts and Bills.

Biscay, Alberoni's fleet ruined in Bay of, 36.

Black Hole of Calcutta, 140.

Blockade, policy of, 101, 102, 156.

Blockades, v. Sieges.

Bohemia, Frederick the Great advances into, 90.

Bolingbroke, Tory Chief, 16. Hampered by Oxford, 16. Works for Stuart Restoration, 16-20. Flies from England and takes service with James II., 20. Intrigues to draw Louis into war with England, 22. Dismissed by James, 25, 27.

Bombay, the Company's Surat factory transferred to, 119. Communication with the other presidencies, 329. Origin of first Mahratta war at, 331. The council treats with Ragoba for Salsette and Bassein.—War declared by Governor Hornby against the regency at Poona.—The Council's decision repudiated by the Governor-General (Hastings).—The British worsted by the Mahrattas at Arras, 332. Hastings sends reinforcements.—The Council attempts negotiations with Poona, 333. Blunders of the council, 333, 371.

Boscawen, Admiral, defeats the French off Newfoundland, 97; at Lagos, 104. At Pondicherry, 126.

Boston, leads colonial resistance, 251, 259. The massacre.—Tea sunk in the harbour, 257. Head-quarters of Sir W. Howe.—Evacuation, 285. Entered by Washington, 286.

Boston Port Act, 258, 259.

Bourbon, Duke of, at the head of French affairs.—Breaks off the Spanish match, 38. His dismissal, 40.

Bourbons, danger of alliance between Bourbon dynasties. — Temporary alienation, 42. First family compact, 45. Design of Bourbon alliance, 45-58. Their gradual advance in Italy, 33, 46, 56. Acquisition of Naples and Sicily, 44; of Parma and Piacenza, 70. The Second Family Compact, 150, 153. Their position at the time of the American war, 298.

Braddock, General, 96, 97.

Braithwaite, Colonel, 336.

Brandenburg, threatened by the Russians, 90.

Brandywine Creek, battle of, 293.

Bremen acquired by George I., from Denmark, 30.

Breslau, Peace of, 57. Secured by the Austrians, 88. Again threatened by Laudon, 95.

Breton, Cape, captured by the English, 102.

Brest, a squadron fitted out to invade England, 103. The fleet blockaded by Hawke, 104, 105.

Broglie, Duc de, in command on the Rhine, 91. Defeated at Kirch Denkern, 95.

Brooklyn, battle of, 291.

Browne, Marshal, in Saxony, 83. Killed at the battle of Prague, 85.

Bruce, Captain, routs Sindhia, 334.

Brunswick, left unguarded, 36.

Brunswick, Ferdinand of, in command of Hanoverian troops, 89. His victory at Minden, 91, 92; at Kirch Denkern, 95.

Buckingham, Marquis of, Viceroy of Ireland, 358.

Bulwunt Singh, Rajah of Benares, 328, 348.

Bunker Hill, battle of, 283.

Burdwan, the Rani of, 343.

Burgoyne, General Sir John; his expedition, 293. His surrender at Saratoga, 293, 366.

Burke, Edmund, secretary to Rockingham, 227. His attitude towards

INDEX. 393

colonial resistance, 260, 261; to Warren Hastings, 351. His Economic Reform Bill, 367. Paymaster-general, 369. His share in Fox's India Bill, 372. Opposition to Pitt, 374.
Burkersdorf, battle of, 149.
Bushe's Irish Mutiny Bill, 357, 358, 360.
Bussy, captures Gingi, 130. Controls the Nizam, 131. Quarrels with Lally, 136. Taken prisoner at Wandewash, 138. A veteran at Cuddalore, 337.
Bute, Lord, favourite of George III., 110. His dangerous influence on the king, 110, 221, 235. His antagonism to Pitt, 150, 222, 233. Is forced to declare war on Spain, 150. His desire for peace, 151. His pusillanimity, 152. Devoid of political or parliamentary knowledge, 222. Secretary of State, 223. Will not renew the Prussian subsidy, 223, 296. Triumphant, 224. His resignation, 225. His shameless bribery, 225, 235. Abused by Wilkes in the "North Briton," 239.
Byng, Admiral, Lord Torrington, defeats Alberoni at Cape Passaro, 34, 98.
Byng, Admiral (son of Lord Torrington), fails to relieve Minorca, 98.

Cadiz, Spanish flotilla blockaded at, 58.
Calcutta (Fort William), Headquarters of future Presidency, 119, 139. Preparations against the French.—The Nawab of Bengal marches into, 139. The "Black Hole." — Surrender. — Clive and Watson. — Suraj-ud-daulah advances on, 140. Head-quarters of British Government, 270, 340. The Supreme Court of Judicature, 270. Constitution of the Council, 351.
Camden, Lord (v. Pratt).
Cameron of Lochiel, 65.
Canada :—
(1) Period of French occupation :—
Geographical position, 3, 76,

77, 203. Military organisation.—Popularity of French colonists with the Indians, 77. Commencement of intercolonial war, 97. Effects of Pitt's naval policy.—Routes to, 102. Montcalm, 102, 106-108. Ticonderoga, 103. Siege of Quebec, 103, 107, 108. Capitulation of Montreal.—Conquest completed, 109.
(2) Under English dominion:—
The Peace of Paris, 152. Roman Catholicism and the Quebec Act, 258. Military correspondence from Massachusetts, 260. American expedition into, 285, 288. Feeling against Americans, 286. Not drawn into the Revolt, 286. Proposed American expedition to, 305. Franklin's suggestion, 368.
Cap Français, 323.
Cape Finisterre, 97.
Cape of Good Hope; result of its discovery, 117. Suffren at, 320.
Cape St. Vincent, 151.
Carleton, Sir Guy, at Crown Point, 291, 292. Brings overtures to Congress, 325.
Carlisle, town of, surrenders to the Highlanders, 66.
Carlisle, Lord, in America, 301. Viceroy of Ireland, 358. Privately advises concession, 359, 360.
Carlos, Don, son of the Queen of Spain; recognised as heir to Italian duchies, 33, 41. Proposed union with Maria Theresa, 39. Naples and Sicily assigned to.—Resigns Parma and Tuscany, 44. Coerced into neutrality, 58. King of Spain, 110.
Carnatic, the Nawab subordinate to the Nizam of the Deccan, 113, 111. Position of English and French settlements in, 119, 123. The theatre of war, 123. Dupleix and La Bourdonnais, 120. The Nawab's friendliness to the French, 124, 209. Defence of Pondicherry, 126. Rivals for the Nawabship, 128-133. Successes of Dupleix, 129-131. Clive at Arcot, 132. Battles

of Arnee and Trichinopoly, 132, 133. Chunda Sahib killed at Trichinopoly, 133. Mohammed Ali proclaimed Nawab, 134. Lally and D'Aché, 136, 137. Capture of Fort St. David.—Siege of Madras, 137. Battle of Wandewash, and surrender of Pondicherry, 138. French power crippled, 143. Compared with Bengal.—The Nawab and the Nizam under English control, 146. Devastated by Hyder Ali, 335. British existence threatened, 335, 336. The Nawab of Tanjore, 345.

Carnwath, Earl of, joins in proclaiming King James, 23.

Carolina, Militia corps raised in, 260.

Carolinas, the ; landholders in, 202. Expedition to recover, 305. Rising of the colonists.—Cornwallis in, 313.

Caroline, Queen, her loyalty to Walpole, 41, 164, 177. Her death, 165.

Carpenter, General, 23, 24.

Cartagena, blockade of, 41, 55.

Carteret, Foreign Minister after Walpole, 58. His foreign policy, 59, 165, 217. Driven into opposition by Walpole, 163. Antagonism to Walpole, 177. Replaced by the Pelhams, 73.

Catherine of Russia, v. Czarina.

Catalans, the, 17.

Catholics ; the English Emancipation Act, 365, 376.

——, Irish, the chief part of the Irish population, 194. Debarred from education and parliamentary representation, 193, 197, 274. Oppressed by the land-laws, 194. Protestant guardianship, 197. Their loyalty towards Britain, 271, 272, 352. Relaxation of the Penal Code, 352, 353, 360. The Bishop of Derry's efforts for their political emancipation, 361, 362. Their enrolment among the Volunteers, 381.

——, Canadian ; population, 258. The Quebec Act, 258, 365.

Ceylon : Trincomalee, taken by the English from the Dutch, 320 ; captured by Suffren, 321, 329 ; restored to the English, 336.

Champlain, Lake, Lord Amherst checked on, 106.

Chandernagore, French settlement at, 119, 139. Dupleix governor, 122. Captured by Clive, 141 ; by Hastings, 334.

Charlemont, Irish volunteer chief, 361. Attends the Dublin convention, 362.

Charles, Edward, the young Chevalier, 60. Compared with James, 61. Lands in Scotland.—At Moidart. —Captures Edinburgh. — Preston Pans, 65. His march to Derby, 66, 180. The retreat. Victory at Falkirk, 67. Final defeat at Culloden, 68. Effect of his failure, 188. The magic of his personality, 65, 188.

Charles VI., Emperor ; his election and succession to the Hapsburg dominions, 14. Insecurity of the succession, 38. His death, 56.

Charles VI., King of Naples (v. Don Carlos).

Charles XII., King of Sweden, coalition against, 30. Enmity to George I., 32, 33. Killed at Friedrichshalle, 35.

Charles, Prince, nominal commander of Austrian troops, 59. At Prague, 85. At Leuthen, 88.

Charleston, 307.

Charlestown, the burning of, 284.

Chatham, v. Pitt.

Chesapeake, Lord Cornwallis at the, 313. De Grasse and Du Barras, 316, 317.

Chesterfield, Earl of, driven into opposition by Walpole, 163. His opposition to the Excise Bill, 166. His viceroyalty of Ireland, 198.

Chevalier, v. James Stuart.

Cheyte Singh, Rajah of Benares, 348, 349.

Chinsurah, Dutch settlement in Bengal, 139. Captured by the English, 145.

Choiseul, Duc de, his accession to power, and energetic war-policy, 91, 103, 217, 218. Encourages naval development, 219, 220.

Chunda Sahib, a prisoner of the "Peishwa."—Claims the nawabship of the Carnatic, 128. Supported by Dupleix and established

as Nawab, 129. In alliance with Muzuffar Jung, 130. Defeated by Clive at Trichinopoly, and killed, 133.
Cider Tax, Dashwood's measure, 225. Repealed, 228.
Circars, the Northern; granted to the French, 131. 137. Expulsion of the French by Forde, 137, 143, 145. Capture o· Masulipatam, 143. Chief source of Indian revenue to the French, 143. In British possession, 268, 327.
City of London; nature of the constituency, 237. Wilkes's candidature for, 241. Its championship of Wilkes.—Collision with the Houses of Parliament, 243.
Clan system, 182, 189, 190.
Clavering, General, member of the Calcutta Council, 342. Collision with Hastings.—His death, 344.
Clermont, General, defeated at Crefeld, 91.
Clinton, at Brooklyn, 291; up the Hudson, 294, 316; at Philadelphia, 303; at New York, 303, 307. Correspondence with Benedict Arnold, 312.
Clive, Robert; popular notions about him, 111. Comes to the front, 131, 132. Capture and defence of Arcot. —Battles of Arnee and Kaveripak. Rids North Arcot of native enemies, 132. Relieves Mohammed Ali at Trichinopoly, 132, and establishes him as Nawab, 134. Illness, 133. Begins the conquest of Bengal, 135, 136. Letter to Pitt, 138. Capture of Calcutta, 140. Mistrusts Suraj-ud-daulah, and determines to remove him, 140, 141. Intrigues with Meer Jaffier, 140. Makes use of Omichund, 141. The Red and White Treaties, 142. Defeats Suraj-ud-daulah at Plassey.—Sets up Meer Jaffier as Nawab, 143. Drives back Shah Alum's invasion, 144. Adopts Dupleix's native policy, 146. His first administration in Bengal, 262, 263. His absence in England and contest with the Directors of the Company, 264; 265. Returns and institutes reforms, 265. His foreign policy, 266. Final departure, 267.

Parliamentary inquiry into his conduct.—His death, 269.
Coalition, between Pitt and Newcastle, 99.
—— between Fox and North, 370.
Colbert, 119.
Colonial Theory, 203, 246.
Colonies, British (v. America, North).
——, French, 3, 4, 76, 77, 96, 97, 102.
——, Spanish, 2, 151-153, 297, 326.
Coltbrigg, 65.
Commerce, rivalry with foreign powers; in America, 2 (v. America, North); in India, 3, 117-120; in the South Seas, 4. Origin of the wars of the period, 2-7.
—— Companies; East India, 118-121. Ostend, 38, 41, 118. South Sea, 5, 29, 50, 52, 171.
——, Colonial; Walpole's attitude, 205, 206. Smuggling, 251, 254, 256. Restrictions on, 205; increased, 248, 252, 256. Chatham's attitude, 230. Exclusive dealing, 259, 260.
—— English; Mercantile theory, 14. Walpole's excise scheme, 174, 175. Pitt's economics, 378, 379. Commercial prosperity, 28, 158, 179, 181, 386.
—— Scottish, 181, 185, 191.
——, Irish, 193-195. Relaxation of restrictions, 278. Demand for commercial equality, 353-356. Failure of demand for Free Trade with Great Britain, 381-383.
Commercial treaties: Assiento, 5, 50. Bolingbroke's, 14. Pitt's, 378.
Concord, colonial depôt for military stores, 282.
Congress, General, at New York, 251, 255, 259.
—— "Continental" at Philadelphia, 259, 290. Its attitude endorsed by Chatham and Burke, 260. Its significance and its consequences, 261. Votes for continental army.— Appoints Washington commander-in-chief, 283. The "Olive Branch" petition, 284. Adopts Declaration of Independence, 289, 290. Commissioners from, confer with Lord Howe, 291. Support of Washington, 292. Departure from Philadelphia, 294. Scheme of confederation, 300. Refuses to treat, 304.

Financial difficulties. — Overtures from the Government.—Address to Washington.—Its commissioners in Paris, 325. Final treaties.—Attitude to the Loyalists, 326.
Congress, Provincial, of Massachusetts. Preparations for war, 260. Defies the governor, 283.
Connecticut, sends militia contingents to Massachusetts, 282.
Contades, sent in command to the Rhine, 91. Defeated at Minden, 92.
Conway, leader in the House of Commons, 228. His retirement, 231.
Coote, Sir Eyre, urges Clive's advance on Plassey, 143. Victory of Wandewash, 138. Commander-in-chief and member of the Bengal Council.—Despatched to Madras against Hyder Ali, 335. Victories of Porto Novo and Pollilore, 336. Ill at Calcutta.—Return to Madras, and death, 337.
Cope, Sir John, commands army against Charles Stuart, 65.
Corah, assigned to the Mahrattas, 329. Transferred by Hastings to the Vizier of Oudh, 330.
Cornwallis, Lord, in the Southern States of North America, 307, 312. At the Chesapeake, 313. Surrenders Yorktown, 317. First Governor-General of India under Pitt's Act, 385.
Corsica, acquired by France from Genoa, 219, 232.
Cossacks, 90.
Council, Bombay, the, exceeds its powers.—Its decision repudiated by the Governor-General, 332. Its blunders, 333, 341, 342, 371.
——, Calcutta, the, its constitution, 340, 341. Its treatment of Hastings.—Relations with Oudh, 342. Attempts to upset Hastings's administration, 343. Hastings at last predominant, 344. Quarrels with the Supreme Court of Judicature, 347. Reconstituted, 385.
——, Madras, the, offends the Nizam, 335. Struggle with Pigot, 345.
——, Privy (English), Dukes of Argyll and Somerset, 18. Its powers over the Irish Parliament, 193, 273, 356, 360.

Council (Irish), 193, 273, 356-360.
Cowpens, battle of, 313.
Crefeld, battle of, 91.
Crosby, Lord Mayor, 244.
Crown Point, Sir Guy Carleton at, 291, 292.
Cuddalore, Hughes and Suffren at, 321, 338. Captured by Tippoo Sahib, 336. Invested, 337. Restored by the Peace, 338.
Culloden, battle of, 67, 68.
Cumberland, William, Duke of, in the Low Countries, 60, 69. In command against Jacobites, 66. Charles Edward escapes from, 66. Replaces Hawley, 67. At Culloden, 67, 68. His cruelty, 68. Joined by William of Orange, 69. At Hastenbeck, 86. At Kloster Seven, 89. Recalled, 89.
Czar Peter the Great, seeks aggrandisement, 30.
Czar Peter III.: Devotion to Frederick the Great.—Deposed by Catherine, his wife, 149.
Czarina Elizabeth, her hatred of Frederick the Great, 78. Expected to die, 89, 93. Death, 149.
Czarina Catherine II., deposes her husband Peter III.—Withdraws support from Frederick the Great, 149.
Czernicheff, Russian commander, 149.
Czeslau, battle of, 57.

D'Aché and Pocock, 136. Second action and departure, 137.
Dashwood, Chancellor of the Exchequer, 225.
Daun, Count, at Kolin, 85. In Silesia, 88. At Hochkirchen, 91. After Kunersdorf, 93, 94. At Burkersdorf, 148.
Deane, Silas, 298.
Deccan, the: and the Carnatic, 113, 123. Mahratta invasions of, 119. Under French control, 131. Under English control, 147. (*Vid.* Nizam.)
Declaration of American Independence, 289, 299, 300. Its reception in France and Europe, 299. Signed by the thirteen colonies, 300.
—— of Irish Legislative Independence, brought forward by Grattan, 357.

Declaratory Act (Irish), George I.'s, 356, 357. "Simple Repeal" of, 360, 361.
—— (American), 228, 251, 252.
De Grasse, Admiral, at Martinique, 315. At Yorktown, 317. Takes St. Kitts, 322. Captured with his flag-ship at "The Saints," 323.
De Guichen and Rodney in the Antilles, 311, 312. Departure, 314.
De la Clue, Admiral, 104.
Delaware Bay, Lord Howe at, 303, 307.
Delaware Colony, 202.
Delaware River, 290, 292.
Delhi, Head-quarters of the Mogul Empire, 113. The Padishah, 144. Shah Alum restored to the throne, 329.
Democrats, rise of the, 169; in Ireland, 381.
Denmark, cedes Bremen and Verden to George I., 30. Subsidised by England, 52.
Derby, Charles Edward's march to, 66, 180.
Derby, Admiral, 318, 319.
Derry, Bishop of, 361.
Derwentwater, Lord, joins in proclaiming King James, 22.
Dessau, Prince Maurice of, 85.
D'Estaing, Admiral, out-generalled by Lord Howe, at New York, 303; and Rhode Island, 304. Sails for the West Indies, 304. Lets Barrington take St. Lucia.—Captures St. Vincent and attacks Grenada, 308. Attack on Savannah and departure, 309.
D'Estrées, General, defeats Cumberland at Hastenbeck, 86.
Dettingen, battle of, 59.
Devikota, fortress of, 129.
Devonshire, Duke of, Pitt's remark to, 100.
Diwance, the, 266.
Dominica, taken by the French, 307.
Dorchester Heights, 286.
D'Orvés, 320, 336.
Drake, governor of Fort William (Calcutta), 139. The "Black Hole," 140.
Drapier's Letters, the, 200.
Dresden, captured by Frederick the Great, 84. Recaptured, 94.
Du Barras, Admiral, at Newport, 314.

Sails for the Chesapeake, 316, 317.
Dublin, Volunteer convention at, 362.
Dubois, with Stanhope arranges the Triple Alliance, 31. Discovers the Anti-Orleanist conspiracy, 36.
Duff, 105.
Dumas, governor of Pondicherry, 120.
Dungannon, Volunteer meeting at, 359.
Dunkirk, 31, 106.
Dunmore, governor of Virginia, 287.
Dunning's resolution, 367.
Dupleix, leads the way to European rule in India, 117. Governor at Pondicherry, 120, 122. Aims at expulsion of the English, and French predominance in India, 117. The war between England and France in 1744. His opportunity. —Weakness of his position.—Disregards pacific instructions of the Directors, 123. Gains the support of the Nawab.—Strengthened by La Bourdonnais's squadron.—Disagrees with La Bourdonnais, 124. Rupture with the Nawab, 125; on good terms again, 126. Success at Pondicherry.—Proceedings checked by the Peace of Aix-la-Chapelle, 127. Encourages native rivalries. —Supports Chunda Sahib, 128. Defeats Anwar-ud-din, 129. Intrigues with Nadir Jung's nobles.— Succeeds in setting up his candidates, 130. The tables turned against him by Clive, 131-133. Battles of Bahur and Trichinopoly. His recall, 133.
Duquesne, Fort, established by the French on the Ohio, 96. Captured by the British and renamed Pittsburg, 108.

East Indies, English fleet in, 151. Dutch trade in, 117, 118.
East India Companies, 118, 119.
—— (English), locations of its factories, 118. Its policy, 119. Its objects, 120. Its character, 120, 121. Its status at the accession of George I., 211. Its power after Lord North's Act, 384. Under Pitt's Act, 385.
—— (Dutch), 118.
—— (French), formation of, 119. Its

objects.—Compared with the English Company, 120.
East India Trade, its importance to England, 121.
Economic Reform, 367.
—— Bill, Burke's, 367.
Edinburgh, capture of, 65. Porteous mob, 187.
Egremont, Lord, 225.
Elizabeth Farnese, heir of the Farnesi, marries Philip of Spain, 10. Her hostility to Austria, 10, 11; to the Emperor and the French Regent, 31. Dominates Alberoni and Spain with her Italian policy, 31.
Elizabeth of Russia, v. Czarina.
Ellis, at Patna, 265.
Emperor Charles VI., v. Charles VI.
—— Charles VII., v. Bavaria.
Europe, relative position of the Powers after the Peace of Utrecht, 7, 11. Spain and the Northern Powers, 32. Austro-Spanish alliance, 38. Treaty of Vienna, 41. War of Polish succession, 43. First Family Compact, 45. Rise of Prussia, 56. War of Austrian succession, 56-60, 69, 70. Austria and Prussia, 78. The Seven Years' War, 82-95, 148-150. Second Family Compact, 150. Peace of Paris, 153. Subsequent isolation of Britain, 218. Attitude of Powers towards American colonies, 296-299. Europe before the French Revolution, 377.
Excise scheme, Walpole's, 174, 175.

Falkirk, battle of, 67.
Family Compact, the First, 45, 47, 48. Known to Walpole, 52.
——, the Second, 150, 153.
Farnese, Elizabeth (v. Elizabeth).
Ferdinand of Brunswick, Prince, in command of the electoral troops, 89, 95. Victory at Minden, 91, 92. Defeats Soubise and Broglie at Kirch Denkern, 95.
Ferdinand of Spain, succeeds his father Philip, 69.
Fermor, Count, threatens Brandenburg.—Defeated at Zorndorf, 90.
'Fifteen, insurrection of the, 22-26. Rising of the clans under Mar,

22; on the English border, 23. Surrender at Preston, 23. Sheriffmuir, 24. Collapse, 25. Results, 25, 185. Its character, 26.
Finck, General, 93, 94.
Fleury, Cardinal, First Minister of France, 40. His peace policy, 41, 44, 45; in harmony with Walpole's, 42. Effects a reconciliation with Spain, 43. His real aim, 47. Devotes his attention to the advancement of the Bourbons, 47, 216. Break-down of his policy, 49. Neglect of the navy, 58, 216. Death, 59.
Flood, Henry, Irish parliamentary leader, 278. Vice-Treasurer.—Carries amendment to Irish Free Trade Resolution, 355. Split with Grattan, 361. His Irish Parliamentary Reform Bill, 362, 363.
Florida lost by Spain, 153. Restored, 326.
Fontenoy, battle of, 60.
Forbes, Lord President, 66, 188.
Forde, Colonel, in the Northern Circars, 143. Capture of Masulipatam, 143, 211; of Chinsurah, 145.
Forster, Thomas, 22-24.
Fort Duquesne, 96, 103 (v. Pittsburg).
Fort Lee, 291.
Fort Moultrie, 288.
Fort Royal, 308, 315, 322.
Fort St. David, 126, 131, 136.
Fort St. George, 118.
Fort Washington, 291.
Fort William, 118 (v. Calcutta).
'Forty-Five, the, compared with the "Fifteen," 61. Importance of its failure, 62-64. Charles Edward lands in Scotland, 65. Inaction of English Jacobites.—The march to Derby, 66. Siege of Stirling and battle of Falkirk, 67. Culloden, 68. Results, 70, 188.
Fox, Charles James, joins the Rockingham Ministry. — Powers of debate, 365. The king hostile to him. — Foreign Secretary, 368. Resigns, 369. Coalition with North, 370. India Bill, 371, 372. The coalition in opposition, 374. Defeat at general election, 375. Attitude to Pitt's Commercial

Treaty, 378; on the Regency Bill, 380; on the Irish Commercial Bill, 383.
Fox, Henry, 74, 75. In office under Newcastle, 97. Appointed Paymaster, 99. Becomes Lord Holland, 225.
France, after Treaty of Utrecht, 1, 2, 10, 71. Desire for continental aggrandisement, 2, 8, 46. Colbert and maritime expansion, 119. Naval inefficiency, 7, 46, 49, 58, 101, 102, 214, 217. Naval improvement, 219, 220. The Duc de Bourbon, 38-40. Fleury, 40-50, 59. Madame de Pompadour's influence, 79, 217. Choiseul, 91, 103. Theoretical Republicanism, 296. Coming of the Revolution,377. Relations with England:—
(1) Friendly.—Mutual support with regard to succession, 10, 11, 212. Dynastic alliance with England, and Triple Alliance, 31. Joins with England in mediation between Austria and Turkey, 32; in war against Spain, 36, 37. Treaty of Hanover, 39. Commercial Treaty, 373.
(2) Hostile.—Motive to friendship removed, 213. First Family Compact, 45-48, 52, 214. Declares war against England, 59. Encourages Stuart insurrection, 60. Peace of Aix-la-Chapelle, 70, 71. Opposed to England in the Seven Years' War, 84. Second Family Compact, 150, 153. Colonial rivalry in America and India, 2-6, 72, 76, 77, 79, 213, 215.
Anglo-French contests in America and India, and expulsion of French from America and India, v. (1) America, (2) India.
Attitude towards American war, 296, 297. Intervention and the Franco-American Treaty, 298, 300.
Relations with Spain:—
(1) Hostile.—Fear of Philip's succession to the throne, 9, 10, 30, 31. Anti-Orleanist conspiracy, 33. Pyrennean campaign, 36, 37. Spanish match broken off, 38.
(2) Friendly.—Cause of animosity removed, 42, 213. Allied with Spain in the Polish war, 43. First Family Compact, 45-48, 53, 214. Negotiates with Spain, 110. Second Family Compact, 150, 153. Influences Spain to join in the American war, 310.
Francis, Sir Philip, member of the Calcutta Council, 312. Opposition to Hastings, and duel with him.—Leaves India, 344.
Frankfort-on-Maine, captured by Soubise, 91.
Franklin, Benjamin: his attitude towards colonial taxation, 252. Colonial agent in London, 257. Circulates the Whately correspondence, 258. A hero in Paris, 299. Peace commissioner in Paris, 325. Proposes that Canada should be transferred to the United States, 368.
Frederick the Great: his personality, 72. His methods of war, 155. Attacks Silesia, 56. Compact with Nieperg, 57. Battle of Czeslau, and Peace of Breslau, 57. Renews war with Austria, 59. Withdraws, 60, 69. Recovers Silesia by the Treaty of Aix-la-Chapelle, 70. Relations with Austria.—with Russia, 78. Accepts overtures from England, 79. Treaty of Westminster, 80. Prepared for war, 81. Opens the Seven Years' War, 83. Captures Saxony and the Dresden archives, 84. Victory at Prague, 85. Defeat at Kolin, 85, 86. Retreat to Saxony, 86. His position becomes alarming, 87. Retrieves it at Rossbach and Leuthen, 88. English subsidy, 89. The nature of his task, 89. Failure at Olmütz.—Victory at Zorndorf.—Relief of Saxony, 90. Defeated at Hochkirchen, 91. His position at the close of 1758, 92. Defeat at Kunersdorf.—Contemplates suicide, 93. Recovers from exhaustion, 94. Victories at Liegnitz and Torgau.—His difficulties

400 INDEX.

increased by political changes in England, 95. Odds against him, 148. Scale turned by accession of Peter III.—Recovers Silesia, 149. Peace of Hubertsburg, 153. Subsequent hostility to England, 295. Partition of Poland.—Fürstenbund. —Death, 377.
Friedrichshaile, Charles XII. killed at, 35.
Fürstenbund, 377.

Gage, General, governor of Massachusetts, 282, 283, 285.
Ganges, Provinces of, 113, 114.
Gardiner's dragoons at Coltbrigg, 65.
Gaspee, the schooner, boarded and burnt, 257.
Gates, General, at Saratoga, 293. Retains Washington's troops, 294. At Camden, 313.
Genoa, transfers Corsica to France, 219, 231.
George I. : proclaimed king, 19. Arrives in England, 20. His unpopularity and insecurity on the throne, 21. His boorishness, 26. Results of his Hanoverian predilections, 28-30. Withdraws to Hanover, 29. The tool of the Whigs.—His personality, 160. Conditions at beginning and end of his reign compared, 161, 163. His jealousy of the Prince of Wales, 162. His death, 41.
George II., as Prince of Wales, left in England with Walpole and Townshend, 29. His accession, 41. His Austrian sympathies, 43, 44, 79. Anxiety for Hanover, 57. Personal valour at Dettingen, 59. Anxious to prolong war, 69. His preference for Carteret, 73. Attitude to Walpole, 164; to subsequent ministers, 165. Accepts Pitt, 100. Death, 109.
George III. : Accession, 109. Influence of Bute, 110, 221. Attack on the Whig oligarchy, 167. Strength of his position, 168. Monarchists and democrats, 169. Rise of the " King's Friends," 234. Use of corruption, 235, 367. Illness and Regency Bill, 226. Compelled to recall Grenville and Bedford,— to accept Rockingham, 227. Return of Pitt, 229. Disruption of Whigs, 234. The king and his ministers, 236. Attitude to Wilkes, 238, 241. Attacked by Junius, 245. Anti-colonial attitude, 236, 257, 284, 295. Effects of Saratoga, 300; of Yorktown, 318. His twelve years' rule through North, 364–368. His personal courage, 366. Attitude to the Rockinghams, 368 ; to the coalition, 370 ; to Pitt, 375. His unconstitutional action with regard to the India Bill, 378. Second illness, and Regency Bill, 380.
Georgia, colony of : French and English limits undefined, 3. Its landholders, 202. Cornwallis, 313.
Ghazipur, its cession demanded, 342.
Gibraltar, acquired by England, 1. Spanish desire to recover it, 37, 39, 45, 213, 297, 310. Attempted siege, 41. Chatham proposes to cede it, 101. Prolonged siege : relief by Rodney, 310 ; by Derby, 315, 318. Grand attack, and find relief by Lord Howe, 319 ; its effect, 370.
Gingi, captured by Bussy, 130.
Glatz, 57 (*v.* Silesia).
Goddard, Colonel, and the Mahrattas, 333, 334.
Godeheu, supersedes Dupleix in India, 133.
Gohud, cleared of the Mahrattas by Popham, 334 ; abandoned to Sindhia, 337. Cause of quarrel between Hastings and Francis, 344.
Goree, captured by England, 103. Restored to France, 153.
Görtz, Swedish Minister, 32. His fall, 34.
Grafton, Duke of, deprived of his Lord-lieutenancy, 236. In Pitt's ministry, 229. Prime Minister, 231. Proposes repeal of Townshend's measures, 231. Resigns, 232. Chatham's influence, 234. Abused by Junius, 245.
Granby, Lord, appointed Commander-in-Chief, 227. Supports Chatham, 232.
Granville, Lord (*v.* Carteret).
Grattan, Henry, 353. His demand for free trade in Ireland, 355 ; and for legislative independence, 356, 357. The Mutiny Bill, 357. At

Dungannon, 359. Success of his policy, 360. His disagreement with Flood, 361.
Graves, Admiral, at Yorktown, 317.
Great Meadows, battle of, 96.
Greene, General, 291, 313.
Grenada, attacked by d'Estaing, 308.
Grenville, George, Treasurer of the Navy, 166. The Triumvirate.— The Bedford Ministry, 225. Attack on Wilkes, 226, 239, 241. Stamp Act, 226, 248. View of colonial taxation, 249, 250, 252. Regency Bill, 226. Reconciliation with Temple, 227. Want of tact, 252, 254.
Guadaloupe captured by England, 108. Restored to France, 152.
Guastella, Duchy of, 84.
Guildford Courthouse, battle of, 313.
Gwalior captured by Popham, 334.

Haarlem, Heights of, 291.
Haddock, Admiral, in the Mediterranean, 57.
Habeas Corpus Act, Irish demands for it rejected, 275, 276, 278. Passed, 359.
Hancock, John, 283.
Hanover: Effects of the Hanoverian connection, 9, 212; George I., 30, 39; George II., 57, 59, 61. In the Seven Years' War, 84-86, 91, 92.
Hapsburgs, v. Austria and Maria Theresa.
Hardwicke, Lord, on the libel question, 244.
Harcourt, Lord, Viceroy of Ireland, 277, 353. Behaviour with regard to Absentee Tax, 278.
Harley, v. Oxford.
Hastenbeck, battle of, 86.
Hastings, Warren, nature of his task, and its effect on his methods, 330, 331, 346, 350. Foreign policy to strengthen Oudh, but not expand, 330. British Resident at Meer Jaffier's Court, 144. Governor of Bengal, 330. The Rohilla war, 331. Becomes Governor-General, 332, 342. Bombay and the Mahrattas, 332, 333. Seizes Chandernagore and Pondicherry, 334. War in the Carnatic, 335. Contest with the Council, 342. Nuncomar, 343. Contest with Clavering.—

Duel with Francis, 344. Financial difficulties, 345, 350. Temporary breach with Impey, 347. The Rajah of Benares, 348. Attack on the Oudh Begums, 349. Political reorganisation in Benares and Oudh. — Retirement, 350. Summary, 350. Impeachment, 351.
Havanna captured from the Spanish, 151. Restored, 152.
Haviland, Colonel, 109.
Havre, 106.
Hawke, Admiral, naval victory, 69. Blockades the Brest Fleet, 104. Quiberon, 105.
Hawley at Falkirk, 67.
Henry of Prussia, Prince, in Saxony, 90.
High Church Party, 61, 176.
Highlanders, their attitude on the 'Fifteen, 22; on the 'Forty-Five, 65, 188 (v. Clan System).
Highland regiments formed, 191, 239.
Highlands, the (v. Scotland and Clan System).
Hillsborough, Lord, Secretary for the Colonies, 257. Inclines to legislative union for Ireland, 357.
Hochkirchen, battle of, 91.
Holbourne, Admiral, 99.
Holkar, Mahratta Chief at Indore, 263.
Holland, limits of expansion, 2. Triple Alliance, 31. William of Orange appointed Stadtholder.— Negotiations with Louis XV., 69. Position, 71, 72. Trade with the East Indies, 117, 118. Settlement at Chinsurah, 139. Attempts to check the British in India, 145. Capture of Chinsurah, 146. The Dutch in America, 202. Annihilated in India, 262. Joins "Armed Neutrality," 315. War declared by England, 315, 316. Dutch West Indian islands captured by Rodney.—Preliminaries of peace signed, 315. Negapatam given up, 326.
Hubertsburg, Peace of, 153.
Hudson Bay Colony, 76.
Hudson River, Clinton's advance up the, 294.
Hughes, Admiral, at Madras, 320. Battles with Suffren, 321, 338.

Hutchinson, Governor of Massachusetts, 257. His correspondence with Mr. Whately, 258.
Hyderabad, head-quarters of the Nizam of the Deccan, 123. The Nizam controlled by Bussy, 131, 146. French control removed from, 136.
Hyder Ali of Mysore, 114. His origin, 267. His neutrality, 138. First Collision.—Alliance with the British, 268. Conflict with the Mahrattas, 329. Ravages the Carnatic, 335. Conflict with the British, 335, 320, 321. Defeated by Sir Eyre Coote at Porto Novo and Pollilore, 336. His death, 337.

Impey, Sir Elijah, Chief Justice of the Supreme Court of Judicature at Calcutta, 342. Position of the Court, 341. Nuncomar, 345. Relations with Hastings, 347. Censured by Parliament, 372.

India :—
(1) European trade and trading companies, 4, 117-121, 139.
(2) *Anglo-French contest* — first stage.
Dupleix governor of Pondicherry, befriended by the Nawab of the Carnatic, 124. Naval co-operation of La Bourdonnais, 124. Capture of Madras, 125. Lawrence at Fort St. David, 126. Boscawen at Pondicherry, 126. Peace of Aix-la-Chapelle, 127.
(3) *Anglo-French contest*—second stage.
English and French championship of rival native claimants, 128. Chunda Sahib supported by the French against Anwar-uddin, 129. Mohammed Ali, 129-133. Clive in the Carnatic, 132. Dupleix recalled, 133. Resulting position of English and French, 134.
(4) *Anglo-French contest* — final stage.
Lally at Fort St. David, 136.

French control removed from Hyderabad, 136. Lally defeated by Sir Eyre Coote at Wandewash, 138. Capture of Masulipatam, and expulsion of the French from the Northern Circars, 143. The English without European rivals, 138.
(5) Conquest of Bengal (*v.* Clive).
Conflict between the Mahrattas and the Afghans in Upper. — Battle of Paniput, 263, 264.
(6) British rule to Warren Hastings :—
Bengal: Clive's first administration, 260, 262. British misrule in Bengal on his departure, 264. Clive's return and reforms, 265. The Diwanee. Clive's foreign policy, 266. Final departure of Clive, 267. Famines, 269.
Madras: Complication with Hyder Ali—with the Nizam —with the Mahrattas, 268.
(7) Under Warren Hastings, *v.* Hastings.
The Mahratta war, *v.* Mahrattas. War with Mysore, *v.* Hyder Ali.
(9) The Home Government and the Company.
Independence of the Company, 118, 120. Secure of naval support, 121. The Company as a territorial power, 266. Clive's idea of transferring control to the crown, 220, 267. First Parliamentary inquiry, 269. Second inquiry, 269. North's Regulating Act, 270, 340. Recall of Hastings, 350. Fox's India Bill, 371. Pitt's India Bill, 385.
(8) The Native States :—
Main divisions of the Peninsula, 112-114; after establishment of the British, 327-329. Break-up of Mogul Empire, 113, 207. Afghan invasions, 115, 263, 328.

INDEX.

Dynastic struggles in the Deccan and the Carnatic, 128–133. Mahratta advance checked at Paniput, 262, 328. Mysore, the Nizam, and the Mahrattas in the south, 268. Growth of the Sikh confederacy, 328. Mahrattas, Rohillas, and Oudh, 329. British Mahratta war, 332–337. War with Mysore, 268, 334–337.

Ireland, compared with Scotland, 193, 199. Catholics (*v.* Catholics, Irish). Commerce (*v.* Commerce, Irish). Education, 197. Emigration, 198. Land-system, 195, 272, 277, 353. Judges, 273, 276. Loyalty during rebellions, 198; during American War, 354, 355, 359. Parliament, subordinate position, and struggle for independence (*v.* Parliament, Irish). Standing army, 275. Undertakers, 274. Viceroys: Chesterfield, 198; Townshend, 275–279; Harcourt, 277, 278, 353; Buckingham, 358; Carlisle, 358–360; Portland, 360; Temple, 361; Northington, 361. Volunteers (*v.* Volunteer movement). Wood's Patent, 200.

Isle of Bourbon, La Bourdonnais governor of, 120.
Isle of France, Suffren joins D'Orves at, 320.
Isle of Orleans, Wolfe established at, 107.
Isle of St. John, falls to the English, and is re-christened Prince Edward's Island, 109.
Italy, 58, 213 (*v.* Austria and Bourbons).

Jacobites, section of Tory Party, 13. Dominate Tory Ministry, 18; overthrow on Anne's death, 19. Rising of the 'Fifteen, 21–25. Dependence on France, 22. Want of organisation, and inaction, 22. Scheme for Swedish aid, 33. Chance of rising on accession of George II., 41. Rising of the 'Forty-five, 60–68. Inaction general in England, 63, 66; partial in Scotland, 65, 66, 188. The end of Jacobitism, 70.

Jacobitism, identified with Toryism, 163. James II., ejected by the Whigs, 12. James Stuart, the Chevalier, 13, 16, 17. His proclamation urged by Atterbury, 19. Joined by Bolingbroke and Ormond, 20, 21. In the 'Fifteen, 22, 25. His dismissal of Bolingbroke, 25. Compared with Charles Edward, 61.
Jamaica, 55, 322.
Jenkins's ear, 51.
Johnstone, Governor, commissioner to Congress, 301. Accused of bribery, 302.
Jones, Paul, 314.
Juggct Seit, Financier to Meer Jaffier, 141.

Justices, Lords: George I.'s Whig list, 20.

Kaunitz, Count, Austrian Minister, 79. His designs, 84.
Kaveripak, battle of, 132.
Kenmure, Lord, joins in proclaiming King James, 22; beheaded, 25.
Keppel, Admiral, at Ushant, 305.
Khevenhüller, 57.
Kirch Denkern, battle of, 95.
Kloster Seven, convention of, concluded by the Duke of Cumberland, 87. Not ratified by the Government, 89.
Kolin, battle of, 85.
Kunersdorf, battle of, 94.

La Bourdonnais, governor at the Isle of France, 120, 123. His grasp of the situation, 120. His squadron ordered home, 123. Joins Dupleix and saves Pondicherry, 124. Captures Madras, 125. Breach with Dupleix, 125.
Lafayette, Marquis of, serves as volunteer in the American war, 298, 314.
Lagos, battle of, 104.
Lahar, taken by Popham, 334.
Lally, brings reinforcements to the French in the Carnatic. Captures Fort St. David. Quarrels with Bussy, 136. His failure before Madras.—Isolated in the Carnatic, 137. Defeated at Wandewash, 138.
Lancashire, Charles Edward's army marches through, 66.

Langara and Rodney: naval battle, 311.
Laudon, comes to the fore, 90. Joins Soltikoff at Kunersdorf, 93. Hampered by Daun, 94. Defeated at Liegnitz, 95.
Lawrence, Stringer, in command at Fort St. David, 126. Sent to support Nadir Jung, 130. Obliged to return to England, 130. Returns to India and joins Clive. Relief of Trichinopoly, 132. Victory at Bahur, 133.
Lee of Virginia and John Adams bring proposal of American independence before Congress, 289.
Lee, General, 303.
Legge, Chancellor of Exchequer, removed by Bute, 223.
Levy, Point, Wolfe at, 107.
Lenoir, one of the Pondicherry governors, 120.
Leuthen, battle of, 88.
Lexington, battle of, 282, 283.
Leignitz, battle of, 95.
Libel, law of, 214, 245.
Lisburn, volunteer assembly at, 362.
Lobositz, battle of, 83.
London, the Preston captives march through, 26.
——, City of (v. City).
Lords Justices, Whig list drawn up by George I., 20.
Lorraine, succession of secured to France, 44.
Loudoun, British commander in Canada, 99. Recalled, 102.
Louis XIV., his continental policy a hindrance to the development of the navy, 119. Attitude to Jacobites, 21, 22. Death, 22, 27, 30, 212.
Louis XV., his succession and minority, 9, 30. Betrothed to the Spanish Infanta. — The match broken off.—His marriage with the daughter of Stanislaus, 38. Consequences of his marriage, 38, 42, 213. His change of attitude to the Stuarts, 61. Negotiations with Cumberland and the Dutch, 69. Madame de Pompadour, 79. Treaty of Versailles, 80. His last years, 219.
Louis XVI., succeeds his grandfather, 220.

Louisburg, taken by the English, but restored to the French in exchange for Madras, 70. Captured and retained, 102.
Lovat, Lord, 66.
Louisiana, 3, 76, 77, 153, 203.
Luttrell, Colonel, government candidate opposed to Wilkes, 243.

Macaulay, on the cruelties of the Rohilla war, 331.
Macdonald of Clanranald, 65.
Macdonald of the Isles, 65, 66.
Macdonald of Kinlock Moidart, 65.
Mackenzies of Seaforth, 24.
Macleod of Macleod, 65, 66.
M'Intosh, Brigadier, 23.
Madras, headquarters of future Presidency established at, 119, 123, 327. The harbour, 123. Anglo-French contest begins there, 123. Captured by La Bourdonnais, 125. Restored to the English, 127. Besieged by Lally, 137. Fear of the Mahrattas, 268. Complications with the Nizam and Hyder Ali of Mysore, 268. Offends the Nizam and Hyder Ali, 334, 335. War with Hyder Ali, 335-338 (v. Hyder Ali). Quarrel of council with directors and Pigot, 345.
Mahrattas, a Hindu confederacy. 114. Growth of their power, 114, 263. The chiefs and their head-quarters, 263. Their raids into the Deccan, 119, 263, 269. Conflict with the Mohammedan Afghans, and battle of Paniput, 263, 323. The chief source of danger to British, 328. Allahabad and Corah assigned to them by Shah Alum, 329. Conflict with Hyder Ali, 329. The company threatened by them, 330. Ragoba and the Bombay authorities, 332. At war with the British, 332, 334, 341, 345, 348. Battle of Arras, 332. They receive overtures from the French.--The Convention of Wargum, 333. The Bhonsla refuses to deal with Hastings, 334, 336.—Sindhia attacks the Rana of Gohud. — Successes of Goddard, Popham and Bruce, 334. The Bhonsla threatens Bengal, 336. Peace concluded, 337. Salsette and Bassein ceded to the British.

—Gohud abandoned to Sindhia, 337.
Manilla, capture of, 151.
Mannstein, General, at battle of Kolin, 85.
Mansfield, Lord (*v.* Murray).
Mar, Earl of, leader of the "Fifteen," 22. Defeated at Sheriffmuir, 24. Escapes to France, 25. His military incapacity, 26.
Mardyke, fortifications at, 31.
Maria Theresa, and the Hapsburg succession, 9. The Pragmatic Sanction guaranteed, 38, 41, 56. Proposed marriage with Don Carlos, 39. Betrothed to the Duke of Lorraine, 44. Accession to Austrian inheritance, 56. Refuses to treat with Frederick the Great, 56. Appeals to her Hungarian subjects, 157. Surrenders nearly all Silesia with Glatz, 57. Her warlike attitude, 69. Obliged to come to terms, 70. Treaty of Aix-la-Chapelle, 70. Personal rancour against Frederick the Great, 81 (*Vid.* War of Austrian succession, and Seven Years' War).
Marion, commander of colonial insurgents, 313.
Marlborough, Duke of, his power curtailed, 14. His double dealing, 20. His complicity with the Jacobites, 27.
Martin, Captain, coerces Don Carlos into neutrality, 58.
Martinique, captured from the French, 150. Restored at Peace of Paris, 152. Blockaded by Hood, 315.
Maryland, new England colony.—Its land-holders, 202.
Masham, Mrs., hostile to Oxford, 18.
Massachusetts, New England colony, 202. Governor Bernard in opposition to Boston Assembly, 256. Governor Hutchinson's correspondence with Whately, 258. Revision of Charter, 258. Repressive Acts against, 259, 260. Warlike measures, 260, 282. General Gage, Governor of, 282, is defied by the Provincial Congress of, 283.
Masulipatam, captured by Forde, 143, 211.
Matthews, Admiral, in command in the Mediterranean, 58.
Maurice of Dessau, Prince, 85.

Mauritius, the, 120, 320.
Maxen, battle of, 94.
Mecklenburg, threatened by the Czar, 30.
Mediterranean, fleet sent there under Byng (Lord Torrington), 34. Under English control, 41, 45, 58. Fleet sent by Walpole, 52. Highway between Spain and Italy, 58. Squadron commanded by Boscawen, 104. France's position is strengthened by the acquisition of Corsica, 219.
Meer Jaffier, Chief Captain of Suraj-ud-daulah, 141. Proclaimed Nawab of Bengal by Clive, 143. Deposed by the Council, 264. Reinstated, 265.
Meer Cossim, finance minister to Meer Jaffier.—Nawab in place of Meer Jaffier, 264. Ejected, 265.
Messina, siege of, 34. Surrender, 35.
Middlesex elections, 241-243.
Milanese, the, Spain's claim on, 33.
Minden, battle of, 91, 92, 103.
Ministries : Tory ascendency in the Commons, 13, 14. Renewed (in 1714), 15. Semi-Jacobite ministry, 16-18. Jacobite ministry, 18. Whig *coup-de-main*, 19. Whig supremacy —united Whigs, 20-29. Stanhope and Sunderland, 29. Townshend and Walpole, 173. Walpole's supremacy, 173-179 (*v.* Walpole). The Pelhams, 73, 180. Newcastle, 74. Pitt, 76 (*v.* Pitt). Bute, 221. Grenville and the Bedfords, 225-227 (*v.* Grenville and Wilkes). Rockingham, 228. Chatham, 229-231. Grafton ministry, 231. North, 364-368. Second Rockingham ministry, 368. Shelburne, 369. Coalition, 370. Pitt the Younger, 373 (*v.* Pitt).
Minorca, acquired by England, 1. Demand for its restoration, 39. Lost by Byng, 98. Recovered in exchange for Belle Isle, 153. Loss of, 318.
Mirabeau, 299.
Mississippi, the, 109.
Mogul Empire, over India.—Constructed by Baber and Akbar, 113. Disintegration at the death of Aurungzebe, 113, 119, 207. Headquarters at Delhi, 113.

2 E

Mohammedan dynasties, ruled at Delhi and at Mysore, 113. In the Provinces of the Ganges, the Central Provinces, and on the East Coast, 114.
—— Viziers, 113.
Mohammed Ali, son of Anwar-uddin, 129. His claim to the nawabship of the Carnatic supported by the English, 129. Established as Nawab by Clive, 132–134.
Mohun Persad, his accusation of Nuncomar, 343.
Mollwitz, battle of, 56.
Monmouth, battle of, 303.
Monson, member of the Calcutta Council, 342. His death, 343.
Montcalm, commander of the French in Canada, 99. Foils Abercrombie at Ticonderoga, 103. Defence of Quebec, 106–108. His death, 108. His foresight, 158.
Montreal, capture of, 109.
Moorshedebad, the capital of the Nawab of Bengal, 143.
Moravia, siege of Olmütz, 90.
Morris, Robert, American Superintendent of Finance, 313.
Morse, governor of Madras, 123, 125.
Munro, Sir Hector, victory of Buxar, 265. Defeated by Hyder Ali, 335.
Murray, Attorney-General (Lord Mansfield). In the House of Commons, 74. Attacked by Wilkes, 242; by Junius, 245. Opinions on libel, 244, 245.
——, General, attacks Montreal, 109.
Mutiny Bill, Bushe's Irish, 357, 358, 360.
Muzaffar Jung, appointed Nizam of the Deccan, 128. His right disputed by Nadir Jung, 128. Supported by the French.—Battle of Ambur, 129. Acknowledged as Nizam, 130. His death, 131.
Mysore, southern division of India, 114, 328. Ruled by Hyder Ali, 114, 267. British forces in, 337 (v. Hyder Ali).

Nadir Jung, claimant for the Nizamship of the Deccan, 128. Killed, 130.
Nadir Shah, invades India, 115.

Nagpore, headquarters of the Bhonsla, 263.
Naples, in Austrian possession, 10, 34. Allotted to Don Carlos, 44. Captain Martin at, 58.
Napoleon, his birth in Corsica, 219.
National Debt, 171.
—— party in Ireland, and modern Nationalists, 278.
Nawab of Arcot, or Carnatic, 113, etc. (v. Carnatic).
—— of Bengal, 114. Aliverdi Khan, 139. Suraj-ud-daulah, 139, 143. Meer Jaffier, 143, 264, 265.
—— of the Carnatic (v. Carnatic).
—— of Oudh, 114. Shujah Daulah, 265, 327, 328. Asaph-ud-daulah, 342, 349, 350.
Negapatam, ceded by Holland to England, 326, 336.
Neisse, siege of, 91.
Netherlands, the, French campaign in, 60, 61, 69. Proposed partition between France and Spain, 84.
New England colonies, 202. Trade restrictions, 260, 299.
Newcastle, anti-Jacobite troops at, 66.
Newcastle, Duke of: his character, 73, 74. Coalition with Fox, 75. Prime Minister, 74, 75. Resignation, 76, 98. Coalition with Pitt, 76, 89, 99, 221, 370. Seeks George III.'s favour, 222, 223. Opposition to Bute, 224.
Newfoundland, acquired by England, 1, 76.
New Hampshire, New England colony, 202.
New Jersey, colony of, 202, 292. Invaded by Washington, 292.
New York, Congress held at, 255, 259. Washington's headquarters at, 288. Geographical position.— British and colonial armies at, 290. General Clinton and Washington.— Abandoned by Washington, 291. Secured by the British, 292. Clinton's headquarters at, 293, 294, 303, 307, 312. Hotham sails from, 304, 307. Sends reinforcements south, 307. Troops sent back by Cornwallis.—Rodney's arrival, 314. Distribution of military and naval forces at, 316. Hood proceeds there, 317.

New York Colony.—Its Dutch element, 202. Resistance to the Mutiny Act, 256. Independent colonial attitude. 260, 289. Protest of loyalty to the government, 260. Holds aloof from signing the Declaration of Independence, 289.
New York Harbour, Lord Howe in, 303.
New York Island, Washington at, 291.
Niagara, captured, 106.
Niepperg, General: secret compact with Frederick the Great, 57.
Nieuport, allotted to France, 81.
Nithisdale, Earl of, joins in raising the standard of King James, 22.
Nizam of the Deccan, 128. Extent of his sway, 211. (*Vid*. Muzaffar Jung, Nadir Jung, and Hyderabad.)
Nizam-ul-Mulk (*v. supra*).
Nonconformists: the Schism Act, 17. In favour with the Whigs, 170. Conciliated by Walpole, 176, 205.
Norfolk burned, 287.
Norris, Admiral Sir John, in the Baltic, 35. In the Channel, 36. Sent to the Tagus, 44. Prevents invasion, 60.
North, Lord, Chancellor of the Exchequer, 231. Prime Minister, 232, 234. Leader of the King's Friends, 236. His subserviency to the king, 295, 364. Head of the Anti-colonial party, 364. Popular but misguided policy, 365. His conciliatory Bills, 261, 300, 301. Not allowed to resign, 301, 366. His Regulating Act, 330, 332, 340. Inclines to Free Trade for Ireland, 353. Resignation, 318, 366, 368. Coalition with Fox, 370, 373. Opposition to Pitt, 374. Qualifications as a Minister. 364.
North Briton, the, Wilkes's newspaper, 226, 239, 240.
Northington, Viceroy of Ireland, 361.
Norway, 33, 35.
Nova Scotia, acquired by England, 1. French and English limits unsettled, 3, 76.
Number Forty-five, 226, 239, 240.
Nuncomar, a Brahmin, brings personal charges against Hastings, 343. Accused of forgery; tried and hanged, 343.

Octennial Bill, the, for Ireland, passed, 276.
Oder, Soltikoff's advance, 93. Presence of the Russian army, 95.
Ohio Company, formation of, 96.
Ohio, Basin of, French and English claims, 96, 103.
Olive Branch Petition brought over by Penn, 284.
Oliver, Alderman, committed to the Tower, 244.
Olmütz, siege of, 90.
Omichund, Clive's tool in intrigues against Suraj-ud-daulah, 111. Victim of Clive's fraud, 142, 262, 269.
Orange, William of, 69.
Orissa, 113. Under English rule, 266.
Orleans, Duke of, regent and heir presumptive, 30. His death, 38.
Orleans, Louis, Duke of, succeeds his father as heir presumptive.—The exclusion of his succession, 38.
Orleans, Isle of: Wolf's army there, 107.
Ormond, impeachment of, 20, 21. Follows Bolingbroke to France, 21.
Ostend Company, the, 38, 118.
Oudh, a province of the Ganges, under Mogul suzerainty, 113. Ruled by the Nawab Shujah Daulah, 265, 327; by Asaph-ud-daulah, 342. Clive's treaty with, 266. A barrier against the Mahrattas, 328-331, 350. Supports the Rohillas, 329. Rohilla war, 330. Allahabad and Corah transferred by Hastings to the Vizier of, 330. The Begums of, 342, 349. Administrative reforms by Hastings, 350.
Oxford, Lord, Tory Chief, 14. His indecision with regard to the succession, 16, 17. His share in the Schism Act, 17. Out of favour with the queen.—Mr. Masham's hostility.—His fall, 18. Impeachment of, 21.

Padishah, the, at Delhi, 139. A prisoner of his vizier, 144. Shah Alum attempts to recover empire, 144. (*Vid*. Shah Alum.)
Palatinate, the, and the Treaty of Versailles, 84.
Paniput, battle of, 263, 264, 328.

Paris, Benjamin Franklin in, 299. American commissioners in, 300. English representatives at, 368. ——, the Peace of, 152. Its effects on France and England, 218. On the American colonists, 206, 247.
Parliament (Great Britain). Life prolonged to seven years, 161. Peerage Bill thrown out, 162. Ministerial responsibility, 165. Corruption under Walpole, 178; under the Pelhams, 180; under Bute, 224, 235, 236; by the crown, 236, 367. Opposition to reform, 367, 379. Privileges, 237, 238. The House and the electors, 241-244. Control by Whig oligarchy, 166; attacked by Pitt (Chatham), 167; by George III., 167, 168; by Democrats, 169 (v. Wilkes). Subordination of crown to, 160. Attempts of crown to regain power, 167, 168, 364. Press and Parliament, 244. (Vid. Ministries, and Parliamentary Acts, etc.)
——, (Ireland). Character of Representation, 196. Subordination to Westminster, 199. Control of English and Irish Privy Councils, 199, 200, 273. Duration, 273. Corruption, 274, 276, 358. Undertakers, 274. Octennial Bill, 276. Flood, 278, 361-363. Demand for Legislative Independence, 355-360. Grattan, 353, 357-361. Bushe's Mutiny Bill, 337-360. Constitution of 1782, 360. "Simple repeal," 360. Renunciatory Act, 361. Pitt's Commercial Bill, 383. Resistance to Parliamentary Reform, 362, 381. Volunteers and Parliament, 361-363.
Parliamentary Acts, etc. (Great Britain). Boston Port Act, 258, 259. Catholic Relief, 366. Cider Tax, 225; repealed, 228. Declaratory Act (American), 228, 252. Dunning's resolution, 367. Economic Reform Bill, 367, 369. General Warrants, 241. India Bills: (1) North's (v. North's Regulating Act); (2) Dundas's, 372; (3) Fox's, 371, 373, 384; (4) Pitt's, (a) 375, (b) 384. Massachusett's Charter, 258, 259. Mutiny (American), 256. Navigation Acts, 181, 184, 195, 203, 205, 354. North's Conciliatory Bills (America); (1) 261, (2) 360. North's Regulating Act, 270, 330, 340, 381. Parliamentary Reform; Pitt's motion for, 369; Pitt's Bill, 380. Peerage Bill, 162, 176, 187. Quebec Act, 258, 365. Regency Bills: (1) 226, (2) 380. Rights (Bill of), 253. Schism Act, 17. Settlement, Act of, 16. Stamp Act, 166, 226, 248; repeal of, 228, 232, 251, 255. Union (Scottish), Act of, 184.
—— (Ireland). Absentee Tax, 277, 354. Augmentation scheme, 275, 276. Bushe's Mutiny Bill, 357-359. Catholic Relief, 353. Constitution of 1782, 360. Habeas Corpus, demand for, 273, 275, 276, 278, 358; granted, 359. Judges' tenure, 273, 276. Money Bills altered in England, 275, 276, 278. Nonconformist Relief Bill, 355, 356. Mutiny Bill, 357-359. Parliamentary Reform Bills, 362, 363. Penal Code, 194, 195, 197; relaxation of, 352, 360. Pensions, 276. Renunciatory Act, 360, 361. Supply for six months, 355. Yelverton's motions against Irish Privy Council, 357, 359.
Parma, Duchy of; succession of Don Carlos to, 33. Restored to Austria, 44. Allotted to Don Philip, 70. To be exchanged with Austria for part of the Netherlands, 84.
Parma and Piacenza, Duke of, uncle to the Queen of Spain, 10.
Passaro, Cape, battle of, 34.
Patna, English factory at, 265. Besieged by Shah Alum, 144. Massacre at, 265.
Peerage Bill, the, 162, 163. Opposed by Walpole, 176; in Scotland, 187.
Peishwa, the, at Poona; chief of the Mahratta confederacy, 118, 328. Nature of the office. — Infant Peishwa, 332. Attempt to set up Ragoba in his place, 332, 333.
Pelham, Henry, his character, 73. His ministry, 74. Death, 74.
Pelhams, the (v. Newcastle), 73, 165, 205, 217.

Penal Code, 194, 195, 197. Relaxation, 352, 360.
Penn, William, brings over the "Olive Branch" petition, 284.
Pennsylvania, its Quaker origin, 202. Opposed to separation, 285. Washington driven into, 292. (*Vid.* Philadelphia.)
Penobscot, British Fort at, 306.
Perth, the Jacobites at, 24.
Peter the Great, *v.* Czar.
Peter III., *v.* Czar.
Peyton, 124.
Philadelphia, continental congress at, 259 (*v.* Congress). Capture of, 293. Evacuated, 303.
Philip, King of Spain: his marriage with Elizabeth Farnese, 10. Renunciation of claim to the French succession, 30, 31. His death, 69.
Philip, Don, acquires the duchies of Parma and Piacenza, 70; to be exchanged for part of the Netherlands, 84.
Philippines, the, Capture of Manilla, 151. Restored by England to Spain, 152.
Piacenza, Duchy of, Don Carlos recognized as heir to, 33. Allotted to Don Philip by the Treaty of Aix-la-Chapelle, 70. To be exchanged with Austria for part of the Netherlands, 84.
Pigot, Lord, Governor of Madras, 345.
Pitt (Lord Chatham): His character, 75, 154, 180, 229. His imperial views, 2, 100, 158, 218, 230. His naval policy, 100, 101, 102, 156; its effects, 156, 158. His theory of Government, 167. His colonial theory, 230, 296, 301. Views on Taxation, 228, 251, 277.
Position under Walpole, 177. Takes office under Pelham, 74. Position under Newcastle, 75. First administration, 76, 99. Coalition with Newcastle, 76, 99. Policy and methods, 100–102. Its effects, 156–158. Proposal to cede Gibraltar, 101. Desire to declare war with Spain, 110, 150. Thwarted by Bute, 110, 150. Resignation, 110, 223. Attitude in Opposition, 223. Refuses office, 225, 227, 228. Takes office and becomes Earl of Chatham, 229. His health breaks down, 231. Resignation, 231. Reappearance, 232. Attitude to colonial resistance, 251, 269, 295, 365. Desire for his leadership, 301, 365. Last speech and death, 301, 365.
Pitt, William (the younger), his career, 376. In the House of Commons, 368. Chancellor of the Exchequer, 370. Prime Minister, 373. Struggle with the coalition, 373–375. The Clerkship of the Pells, 375. Triumph, 375. Foreign policy, 377. Finance, 377, 379. Parliamentary Reform, 369, 379. Regency Bill, 380. Irish policy, 381, 383. India Bills, 375, 384.
Plassey, battle of, 142.
Pocock, commands a squadron off the Carnatic, 136–138. Expedition against Havanna, 151.
Poland, succession to the throne disputed by Stanislaus and Augustus of Saxony, 43. Augustus recognised king, 44 (*v.* War of Polish succession). Partition of, 219, 399.
Pollilore, battle of, 336.
Pompadour, Madame de; her animosity to Frederick the Great, 79. Her favourites, 217.
Pomerania, 85, 89, 90, 95.
Pondicherry, French settlement in the Carnatic, 119, 123. Its harbour, 123. Dupleix governor of, 120. 122. Beginning of Anglo-French contest, 125. Blockaded by English squadron.—Relieved by La Bourdonnais.—Besieged unsuccessfully, 126. Surrenders to Sir Eyre Coote, 138. Captured by Hastings, 334.
Poona, headquarters of the Peishwa, 263, 328. Council of regency at, 332. War declared by Governor Hornby (*v.* Bombay). The Chevalier St. Lubin brings overtures from the French.—Troops sent by Hastings to set up Ragoba as Peishwa, 333. Promises to support the British in suppressing Mysore, 337.
Popham, Captain, captures the fortress of Gwalior, 334. Takes Labar, 334.
Portland's ministry, 371.
Port Mahon, siege and surrender of, 318. Importance of its loss to England, 324. (*Vid.* Minorca.)

INDEX.

Porto Bello, captured by Vernon, 55.
Porteous Riots, 187.
Porto Praya, British squadron at, crippled by Suffren, 320.
Portugal, her position relative to oceanic commerce, 2. Trade with England, 15. Quarrel with Spain, 44. Pioneer in trade with the Indies, 117. Disappears as a rival, 118. Rejects Spanish overtures, 151. The earthquake at Lisbon, and England's assistance, 151. Good will to England, 151.
Pragmatic Sanction, the, guaranteed by Spain, 38; by Walpole, conditionally, 41; by France, 44; by all the great powers except Bavaria, 56.
Prague, battle of, 85, 86.
Pratt (Lord Camden), Chief Justice. Liberates Wilkes, 240. Removed from the Chancellorship, 232. On the Libel question, 244.
Press, the, 246.
Preston, battle of, 23, 24.
Preston Pans, battle of, 65.
Pretender, v. Charles Stuart and James Stuart.
Prince of Wales, George, (v. George II.).
Prince of Wales, Frederick, in opposition to George II., 164.
Princess of Wales, the Dowager (Augusta), 221. Her name omitted from the Regency Bill, 280.
Prince Edward's Island, 102.
Privy Councils, v. Council.
Prussia, its early organisation proceeding, 9. Alliance with France, 39. Established as a first-class power, 70. Upsets the balance of power in Europe, 72, 78. Its position due to Frederick the Great, 72. (*Vid.* Frederick the Great.)
Pulteney, his opposition to Walpole, 163, 177. Becomes Lord Bath, 165. His brief period of ascendency, 73.
Punjaub, the Sikh confederacy in the, 114, 328.
Putnam, replaces Commander Greene, 291.
Pyrennean campaign, 36.

Quadruple Alliance, 34. Its terms insisted on, 37. Philip's accession to it, 38.
Quakers in Pennsylvania, 202, 303.

Quebec, capture of, 103, 106-108. Attempt of the French to recover it, 109. Attacked by Benedict Arnold, 2-5.
Quebec Act, 365.
Queen Anne, v. Anne.
Queen Caroline, v. Caroline.
Queen of France, daughter of Stanislaus, ex-king of Poland, 43.
Queen of Spain, v. Elizabeth Farnese.
Quiberon, blockaded by Duff, 105. The French navy shattered at, 103, 105. The destinies of India decided at, 121.

Ragoba (Ragonath Rao), 332, 333.
Rajah of Benares, Bulwunt Singh, 328. Cheyte Singh, 348.
Rajah of Tanjore, ejected by the Madras Government, 345.
Rajputs, 114, 208.
Rajputana, Hindu states of, 114.
Raua of Gohud, 334, 344.
Rani of Burdwan, 313.
Regency Bills, 226, 380.
——, Council of, at Poona, 332.
—— of Orleans, v. Orleans.
Reggio, 34.
Regulating Act, Lord North's, 270, 330, 332, 340.
Renunciatory Act, 361.
Rhine, the emperor's reverses on the, 43. Contades and the Duc de Broglie sent to the, 91.
Rhode Island, a New England colony, 202. Militia corps formed there, 260.
Richelieu, Duke of, 86, 87.
Richmond, Duke of, proposes withdrawal of fleets and armies from America, 301. Attitude to Shelburne, 370.
Robinson, Sir Thomas, 75.
Rochambeau, 312, 313, 316.
Rochefort, 102, 105.
Rockingham, Marquis of, deprived of his lord-lieutenancy, 236. First ministry, 227, etc. In opposition, 365, 366. Second ministry, 368. His death, 369.
Rockingham ministry (first): characterised, 228, 233, 234. Grafton and Conway, 229. Reinstates General Conway, 236. Support of Wilkes, 238. Colonial policy, 255.

INDEX. 411

Rockingham ministry (second), 318. Composition and policy, 368, 369.
Rodney, Admiral, despatched to West Indies, 309. Defeats Langara, 311. Relief of Gibraltar, 311, 319. De Guichen, 311, 312. Sails for New York, 314; for England, 316. Returns to the West Indies, 322. Defeats De Grasse at the battle of "The Saints," 323.
Rohilcund, Hindu province ruled by the Mussulman Rohilla chiefs, 328.
Rohilla war, 330, 342.
Rossbach, battle of, 88.
Roydullub, 141.
Russia united with Sweden in enmity to England, 30, 33, 35. Checked by an English fleet in the Baltic, 35, 41. Her enmity chiefly to Hanover, 30, 39. Alliance with Austria in support of Augustus of Saxony's claim to the throne of Poland, 43. Her attitude to Prussia, 70, 78. Subsidising treaty with England, 79, 89. Negotiates with Austria for the partition of Prussia, 80. Treaty with Austria, 84. Her policy influenced by the expectation of the Czarina's death, 89, 95. Russians at Zorndorf, 90; at Kunersdorf, 93. The army duped by Frederick the Great, 95. Her attitude to Prussia changed by the death of the Czarina Elizabeth, 149. Withdraws from the contest, 150. Accession of Peter III., and his deposition, by Catharine his wife, 149. Joins with Prussia and Austria in dismembering Poland, 219, 377.

Sacheverell Riots, 175, 176.
Sackville, Lord George, at Minden, 92.
St. Charles, river, 106.
St. Christopher, v. St. Kitt's.
St. David, Fort, English station in the Carnatic, 119. Futile attack by Dupleix, 126. Saunders governor at, 131. Surrenders to Lally, 136, 137.
St. George, Fort (Madras), English factory at, 118.
St. John (v. Bolingbroke).
——, Isle of, 102.

St. Kitt's (St. Christopher), Hood and De Grasse, at, 322.
St. Lawrence (river), commanded by Louisburg, 99. Route to Canada by the. — French squadron on the, 102. Unnavigable, 106, 109. Junction with the St. Charles, 107. Positions of British and French armies on. — Commanded by the British, 107.
St. Lubin, the Chevalier de, 333.
St. Vincent captured by D'Estaing, 308.
Salsette, 332, 337.
Sandwich, Lord, 240.
Sandy Hook, 289.
Sant Iago, siege of, 55.
Santa Lucia captured by Barrington, 308.
Saratoga, surrender of, 293.
Sardinia in the possession of Austria, 10. Spanish attack on, 32. Transferred by Austria to Duke of Saxony in exchange for Sicily, 32.
Saunders, Admiral, 106, 108.
Saunders, British Governor at Fort St. David, 131.
Savannah, D'Estaing at.—Capture of, 306.
Savoy, Duke of, in possession of Sicily, 10 ; which is exchanged for Sardinia, 32.
Saxe, Marshal, to command invasion of England, 60. In the Netherlands, 60, 69.
Saxony, supports Duke of Bavaria, 57. Friendly to Austria, 80. Frederick the Great captures it, 83, 95. Battle of Rossbach, 88. Hochkirchen, 91. Dresden recaptured, 94. Relinquished by Frederick at the Peace of Hubertsburg, 153.
Schism Act, the, 17.
Schwerin, General, killed at Prague, 85.
Schweidnitz, captured by the allies, 88. Recovered by Prussia, 89. Retaken, 95. Recovered again, 150.
Scotland, the insurrection of the 'Fifteen, 22-25 ; its effects, 185. The battle of Sheriffmuir, 24. Arrival of James Stuart, 24. The insurrection of the 'Forty-Five,

60-68; its effects, 188. Landing of Charles Edward.—Capture of Edinburgh, 65. Battle of Preston Pans, 65. Lord President Forbes, 66. Battle of Falkirk, 67. Battle of Culloden Moor, 68. Before the Union, 181, 183. Effects of the Union, 184, 185. Its unpopularity, 187. Religion and education, 184. Commerce, 185. Land laws, 189. The clan system, 182, 186, 190; broken up, 190, 191. Effects of the 'Fifteen, 185; of the 'Forty-Five, 188. Scots and English, 183, 192, 239.
Scots, their indignation at Sunderland's Peerage Bill, 163. Abused by Wilkes in the *North Briton*, 239.
Sea-Fights, v. Battles (Naval).
Senegal captured by the English, 103.
Septennial Act, the, passed in England, 162. Demands for one in Ireland, 273, 275, 276.
Settlement, Act of, and Steele's pamphlet, 16.
Seven Years' War, v. Wars.
Seville, Treaty of, 4.
Sieges, blockades, and surrenders:—
Boston, 285, 288.
Cadiz, 58.
Cartagena, 44, 55.
Dresden, 94.
Edinburgh, 65.
Gibraltar, (a) 41; (b) 311, 318, 320, 334.
Louisburg, 70; 102.
Madras, 137.
Messina, 35.
Montreal, 109.
Neisse, 91.
Olmütz, 90.
Patna, 95.
Pirna, 83.
Poudicherry, 126.
Port Mahon, 98, 318.
Porto Bello, 35.
Prague, 85, 86.
Quebec, 106-108; 285.
Rochefort, 102.
St. Malo, 102.
Sant Iago, 55.
Schweidnitz, 149.
Stirling, 67.
Ticonderoga, 103; 106; 283.

Shah Alum, son of the Padishah at Delhi, 144. Attempt to recover empire, 144. Invades Bengal, 144. Defeated by Clive at Patna, 144. Allahabad and Corah conferred on him, 328. Restored to the throne of Delhi by the Mahrattas, and forced to assign Allahabad and Corah to them, 329.
Shelburne, Lord, 231, 257, 277. In the second Rockingham ministry, 368, 369. Prime Minister, 369. His character, 370. Resignation, 371.
Sheridan, 374.
Sheriffmuir, battle of, 24.
Shrewsbury, Duke of, Lord Treasurer, 18, 19.
Shujah Daulah, Nawab of Oudh, 265, 327. Invades Bengal.—Defeated by Sir Hector Munro at Buxar, 265. Suzerain of Benares, 327, 328. His death, 342.
Sicily, owned by the Duke of Savoy, 10. Exchanged for Sardinia, 32. Spanish attack on, 34, 35. Secured to Don Carlos, 44.
Sicilies, the, 10, 33, 70.
Sikhs, the, a Hindu confederacy in the Punjaub, 114. A barrier against the Afghans, 328.
Silas Deane, 298.
Silesia, Austrian province of Maria Theresa.—Coveted by Frederick the Great, and invaded by him, 56. Battle of Czeslau.—Peace of Breslau.—Nearly all the province surrendered to Frederick, 57. Maria Theresa determined to recover it, 78. Daun's progress is checked at Leuthen, 88. In Prussian hands, 89, 95. Neisse relieved by Frederick, 91. Laudon's progress is checked at Liegnitz and Torgau, but continued next year, 95. Recovered after Burkersdorf, 149.
Sindhia, Mahratta chief at Gwalior, 263, 328. Supports the Poona Regency against Bombay, 332. Ragoba surrendered to him, 333. Attacks the Rana of Gohud, 334. Gohud given up to him, 337.
Slave-trade, 5, 376.
Smith, Adam, Pitt and Shelburne, disciples of, 378.

Soltikoff, General, at Kunersdorf, 93.
Somers, Lord, 20.
Somerset, Duke of, with the Duke of Argyll surprises the Tory Council, 18.
Soubise, Prince de, marches on Saxony, 87. Defeated at Rossbach by Frederick the Great, 87, 88. Captures Frankfurt, 91. Defeated by Prince Ferdinand at Kirch Denkern, 94.
South Sea Bubble, 29, 171.
South Sea Company, instituted by Harley, 171. Monopoly of the slave-trade conferred upon it by the Assiento, 5, 50. Debt to Spain, 52.
South Seas, English and Spanish commercial rivalry in, 5. Limited nature of English trade in, 171.
Spain: Results of war of Spanish succession, 1, 2. Position after Treaty of Utrecht, 1, 2, 71. Dynastic connection with France, 9, 10, 30, 31. Oceanic commerce, 2. Monopolies, 2, 4, 5. Foreign possessions, 2, 151-153, 297, 326. Naval deterioration, 7, 8, 45, 49. A disturbing influence in Europe, 9. Philip's marringe and its effects on policy, 10, 11, 31, 32. Alberoni, 31-37. Quarrel with Portugal, 44; 151. Death of Philip.—Accession of Ferdinand and end of Italian influence, 69. Position after Treaty of Aix-la-Chapelle, 70-72. Under French influence, 310. On the verge of bankruptcy, 325.
—— and *Austria:* Rival claims of the queen and Austria in Italy, 10, 11, 46, 56. Attack on Sardinia, 32. Don Carlos and a compromise, 33. Alberoni's intrigues, 34. Siege of Messina and battle of Cape Passaro, 34, 35. Withdrawal from Sicily and Sardinia, 37. Alliance with and concessions to Austria, 38. Secret articles.—Proposed marriage of Don Carlos and Maria Theresa, 39. Treaties, of Seville and Vienna, 41. Opposed to Austria in the Polish war, 43. The Sicilies secured to Don Carlos, 44. Renewed attacks in Italy, 57, 58. Treaty of Aix-la-Chapelle, 70.
—— and *France:* In opposition, 6, 7. Chance of Philip's succession to French throne, 9, 10, 30, 31. Anti-Orleanist conspiracy, 33. Pyrennean campaign, 36, 37. Franco-Spanish match broken off by the Duke of Bourbon, 38. Reconciliation, 42. Allied in the Polish war, 43. First Family Compact, 45-48, 53, 214. France negotiates with, 110. Second Family Compact; joins in the Seven Years' War, 150. Obtains Louisiana from France, 153. Pressed into American war, 309.
—— and *England:* Cedes Gibraltar and Minorca, 1; attempts to recover Gibraltar, *v.* Gibraltar. Rivalry with England in colonial enterprise, 2, 5; in the South Seas, 5, 42, 47, 50. The Assiento, 5, 50. Alberoni's English policy, 31, 32. England's mediation between Spain and Austria, 32, 33. Abortive schemes against England, and naval disasters, 34, 36. Humiliating terms, 37. Austro-Spanish alliance, 38, 40. Secret Articles, 39. Blockade of Cartagena.—Treaty of Seville, 41.—Sir John Norris, 44. First Family Compact, 45-48, 58. War of Jenkins's Ears, 50-57. Money claims on South Sea Company, 52. Don Carlos and Captain Martin, 58. Second Family Compact, 150. Intervention in American war, 309-312, 315.
Spanish America, *v.* America.
Spanish American trade, 50.
Spice Islands, Dutch settlements and trade in, 118.
Stade, Cumberland's retreat to, 86, 87.
Stadtholder, William of Orange appointed, 69.
Stamp Act, imposed by Grenville on the American colonies, 226. Repealed, 228. (*Vid.* Grenville.)
Stanhope, General, Secretary of State, 20. Goes with George I. to Hanover, 29. Disloyal to Townshend, 29. His view of foreign policy, 29, 162. With Dubois effects the Triple Alliance, 31.
Stanislaus, ex-king of Poland: Father-in-law of Louis XV., 38. His election to the throne contested

by Augustus of Saxony, 43 (v. War of the Polish succession).
Staten Island, 290, 291.
Statutes, v. Parliamentary Acts, etc.
Steele, his pamphlet attacked by the ministry, 16.
Steinhorst, fortress of, 52.
Stirling, siege of, 67.
Stuarts, their restoration destructive to the Whigs, 12, 62. Command the sentiment of the nation, 13. Their dependence on foreign support, 28, 31–33, 48, 60, 61. Their inspiring personality, 61. Their obstinacy, 62. Reasons for fearing them, 64. End of their hopes, 68, 70, 71.
Subadhar, title of the Nizam of the Deccan, 113.
Suffren, Admiral, in India, 146. Compared with other French officers, 320. His encounters with Hughes, 321, 338. Capture of Cuddalore, 338.
Sumpter, leader of colonial insurgents, 313.
Sunderland, son-in-law of Marlborough, 20. In power, 29. Peerage Bill, 162.
Supreme Court of Judicature, at Calcutta, 270, 341. Its quarrels with the Council, 347. (Vid. Impey and Hastings.)
Suraj-ud-daulah, Nawab of Bengal.—Marches on Fort William, 139. The "Black Hole" of Calcutta.—Negotiations reopened by Clive, 140. Deposed by Clive, 141. Battle of Plassey, 142. Escapes from Moorshedabad, and is murdered, 143.
Surat, English factory at, 118.
Sutherlands, the, 66.
Sweden, 30, 34, 56, 89, 90.
Swift, his Tory pamphlet attacked by the Lords, 17. "Drapier's Letters," 200.

Tanjore, Hindu kingdom, 113. The Rajah helped by the English to the throne, 129; ejected by the Madras Council, 345.
Temple, Lord: his resignation, 223. Alliance with Grenville, 227. Refuses to join Pitt's ministry without Grenville, 227, 229. Estrangement from Pitt, 229.

Thurot, 106.
Ticonderoga, 103, 106, 283.
Torgau, battle of, 95.
Tories, divided about the succession to the throne, 13. Large Tory majority at the beginning of 1714, 161. Bolingbroke's lament, 20. Impeachment of three Tory chiefs, 21. Toryism identified with Jacobitism, 163. American "Tories," 282.
Torrington, Lord (v. Byng).
Toulon, fleet destroyed at, 104.
Townshend, Charles, Secretary of State, 20. Whig disruption, 29. Resumes power, 30. Makes the Treaty of Hanover, 38. His pacific influence, 40. His quarrel with Walpole, 173.
Townshend, Charles, grandson of the above, Chancellor of the Exchequer, 231. American taxation, 231, 256. His power in the Cabinet, 255. His death, 231.
Townshend, Viceroy of Ireland, 275–277.
Trade, v. Commerce.
Traun, Austrian commander under Prince Charles of Lorraine, 59.
Treaties:—
  Aix-la-Chapelle, 1748; 70–72, 127, 215.
  Armed Neutrality, 1780; 315.
  Breslau, 57.
  Commercial Treaties: Bolingbroke's, 14; Pitt's, 1786; 378.
  Convention of Kloster Seven, 1757: 87, 89, 154.
  —— of Wargum, 1777: 333, 334.
  Family Compact (First), 1733; 45, 47, 48, 52.
  —— (Second), 1761; 150, 152.
  Franco-American, 1777; 300.
  Hanover (1725), 39.
  Hubertsburg, Peace of, 1763; 153.
  Kloster Seven, Convention of, 87, 89, 154.
  Paris, Peace of, 1763; 152.
  Quadruple Alliance, 1718; 34.
  Seville, 1729; 41.
  Triple Alliance, 1717; 31.
  Utrecht, 1713; 1, 14, 71, 76.
  Versailles, 1757; 84.
    1783; 325, 326.
  Vienna, 1725; 38.
    1731; 41.

Wargum, Convention of, 333, 334.
Westminster, 1756; 79.
Westphalia, 1648; 38.
Trenton, taken by Washington, 292.
Trichinopoly, Hindu kingdom, 113. Flight of Mohammed Ali to, 129, 130. Besieged by Chunda Sahib, 131. Relieved by Clive and Lawrence, 132.
Trincomalee, captured by Suffren, 321.
Triple Alliance, between England, France, and the Netherlands, 31; becomes the Quadruple Alliance by the accession of Austria, 34.
Triumvirate, the, 225.
Turgot, opposes French intervention in the American war, 297.
Tuscany, Grand Duchy of, heirship of Don Carlos, 33. His claims resigned, 44.

Undertakers, the: their control of the Irish Parliament, 274, 275. Compared with the Whigs in England, 274.
Union, the Act of, 185 (v. Scotland).
United States, their independence acknowledged, 326.
Upper Provinces of India, the British brought into contact with them, 265; protected from them by Oudh, 266.
Ushant, battle of, 304.
Utrecht, Treaty of, 1, 14, 71.

Valley Forge, Washington winters at, 291.
Vansittart, Governor of Bengal, 264.
Verden, acquired with Bremen by George I. for the Electorate, 30.
Vergennes, his policy of intervention in the American war, 297, 298. His appreciation of Washington, 299.
Vernon, Admiral, 55, 57.
Versailles, Treaty of, 84.
Vienna, Treaty of, 38, 39; 41.
Vigo, 37.
Villars, Marshal, 36.
Virginia, colony of: its landholders, 202. Militia corps formed there, 260.
Virginian Assembly, passes resolutions against British taxation, 251.
—— House of Burgesses, and the Boston Port Act, 259.

Volunteers, in Ireland: their rise, 354; their influence, 355. Policy supported by the movement, 355-361. At Dungannon, 359. Change in their attitude, 360, 361. At Lisburn.—In Dublin, 362.

Wade, General, at Newcastle, 66. Superseded, 67.
Walpole, Robert, First Lord of the Treasury, 20, 172. Removal from office. — Opposition to Stanhope, 29. His return to power, 30, 39, 40, 172. Succeeds Aislabie as Chancellor of the Exchequer, 172, 173. Settles the South Sea Bubble crisis.—Quarrels with Townshend. —Beginning of his rule, 173. His financial schemes, 173, 174. His peace policy, 40, 43, 47, 48, 51, 165, 214, 215. His influence over the queen, 41, 43, 164, 177. Guarantees the Pragmatic Sanction, 41. Keeps England out of the Polish war, 43. His knowledge of the First Family Compact, 48, 52. Is weakened by the queen's death, 51, 165. Break-down of his policy, 49, 50. Declares war against Spain, 53. His unpopularity, 58. His resignation, 59. His opponents, 74, 177. His system of corruption, 164, 178, 235. His opportunism, 175. Causes of his power, 176. Results of his rule, 179. His death, 59.
Walton, Captain, his despatch, 35.
Wandewash, battle of, 20, 138, 145.
Wargum, Convention of, 333.
Wars:—
Alberoni's, 1717-1719.
Attack on Sardinia, 32. Attack on Sicily, 34. Battle of Cape Passaro, 34, 35. Siege of Messina, 35. Intended invasion of England. —Fleet destroyed in the Bay of Biscay, 36. Pyrennean campaign, 37. Quadruple Alliance, 37.
American, 1754.
(1) *intercolonial*.
Anglo-French contest for the Basin of Ohio.—Fort Duquesne established by the French. — Washington defeated at Great Meadows,

96. General Braddock, 97. Boscawen, 97, 102. French reinforcements from Canada. — Engagement off Newfoundland.—French success, 97. Amherst and Wolfe in Canada, 102. Montecalm in Canada, 103. Surrender of Louisburg. — Cape Breton and Prince Edward's Island taken, 102. Abercrombie's failure at Ticonderoga. — Capture of Fort Duquesne, 103; of Niagara and Ticonderoga, 106; of Quebec, 108. Siege and surrender of Montreal. 109.
(2) *Of Independence.* Causes of war, 246-260.
A. *Continental.* Preparations at Boston and Massachusetts, 282. General Gage's proceedings.—Battle of Lexington. — Capture of Ticonderoga. — "Continental" army raised.—Arrival of Burgoyne and Clinton.—Washington appointed Commander-in-Chief.—Battle of Bunker Hill, 283. Burning of Charleston.—The "Olive Branch" petition, 284. General Gage superseded by Sir William Howe, 285. Washington before Boston, 285, 286. Canadian expedition, 285, 288. Capture of Montreal, 285. Evacuation of Boston, 286. General Howe at Halifax.—The Southern States and Governor Dunmore, 287. Washington at New York.—Arrival of Lord Howe, 288. Declaration of Independence, 289, 290. British and colonial armies at New York, 290. British victory at Brooklyn, and further successes, 291, 292. Washington escapes with his army across the Delaware, 291; recovers ground and defeats Cornwallis. 292. Burgoyne's expedition, and surrender of Saratoga, 293. Capture of Philadelphia, 294. French intervention. — La Fayette, 298. Franco - American Treaty, 300, 303. Battle of Monmouth, 303. Clinton at New York, 303-305, 307, 310. Cornwallis in the South, 306. 307, 313. Capture of Savannah, 306; of Charlestown, 307. British fort established at Penobscot, 306. Battles of Cowpens and Guildford Court House, 313. Intervention of Spain, 309, 310. Washington at Middlebrook, 305; reinforced by Rochambeau, 312, 313. Cornwallis at Yorktown. — Washington and Rochambeau attack Yorktown, 314. Surrender of Yorktown, 317.
B. *Naval.* Arrival of Lord Howe, 289. Controls the Hudson, 291. Conveys transports from Delaware Bay to New York, 303. Out-manœuvres D'Estaing at New York and Rhode Island, 304. War transferred to West Indies, *v.* West Indies. Battle of Ushant, 304, 305. D'Estaing at Savannah, 306. Gibraltar besieged, 311. Defeat of Langara and relief by Rodney, 311. Du Barras and Graves at Newport and New York. — Rodney on North American coast, 314. War declared with Holland, 315. De Grasse reaches Yorktown. 316. Surrender of Yorktown, 317. Gibraltar relieved by Derby. — Allied fleets in the Channel.—Fall of Minorca, 318. Grand attack on Gibraltar. — Final relief by Howe, 319. Suffren at Porto Praya and the Cape, —reaches Indian waters, 320. Five engagements with Hughes.—Fall of Trincomalee, 321. Cuddalore, 337. 338. (*Vid.* West Indies.)

INDEX. 417

Austrian Succession.
Frederick invades Silesia.—
Mollwitz. — He joins with
France in supporting Bavaria, 56. Allies joined by
Saxony and Spain.—Maria
Theresa appeals to Hungarians.—Battle of Czeslau.
Peace of Breslau, 57. England joins Austria.—Dettingen.—Frederick rejoins the
war.—Progress of Austrian
arms, 59. Marshal Saxe in the
Netherlands. — Fontenoy.—
Frederick withdraws.—Cumberland recalled, for the
'Forty-Five, 60. Subsequent
campaigns in the Netherlands, 69. Peace of Aix-la-Chapelle, 70. (*Vid.* Indian
Wars (1), and Jenkins's
Ears.)
Civil wars, *v.* 'Fifteen, and 'Forty-Five.
Indian wars:—
(1) French and English Companies.
Attack on Pondicherry forbidden by Nawab.—Arrival
of La Bourdonnais.—Dissensions of La Bourdonnais and
Dupleix, 124. Capture of
Madras. — Nawab attacks
Dupleix, 125. Defence of
Fort St. David and Pondicherry, 126. Peace of Aix-la-Chapelle and restoration
of Madras, 127.
(2) French and English in alliance with native powers.
Rival Nizams and Nawabs,
128, 129. Battle of Ambur,
129. Death of Nadir Jung,
130. Bussy at Hyderabad,
131. Trichinopoly invested.
—Clive's capture and defence
of Arcot,—Arnee, 132. Further successes of Clive and
Lawrence.—Recall of Dupleix, 133. Lally takes Fort
St. David, 136; attacks Madras,—Masulipatam.—Siege
of Madras raised by fleet,
137. Wandewash, 138.
(3) Conquest of Bengal, *v.*
Clive.

(4) Mahratta war, *v.* Mahrattas.
(5) Mysore, *v.* Hyder Ali.
(6) Rohilla war, 330, 331.
Jenkins's Ears, war of (*v.* p. xxi).
War with Spain declared,
58. Anson's voyage, 54.
Vernon takes Portobello.—
Attacks Cartagena and Sant
Iago, 55. Haddock and
Matthews in the Mediterranean. — Captain Martin
at Naples, 58. English
troops on the Continent.—
Dettingen.—France declares
war, 59. The 'Forty-Five,
60-69. Naval victories of
Anson and Hawke, 69. Loss
of Louisburg, exchanged for
Madras at Peace of Aix-la-Chapelle, 70 (*v.* War of
Austrian Succession).
Polish Succession, war of, 43, 41.
Seven Years' War (*v.* Chronological table, p. xxii) :—
(1) In Europe.
Frederick attacks Saxony.
—Lobositz, 83. Fall of
Dresden, 84. Battles of
Prague and Kolin, 85. Hastenbeck, 86. Kloster Seven,
87. Rossbach. — Austrian
progress in Silesia stopped
at Leuthen, 88. Swedes
foiled in Pomerania.—Ferdinand of Brunswick in command at the Aller, 89.
Olmütz and battle of Zorndorf, 90. Hochkirchen.—
Relief of Silesia.—Fall of
Frankfurt.—Minden, 91. Kunersdorf, 93. Maxen, 94.
Liegnitz and Torgau.—
Kirch Denkern, 95. Withdrawal of Russia.—Burkersdorf, 149. Peace of Hubertsburg, 153.
(2) In America.
Fort Duquesne established,
96. Braddock. — French
reinforcements on the St.
Lawrence, 97. Progress of
French, 99. Amherst and
Wolfe, 102. Abercrombie
fails at Ticonderoga.—Fort
Duquesne captured, 103.

418   INDEX.

Wolfe before Quebec, 106. Capture of Quebec, 108. Completion of Conquest of Canada, 109. Peace of Paris, 152.
(3) Naval.
Hawke's vague instructions, 97. Byng fails to relieve Minorca, 98. Hawke and Mordaunt at Rochefort, 99. Blockade of French coasts, 101. Pocock and D'Aché, 136. Toulon fleet destroyed. —Hawke and Conflans, 101. Quiberon, 105. Holmes and Saunders in the St. Lawrence, 107, 108. Spain joins the war, 150. Capture of Martinique, 150; of Havanna and Manilla, 151. Peace of Paris, 152.
Turkish war with Austria, 32, 33.
Washington, George (in the Anglo-French American war), defeated at Great Meadows, 96. Appointed commander-in-chief in the War of Independence, 283. The condition of his army, 285, 286, 292, 325. Before Boston, 285. Sends detachments to Quebec, 285, 286. Causes Howe to evacuate Boston, 286. Removes to New York, 288. Face to face with the British army.—Lord Howe attempts to negotiate with. —His official position not recognised, 290. Driven back from Brooklyn. — Withdraws to New York Island.—Escapes with the army across the Delaware, 291. Endowed with temporary dictatorship.—His raid into New Jersey.— Capture of Trenton.—Headquarters there, 292. Sends detachments to Gates.—Before New York.—Defeated at Brandywine Creek, 293. Joined by French volunteers (La Fayette), 298. Vergennes' appreciation of him, 299. His reasons for opposing an expedition to Canada, 305. Reinforced by Rochambeau, 312. Takes Yorktown, 317. Address praying him to become king, 325.
Watson, Admiral, on the Hooghly, 140. Refuses to sign Clive's " red treaty," 142.

Wentworth, General, 55.
West Indies:—
(1) In the Seven Years' War. French colonies attacked by the British fleet, 102. Capture of Guadaloupe, 108 ; of Martinique and Havanna, 150, 151. Restoration of French islands, 152.
(2) In the American War. Position of French and English possessions, 307. D'Estaing and Hotham sail for Barbadoes, 304, 305, 307. Santa Lucia secured by Barrington. — French capture St. Vincent and attack Grenada. — Byron and D'Estaing, 308. Arrival of Rodney and De Guichen, 309. Their contests.— French numerical superiority in the Antilles, 311. Departure of De Guichen and Rodney. — Rodney's return, 314. Arrival of De Grasse. Capture of Dutch West Indian islands. — Hood off Martinique, 315. De Grasse and Hood, 321. Battle of "The Saints," 323. British mastery of West Indian seas, 323.
Westminster, Treaty of, 79.
Westphalia, Treaty of, 38.
Weymouth, Lord, 242.
Whigs, their policy defeated by Treaty of Utrecht, 2. Out of office, 12. Their attitude to the Hanoverian succession, 13. The Duke of Marlborough, 14. Their dependence on the commercial classes, 15, 170. Their coup de main, 19. Their control of Parliament, 20, 21. Their disruption, 29. The Stanhope Whigs and their foreign policy, 43, 215. Their position under George I. and George II. compared, 159, 160, 163. Danger of defeat, 161. Measures of self-preservation, 162, 163. Want of cohesion, 165, 168, 227, 234. The Whig oligarchy attacked, 166-169. Bound to religious toleration, 170. The first Rockingham ministry, 227. Whig disorganisation, 234. Their prin-

INDEX. 419

ciples of taxation, 249. Ousted by the "King's Friends," 264, 266. The second Rockingham ministry, 368. Division among the Whig peers, 373.
Whiteboys, the, 272.
Widdrington, Lord, Jacobite leader, 25.
Wilkes, member for Aylesbury, 239. Attacks Bute in the *North Briton*, 226, 239. "No. 45" and the king's speech, 239-241. Encouraged by Temple, 239. Prosecuted by Grenville, 239, 240. His arrest, and liberation.—Expulsion from the House, 240. Outlawed, 241. Returned for Middlesex, 231, 241. Sentence of imprisonment and second expulsion, 242, 243. Made an alderman, 243. The Press, 244, 245.
William of Orange, appointed Stadtholder.—Joins the Duke of Cumberland's army, 69.

William III., compared with the Hanoverian kings, 159.
Wills, General of the anti-Jacobite army, 23, 24.
Wilmington, 314.
Windward Islands, 307.
Wintoun, Lord, joins in proclaiming King James, 23.
Wolfe, in Canada, 102, 106. Takes Quebec.—Death, 108.
Wood's halfpence, 200.
Worthington, 231.
Wyndham, Sir William, 22.
Wyoming, 306.

Yelverton, 357, 359.
Yorktown, Cornwallis at, 314. A division of the British army at.—Attacked by Washington and Rochambeau, 316. Surrender. 317, 321, 323.

Zittau, 86.
Zorndorf, battle of, 90.

www.ingramcontent.com/pod-product-compliance
Lightning Source LLC
Chambersburg PA
CBHW051723300426
44115CB00007B/445